My Life & Soft Times

My Life
&
Soft Times

HENRY
LONGHURST

COLLINS
8 Grafton Street, London W1
1983

William Collins Sons and Co Ltd
London · Glasgow · Sydney · Auckland
Toronto · Johannesburg

Longhurst, Henry

    My life and soft times.
    1. Longhurst, Henry   2. Golf–Biography
    I. Title
    070.4'49796352'0924   GV964.L/

    ISBN 0 00 217065 5

First published in Great Britain 1971
by Cassell and Co Ltd

This edition 1983

Set in Imprint
Made and Printed in Great Britain
by William Collins Sons & Co Ltd Glasgow

Contents

Illustrations

Foreword
by Peter Alliss

I remember Henry Longhurst very fondly and I am delighted to write this foreword for the re-issue of his autobiography. It was, in fact, only during the last eight years of his life that I really got to know him. Before that I had been playing golf and he had been writing about it: along with Peter Ryde, Ward Thomas and Leonard Crawley he was one of the great writers on golf of the day; but these men were a race apart and we players never really had the opportunity of getting to know them.

I owe him a great deal, for he encouraged me in my writing. He taught me the importance of being concise at all times and also how to develop a somewhat conversational style of writing. He was a master and craftsman among writers himself. His proud boast was his economy of style: in all the twenty-odd years that he wrote for the *Sunday Times*, he never wrote an article of more than 850 words.

Later, through our television work, Henry Longhurst and I became close friends. At first he frightened me but then he gradually taught me to marvel at the skills of great players, to appreciate their dedication and their hard work; and he taught me how to smile, if wryly, at their misfortunes. Above all, he thought the game of golf should be fun, and I believe something of that spirit is conveyed in the pages of this autobiography. He also believed strongly in the importance of keeping your eyes and ears open, of learning the true art of listening, an attitude reflected in his love of the countryside – of birds, butterflies and flowers. He imparted some of this to me and taught me to slow down a bit – to learn that you don't always have to rush.

Television completely changed his life. His following increased enormously: instead of receiving six or eight fan letters a year he suddenly started to receive as many in a week. A whole new audience appeared through televised golf and all sorts of people started writing to him – old-age pensioners, women from Barnsley and Bodmin. One day he came in to see me with a bundle of letters, and pushed one at me to read. It went something like this: 'Dear Mr Longhurst, I have never played golf but you make it sound so interesting. You take us to so many beautiful places. I just want you to know that I am eighty-four; I have been a widow for forty-seven years. Things are a bit hard, but you bring a great deal of life and colour into my days.'

'What do you think of that?' he said to me, 'Fancy some old bird wasting a five-penny stamp writing to me!'

What else can I say about Henry Longhurst? He loved conversation. He was tough. He was definitely right-wing but he was always fair and disliked pomposity and cant of any kind. There was a roguishness about him. He loved open cars – he bought a lefthand-drive Ford Mustang, of which I am now the proud owner. He wasn't exactly an oil painting, but there was something very attractive about him. He had a marvellous sense of the ridiculous. He was very brave, for he suffered his final illness with great courage. And although he didn't suffer fools gladly, yet he was very mindful of other people in a genuine way and he was kind, very kind, and very modest.

In fact, I miss him very much indeed and I hope that the reissue of his autobiography will do something to keep his spirit alive, to remind people of his very great qualities and maybe introduce him to many more who never had the good fortune to know him, to read his writing or to watch his television appearances and commentaries.

Peter Alliss

Preface

'Vanity,' it has been said, 'is the basis of all autobiographies,' and so, I suppose, it is. Nevertheless, books which enable me to live part of other men's lives without the trouble of actually doing so have always been my favourite reading and in that spirit I have ventured to set down some of the more agreeable aspects of my own. Nature is kind in letting us forget the worries and frustrations and follies endured or committed on the way – hence the manifestly absurd assertion that our schooldays are the happiest of our lives – and in any case nobody wants to read about them, so I have tried to extract from my own by no means invariably soft times only such parts as I think would have entertained me as a reader if they had happened to somebody else.

In a very few cases I have included something of what I wrote about events at the time, perhaps twenty-five years or more ago, either because impressions were fresher then or because in at least one case – namely the appalling episode of Blondin and his manager over the Niagara Falls, on which I have dined out for years – I have since managed to secure a picture. For the rest I have written afresh about life as I look back on it now, with the modest hope of passing on to the reader a little of the entertainment it has given me on the way.

CLAYTON WINDMILLS
HASSOCKS
SUSSEX
June 1971

Henry Longhurst

I

I Remember,
I Remember . . .

My only excuse for starting at the beginning and writing about my childhood is that I have always so much enjoyed reading about other people's. The other day I stopped beside the little white gate leading into the park and down to the Hall in the village of Bromham, Beds. As I paused to gaze nostalgically at the rambling old house on my left, known as Park Cottage, a lady came out and we fell into conversation. 'I was born in that room,' I said, pointing to an upstairs window, 'sixty-one years ago next Wednesday,' so she invited me in, and there I was, a little boy of five again – with the same wicket gate that had been put at the top of the stars to stop me falling down, and the nursery and the schoolroom and the yard where the yeomanry were billeted, as a result of which at the age of five I told my affronted mother and Hilda, the maid, to 'get out of the bloody way'; and the walnut tree, the biggest in Bedfordshire, it was always said, but looking a little elderly now, though the present owner, God bless her, had just refused some philistine's offer of a hundred pounds for it; and hopping about in it a grey squirrel, the fifty-fifth generation in direct line from the one we once captured and kept for a pet. Though the village is largely a dormitory now, by some extraordinary chance this little corner at one end has survived unspoilt, with Park Cottage still flanked on one side by the big, old, unmanageable vicarage, with its stables and walled garden and orchard, and on the other by the lovely limestone farmhouse known to us as 'Skevvy's', after the Skevington family who farmed there, but now occupied by a retired air marshal. The same path leads down across the meadow and over the little stream to the square-towered church, still standing alone in the middle of the park, where I and my son were baptised and where Gray might so well have written his 'Elegy'. I have had one or two lucky numbers turn up in my life, but the luckiest was to be born and brought up in the country.

I suppose I should say something about my family. A rum lot, one or two of them, with the Demon Drink running like a jovial but occasionally destructive thread through both sides, but for the most part sound and worthy citizens.

The Longhurst family [according to some notes written out in a clear hand by my mother at the age of ninety-two] lived in their childhood at Chertsey in a lovely Georgian house, Maybury, in the main street. Grandpa Longhurst was a linen draper and the business was attached to the house – in those days nothing was ready-made and a linen draper stocked materials of every kind and all of the highest quality. He married a widow with three children, Mrs Hewat (born a Carpenter) with two sons and a daughter, Emmie, who married Charles Moore, a highly respected solicitor and Coroner for Leominster, and they lived in a lovely old house called Fairlawn, quite oblivious of the bills owing. Luckily they had a son, Captain Charles Moore, who had great expectations from an Aunt. The Captain came home on leave and paid all the debts, £300 for coal and a little less for the butcher, and in telling us Emmie said it had given them 'such a nice free feeling'.

Six little Longhursts quickly followed, three boys and three girls; Harry, Agnes, Gertrude, Sydney, Ernest and Biddy, but the mother died and Grandpa took on a sour-faced spinster much hated by all and as soon as they could they left home, Harry [my father] to be apprenticed to a well-known business at Cavendish House, Cheltenham, where he met Fred Skinner, his partner-to-be when they moved to Bedford and founded the family business of Longhurst & Skinner. Sydney went in the bank at Richmond and Ernest was apprenticed to Cox's Luck Mill at Weybridge. When Grandpa died, leaving £40,000, the boys were allowed to draw the capital. Sydney left the bank and went round the world. Ernest stuck the Mills for a time but went off and bought a farm in Herefordshire with no knowledge whatever and soon had to get out and buy a smaller one, where unfortunately he was tricked into marrying his housekeeper, Miss Berry. She was a thorough bad lot and took to drink in a very big way and again the farm had to be sold and she appeared at the Sale in only a dressing-gown – well, you know the rest – how she fell down the stairs in the night and broke her neck.

Uncle Ernest after his unfortunate alliance with the housekeeper continued to the end to call her 'Miss Berry'. There seems little doubt that on the fatal night he pushed her down the stairs. When challenged with this in later years, my mother would say, 'I never heard such a thing. Don't be so disgraceful!' but I still suspect an earlier reaction of hers to be nearer the truth, when after a certain hesitation she said, 'Well, we did think it was perhaps fortunate that Charlie Moore was the Coroner.' My mother had a very soft spot for Uncle Ernest and they were always happy in each other's company. I just remember him with us on leave in the First War. When the telephone gave a single ring – our number was Double-One X 1 on a party line of six, so when it gave one ring it meant us, though of course, however many rings it gave, all the other five picked theirs up to listen in – the odds were that it was Mr Quenby at the Swan asking would we send the trap down for Uncle Ernest or should he keep him there for the night?

Uncle Sydney, gay, debonair, lovable and in the end lost, on returning from his venture round the world was taken for a while into the family business, but by this time the devil had got into him and in the end there was nothing for it but the next boat for Australia. Somebody, I believe, put something in his tea and cured him, but by then it was too late. He settled in a place called Narembeen, Western Australia, which we always took to be a suburb of Perth, and in 1953 I paid sixty-eight pounds to fly all night from Sydney and all night the next night back to Melbourne just for the pleasure of meeting for a few hours the legendary Uncle Sydney. I got him with difficulty on the telephone from Sydney. 'Sorry I shan't be there to see you,' said a brassy Australian voice. 'It's four hundred miles and I'm seventy-nine, yer know.' Sadly I got my money back and next year he died.

My friendship with the Longhurst family [my mother's notes continue] began on 14 September 1886, when Biddy and I, both aged nine, were sent to school at Cambridge House, Guildford. She was a shy, very unhappy girl, always in tears, and I took her under my wing. When twenty-one she came into her share and had about £250 a year, a large sum in those days, and insisted on marrying a horrid little German, Rudolph Rosenstock. There is no doubt he was a spy. Things got too hot and he conveniently drowned himself in a pond . . . Soon after Harry and I were married the great Uncle James Carpenter came to stay at Park Cottage. Came into the family estates and lived in great style at a house outside Leominster called Wheelbarrow Castle, where he spent his time hunting and gambling in every form and ran through the lot.

Uncle James, whose name, as Henry Carpenter Longhurst, I have borne so unprofitably for so long, also had a housekeeper, whom he did not marry, he being engaged to a Miss Hughes at the time. Sometimes the housekeeper would find him lying on his back, pink coat and all, with an empty flask after a hard day in the field, repeating, 'Another good man lost! Another good man lost!' 'Yes,' said the housekeeper, eyeing him sternly, 'and if only Miss Hughes could see you now!'

Looking back upon all of which it does seem remarkable that I myself should have turned out to be a life-long near-teetotaller. And if ever I should inadvertently stray from the path, my mother is liable to eye me rather as did Uncle James's housekeeper and say, 'Yes. And your Uncle Sydney had a good brain too.'

My father, alas, died on New Year's Eve, 1933, at only my own present age, having retired to the little Somerset town of Clevedon, and at the moment of writing my mother has now celebrated this melancholy anniversary for thirty-seven years. As he was already forty when he married, I did not know him as well as I should have liked but could sense the respect in which people held him and will quote only what the *Bedfordshire Times* said of him at his death. After recalling that in 1909 he had been 'by common consent one of the best Mayors that Bedford had had for some time', it went on:

> He met with such success that at the conclusion of his year of office the *Bedfordshire Times*, in expressing the town's wish that he should accept the Mayoralty for another year, said, 'He had a very hard row to hoe at first, but his inflexible honesty and straightforwardness and his strong sense of duty carried him safely through and he gained the respect of the Council and the town generally.' It happened that on the day that Mr Longhurst completed his year of office the triennial election of three aldermen took place and the Council paid Mr Longhurst the compliment of appointing him to one of the vacancies, thus securing to the Council and the town his services for another ten years.

At any rate, encouraged by her notes that I have already quoted, I bought my mother a lined exercise-book and said, 'Why don't you amuse yourself making a few notes about the Bromham of my childhood?' This she did and, since it formed the background of my early life, I venture to pass it on, exactly as she wrote it, still in a firm clear hand at the age now of ninety-three.

> Bromham – as pretty a village as any in Bedfordshire with its village green and lovely little thatched cottages nestling round – lovely only to look at outside but inside such conditions as seem unbelievable now. They mostly consisted of a small living-room with an open fire in a little kitchen range and an oven and a back scullery or wash-house where a

large copper would occupy one corner and which supplied all the hot water needed – no water laid on, but a tap outside which would supply one or two cottages, the water coming from a well in a field and worked by a wheel driven by the wind, so if no wind no water. Most of the men were employed on one or other of the two large Farms owned by Howkins or Skevington. Inskip was milkman to Howkins – he was one of the dirtiest men I have ever known and did not think it necessary to wash his hands before milking and took the milk straight away in a revoltingly dirty cart reeking of cows straight to the Hospital. Others on the farm were notable characters, such as dear old Matthew Tebbutt, the shepherd, who just lived for his sheep, his only outing being to the Smithfield Show, where he invariably brought home the Cup for the best of their kind. On one occasion they were of the kind with a black tuft on the head and all were perfect except one whose tuft was not up to standard, so to quote him, 'What did I do but take a tuft off another and fix it on, but I was mortal frit when that there Judge came round lest he should take hold of it.' However, all was well and as usual he brought home the award. He slept in the pen with the sheep. Another well-loved character was old Gardner, the horse-keeper, and his horses were a joy to look at and, when the old man died, they carried him to the Church on the farm wagon, which would have pleased him. We shall never see their like again but it was a privilege to know them.

The Village Post Office was kept by an old woman, Mrs Pepper, and her daughter, Agnes – a shelf was drawn across the entrance to the Cottage which served as a counter but the great attraction was a tame Canadian goose named Traddles, which had been picked up when young by the son, Pepper, a gardener at the Hall, who passed Park Cottage four times a day to and fro with such regularity that the clocks could have been set by him. There were at least three or four gardeners there, notably George Church (head), whose wife also was employed as Cook, but they retired soon after I was there and had the village shop and George was the Carrier – he took you to Bedford three and a half miles for 1s. and parcels for 6d., unless it was what he called a 'purpose journey', when the cost rose a little – they were the most perfect examples of Nature's Gentlefolk who could be found – the cottage attached to the Shop was one of the best in the village and the garden a joy to be in, with a wealth of every flower imaginable.

The Hall, a rambling old house set in a charming Park and on the banks of the River Ouse, which wandered through the grounds and occasionally invaded the Servant's Quarters, compelling them to walk about on planks, was occupied by a Victorian old lady, Miss Rice Trevor, who ruled the village with a rod of iron. She was daughter of a Lord Dynevor, who I think was drowned; anyhow his Ghost haunted the Church, where his helmet and armour hung over his Tomb.

Of course the village had its baker, Mr Bruty, and many Sunday dinners were baked there as the Cottage ovens were too small – his bread was good and he was a cheery person who tramped round with a huge basket. There was also the Village Forge, where the Blacksmith was kept very busy with the farm horses and hunters – all the Farmers and their sons seemed to hunt and many rode in the Point-to-Point races and National Hunt Meetings at Towcester and even Cheltenham. The Forge was a meeting place for a gossip and the delight of the children, who were sometimes ordered out but when the blacksmith, Mr Prudden, a fine old man with a long white beard, was in a good mood they might be allowed to help with the bellows and delighted in making the sparks fly.

The village was not without its fish supply, brought around in an open basket by an incredibly dirty little man, Teddy Whiteman, who was slightly simple and whose cottage was swarming with flies and naturally smelling of fish, and I was assured by the District Nurse that the basket was kept under the bed. She should know, as she brought three or four small Whitemans into the world; however, no one was poisoned!

One great event was the Feast, or Fair as we called it. This was held on another smaller green at the lower end of the village, opposite the Swan, and consisted of a small roundabout, coconut shies and the usual stalls of rubbish. It was a date which influenced certain actions in the garden. Our old gardener called Staffie, short for Stafferton, would on no account sow certain seeds 'while Bromham Feast'. Another annual event was the Flower Show held in the gardens of the Hall and, when Miss Rice Trevor reigned, all money had to be taken to her but all must be well washed before she touched it. Life went on in this peaceful way – the cottagers all apparently quite happy to be in that state of life to which the Lord had been pleased to call them, and then 1914, the peace of the world was shattered and the news came the very day of the Flower Show, with dreadful rumours of all the lovely horses being commandeered and 'men's hearts were failing them for fear'. In a few days the whole village was taken over by the Bedfordshire Yeomanry and every cottage had to find room for at least one man and, as our wandering old house had much room, we were given four Tommies to house and feed and our stables became the Headquarters. This meant that the household consisted of my husband and myself, a Governess and two five-year-old boys [the other my cousin], and, when I look back, I marvel at the wonderful maid I had – a dreadful old kitchener to be coaxed into burning and breakfast to be served for the men at 7.30 and in the Dining-room at 8. Her work went on all day – I did the cooking and the shopping but there was the washing and cleaning – everlasting washing-up – there was no gas or electricity but eleven lamps and three stoves to be done every day. This was my work until Charles came on the scene – he started with us aged ten before and after school and was with us until eighteen. When he was about eleven or twelve I was able to pass the lamps and stoves on to him and at thirteen he left school and became gardener and helped in every way.

After a year or two I was asked to exchange four Tommies for two Officers – this made the work equally hard as it meant a hot meal midday for the children and hot dinner at night. So life went on until 1918 and with the end of the war in sight and with my health failing we moved to Biddenham to a small house rented from someone, I forget who. We were happy enough but our hearts were always in Bromham and so in 1925 the next chapter of our village life began. . . .

My mother, as I have said, wrote the above when she was ninety-three. What an extraordinary thing is extreme old age, especially at the present time when one will have lived through five reigns and three wars! My mother, for instance, was twenty-five at the time of the Relief of Mafeking in 1900 and twenty-six when the Old Queen died. When the subject of Mafeking came up one day, I said to her, 'You must remember Mafeking?' 'Of course,' she said. 'I remember it as though it were yesterday.' She was living at the time with her father and older brother in the little village of Wrecclesham, near Farnham, Surrey. One evening the bells of Farnham rang out and the brother said immediately, 'It must be Mafeking,' so they got out their bicycles, lit the wicks of the oil lamps and sailed down to Farnham, my mother much of the time with her feet up on the front mudguard since they had in those days no free-wheel. In Castle Street, almost unchanged today and still one of the most beautiful streets in England, a large crowd had already collected and the Mayor of Farnham appeared on a balcony, complete with chain of office, and made a speech. He ended with the unfortunate words, 'And now we will all return peacefully to our homes,' to which an unknown voice at the back replied very properly, 'Bollocks!' Somebody knew somebody who kept a shop which sold fireworks, others got busy with material for the bonfires, while the majority celebrated from one hostelry to the other, and the result put a new word into the English language, the verb 'to maffick'.

My father at first bicycled, then motored, in to the business every day, but it must have been in the bicycling days when in the early hours of the morning of 11 January 1912 he was awakened by a shower of stones cast at the bedroom window by our neigh-

bour, Mr Ben Howkins. 'I suppose you know your place is on fire?'
he said. My father, of course, did not, but a glance out of the window and the rosy hue of the distant sky over Bedford told him that
it was only too true. Howkins had had the good sense to retain the
cab which had brought him home and soon my father and his
partner were surveying the biggest fire that Bedford has ever
known.

The *Bedfordshire Times*, as might be expected, went to town on
it with an account of several thousand words, in the unbroken
small print that was the practice in those days:

> It has often been a matter of comment that Bedford has been without
> a really big fire for some years, but it has come at last, and of a magnitude
> that fairly tops the record within living memory. It is our painful duty
> to chronicle the loss by fire, in an incredibly short time in the early
> hours of Thursday morning, of that splendid building – the finest
> business premises in Bedford – known for many years as The Pan-
> technicon and occupied by Messrs Longhurst and Skinner, by whose
> perseverance and enterprise a great and successful house-furnishing
> business has been carried on there.

The fire was detected at about three in the morning and a policeman broke into the back of the premises with his truncheon. Only
a few years ago one of his family presented us with this very
truncheon, somewhat battered, and it hangs on our office wall
today. He was too late, however, for nearly everything on the four
floors was of wood or fabric and as dry as tinder, and it was not
long before the glow was seen by a Midland Railway driver twenty
miles away at Luton. Next door was, and is, the little pub known
as the Nag's Head, through whose roof and bar a huge lump of
masonry fell, wrecking both. Furthermore, said the *Beds Times*,
'A quantity of bricks fell on a bed in one of the rooms – some say a
ton, some say two, but we have not weighed it and cannot tell to an
ounce. A truck in the yard received an unexpected load of bricks,
and was somewhat bent, not to say broke.' On the other side the
Golden Lion caught fire and was extinguished, but the main
anxiety was for Jarvis's Brewery. We seem, in fact, surrounded by
places of refreshment and no wonder poor Uncle Sydney had to
go to Australia. Mr Talbot Jarvis, an old friend of my father's,
was returning from a Primrose League dance at Elstow School –
rather late, one would have thought, for a function of that kind –

and was inspired to deeds of sterling valour at the thought of losing his Brewery. Quoting again from the *Beds Times* – and if only we had the same amount of space today!

> The heat, however, was awful and at first baffled him, until he took his overcoat off, wrapped it over his head, and sprinted for all he was worth for Hassett Street. The intensity of the heat may be imagined from the fact that his left foot was scorched by the heat where the trousers and the dancing pump left it unprotected and several great blisters were raised on it. His dress suit caught fire from the sparks that were falling everywhere, and he had to take off his coat. It presented a pretty picture later in the day. Holes were burned through in many places, molten lead adhered to the back, and it was soaked through and through, as of course was Mr Jarvis himself. In Hassett Street he got P.C. 43 to give him a leg up and scrambled over the gates, using his overcoat to protect him from the spikes. . . . There can be no doubt that the promptness, presence of mind and courage of Mr Jarvis saved the Brewery from extinction.

Wonderful what these brewers can do when really pressed!

On another page there appeared a column of miscellaneous items headed 'Sparks from the Fire', from which I pass on the following gems:

> We have been asked if we remember 'sale stock' ever having been 'cleared' so effectively as on this occasion? Our reply is a polite negative.
>
> A brewery, two public houses and a wine merchant's suffered considerably from the fire. We understand no blame is attached to Mr Lloyd George.
>
> When the contents of the fruiterer's window parted company and oranges littered the roadway, a wag suggested that that part of Midland Road resembled a part of South Africa. Every Orange seemed Free and was in a State.

The story ended, however, on the happy note: 'We understand that the building and stock were insured. About eight months ago Messrs Longhurst and Skinner, though reluctant to do so, were strongly advised to insure against loss of profits, and are now very glad that they did so.'

At about five in the morning the main walls collapsed and, when daylight came, sightseers in their hundreds surveyed a pile of rubble no more than a few feet high where once the proud Pantechnicon had stood. From the ashes, however, arose the present even more imposing edifice, once again, as we like to think, 'the finest business premises in Bedford'.

Bernard Darwin called his last autobiographical volume *The World that Fred Made*. Fred was the gardener-handyman and hero to Bernard's young nephew, Philip, who once asked, 'Could Fred make the world?' The Charles mentioned by my mother was the Fred of my early life and I could well have entitled this book *The World that Charles Made*. Charles was one of seven children of the Flute family who farmed the Lower Farm, down on the other side of the railway bridge under which roared the red Midland Expresses, sometimes with two engines, and beside which there was always a yellowhammer's nest in the hedge. My mother, I was sure, was capable of many things and so, of course, was my father, but Charles, so far as I was concerned, could do everything. Among other things he was the master-craftsman at making catapults, and I can recapture it all today, the search for the suitable Y-shaped prong and the peeling thereof, and the soft leather to bind onto the shafts of the Y, and the surreptitious purchase of catapult elastic and the pocketful of selected round stones. Since he is now sixty-eight to my sixty-two, Charles would have been eleven to my five when my hero-worshipping days began. He taught me to ride my first new bicycle – a thrill exceeded by positively none other since – and for a few precious years we grew up together, inseparable.

It was not too difficult for me to imagine what life was like in Edwardian days, but it must be almost impossible for young people these days to imagine what life was like in darkest Bedfordshire before the days of electric light, wireless, television, tractors, or, except for the few, the motor car. The land was still ploughed by horses, though the bigger farms hired an exciting apparatus known as the Cultivator, or in local dialect, one of the ugliest I fear in the whole country, 'the ol' cul'iva'or'. This consisted of two traction engines, each with a drum of cable which hauled a plough across from one to the other, each moving up a stage at a time and whistling to the other when they were ready.

Everybody in the village was distinguishable not so much by class, which is a 'bad' word these days, as by what could more properly be described as rank. Olympian in the distance was the Old Duke at Woburn, of whom I shall permit myself a word or two later, followed by 'The County', who probably hunted with the Oakley and in Bedfordshire were not, I suspect, quite so grand as some of them may have cared to imagine. Bromham was not big enough to aspire to any members of the County, and the Big House was occupied by Mr Allen, founder of the great Bedford engineering works of W. H. Allen. Then came professional men: doctors, lawyers, retired colonels and the like; followed very definitely lower in the social scale by 'trade', to which my respected father belonged, and 'gentleman' farmers. However, as there were no County and no professionals in our little village, we stood higher than we should otherwise have done and ranked almost equal second after, though a long way after, the House and the Hall. So perhaps I was lucky to be born in the humble county of Bedfordshire rather than, say, Gloucestershire, where we should have ranked nowhere. My mother worked assiduously in charitable works, relieving distress, visiting the sick, and raising support for the Waifs and Strays or, her main 'cause', the Disstrict Nurse, who would think nothing of being called out in the middle of the night and bicycling three miles through the snow to deliver the eleventh infant of some already poverty-stricken cottager. Nevertheless, it was the only life that people knew and few, I fancy, sought much to change it, though there may have been a few red revolutionaries in the town. Every Sunday we prayed, and meant it, that we might be rendered content with that state of life into which it had pleased God to call us, and most people were. Unfashionable as it may be to say so, there is still something to be said for rank. At least you knew where you stood.

In the meantime I grew up under the wing of the great Charles, roaming the unspoilt countryside and learning about Nature without knowing I was doing so, or what a solace it was to be in later life. In spring the Big Wood (now a council estate) was carpeted with anemones, primroses and bluebells, and white and purple violets grew in the hedges, and, when the early corn showed through in April, it was time to quarter the fields in search of plovers' eggs. At least as great a delicacy, however, are moorhens' eggs, of which I dare say Charles and I can claim in our time to have brought home and eaten for tea more than anyone still alive in Bedfordshire. Sometimes the detection of a feather or a speck of down would lead to the discovery of a wild duck's nest up a willow tree, and once we brought a whole clutch of eggs home and hatched them out under a hen.

When the First War came, thousands of Scottish troops were billeted in Bedford and the sound of their pipes coming up across

the river from Bromham Bridge was the signal for furious activity
with jugs and cans of water with which to refresh them when they
fell out beside the little green behind Park Cottage. One day, and
what joy to a small boy, ·they even unhitched a battery of real
howitzers and levelled them up behind a bank, pointing at
Clapham.

Not that all of life was idyllic for a boy in a rural Bedfordshire.
For one thing there settled over the scene for days at a time,
especially in winter, what I came to think of as the 'country
colour', a sort of uniform grey – the sky grey, the roads grey, the
telephone wires grey, and even, as it sometimes seemed, the grass
grey. Again, I was an only child, forced back on my own resources
at a time when one has not normally created many, and I can see
now what a great effect this had on my life and character. I have,
I like to think, developed a few agreeable qualities, but selflessness
and gratitude are not among them. I am aware of accepting favours
and then, once they are safely received, omitting to thank people
for them as I should. Again, as an only child, your toys, and later
in life your more valuable possessions, are your own. You have
never been compelled to share them with brothers or sisters, so
why should you share them with anyone now? I remember acutely
to this day the affront I felt when, having been forced to let some
visiting boy play with my train, I found that he had actually broken
my signal; or when, having been persuaded to lend to a family
of four Irish children my ultra-precious bound volumes of *Railway
Wonders of the World*, which I enjoy to this day, they had actually
torn almost in half the coloured plate of the Scotch Express
thundering across the Forth Bridge. The fact of being an only
child, and in a remote countryside, coloured one's whole life and
some day some learned psychologist, though not I, might write a
treatise on it. In the meantime I can only hope that to understand
is to forgive.

I remember long ago seeing an article by a number of distinguished authors on 'The Book I never Wrote'. There is nothing
to stop less than distinguished authors joining in and, if I do so,
it is because mine is so clear in my mind. It is called *The Spacious
Days* and would be what is now known as a coffee-table book, an
anthology in writing and pictures of the sort of life led by 'them',
the aristocracy, in late Victorian and Edwardian times. I should
not in fact have written it, only have edited it, but I like to think

of the unbelievable beauty of the surroundings in which they lived in unspoilt rural England and the stately homes, particularly the minor ones, and the parks and gardens, and the often preposterous way their owners carried on. Since all is over, or nearly over, I should not allow myself to spoil the picture by mentioning that the labourers in their fields were paid twelve shilings a week.

All this occurs to me because, living where we did, I was ever conscious as a boy, of Woburn Abbey and what people of my generation still think of as the 'Old' Duke, that is Herbrand, 11th Duke of Bedford and the present one's grandfather, by no means to be confused with the present one's late father. People of our level, of course, never got to see the Abbey, though one or two chimney-pots were just to be detected through the trees, but the proles were allowed to drive through the park so long as they kept to the roads and did not stop. (When my mother, soon after my birth, was invalided out to a cottage somewhere on the Woburn Estate, she was given written permission to say that, when walking along the path through the woods, she might sit down if she were tired!) These Sunday drives through the park were naturally a tremendous thrill to a boy. There were all kinds of deer, and bison and llamas and golden pheasants and emus, sometimes with a family of a dozen little emulets right beside the road, and, even if you weren't allowed to stop, there was nothing to prevent your driving very, very slowly.

Sometimes we went to church at Woburn, where I was terrified of the gargoyles peering down over the edge of the tall, square tower – and to tell the truth I do not really like the look of them today. I cannot quite remember whether we stood up when the vicar came in: it is my impression that we did not. What the congregation was really waiting for was the stir at the back of the church which heralded the arrival of His Grace and his poor, patient, deaf Duchess, the 'Flying Duchess', who ran a hospital in Woburn and eventually perished in her aeroplane in the North Sea. That, though, was in the future and for the moment, whether or not the congregation stood up when the vicar came in, we all stood dutifully up when the Old Duke did. Nor did anyone think this odd in the still Spacious Days.

To retain the privacy fit for persons of their station the Old Duke's forebears built an eleven-and-a-half-mile wall round Woburn. Castlerosse's grandfather did the same at Killarney, only seven-odd miles, but the record, I believe, is the one at Petworth, some thirteen miles and, let us be fair, constructed by the Lord Leconfield of the day to give work in the hard-times of the Napoleonic wars. The Old Duke, however, went one better. When he built cottages for the estate workers outside the wall, he built them in rows of eight or so, set back from the road and with gardens in front. The keener-eyed passer-by may, however, notice something strange about them. Look again and you see that there are no front doors. All the doors are round at the back. 'Put 'em at the front and the first thing you'd see is the women gossiping at the doors, and you don't want that sort of thing as you drive round your own place.'

Inside the Abbey fifty or sixty servants ate their heads off, no fewer than eight of them waiting on the Old Duke and the Duchess, one at one end of the table unwilling to speak, the other at the other unable to hear, and all was over in twenty minutes. All the housemaids had to be five feet ten or better, which must have been splendid for the footmen, and between them in winter the servants lit seventy or eighty fires every day, since the Old Duke would only have central heating installed in the corridors. If you came as a guest from London, you travelled with a chauffeur and footman in one car, followed by your luggage with a chauffeur and footman in another. These took you as far as Hendon, where two of the country cars were waiting to take you and your luggage the rest of the way. All the above and much more you will find in the present Duke's book *A Silver-Plated Spoon*,* and a more entertaining, tolerant, forgiving and good-humoured account of the dastardly treatment meted out to him by his father, largely in connivance with the Old Duke, you could never find. It was not until he was sixteen and noted a picture of the Flying Duchess in the paper and a little housemaid said, 'But that is your grandmother,' that he realized who he really was.

Between them they did their best – though heaven knows why, since Woburn has been in the Russell family for more than four hundred years – to deprive him of his inheritance, and today it does not belong to him. Yet now, where the last two Dukes shared their treasures with no one, the present incumbent through a form of Trust shares them with more than half a million people a year, and for this, if he were not a Duke already, he ought to be made one. As proof of which, let me quote one passage from his book:

* Cassell 1950.

Woburn is one of the loveliest of England's stately homes. It stands as a monument to the architectural genius of Inigo Jones and Henry Holland. Its treasures include Canalettos, Van Dycks, Holbeins and the Armada portrait of Queen Elizabeth, all relics of the part the Russells have played in the history of England. It gives more people pleasure than any building of its kind in the whole country. The lakes where my ancestors used to shoot ducks in moody solitude are now thronged by happy children in little paddle boats. The eleven and a half miles of wall which my forbears built to keep their neighbours at bay now serves to protect herds of rare animals in their natural surroundings for the delight of our innumerable guests. From the dusty suburbs of London and the Midlands thousands of people find an oasis of green which helps them to return to their week's work refreshed. Our visitors come from all over the world. By making them welcome we try and share the happiness we enjoy in possessing such a unique establishment.

I must end my little diversion to Woburn by an episode related by a contemporary who as a young man was in the Estate Office in the Old Duke's day. It concerns the young assistant under-gamekeeper who had got a girl in Woburn into what in those days they called 'trouble' and was brought up on a charge in front of the Duke. Probably he had never been farther inside than to deliver fifty brace of pheasants at the back door. Now here he is in his best blue serge suit, nervously twiddling his cap in his hands, and escorted by the head gamekeeper, Mr Young, first through the lower servants' quarters, then through the upper servants' quarters, then through the green baize door and along the corridor from whose walls eleven Dukes of Bedford follow him along with censorious (or in some cases, I dare say, sympathetic) eyes. At last he is in the Presence. The evidence is heard and he is sent from the room to await the verdict. Whereupon the Old Duke says slowly, 'Well, on the whole I don't think I should sack him, Young. After all, he did it in his own time.'

2
Messing About
in Boats

My entire boyhood was enriched by, and in the summer revolved around, the River. I suppose that, if I had given it a thought, which I didn't, I should have appreciated that other boys managed to get through life without the River, but what a deprived and miserable existence theirs must have been! The River was the Great Ouse and it made its leisurely way in great loops, in so far as I knew it, past Lord Ampthill's at Oakley, under Oakley Bridge, round past Clapham and under the viaduct where the Midland Railway crossed it just north of Bedford, along through the gardens of Bromham Hall, from whose lawn could be seen on a summer evening the fins of a shoal of bream cruising up and down – 'as big as babies', it was once said – then along past the Osier Beds, where the Hunt nearly always found a fox on Boxing Day, and over the Big Weir, where in summer you could walk across the narrow parapet dry shod while the water went over the Little Weir down to the Mill; then under Bromham Bridge, past the Island, through the Rapids, and eventually out to the long open stretch leading to Kempston, where we parted company, leaving it to wind its way round to Bedford and the Embankment, with all the punts and skiffs and the School Eight and the pleasure steamer and the Suspension Bridge, off which a friend of my father's, who was Mayor at the time, once threw a rude fellow from Luton for expectorating upon respectable ladies in punts below.

Sometimes the River was not so leisurely and the news 'the floods are up' sent us down to Oakley Bridge to see huge volumes of brown water swirling inexorably down. If you are ever in that part of the world, make a diversion to Oakley Bridge, of grey limestone, unbelievably beautiful, irretrievably doomed by the motor car, and take note of the pillar, several feet higher than the parapet, at one end. The top of this pillar represents, believe it or not, the height of the floods of 1881.

I started my fishing career off the solid wall overhanging the mill stream at Bromham Mill, fishing for minnows and gudgeon, often destined for the bait-can to be used as live bait on the morrow, when the can would be carried, swinging from the handlebars, down through the fields to a pool under the willows below Oakley Bridge – of which I permit myself to write because, though I have fished rivers with resounding names since that time, these were the only times when the result was a certainty. You had only to lower the 'paternoster' – an affair with a lead weight, a couple of luckless minnows or gudgeon on separate hooks, a fixed float under water and a 'bobble' float on the surface – when some voracious perch would dash out and in a moment the line would be disappearing through the bobble. Often it would be a comparatively small one, since the perch thinks nothing of trying to swallow another fish almost its own size, but sometimes it would be a three-pounder, and what a magnificent fish at that – broad handsome red stripes, sharp spikes in its dorsal fin strong enough to get its own back by slitting up the loose skin between your forefinger and thumb, and almost the only coarse freshwater fish really good to eat.

I must have been about nine when my father acquired first a punt, then a dinghy, and these were moored just below Bromham Bridge, with the punt cushions and paraphernalia kept in a hut belonging to Mr Quenby of the Swan, from which my Uncle Ernest had had so often to be rescued. My father, as a good Chertsey man, was adept with the punt pole and had indeed entered races on the Thames – and, if any of the modern daredevils who roar round seaside resorts making a fiendish din at forty-five miles an hour in their power-boats think poling a racing punt on the Thames is a pushover, the answer is that, literally, it very often is! It seems inconceivable today that our two craft, with the single exception of a rowing-boat belonging to two elderly ladies farther up and scarcely ever used, should have been the only boats on three miles of absolutely virgin and unspoilt river, many stretches of it invisible from the bank, its very existence secret and unexplored.

What a paradise for a boy! Soon I became adept at four navigational arts: poling the punt – without crossing the hands on withdrawing the pole or dropping water down the neck of the passenger just in front or getting stuck and finishing up in the water hanging on the pole; paddling the punt and keeping it straight single-handed; rowing the dinghy; and eventually sailing the dinghy as well. Once, so enthralled that it might have been yesterday, I stood motionless in a sallow bush and watched at a range of no more than three feet a kingfisher, darting into the water, coming out with a minnow, and tossing it up to straighten it in its beak before swallowing it. On another occasion I saw a family of six sitting side by side on the branch of a willow.

I have had the luck to watch a number of master craftsmen in my time, men like Joe Davis, for instance, who was probably better at snooker than anyone else in the world by a bigger margin than anyone has been better than anyone else at any other game, or Ben Hogan, of whom certainly no more than three other golfers have been the equal. No doubt memory and the hero-worship of boyhood play me false but I shall always, when it comes to fly-fishing, think of Mr Odell as being in their class. He was pronounced 'Odle' and drove a taxi in Bedford, it must have been for thirty or forty years, since he was still to be found and reminisced with on the station rank in the 1950s. Sometimes I would be allowed the immense privilege of punting him up the river on my own as far as the Rapids, towards which we would creep silently, he kneeling in the front and I now sitting at the back paddling furtively without taking the paddle from the water. The river narrowed down at what we called the Rapids and swirled through a narrow gap with overhanging trees and reeds on one side and quite tall bushes on the other. It was under these bushes that our quarry lay, the big fat timid chub. Odell would whisper instructions as to where I was to manoeuvre the punt and then would begin an exhibition of skill that I am sure is rarely exceeded on the Kennet or Test. His problem was to avoid getting caught up in the ash trees and reeds on the right, to avoid plucking out the eye of the boy behind him, and to drop the fly a matter of inches short of the bushes on the left so that it floated gently beneath them as though having just dropped off the branches. After that, the result seems in retrospect to have been inevitable. A swirl, followed by frantic flashes of silver to and fro under the water, and minutes later a breathless eleven-year-old is leaning over with the net and heaving into the punt an enormous chub. One was four-and-a-half pounds. It never even occurred to me that going out with Odell would not mean coming in with a bigger fish than I had ever caught myself, and of course it never did.

By the time I was introduced to *The Wind in the Willows*, which at once became my favourite book and has been my travelling-companion and ever-present solace in times of trouble ever since, I was already on terms with the principal characters and could identify myself completely with the Water Rat when the Mole said to him, 'So-this-is-a-river?' and he corrected him with, '*The* River'; and when he uttered his famous lines, which I hope will remain the familiar quotation they have already been for more than sixty years, 'Believe me, my young friend, there is *nothing* – absolutely nothing – half so much worth doing as simply messing about in boats.' *The Wind in the Willows* was written in 1908 by Kenneth Grahame, a man of great personal charm (how could it be otherwise?), who of all things was Secretary of the Bank of England, and it was at first somewhat coldly received through being different from his already famous *Dream Days and The Golden Age*. One of those who helped to popularize it was Theodore Roosevelt, President of the United States, where the Americans in turn took the Water Rat, Mole, Toad, Badger and the Otter to their hearts – so much so that a publisher who had turned the book down two years previously retired to the Adirondack Mountains and called his house Toad Hall. All of which now allows me to blow a small blast on my own trumpet.

Although Ernest Shepherd captured so much of the charm of Kenneth Grahame's story in black and white, it was obvious that the only man to do so in colour would have been Arthur Rackham, and he had refused the job in 1908, when the book was still to be called *The Wind in the Reeds*. Imagine my delight and astonishment when in 1949 I found in the home of a friend in Detroit a copy illustrated with twelve of the most lovely water-colours and fifteen line drawings – by Arthur Rackham. Restricted by illness to a short period of work each day, he had decided to devote the rest of his working hours on this earth to *The Wind in the Willows*. In 1939 he handed his labour of love to a director of the Limited Editions Club in New York, and before it had crossed the Atlantic he was dead. I respectfully drew this to the attention of Mr J. A. White, the head of Methuen, who publish the book in England (it was even then in its hundredth edition), and within the year he had not only published the Rackham pictures for us in England but was kind enough to send me the first copy. It is absolutely beautiful and I can only beg you to lay hands on one.

3
Queen of the Sky

All we Bedfordians took an almost proprietary interest in 'the airship'. Whichever might be the current occupant of the gigantic hangar at Cardington, bigger than St Pancras station, we felt that it was *our* airship. Others might read about it and see pictures of it, but to us who saw it every time it flew it became almost a living thing. You get fond of an airship in quite a different way from an aeroplane, and to us the R.101 was undisputed Queen of the Sky. Furthermore, my family had friends at Cardington who knew how everything worked and we used to hang on their words – one a designer and the other the expert on the gas.

Though Bromham was on the opposite side of the town from Cardington, the airship was a familiar sight, since it always circled the town, whether on a trial flight or at the beginning of a journey, and the smooth hum of its motors would bring everyone to their doors or windows to admire its silver sheen and elegant lines. The evening of 4 October 1930 was no exception. 'Quick. It's the airship.' My parents and I rushed out into the garden and, looking up into the dusk, saw the massive cigar-shaped ship, with gondolas lit up, making its stately way across the sky no more than half a mile away.

After a certain amount of public controversy and a great deal more behind the scenes, the R.101 was on its way to show the flag in India. It was a moment at least as moving as when a great ship of the sea departs on its maiden voyage. We had seen it many times, and now we could not help noticing that its nose was dipping at a rather unusual angle. After gazing at it for sometime with an almost personal affection, we found that my mother was silently in tears. 'I can't bear to think of their poor wives and families,' she said. This was, of course, shot down by my father and myself. Far from being sorry for their wives and families, we said, what would we not give to be going in their place?

32

News travels fast even in darkest Bedfordshire, and it was not long after six on Sunday morning that the milkman woke the household with: 'The airship's down and they're all dead.'

I gather that the R.101's voyage was a political scandal of a fairly disgraceful order, but that will have been no consolation to the men whose charred remains lie in their communal grave at Cardington or to those they left behind. And for the rest of us we shall never see another Queen of the Sky.

4
St Cyprians, Eastbourne

I suppose I had what is known as a Good Education, of the type which people will still pinch and save in order to afford for their children despite every effort by the State to prevent them. It began somewhere around the beginning of the First War with a succession of governesses, Miss Crawley, Miss Brown and Miss Bridgeman, of whom I can remember with any distinction only Miss Brown, a stern and fearsome little woman who had once been headmistress of a girls' school. How she had descended to teaching a solitary small boy in a remote Bedfordshire village I still do not know, but she soon had me learning Latin and asked my parents when I was six whether it would be all right to start me on Greek. She came from Harpenden, and to this day, as I pass through the town in the train on my way to the family business in Bedford, the thought never fails to come to my mind: 'Ah, Harpenden. That's where Miss Brown lived.' I was rather afraid of her, but it was a stroke of luck to be forced out of the starting-gate, so to speak, at so smart a pace.

When the last of the governesses had packed her things, I graduated to the junior school, known as the Incubator or 'Inky', of what is now Bedford School and was then Bedford Grammar. It was the cheap but excellent education afforded by this fine school that attracted so many impecunious officers and empire-builders to settle in Bedford and to lend it in those days a character similar to that of Cheltenham. That aspect of the town has vanished, of course, almost without trace – it is said that, when one of the big old houses in the 'best' part of the Town caught fire the other day, forty-two people came out, lamenting in eight different languages – but the school still lends dignity to the scene and itself goes from strength to strength. To attend the Incubator, however, meant harnessing the pony early each morning and a drive of

At St Cyprians we learned, inter alia, *to shoot with a rifle (I am holding it in this picture), put on puttees, slope arms and stand still in the ranks when inspected by a visiting general.*

My entire boyhood was enriched by, and in summer revolved around the river – the Great Ouse, here seen near the Big Weir. In summer you could walk across the parapet dryshod while the water went over the Little Weir to Bromham Mill.

some four miles, and a similar procedure again in the evening, complete with oil lamps on the trap. After two terms, at the end of which it cannot be too widely known that I finished top of Miss Godfrey's bottom form, this proved too much of a good thing, and so in September 1915 I found myself in my best Sunday suit setting off from Victoria, unchanged almost these past fifty-five years – Victoria, I mean – en route to St Cyprians, Eastbourne. I was six and three-quarter years old.

We were transported from Eastbourne station in a charabanc run by a gas balloon on the roof and met at the door by the most formidable, distinguished and unforgettable woman I am likely to meet in my lifetime. This was Mrs L. C. Vaughan Wilkes, or 'Mum', the undisputed ruler not only of about ninety boys but of a dozen masters and mistresses, a matron, under-matron, several maids, a school sergeant, a carpenter, two or three gardeners, Mr Wilkes, and their two sons and three daughters. Here was the complete matriarchal society and, on looking back, no bad thing for boys of seven to thirteen a long way from home.

Morning revealed St Cyprians to be a vast, gabled, red-brick house with a sunken playing-field, complete with cricket pavilion, known as the Armoury, and twenty-five-yard rifle-range. On the far side was a high bank; then the road; then another bank, and above it the first fairway of the Royal Eastbourne Golf Club, the silhouetted figures on which gave me my first sight of the game of golf and thereby determined much of my life. On our left was the bigger and rather barrack-like Temple Grove, attended just after my time by Douglas Bader, who was destined to attain world-wide fame in the next war, and on our right Cholmondley House, a smaller building similar to our own and now, as Beresford House, a capital girls' school which my daughter attended for some years. We played all three games against Temple Grove, but none against Cholmondley House, the rumour being that the headmasters had once fallen out and/or that one of their masters when refereeing or umpiring a match had given such a vilely partisan decision against us that we never played them again. Eastbourne, it turned out, was *the* town for preparatory schools and there was one for every week – or was it every day? – of the year.

At that age you don't ask many questions. You take life for what it is, and on the whole, by today's standards, it was pretty spartan, not only from the point of view of washing in very cold water and having to do a length of the swimming-pool every morning, followed by P.T., which put me off every form of artificial physical exercise for life, but also because the food rationing was far less expertly managed in the First War than in the Second and the Wilkeses must have had a hard job feeding a hundred appetites made ravenous by the sea and downland air, to say nothing of 'runs' the whole way to Beachy Head and back.

It is one of the more merciful dispensations of providence that one tends to forget the hard times and remember the good – hence 'time, the great healer', which it is, and 'your schooldays are the happiest time of your life', which they assuredly aren't. Some of the scars remain, but not many. Among them I should put the cold pewter bowls of porridge with the thick slimy lumps, into which I was actually sick one day and made to stand at a side table and eat it up; the liquefied orange-coloured maize pudding with the coarse husks floating on the top; and the Thursday agony when the raisin pudding ran out and the last three at the long table got rice instead. If only we had had Second War rationing with the much-despised Spam, which I still dote on, and that supremely versatile dehydrated egg power, what a difference it would have made!

All the same there was much to be revelled in and, if it lasts in the memory so long, there must have been something to it. Gavin Maxwell, every word of whose books I have read, seems somehow to have been destined for a life of unhappiness. Having had to be taken away from his first preparatory school, he also after two years had to be taken away from St Cyprians – ten years after my time, when conditions must surely have become less spartan. In his autobiography he gives the school a long lambasting, yet in the middle writes:

Flip [Mrs Wilkes] would have liked to have kept me in favour but I was just too much of an oddity for a busy woman to cope with. She started to do her best the day after I arrived, which was either a Sunday or for some other reason a holiday. She took me, another boy . . . and her daughter Robina, all of an age, to go blackberry picking. We packed into her Willys Knight (two-seater and dickey, all painted in two shades of brown) and drove off up the chalk downs and parked the car and wandered in briar-choked disused farm lanes where the chalk was everywhere like dirty snow underfoot and there was sunshine and big white cumulus clouds blowing on the early autumn wind. We filled our baskets with blackberries, and Flip gave us cake, and coffee from a thermos; it ought to have been a wonderful start, and I don't see what more she could have done.*

Nor for that matter do I.

These expeditions on the Downs remain one of the highlights of my life, and perhaps because of the contrast with the flatness of rural Bedfordshire, which gave me a sore throat every single holidays the moment I came home, causing me to have my tonsils removed twice by butchers and the third time by an expert, they lured me back when the time came forty years later to move out of London. Our clothing, the green jerseys with light blue collars and the corduroy breeches plus football boots or sneakers, and Maltese Cross cap-badge, was ideal for the purpose and, if you substitute a coat for the jersey, almost identical with what beaglers wear today. Often we were allowed to make a day of it and walk to Jevington, wandering at will through the gorse and the blackberry bushes and the innumerable wild flowers, being greeted in the village with gaseous bottles of 'Cherry Cider' or 'Ice-Cream Soda', the ones with marbles in the end into which your tongue always got stuck until you learnt the knack. Sometimes the older boys would walk on all the way to Alfriston, there to be picked up in the car of the day by Flip – no mean tramp for a twelve-year-old boy with legs as short as mine. Sometimes there would be a walk right across to Birling Gap and a bathe and picnic, or simply down to Holywell on the front, and sometimes to Pevensey, plus a visit to the Castle after a good briefing on who built it and when and why. It was in the course of one such expedition, I fancy, that I lost the first of my nine lives, when I was allowed to sit with my legs dangling over Beachy Head where a very slight dislodgement of chalk turf would have sent me six hundred feet to eternity.

On Saturdays it was nothing to field four elevens against some other school, half at home and half away, and against St Andrews we actually used to field eight. Lest I seem too eulogistic, let me add that teams which won got hot sausages for tea and the others didn't, which seems as damnably unfair now as it did then.

Nearer home the formidable Mrs Wilkes enabled us to touch life at many another point. During the war, for instance, we all knitted furiously for the soldiers at the front, keeping the ball of wool under

* Gavin Maxwell, *The House of Elrig* (Longmans, 1965).

the jersey and hauling it out as required through the neck (than which I doubt whether a better method has yet been devised) and graduating through simple long khaki scarves to three-needle socks and plain-and-purl Balaclavas. Again, a man may be nervous at the prospect of making a maiden, or even after-dinner, speech, but never to quite the same degree if years ago he has had to read the lesson in chapel at half-term in front of not only the entire school but all the assembled parents – and Flip. On Sunday evening nearly all of us would gather in a room known as the Band Room and would in turn choose hymns, which we sang with gusto to Flip's accompaniment on the piano. 'To sing a grand old hymn in company,' wrote A. P. Herbert, 'is to feel yourself a member of something more important than yourself' – and so it is. I can never hear the haunting refrain of 'The day thou gavest, Lord, is ended' without its taking my mind straight back to the Band Room fifty years ago. When the hymns were done and the rest had trooped to bed, three or four of the older boys would be permitted to stay up and wait on Flip and the masters at supper, which meant not only staying up agreeably late, but also being rewarded with a large plate of fruit salad or some such. This, it may be said, and certainly would have been said by George Orwell (of whom more later) was very convenient, since they made a cheap substitute for the maids on their Sunday night out. That may be so, but here was one of the lessons of life. Either you have been a waiter or you have not. We had, and I for one never needed anyone in after-life to tell me not to be rude to waiters. Other minor lessons were to be learnt too, one of them that it is physically impossible at the age of twelve to pull off a turkey leg with your bare hands.

The outstanding character at the school apart from the in-domitable matriarch herself was the second master, Robert L. Sillar, about whom even poor Orwell could scarce have found anything vile to write, though I cannot say, for I only picked his book up casually in a bookshop in Honolulu and was so shocked that I never read it again. Mr Sillar – he had no nickname – looked the gentle soul that he was, rather like, with his white hair and long moustaches, that other gentle soul, Kenneth Grahame. Mr Sillar taught art and geography and natural history and helped us with our butterflies – truly the Mr Chips of St Cyprians, corny as it may sound to say so. Maxwell wrote of him:

When I finally left . . . in a quaking jelly of misery and self-pity, he said: 'Just remember your luck will change – and never give up your interest in natural history.' . . . He nurtured and fostered my interest in natural history ('No one can understand simpler things like animals and birds first') during my two years [there], so that during the holidays, when I was restored to my normal existence in the family, it became my centre-point.*

Hence perhaps *Ring of Bright Water*. To many of us, however, Sillar will be for ever remembered for his lantern lecture on Dickens's *Christmas Carol* during that most agonizing time in a small boy's life, the few days that separate him from Home For Christmas. 'Where in a week's time shall we be? Not in this Acadamee.' Scrooge and the door-knocker turning into the ghost of Marley; the Ghosts of Christmas Past and Christmas Yet to Come; Bob Cratchit and Tiny Tim – if anyone produced one of those slides today I could identify it instantly. And above it all, unseen behind the light of the lantern, Sillar's melodious yet dramatic voice reading the story.

Looking back as what I hope I have now become, namely a 'freethinker', all passion spent, all bitterness gone, I conclude that St Cyprians was a very good school indeed, despite the fact, to which I shall return, that three of my more celebrated contemporaries, or near-contemporaries, have written so vitriolically about it as to make one wonder whether we are writing of the same institution. It is true that Mum Wilkes's dominant and sometimes emotional character caused one's whole existence to depend on whether one was 'in favour' or otherwise, and indeed the expression became a normal part of one's daily life without, so to speak, the inverted commas. If you were in favour, life could be bliss: if you weren't, it was hell, and no doubt this should be chalked up on the debit side. On the other hand it taught you the hard way one of *the* lessons of life – that, if you don't 'look after Number One', no one else will.

This was somewhat confirmed by one of the three critics I have in mind, Cyril Connolly, a fellow-contributor, though on more elevated subjects, to the *Sunday Times*. The other two were George Orwell, of *Nineteen Eighty-Four* and *Animal Farm* fame, whose real name was Eric Blair, and Gavin Maxwell, whom I have already quoted. Writing on Orwell's *Collected Essays* in 1968,

* *The House of Elrig.*

Connolly said: 'There one is, back again, among the cramming and the starving and the smells, a little boy in corduroy knickers and a green jersey. Horror upon horror – and yet we are determined to survive.'

Connolly went on to admit that later, on getting possession of his school reports and Mr Wilkes's letters to his father and his own letters home, they 'revealed a considerable distortion between my picture of the proprietors and their own unremitting care to bring me on'. Orwell, he added, 'rejected not only the school but the War, the Empire, Kipling, Sussex and Character' – hardly perhaps an endearing 'reference' for one's hero. Orwell himself sank from Eton via service in Burma and the Spanish Civil War to a life among the down-and-outs in Paris, and those who have read his book about it may share the charitable opinion that by this time he was mad.

Anyway, whatever my distinguished fellow-sufferers may say – and it is my impression that Connolly was nearly always 'in favour' and that I practically never was – I looked back on St Cyprians as having given us a very good education, with a small e and in the sense of a preparation for life, though of course any boarding school, including Borstal, will teach you more about life than any day school, state or private. Indeed, you almost certainly learn more about life during out-of-school hours than in.

'The happiest people,' said Theodore Roosevelt, 'are those who touch life at as many points as possible,' and it is fair to say that schools like St Cyprians enabled us to do so. We played the three compulsory games, of course: soccer in the winter term, rugger in the Easter and cricket in the summer. There is nothing wrong in not liking any or all of them, but years of enforced experience do at least enable you to enjoy the finer points of them later on and to sense when a critic, not similarly fortunate, is writing rubbish. Thus, though I can sense that cricket is, or at any rate was, a great and noble game, it seemed to me, even at that age, to be too often completely inactive. In soccer, of course, you played in goal – a game within a game, as putting is in golf – and let the others do the running about; while in rugger, especially if you were small, as I was, you played scrum half and let the muddied oafs do the shoving.

These games taught me something else, though, which I like to think may have been valuable later on when I fell into becoming a commentator. I once kept wicket in a needle game against St Anthony's and with the last man in they needed one to tie, two to win. Supposing I could bring off a catch? Supposing I dropped one? Supposing I let through a boundary bye? Not, I dare say, a milestone in the history of cricket, but the *intensity* of feeling has never been exceeded since, however desperately I have wanted to win at golf or any other game. So at least you know, as a commentator or critic, that the man lining up the putt to tie for the Open is not just the figure you see on the telly. You know how it *feels* to want more than anything in the world not to drop a catch against St Anthony's, and the commentator and the victim become brothers under the skin. 'A man may miss a three-foot putt,' wrote Bernard Darwin, 'yet be a good husband, a good father and an honest Christian gentleman.'

Such were the standard pursuits, but some of us also did carpentering with George, who helped me, or perhaps the other way round, to make a very fine glass-fronted bookcase; and rode on the Downs; and learned to shoot with a rifle, and to put on our puttees and slope arms and stand still in the ranks when inspected by a visiting general. Some, though not your humble servant, even learnt to play in the band and render the General Salute. Above all, perhaps, we learnt about the Downs.

We used to go riding in threes with a man from the riding-school and often one of my companions would be a pale, rather lanky boy, no great shakes at games, known as Milksop Mildmay. Years later, if his rein had not broken at the crucial moment, he would almost certainly have won the Grand National. He was drowned while bathing and the Mildmay Stakes commemorate his name. He was, of course, by that time Lord Mildmay, among the last of the Corinthians of steeplechasing and much loved by the Aintree crowds as 'M'lord', and indeed by the press as well, who still prefer a lord to a commoner, as the popular gossip columns make abundantly clear. One of the charges levelled against the Wilkes family by the critics I have mentioned was that of 'snobbery', in that they liked to have in the school the offspring of the aristocracy, and indeed I think they did, but for the life of me I cannot see why they shouldn't – especially when it is remembered that they cheerfully accepted the rather uncouth offspring of a modest, though worthy, retail house furnisher. I claim to have grown up absolutely 'classless', but if someone said, 'Tomorrow you may meet either a Duke or a dustman but not both,' I should choose the Duke, not to dine out on the fact that I had met him but because he would surely be the more interesting company of the two. Boys on the whole are not themselves aristocracy-conscious, as proof of which I might say that we had at St Cyprians a number of Cavendishes, a great 'capture' by any standard and, though I remember at least one of them, I could not for the life of me tell you whether he is, or became, the Duke of Devonshire. Another scion of the aristocracy was Reggie Malden, who remains a crony of mine to this day, and I am sure we still see each other more as the original small boys in green jersey and corduroy breeches than as a couple of increasingly portly gents having a drink in the Bath Club. We knew that Reggie Malden was really Lord Malden and presumably would one day be the Earl of Essex (it took him the best part of forty years!) because his father, as Earl, captained the fathers in the Fathers' Match, but the real snobbery lay in the pride we took in having among us a boy called Case, whose stepfather also captained the Fathers. Now there *was* aristocracy for you, for his stepfather was the great Test captain J. W. H. T. Douglas.

It was also held against the Wilkeses that they were over-keen on boys getting scholarships to their public schools, and above all to Eton, and perhaps they were, but this, after all, was one of the main measurements of a school's standing in the preparatory schools' League Table, just as one reads about how many university scholarships various public and grammar schools attain today. As to Eton, a contemporary of mine, Arthur Colver, who came of a Harrovian family, recalls as though it were yesterday the unfortunate episode in Flip's history form, when the subject under discussion was 'bad' kings. John, Richard III and one or two others had been accepted in this category, when the unhappy Colver suggested Henry VI. The reply was a thunderous roar, he says, of '*He founded Eton!*' and he was forthwith sent to bed without supper. She could indeed be rough at times. Another witness was also a contemporary in the person of David Ogilvy, of whom the Alma Mater may well be proud, for he is one of the very few Englishmen who have singed the Americans' beard and taken them for a monumental ride at their own game. In the course of building up what must be almost the most successful advertising agency on Madison Avenue, he put across three stupendously successful gimmicks: one by putting a black patch over one eye

43

of a male model to sell shirts; another by putting over the bearded Commander Whitehead as the emblem of Schweppes' Tonic Water; and the third with his slogan: 'The only sound at sixty m.p.h. in the new Rolls-Royce is the ticking of the electric clock.' In his book *The Confessions of an Advertising Man** he revealed that the revenues of his nineteen clients in 1963 were greater than the revenue of Her Majesty's Government. He also wrote on the first page:

> At the age of nine I was sent to board at an aristocratic Dotheboys Hall in Eastbourne. The headmaster wrote of me: 'He has a distinctly original mind, inclined to argue with his teachers and try to convince them that he is right and the books are wrong; but this perhaps is further proof of his originality.' When I suggested that Napoleon might have been a Dutchman because his brother was King of Holland, the head-master's wife sent me to bed without supper. When she was robing me for the part of the Abbess in *The Comedy of Errors*, I rehearsed my opening speech with an emphasis which she disliked; whereupon she seized me by the cheek and threw me to the floor.

My own experience in *As You Like It* was rather more fortunate. I played the part of Adam, the old man, and can remember only the line: 'Kind master, I can go no further.' Not only did I escape being thrown to the ground but the part involved the eating, on stage, of a splendid free apple. My only other appearance on the stage, it may be noted, was in a charity television show at the Palladium before Her Majesty. What she thought I was doing, dressed in an Olympic Games T-shirt and hitting a plastic golf-ball into the orchestra (I had in fact been summoned on the under-standing that I was to be the announcer) one hesitates to think – if indeed she thought about it at all, which is doubtful.

It was assumed, of course, that almost every boy would follow the normal educational pattern: public school followed by the University – 'the University' meaning, of course, Oxford or Cambridge. Some would go straight to Sandhurst and a sub-stantial proportion, including one of the Wilkeses' two sons, Dick, would give a lifetime to the service of the Empire overseas. His obituary in the *Daily Telegraph* in November 1970 told a typical story:

RICHARD LESLIE VAUGHAN WILKES. At Minehead, Somerset, aged 66. Entered Colonial Service Nigeria, 1928; retired, 1951; C.M.G.,

* Longmans, 1964.

1958. Public Service Commission, chairman, Sierra Leone, 1954–58; Sarawak, 1961–64 and British North Borneo (Sabah) 1963–64.

To which might in the light of present knowledge be added Kipling's:

> Take up the White Man's burden –
> And reap his old reward:
> The blame of those ye better,
> The hate of those ye guard . . .

The highest accolade, and my father's dearest ambition for me, was to be accepted for the Indian Civil Service – classical scholars of a high order, who ruled a vast continent by force of character and ended with the then unprecedented pension of £1000 a year.

One of the oldest school stories is of the teacher asking little Johnnie what are two and two and he says, 'Four,' She says, 'Very good,' to which little Johnnie replies, 'Very good be damned. It's perfect!' and perhaps for this reason I always enjoyed arithmetic and algebra, partly for the almost sensual satisfaction of bringing a sum or an equation to a 'perfect' solution and partly because I often used to get 100% in exams, which is impossible in History and English, where there is no 'correct' solution. Lest this sound a little blasé, I should add that when later they tried to teach me higher mathematics in the shape of differential calculus and analytical geometry – δy by δx and all that sort of thing – I not only no longer got 100%; I could not, and still cannot, understand a single word.

Mum Wilkes herself taught History and English and Scripture, her great ambition being to produce a winner of the Townsend Warner History Prize, but of course much of it – Keats, Shelley, Tennyson, Kipling, Newbolt and the rest – would cut little ice today. She made us keep History Notebooks, filled with jottings of quotations and any bits and pieces that took our fancy, akin to the commonplace book of adult life, and created a high standard of essay-writing, at which I was one of the lowliest and most inarticulate performers, little thinking that I was to earn much of my living by it later on.

Every Sunday we had to learn and recite the Collect for the day, sometimes mercifully short but always in sublime English, and in chapel I graduated to blowing the organ, alone in a little cubicle with Yellow Underwings for company, the irascible organist just visible through the pipes as he exhorted the choir to, 'Sing up. Don't stand there like tom cats with cherry-stones in your mouths.' The idea was to blow sufficiently to keep a weight hanging on a cord between a high and low point. The temptation to see how near the top one could let it go before pumping the handle would have been irresistible to any boy. Half an inch too far and a furious voice – had Flip heard and would one get the sack and have to sit in chapel thereafter with the common herd? – would be crying, 'Blow up, you owl, blow up!' Hasty pumping would then get the weight right down to the bottom, whereupon the organ with a ghastly grunt seized up and the voice – surely it must be heard this time? – shouted, 'Don't overblow, you owl, don't overblow!'

That I was 'crammed' for a scholarship I now have no doubt, and certainly I was not the only one. On the other hand there is also no doubt that I should not have got one without, since I was by nature willing to expend more effort in evading work than would have been required to do the work itself. After much compulsory travail in the holidays, partly by correspondence and partly in person with Mr Sewell, a master at Bedford School and the best coach I ever knew, I was taken for a trial run at Harrow. The exam was a two-day affair and I was not surprised, on looking at the board on the first evening, to find that I was not among those required on the morrow – and, if I seem to hear voices suggesting that I should not have made a very good Harrovian, well, perhaps they are right.

More cramming followed, and the day came when Rosemary Wilkes and I were shoved into the dickey of Mr Wilkes's two-seater and deposited respectively at Wycombe Abbey and Charterhouse. For the next two days the sun shone and I fell in love with the Charterhouse scene. To get a scholarship here really would be something – and they even played soccer, so with luck I could go on playing in goal. Perhaps because of this I played rather better than my handicap, so to speak, and I could point now to the very spot on the Downs at Birling Gap where a group of us were sitting when Mr Wilkes came up with a telegram from my parents. DELIGHTED WITH NEWS FROM CARTERHOUSE [sic], it said. Meanwhile Rosemary had obliged at Wycombe, so we had brought off the double, each of us thereby earning the traditional half-holiday for the school.

Eastbourne remains one of my favourite towns, perhaps because, apart from the truly disastrous high-rise block of flats, which not only ruins the gentle and still dignified façade of the sea front but can actually be seen from the golf-course at Crowborough, twenty miles away, it remains largely unchanged: the same respectable tree-lined streets and avenues and privet hedges (I have a good deal of privet in my downland garden and the almost overpowering scent of it in July never fails to take me straight back to St Cyprians) and the same old Devonshire Park and the Saffrons cricket ground and the station (which Councillor Major C. J. H. Tolley, MC, the great golfer, later wanted to move, for some reason, to the Crumbles – scene in our day of an 'orrible murder by Field and Gray and later an equally famous one by Patrick Mahon). Above all there are the same hotels, from which it was possible to grade the parents by the one at which they stayed. My own parents stayed at the comparatively humble Chatsworth, still there on the front. The rich, possibly with a 'nouveau' in front, stayed in those days at the Grand. The gayer, younger, well-off types – the mother in full glamour, the father perhaps with a dashing motor car – stayed at the Cavendish, but there was no doubt where the aristocracy stayed. They stayed at the Burlington. When I first went to Eastbourne as a parent, we booked in, to cut a bit of a dash, at the Cavendish, and nothing could have been nicer. I told the children to bring as many friends as they liked, the more the merrier, and the barman was expert at making a huge pink and white concoction called a 'Half-term Special', calculated to keep them occupied while the parents had a few nourishing pink gins before lunch. A splendid time was had by all till we got the bill. It came to just over half the term's fees.

Soon after the war St Cyprians was burnt to the ground and, though the name was carried on for a while elsewhere – in fact at Wispers, near Midhurst, a charming old house which the 9th Duke of Bedford had bought as a dower house for the Flying Duchess and to which he added a staff wing as big as the house itself, since he could not envisage anyone living without an army of servants – the blow was too much for the school, and Mum Wilkes retired to what had been the Masters' Lodge at the end of the original St Cyprians drive, where quite often I was able to call and see her. I had often suffered at her hands, but my respect for her grew, till I realized that she was undoubtedly the outstanding woman in my life. A year or two ago, driving by and seeing a light in her window, I thought to myself, 'If I don't stop now, I may never see her again.' She was ninety-one at the time and I found her quite alone, doing the *Times* crossword, which she said she was finding more difficult than it used to be. She produced the ledgers and scrapbooks of all the boys who had passed through the school and we talked of many we had known in common, not forgetting Cecil Beaton and his rendering of 'Tit Willow' from the wings of the gymnasium stage. She remembered every one of them and who they had married and how many grandchildren they had, but for many, alas, the entries were closed. Killed 1914. Killed 1916. Killed RAF 1940. Died of wounds 1944 . . .

'I really am beginning to feel my age a bit,' she said, 'now that my oldest old boy is seventy-four!' A year later she died and I will end on a lighter note which would have given her enormous delight. When I wrote a piece about her in the *Sunday Times*, a boy with whom I had been there half a century before wrote: 'It may amuse you to know that my brother attributes the fact that he emerged absolutely sane and fit from five years as a prisoner of war solely to having been at St Cyprians.'

5

Golf at
First Sight

I have mentioned how at St Cyprians I first became conscious of
the game which was to play such a powerful part in my life, and
indeed, though no longer superstitious nor even, I fear, religious,
I cannot help feeling that these things are somehow 'meant'.
Bernard Darwin, to whom golf and the writing about it became
the abiding interest of his life, has recounted how a certain uncle of
his joined a certain regiment, long before the First War, and if he
had not joined this particular regiment he would not have been
posted to Liverpool, he would not have taken his leave in Aberdovey, and if he had not taken his leave in Aberdovey he would not
have laid out the golf-course there (with flower-pots for holes) –
and, if all this had not happened, he, Bernard, might never have
been introduced to golf. The same may be said of myself, though
by no means through so complicated a chain of events. The first
link was a simple one. If my cousins Michael and Bernard Waterer
(Michael killed in the First War; Bernard now a retired knight!)
had not been sent there, I should never myself have been sent to
St Cyprians, into whose sunken playing-field the golfers of Royal
Eastbourne were prone to slice their opening drives. The golfers
on the skyline with their boy caddies trailing behind them became
a familiar sight and it was not long before I was gazing at them – the
caddies, not the golfers – with the deepest envy as I peered
surreptitiously up from the Greek Unseen, waiting for the familiar
'Will-you-get-on-with-your-work, *Long'st*!' from Mr Wilkes.

The school itself had a strong flavour of golf about it since Mr
Wilkes was a pillar of the club and scratch or thereabouts. His son,
now the Reverend J. C. V. Wilkes and one-time Warden of Radley,
played for Oxford in the mid-twenties and *his* son, J.V., for Oxford in 1965 and 1966. The caddies, however, did not enjoy quite
the life of bliss that I had imagined. There used to hang on the

wall of the billiard-room at Royal Eastbourne, and I hope still does, a document dated 1900 outlining their conditions of engagement and employment. The boys were paid 6s. a week and had to report to the caddie-master at 9.15. Most of the notice consisted of the scale of fines for ten sets of offences – and pretty intimidating they must have been at 6s. a week! Mr Holly the caddie-master (he served fifty years at the 'Royal' and so, very nearly, did the Ranger, Huggett; while Cyril Thomson, the professional, has so far done forty-nine) booked the boys in in turn and, if you weren't there when your turn was called – 'Missing turn through want of attention' – it was 1d. fine for every boy sent out after your name had been called. Throwing stones, fighting (I think Mr Holly must have turned many a blind eye here, for they always seemed to be wrestling and rolling on the grass), using obscene language, shouting and annoying any member or visitor were all 1s. a time. 'Laziness . . . inattention . . . rudeness, incivility or smoking while carrying clubs . . . or asking for gratuities(!) – all carried 1s. for the first offence and 2s. 6d. for the second. The most savage penalties however – 2s. 6d., 7s. 6d. and dismissal – were exacted and constantly risked for 'entering the grounds of any school, or any woods or plantations', and this meant the Duke of Devonshire's spinneys and the steep rough bank down into our playing-field. We regarded such balls as our 'perks' – somewhat supported by Mr Wilkes, who once confiscated a brand new blue-dot Silver King before I had bounced it more than a couple of times in the lavatory – but the caddies made constant forays, and running battles were liable to ensue, conducted under well understood but far from Welfare State rules. The school sergeant, who had once played in goal for Plymouth Argyle, took pot-shots at them with a .22 from the gymnasium window at a range of no more than a hundred and twenty yards, without, so far as I remember, scoring an outer, while two who were apprehended were treated on a par with the sons of the aristocracy in the school and soundly beaten by Mr Wilkes, who, though the mildest of men, would no doubt in this enlightened age be sent to prison.

The second and decisive link in the chain that was to attach me to golf was 'if my parents had not in 1920 decided to take their holiday in a certain hotel overlooking the common in the little town of Yelverton, in Devon'. With us were my cousin Betty Waterer and her splendid mother, my Aunt Gertrude ('It's not a question of whether we can afford to have it, my dear Harry. It's whether we can afford not to.'). It came to the knowledge of my cousin and myself that a couple of boys had cut three holes on the common with penknives – just as the great Horace Hutchinson, the first Amateur Champion, used to do at Westward Ho! in the eighties – and were in the habit of playing their three-hole course in the morning before the grown-ups surfaced for breakfast. We joined them, I with a small sawn-off club, and within a matter of an hour I was hooked for life. A set of three or four clubs was procured for me from the pro at Yelverton, who also gave me a lesson, and thus it was on this charming heath-and-heather course that I hit my first 'proper' shot at golf.

It seemed almost fated that the game of golf and I should be drawn together, since a year or two before I had got the 'bug' into my system at Yelverton the family had moved from Bromham to another little village called Biddenham, ten minutes' bicycle ride from the town, but still, difficult as it is to believe today, completely rural. Scarcely two minutes away was the Bedford Golf Club (now, more grandly, Bedfordshire), just down the lane past the deserted gravel pit where occasionally one could bag a rabbit with a .22 and where once we – or rather they, with me standing well back – took a hornets' nest suspended in a bush by enclosing the whole thing with tied-up sheets and pouring poison on it.

Golf for the young was a good deal frowned upon in those days as not fostering the team spirit, though how one could find twenty-one other boys and a pitch in rural Bedfordshire with whom to indulge in team games was never revealed. The professional at the Bedford club, as his father had been before him, was Jack Seager, and soon, now that Charles Flute had gone off to make his way in the world, he became my hero and friend. My father stood me three lessons a week with him and most of the rest of most days I spent hanging about his shop, with its divine smell of shavings, pitch and glue. Nearly all professionals in those days made clubs and Jack was a very fine craftsman. I must not overdo the 'good old days', but here the young golfers of today really do miss something in never having been promised a new driver for Christmas and never having seen the rough hickory shaft selected from the bundle standing in the corner and the head gradually taking shape in the vice, until at last there is Jack giving it its final coat of varnish till it gleams like a new 'conker'. Then comes the supreme moment when you waggle it in the shop, and it is your very own. (Times do indeed change. During the Walker Cup match of 1949 at one of New York's most opulent clubs one of the British players broke the shaft of one of his clubs. The pro's shop was more like a Bond Street store, with I don't know how many assistants. Not one, however, was able to re-shaft a club and it had to be sent hastily back to the factory. Such is progress!)

Junior members, of course, were not in those days allowed in the club-house, while on the course itself one was always in fear of being chivvied by retired Indian Army colonels with very white moustaches and very red faces, ever liable to report 'that damned boy' for getting in the way. As for the course, fond as my memories may be, it would be idle to claim any great distinction for it, for if the truth be told it was a flat, lush hundred-acre meadow, bounded by the Midland Railway, the River Ouse, the Girls' High School hockey-field, the allotments, a cornfield and Mr Somebody's garden. Furthermore, all these hazards were on the left, so that at the top of the swing, so quickly does the human warning-system work, the small voice would cry, 'Look out. The railway!' or, 'Look out. The allotments!' Add to this the fact that for much of the year it was muddy enough to require a cut-up shot to get the ball in the air at all, and one may sympathize if this golfing baptism left me with a slice that lasted to the end of my days. It is some consolation to think that in the end in quite august circles, including Henry Cotton himself, a shot with an involuntary fade was said to 'have a bit of Bedfordshire on it'. In winter the mud really could be a little beyond a joke, though it gave rise to one minor episode that delights me to this day. One of the regulars, just before the war, was Lord Mandeville (now the Duke of Manchester) from nearby Kimbolton, with whom I used often to play. He was akin to the P. G. Wodehouse character who 'never spared himself in his efforts to do the ball a violent injury', and at the 8th hole during the County Championship, determined to be the only player in the field to reach the green with an iron, he struck at the ball so savagely, and leaned so far forward in the process, as actually to drive it straight into the ground where it lay – a feat of which to this day I have not heard the like. The only muddier course was perhaps Southfield, near Oxford, at which the University played their home matches. The 10th hole was about six hundred straight yards of absolutely damn-all and evoked from a distinguished Walker Cup player, Rex Hartley, visiting it for the first time on a foggy, drizzly day in February, the immortal comment, 'Only two clubs to play this hole with. A rifle and a spade.'

Having been a little candid about my golfing alma mater at Bedford, let me now add not only that surface conditions are much improved through modern greenkeeping knowledge but also that a few years ago there was begun a transformation that has to be seen to be believed. Apart from a row of magnificent poplars down by the river there was not in my young days a single tree or shrub on the course. You could see every hole but one from the clubhouse, and the prospect was later enhanced by the erection of a gigantic electricity grid, complete with pylons stretching out in every direction. One day, greatly daring, they planted a few stunted bushes in the rough at the second, at which next morning two rather short-sighted retired colonels were heard shouting, 'Fore!' under the impression that it was a fourball looking for a lost ball, but for years afterwards unimagination held sway, till one day someone – and may his or their name be blessed! – suggested trees. All I can say now is, if you belong to a flat, uninteresting course, of which geographically there must needs be many, especially in the Midlands, pay a visit to Bedford and see the miracle they have achieved.

There can be no doubt, I think, that the seasons have changed since I was a boy at Biddenham and that the winters these days are not so cold nor the summers so hot. One would not nowadays, for instance, give a boy a pair of skates for Christmas on the assumption that the ponds would freeze over. Again, in the midsummer of 1921 or 1922 there occurred a phenomenon which I took for granted at the time but the equal of which, like Lord Mandeville's self-inflicted 'sucker', I have not seen since. The drought was such as to cause vast cracks to appear all over the golf-course, some of them a foot or more across and many feet deep, so that one's ball, rolling merrily along the middle of the fairway, would suddenly vanish and one tried to mark the exact spot in the exact crack down which it had disappeared. Thus I must remain among the few who have actually seen retired colonels and schoolmasters lying flat on the fairway, the blood going rapidly to their heads as they reach down at arm's length with their niblicks trying to retrieve their ball from the bowels of the earth. Many a ball

*After winning the juveniles'
competition at North Foreland,
aged thirteen.*

*About sixteen, riding my P. and M.
Panther, a very great machine.*

would be hauled to within a foot or two of recovery, only to drop off, like a trout within reach of the net, and vanish out of sight for ever. Some day, perhaps in a thousand years' time, archaeologists will discover some of these balls and will prove, positively beyond question, that golf was played at that level in the Bedfordshire of the 1900s.

After three or four blissful years Jack Seager left for the Rothley Park Club, near Leicester, to be succeeded by a young professional, Bill Moore, whose coming I automatically resented, though my attitude softened to a certain extent when I found that he had come from being an assistant at the same old Royal Eastbourne where it all began and that I actually remembered having seen him giving a lady a golf lesson as we walked across the course to a match against St Andrews. I continued my own lessons with him and as I grew up we became not only friends but, if I have the right word, 'cronies'. With little else to concentrate upon I improved rapidly, and it was soon borne in upon me that as a character-builder, or at any rate character-tester, golf left all the virtuous team games standing. Indeed, one could claim without being pompous that this ridiculous game teaches you all the lessons of life in miniature – no sense in losing your temper . . . never give up till the game is lost, and many others – without the disastrous penalties that await failure in higher spheres. For myself, nearing what my friend Leonard Crawley habitually refers to as the 'close of play', I find myself super-tolerant – dust into dust and nothing and nobody really matters, and what business of mine are another man's shortcomings? – but in the early days failure drove me almost out of my mind, so that to this day I sympathize with the silver-tongued, club-throwing golfers of former times so piously frowned upon today. I was in good company, however, for only after similar years of mental anguish did the great Bobby Jones himself become a model of deportment and the best-loved figure in the history of golf. I will not say that I became a model of deportment but I did eventually develop an aptitude for wrapping myself in a sort of cocoon of concentration – only to have the whole thing split asunder in a few seconds one night on the Leicester road.

Soon I belonged also to the other Bedford club, the Bedford and County, near the village of Clapham, a more up-and-down and more 'sporting' course, where I often played with my father, a keenly indifferent 16-handicap performer and precisely the average golfer for whom all golf writers should to my way of thinking deem themselves to be writing. His game merits only one observation, that he used a most graphic expression which I have never heard since. Even as his club was descending to the ball, he would say, 'Ach! *Smudged 'im!*' Every Sunday they played at Clapham for the weekly 'Spoon' – it really was a spoon in those days, an ornamental tea-spoon, though you never hear the expression now – and I should not care to say how many I won. Week by week they put my handicap down but in a week or a month I had overtaken them and they had to put it down again. I do not think the older members were too pleased, but, Lord, what fun it was to be ever on the upward path, bounding forward to a limitless future, unaware that the day would come when you would put the bloody things in the loft, lower the hatch, remove the steps and creep away!

I suppose what really set me going was the fact that my parents agreed to combine their holiday with the annual juvenile golf tournament at North Foreland, near Broadstairs. This was held on the par-3 course beside the main course, with an age limit of fourteen and two strokes handicap per year below that. Being thirteen I received two. Wing-Commander P. B. Lucas, DSO, DFC, Croix de Guerre, chairman of the Greyhound Racing Association, former Walker Cup captain, and ex-MP for Brentford and Chiswick, being six and a half, received sixteen. I won (65 less 2 – 63, I may say, and I wonder if I could do it today) and he was second with 66, thus beginning a friendship valued equally, I like to think, by each of us. Lucas, incidentally, was born in the clubhouse at Prince's, Sandwich, where his father was secretary, and his intimate local knowledge of the course enabled him, when shot up in the war, to land his crippled Spitfire on the 9th fairway. Some time after this, when we were neighbours at Fighter Command and Anti-Aircraft Command, some excuse was made by which I was able to accompany him in some small aeroplane to visit a Wing at Coltishall in Essex. On the way home to Northolt he allowed me to 'have a go' and in endeavouring to do a turn, 'maintaining altitude and keeping the nose steady on the horizon', I managed to lose twelve hundred feet over the Harrow gasworks and finished up parallel with the Watford Bypass. Meanwhile the nose yawed continuously from side to side and in the end it seemed more like bicycling. Perhaps I was better off in the Army after all.

In the tournament at North Foreland I had for the first time a caddie. His name was Frank Honour and hang it if he was not later a constituent of mine at Acton. He admired a pair of white shoes I was wearing and in a burst of fellow feeling I said that if we won – I am sure I said 'we' and not 'I' – I would give them to him. We did and I did, and R. Endersby Howard wrote so charming a little piece about us in the *Daily Mail* that I venture to quote it in full.

GOLF BOY & HIS CADDIE
Child-like contract and its result

By R. Endersby Howard

Broadstairs, Thursday

Even the seasoned championship follower – setting out to be amused – could not help being seriously impressed by the *sang-froid* and success with which children, whose ages ranged from 6 to 14, played golf in the juveniles' competition on the approach and putting course at North Foreland today.

Henry C. Longhurst, who is 13, and Percy Belgrave Lucas, who has yet to turn 7, were the heroes of the occasion. For their years they performed wonders.

Longhurst, a sturdy little fellow who has just finished his course at a preparatory school at Eastbourne and is going to Charterhouse next term, embarked upon his task with all due circumspection. Before the start he and his caddie – a boy of about the same age and size – had an earnest consultation as to how the holes should be played.

In a final burst of fellow-feeling Longhurst intimated that for every hole he did in 3 he would give the caddie a penny; whereupon the caddie, warming to such friendship, remarked that they were a very nice pair of white shoes that Longhurst was wearing. 'Yes,' said the young principal, 'they cost 4s. 11d., and if I win this competition I will give you them.'

He did win, and the traditions of kings and cobblers who were companions on the links never had happier modern expression than in this round. The caddie would allow nobody to approach his player. 'Don't worry him,' he would say when anybody went near. 'He's doing well, so leave him alone.' Each time he would place his arm on Longhurst's shoulder, point out exactly the best spot on which to pitch the ball, and move silently away.

Longhurst returned a score of 65, less 2 – 63, the homeward half being 30. This was extraordinarily good considering that the holes vary in length from 50 yards to 140 yards. He had nine 3s, seven 4s and two 5s. He hit some particularly crisp and accurate shots with a mashie niblick. He hails from the Biddenham Golf Club, near Bedford.

Percy Lucas – son of the secretary of the Prince's Golf Club, Sandwich, Mr P. M. Lucas, was second with 82, less 16 – 66. This also was an astonishing performance for a boy not yet 7. Standing about the height of a man's driver (42 inches) and dressed in a little grey jersey suit and white socks and shoes, he took complete charge of his father, who carried his clubs.

'Niblick!' he would request imperiously when he hit the ball into a bunker; and his bunker shots were masterpieces of advanced golfing art.

Not only this, but a picture of me holding the Cup appeared on the front page of the London evening newspaper, the *Star*, and elsewhere there were pictures of me being presented with the trophy by Phyllis Monkman, star of the *Co-Optimists*. I gazed steadfastly at the 'coveted trophy', while Miss Monkman, I could not understand why, gazed equally steadily at the camera. Thus was shone upon me for the first time the heady light of public recognition.

6

Charterhouse in the Twenties

Soon after the modest triumph at North Foreland I went back to the bottom of the form again and started the long five-year process of working my passage through Charterhouse, and, looking back, I can honestly think of no school to which I would rather have been. It sits on the top of the hill outside Godalming, with the three so-called 'block' houses, the chapel, and classrooms all on the hill, in yellow limestone, architecturally somewhat in Palace of Westminster style, which is much more impressive to the youthful mind than the modern glass-box affairs. The rest of the houses are on the other side of the road down to Godalming, of somewhat 'institutional' appearance and in red brick. All except one, still known as Gownboys after the original scholars in the City of London, are called something or other '——ites', e.g. Saunderites, Hodgsonites and so on. Gownboys is in the centre of the block houses and it was to Gownboys that I reported as a rather indifferent classical scholar, in September 1922. Each house had one classical scholar per year, known, since work was known in the school jargon as 'hash', as the 'hash-pro'. Who allotted me to Gownboys I do not know, but I thank him in retrospect not only because it was probably at that time as good a house as any in the school but also because you didn't have to run for about five minutes to get to school, as they did from the more remote houses. You were already there.

The housemaster was the Duke, in other words Mr Stephen Langton. Many schoolmasters have nicknames but few in my memory have had one by which they were not only known but normally thought of. You did not think of 'Mr Langton', or even 'Langton'. You referred to him in mind and speech automatically as 'The Duke'. If ever a man was house-proud, the Duke was – and what is wrong with that, anyway? He was not, I confess, allocated a particularly brilliant 'hash-pro' in 1922, but we did win more than our fair share of sporting and other events, due largely, I always suspected, to his keeping so sharp an eye on preparatory schools who might be able to furnish a good round-the-wicket left-arm bowler who would come in useful in a few years' time. Our success, due at least partly to weight of numbers, tended to cause a tinge of envy in smaller houses and it was to correct this and a certain piety of outlook on the part of the Duke himself that in my last year we finished almost deliberately last-but-one in the drill competition. He was both affronted and ashamed. 'My Gownboys,' he said at Prayers that night. '*My* Gownboys!'

Headmaster in my time was Frank Fletcher, upon whom it may safely be said there were no flies whatever and whose personal motto might well have been *Nemo me impune capit the mickey*. Public schools, like so many institutions, have their ups and downs, while to the outward world remaining the same, and I believe that Charterhouse, just before my time, had been allowed to run a bit wild and that Fletcher was the new broom appointed to sweep it clean. This process had been accomplished by the time of my arrival and I therefore am able to reveal none of those lurid or painful experiences described by Robert Graves and Simon Raven, of Charterhouse, or Cyril Connolly and David Benedictus, of Eton. I think it was just a very good, 'straight' school, its products not so immediately identifiable as those of Eton, Winchester or Harrow, yet, when you think that from the smallest house there emerged such widely diverse characters as Ben Travers and Harry Oppenheimer, it must surely have had something.

No reminiscences of English public school life are complete without dark and sometimes salacious allusions to corporal punishment, on which more rubbish is talked than on foxhunting and South African tours, which is saying something. The greatest rubbish is talked by the modern psychiatrists and politicians who are able to prove that it is 'no deterrent'. One such, a former Minister of the Crown, solemnly declared to this effect when he was a law officer in the Commons. The press somehow got hold of the fact that, while at Eton, he had received eight of the best from the Hon. Gentleman for Thirsk, Mr Robin Turton, an event which both parties remembered with the greatest clarity, and it furthermore transpired that this particular non-deterrent was administered for bullying small boys. One would have liked to ask the Rt Hon. Gentleman, (1) What other correction did he remember with such clarity after forty years? and (2) May we take it that, since it is no deterrent, he continued to bully small boys? At Charterhouse the head monitors of the houses were issued by the school sergeant with ash sticks, with which they ran at the kneeling victim and delivered such a blow as nearly always broke the stick. The prospect of this I found to be deterring, as would, I suspect, young breakers-up of railway carriages today, and it is a pity for their own sakes that they cannot be subjected to this cheap experiment – eight for the first carriage, twelve for the second – before being sent to a life of lonely sodomy and resentment in an institution.

Housemasters could also beat their own inmates and one at least, I am reasonably certain, only became a housemaster for the pleasure of doing so. Most, however, and certainly my own, were sparing of this particular privilege, for which relief much thanks. The most deterring was, appropriately enough, Frank Fletcher himself, and one's fear of being 'called up' when the weekly form order was read out was, to one idle scholar at least, a very real one. Only the other day I met a well-known racehorse-owner, now aged about sixty-seven, who made the error of deleting from some list or other a mark against his name indicating that he had been absent. This, as the Inland Revenue narks put it, 'came to light', as a result of which an appointment was made with Fletcher and he got eight. This was almost precisely half a century ago, but he remembered it with a shudder as though it were yesterday. No deterrent indeed! You ought to have seen the boys' bottoms at the Baths, multicoloured like baboons'. You could always tell when the damage had been done by Fletcher. He left a neat series of purple and yellow stripes on their legs.

I do not know where he ranks in the opinion of the profession but Fletcher seems to me to have been a very considerable headmaster, particularly in that there was no doubt in anybody's mind – including, I am sure, both senior and junior masters – as to who was in charge. *He* was. The same applied in the Sixth Form Classical, where I spent a respectful year under his eagle eye and scathing tongue. One's only hope, when he looked round for someone at whom to throw a question, lay in self-effacement and, if one got precisely behind the boy in front, one nearly always escaped. We were doing Thucydides' *War in Plataea*, and I fear that both my attention and my vigilance had strayed. When I was last attending, the war was being carried on, or so I thought, in Sicily. It had now reached a place called Decalaea. 'Decalaea, yes. Where's that?' I was gazing at the ceiling and my face must have stood out a mile. In a flash I realized the peril, but too late. '*Longhurst!*' I nudged my next-door neighbour, later to become my insurance agent, but to no avail. 'Well, er, Sicily, sir.' I mumbled. There was a long pause. 'Sicily? Did you say *Sicily*? Speak up, boy. *I* thought he said Sicily. He can't have said Sicily. Can anyone tell us how long ago we were in Sicily? . . .' Later, in one of the semi-underground magazines that were a source of much innocent fun, a fellow scholar, whom I met for the first time since and instantly recognized only the other day, provided the rather splendid limerick:

> An unwisely courageous back-bencher,
> When asked, drew a bow at a venture.
>   Decalaea, um, er,
>   It's in Sicily, sir.
> Moral: silence is better than censure.

Fletcher had what we were always told were the two best grass courts in Surrey and older boys were sometimes invited to play with him. He had little style but a devastatingly good eye which enabled him to place the ball with great accuracy anywhere you didn't happen to be, after which he would say, 'Run up, boy. You don't run!' This riled me so much on one occasion that I hit one straight at him as hard as I could as he stood peering over the net. Without moving, he chopped it nonchalantly down with such backspin that it actually bounced back into the net. 'Run up, boy!' he said. 'You don't run!' He was an extremely caustic man, a characteristic which schoolboys are often said to resent, though I did not. One day he observed that our House Tutor, Mr Reginald Poole, had put a boy in extra school.

'I see you've put so-and-so in extra school,' he said. 'What was he doing?'

'He was reading history, Headmaster, during my science period.'

'Oh, what was he reading?'

'Macaulay, sir.'

'Macaulay?' said Fletcher. 'That's worse. That's fiction!'

Charterhouse, like any other school, numbered among the masters a mixture of the dedicated and the eccentric, including such characters as the fantastically absent-minded Lt-Col. F. W. B. Smart, who ran the OTC and once threatened that, if the marching did not improve, he would make them mark time all the way to Puttenham. To an Old Carthusian he is reputed to have said, 'Now, let me see. Was it you or your brother that was killed in the war?' In my own presence he said, 'Get out your pencils and paper and take a dictation,' and then, having for some minutes gazed out of the window, turned and said, 'Now we'll correct what we've done.' At the other end of the scale there was Oswald H. Latter, whom I mention partly because he was probably a greater teacher of zoology than anyone before or since and partly as an excuse for saying that I got 84% in that subject in the Higher Certificate, largely, I fancy, through possessing some coloured pencils with which to 'compare the nervous systems of the earthworm and the frog'.

All schools have their own expressions for pushing off when a master fails to arrive in time. Ours was 'raising a cut'. When everyone was agreed that ten minutes had passed, you could fold your tents like the Arabs, so to speak, and silently steal away. I mention it because I like to think, and indeed am certain that I am among the survivors of about twenty boys who in 1926 set a record which now, since there is no longer any early school, can never be equalled. On a winter Monday the schedule was early school before breakfast; then two periods before the morning break and one afterwards, followed by two afternoon periods from 4.00 till 6.00. To raise a cut on early school was hardly worth mention, for masters after all were only human and could oversleep as well as the next man. There was little comment, then, when the Fifth Form Classical raised a cut on Mr Ivor Gibson, a man of minute stature who later became housemaster of Gownboys. To raise a cut at any time other than early school was, however, quite an event. On this Monday Mr Gibson failed again to turn up after breakfast, or for the second morning period either. Already this was probably a record, but secrecy was enjoined in case by some fantastic chance we might complete the whole morning, which in fact we did. Security must have been remarkably good, for it only needed a boastful word at lunchtime in any of the eleven houses for the secret to leak out. There being another form-room just opposite we tiptoed in like mice at 4.00 o'clock, tiptoed out at 4.10, tiptoed back at 5.00, crept out at 5.10, and scattered into the unknown. Poor little Mr Gibson, it transpired, had gone to London under the impression that all arrangements had duly been made. I would willingly give a fiver for a recording of his subsequent interview with Frank Fletcher!

On the whole the best master under whom I sat, anywhere, was Humfrey Grose-Hodge, who took the Under-Sixth Classical and paid one the compliment of treating one almost as an adult until proved otherwise. He had been at one time in the Indian Civil Service or some such and, having travelled the world, would leaven Latin and Greek with reminiscences of the 'real' life to come. Later he became Headmaster of Bedford.

Writing the best part of thirty years ago I see that I was critical of the fact that no one ever taught us the Art of Working, but on looking back I think this may have been less than fair, for I had already, before I got there, developed to a high degree the art of never putting off till tomorrow what could be put off till the day after. In other words if the stuff has to be shown up at early school in the morning, never do it this afternoon, when you have plenty of time, or during the regulation period this evening. Stay up far into the prohibited hours of the night or, better still, get up at crack of dawn and do it then. On the other hand the two most important things in a man's life are three-letter words ending in x (the other one, of course, being tax) and it is fair to say that in a long and expensive education nobody taught me a thing about either, with the result that I missed many interesting experiences on the one hand and on the other got done by two hatchet-faced tax-collectors for a vast sum of money which I didn't owe but couldn't prove it. Perhaps things are different now and maybe some of the boys could teach some of the masters things about sex which would make their hair stand on end. Due largely, I suppose, to good feeding, which strangely enough started, or so I believe, with the lessons learnt from communal catering in the war, boys these days are giants compared with my day. Not long ago, on ticket leave from the annual starvation cure at Enton Hall, I attended a soccer match at Charterhouse against Winchester and nearly every so-called boy on both sides seemed to be about six foot four, absolute giants beside, say, Bobby Charlton or George Best, and all with hair of which Samson would have been proud before Delilah did him.

What seemed to make Eton so superior to other schools in the time of which I am writing – I wonder if Etonians of my vintage would agree? – was the fact that boys appear to have been permitted to take up almost anything that legitimately interested them, whereas in most schools, including Charterhouse, it was virtually compulsory to stand shivering on the touchline on a precious Saturday afternoon, shouting with ever-diminishing enthusiasm, 'Charter*house!*' at the footballers. All this seems to have changed and interests to have widened enormously. One by one the houses have been modernized, the boys moving out for a year, so that now even the most insignificant boy has a small space that he can call his own and can plaster with pin-ups of spacemen, racing motor-cyclists or Brigitte Bardot, according to his stage of development. Gownboys being among those already 'done', the head of the house was detailed by the present headmaster, Mr Oliver Van Oss, during the football match to show me round and I must say that by comparison with my day the house was a damned disgrace. More like Claridge's.

The successes of Old Carthusians in the Halford-Hewitt tournament before the war led people to think we must have been allowed to play quite a lot of golf at school, but this was not so. The winter afternoons did not allow time and in summer it was difficult to get off cricket, which I enjoyed to a certain extent but treated with the selfishness ingrained in an only child. Compulsory day-to-day school cricket can be a most ghastly bore, not-batting yourself for most of the time and fielding without touching the ball for the rest, and even at St Cyprians I decided to get, as the Americans say, 'where the action is', in other words to be a slow bowler – therefore being kept in action longer than the others – or, better still, keep wicket and be in action all the time. When batting I continued with the regrettable philosophy that, if you kept your eye on the ball and never in any circumstances tried to score in front of the wicket or anywhere on the off-side, you were liable to be in action for a very long time. If you keep your eye on the ball, let it hit the bat with a dull thud and then walk away while the wicket-keeper comes all the way up, maybe six times in one over, to collect it and throw it back, you can break the heart of the fiercest and fastest schoolboy bowler in half a dozen overs, so eventually I used to be sent in first, accompanied by a proper player, in order to do just this thing. They also serve who only stand and block.

So at any rate it was only during the Easter term, or 'quarter', as it is called, that we got the occasional chance to play golf, sometimes on the charming little heath course at Puttenham but mainly on the West Surrey course at Enton. The rigours of getting there and back, cheerfully endured at the time, appal me now. It must have been every bit of four miles and I had an enormous bicycle, the sort one used to associate with village constables, known as the Golden Sunbeam with the Little Oil Bath, on which my esteemed father had pedalled to and from Bedford. Shouldering the bag of clubs, lovingly polished and re-polished in the study, one sailed down Charterhouse Hill to Godalming, turned right at the 'Pepper Box' onto the Portsmouth Road, and there waited to see what chance might bring in the shape of a lorry onto which one could attach oneself like a parasite at the back. Sometimes the driver would be bloody-minded and try to throw us off and the thought of hanging on for dear life to a swerving lorry at thirty miles an hour with the left hand and trying to control with the right not only the Golden Sunbeam with the Little Oil Bath but a bag of clubs whose sling was now up round one's neck makes me wonder how all of us lived to tell the tale. Normally we had to break away from our 'host' at Milford and do the remaining mile under our own steam. Sometimes, of course, one did not pick up a 'host' at all. On the other hand once – oh, blessed day! – not only did I pick up a coal truck in Godalming and not only did it turn left at Milford: it actually delivered its coal to the clubhouse!

In the winter we played soccer, the ground being too hard, for which the Lord be praised, for rugger, which of all games that I have been forced to play I loved the least. Soccer, as the television has abundantly shown, can be a game of supreme artistry, but here again the 'looking after Number One' that my friend found so useful as a prisoner of war told me that goal was still the place to play – though to perform behind R. L. Arrowsmith as right back was something of a trial. Though a first eleven cricketer and crafty slow bowler – also a first-class classical scholar and pretty well word-perfect on Boswell's *Johnson* – he failed to develop similar talent on the football field. What counted, however, was that he was not only Head of the House but Head of the School, and that, to a boy in only his second year, is saying something. Fancying myself as Hibbs, the goalkeeper hero of the day, I would position myself to narrow the angle and anticipate the shot, possibly from Richard 'Stinker' Murdoch dashing down the right wing and trying not to trip over the ball, but all too often a vast boot would deflect the ball at the critical moment into the far corner of the goal, where Hibbs in all his glory could not have got a finger to it. 'Sorry!' 'Oh, not at all, Arrowsmith, not at all.' Thinks: 'You clumsy great ——!' There are eleven houses at Charterhouse and in his time Bob Arrowsmith managed inadvertently to score for them all – including, on one memorable occasion, let it be said, our own. He became a lifelong Carthusian, Classics master, housemaster, and pillar of the school Establishment.

Two or three years later my career between the uprights came to an untimely end. The professional goalkeepers of today never seem to advance from their goal and simply kick the ball, the thing to do being to gather it up to one's bosom and claim to be untouchable. In my day, however, even the best of them would run out and get rid of it by a direct kick without stopping to pick it up. It was a wet muddy day, with the ball like a lump of lead, when I advanced nobly from my goal and one of the onrushing forwards got there at exactly the same time. We each kicked the lump of lead with a resounding thud at the same moment and each fell over it forwards. He got up and I did not. I hobbled back in agony and repaired to the school doctor, Charles Leatham, the amateur rackets champion, who after a great deal of measuring-up declared it to be an internal cartilege. He arranged for me, a little furtively it seemed, though I did not understand why at the time, to go and see a Mr Blake, who performed his miracles from some humble premises in the City, in Charterhouse Square. He was, I believe, the son of a Northumberland miner and considered that his was a divine gift. He was frowned upon, naturally enough, by the regular medical profession, who had not themselves been thus endowed, and was not allowed to have even a qualified practitioner to administer an anaesthetic. This explained the slightly furtive air about my appointment, and I have no doubt that it took moral courage on Leatham's part in sending me to him, for which I shall ever be grateful.

I hobbled up to London like a cripple and eventually in a thick pea-soup fog found the modest premises of the great man, where I was shown into a waiting-room with benches round the walls. From time to time a victim would return, pale and trembling, to retrieve his hat and coat and the next would be summoned and shown into one of a row of half a dozen curtained cubicles, up which Blake could be heard but not seen making his way. From time to time a cry of anguish would go up from along the line and I remember his voice saying, 'Well, madam, I am afraid if you cannot bear a little pain . . .' Eventually he swept in to my cubicle, turning out after all this to be an unobtrusive little man in a black alpaca coat, such as barbers wear, with four pencils stuck in the breast pocket. I had already been detrousered and unbandaged and was sitting with my legs hanging over the edge of the couch. I muttered something about its 'seeming to be rather better'. He ran his fingers gently over my knee for perhaps five seconds, certainly no more, and said, 'No, it isn't. And your kneecap is out of place too. You can watch it go back.' 'Christ,' I thought, 'I don't fancy this one,' but I watched fascinated as my kneecap moved painlessly about an inch to one side and gave a sort of click. The rest, however, remains acutely in my memory at a range of more than forty years. I lay on my back, a nurse came and prostrated herself on my other leg, Mr Blake took my thigh in one hand and ankle in the other, rotating the latter on the ground that he was 'just testing', and a moment later flung himself violently upon me, bending my leg so far back that my foot nearly hit the pillow behind. I let out a horrible yell, which can have lent no great encouragement to the occupants of the other cubicles awaiting their turn, and then he did it again. He felt it for a moment, apparently satisfied, and with a curt, 'Two guineas. Pay at the desk,' moved on to the next patient. I paid my two guineas to a young lady with celluloid cuffs and tottered out into the fog, thinking that here was a remarkable man, a very remarkable man indeed. Nor did I ever have any trouble with my knee again.

Each generation likes to think that times were harder in its own day and if one were comparing, say, the Rugby of Tom Brown's day that would undoubtedly be true, but I do not think that, apart from the icy horrors of early school in winter, my own generation had much to complain about. An exception that comes to mind, however, is what was known as the Dead Cart, by which the ailing pupil was trundled down to the Sanatorium in Peperharow Road. The Dead Cart, and I can still hardly credit that I am telling the truth, was an old black four-wheeler with horse and cabbie to match, which might have come straight out of the pages of

Sherlock Holmes, and I remember only too well its pulling up at the door of Founder's Tower to take me away. For casting an air of gloom and despondency over the patient it must have been unique. Awaiting the victim at the San. was Miss Abrahams, whose leg was unmercifully pulled by some of the older layabouts in her care, such as J. T. Morgan, the celebrated cricketer, who on the arrival of Seligman, R. J. (Lockites, 1926) informed her that he, Seligman, was Captain of Cycling. In answer to Miss Abrahams's solicitous inquiry Seligman to his credit replied that the school had a particularly fine team, as he had several 'Old Wheels' left over from last year.

At the beginning of my last year I went to Cambridge, staying in the beautiful but as yet uncompleted New Building of Clare College on the other side of the Backs, to try for a Classical Scholarship, but I sensed that I had not the class and anyhow that my days with the Classics were drawing to an end. I failed for the scholarship but the authorities at Clare were kind enough to intimate that they would accept me as an amateur without further examination, so, with that settled, I left to spend my last summer term not at Charterhouse but at Lausanne, where I was to stay with a family and learn French. I am afraid the French was a failure but the golf rapidly improved. The Lausanne course was a few miles up in the hills and I used to go by tram, sometimes transferring to a friend's open car at about 30 m.p.h., with one foot on the tram, the other on the car and the clubs once again hanging round the neck, rather like the lady at the circus riding two horses round the ring. Sometimes I played for the club and half a dozen of us would cross the lake to play the Evian club, whose course was laid out among cherry orchards on the side of the hill, coming home by the steamer in the evening with the lights of Lausanne twinkling on the dark water. I felt I was growing up at last.

7
Halcyon Days

I went up to Clare College, Cambridge, in the autumn of 1927 and fell at once into a different and heavenly world, for of all the transitions that one undergoes in this life that of schoolboy to undergraduate is assuredly the best. At some schools, Winchester I believe is one of them, the boys talk of each other as 'men', though they must know well enough they are not. At Charterhouse we were 'fellows' – the word 'chaps' being a most frightful solecism – but now at last one was out on one's own, a man. At Cambridge you live out of college at first and move in later. At Oxford it is the reverse, which must surely be better, namely living in the college as a freshman, getting to know other members of your own year, and going out later when you know your way about. However that may be, I found myself lodging in Park Street, which was then a little street off Jesus Lane, under the roof of Miss Hardstaff. Though these were comparatively modest rooms, her other lodger was none other than Prince Alex Mdivani, a member of a family known on account of their matrimonial adventures as the Marrying Mdivanis. When Miss Hardstaff admired the portraits of two exceptionally beautiful women in his bedroom, Alex said, 'Ah, yes. They are my sisters-in-law.' They were the two great film stars of the day, Pola Negri and Mae Murray.

Autumn is my favourite time of the year and I can think of nothing more nostalgic than walking through the narrow streets in the evening to dine in Hall, leaning for a few minutes perhaps over Clare Bridge, with the smell of wood smoke coming up from the Master's Garden and the light of coal fires flickering from rooms in the Old Court. Authority was wielded ultimately by the benevolent Master, Henry Thirkill, known universally as 'Thirks' – now Sir Henry, and quite right too – and more immediately by the Dean, the Rev. F. Telfer, whose name must have been signed in the books of more night-clubs than any man alive. In the town, especially in the evening, it was the Proctors who would:

> Sail in amply billowing gown
> Enormous through the sacred town

each accompanied by his two top-hatted tail-coated 'bulldogs', or 'bullers', who were college servants noted for their fleetness of foot. All these authorities were accepted in principle, though evaded from time to time in practice, without question. The proper function of the student, it would have been held, had anybody thought to raise the question, which they didn't, was to study. How much he did of it and what form it took was largely his affair. Any suggestion of joining an organization called the National Union of Students (in any case we were undergraduates, not students) would have been laughed out of court and there would have been many an unseemly jest if its president had turned out to be called Jack Straw. A year or two ago, I noted, a mixed bag of Town and Gown tried to turn Mr Harold Wilson's car over when he visited Cambridge and pictures of them in action appeared in the papers. Mr Wilson at the time was Her Majesty's Prime, or First, Minister. Nothing much appeared to happen about it, but I can say with absolute certainty that at the time of which I am writing the college porter would have come round and said, 'The Master, sir, wishes to see you sir.' 'Thirks' in his most courteous way would have said, 'Is this your picture, sir, that I observe in the paper?' and, on your replying in the affirmative, would equally courteously have said, 'In that case, sir, I fear that I shall require your rooms within twenty-four hours.' A moment later the porter would be saying, 'Can I help you with your bags, sir?' and a vacancy would have occurred at Clare which several thousands of young men would have given anything to fill. Now that I come to think of it a vacancy did occur in Clare only the other day when the incumbent was removed to Borstal for helping to break up a hotel, doing £2000's worth of damage and putting women in such fear of their lives as to cause them to lock themselves in the lavatories – but he was sent there not by the Master but by Mr Justice Melford Stevenson.

Now I see that they want to do away with the Proctors altogether and there is much talk of where authority in the University should lie, and even, grotesquely, of 'Student Power'. I never heard any-one of my vintage even discussing such things and most, I suspect, would have found it an infinitely boring subject. There was too much else to be getting on with. On the other hand the abolition of the Proctors marching the streets at night with their attendant bullers would have been much resented as taking away a distinctive item in undergraduate life. One was meant at night to wear a cap and gown – and why not? – and it was 6s. 8d. for being 'improperly dressed' without cap, 13s. 4d. for the pair. One was often minus at least the cap and this led to an inspiriting sense of hazard as one made one's way about the streets after dark, never sure whether a Proctor might be encountered marching briskly round the next corner, in which case one had a split-second decision to make as to whether to nip back and run for it or declare a 'fair cop'. Some-times an undergraduate would appear from nowhere, going like the wind, with the buller flat out just behind, like a bull terrier after a cat, and one stepped discreetly aside to let them pass. At others a properly dressed undergraduate would mutter, out of the corner of his mouth in passing, the magic word, 'Progs!' in which case one knew one had but seconds to vanish up the nearest bolthole. One night there was a commotion at our front door in Park Street, the panting Prince claiming sanctuary, an equally out-of-breath buller claiming a dead heat on the doorstep and Miss Hardstaff emerging from below stairs wringing her hands that such a thing should have happened in her house. All Keystone Cops stuff – but I smile at the recollection and it makes me feel young again.

One night a friend of mine, George Francis, now a pillar of the commercial life of Christchurch, New Zealand, came late into my rooms, then in the New Building, and leant against the mantel-piece muttering rather thickly, 'Four kings and a bloody ace. Go home!' I formed the opinion, as police witnesses say, that he had enjoyed a not wholly teetotal evening. 'What's all this, George?' I said. 'Four kings and a bloody ace,' he said. 'Go home!' Gradually the tragic tale came out. He had been playing an innocent game of poker in some rooms overlooking the Market Square and it was the evening of November the Fifth. The Market Square was always a scene of lively activity on Guy Fawkes' Night and this was turn-ing out rather a good one. Meanwhile, George and his companions had been having a jackpot, for quite worth-while stakes, and on picking up his hand George saw in it four kings and an ace. Somebody opened, George doubled, somebody the other side raised the ante, George raised it again, and the whole lot of them came in. Life to George, as he gazed inscrutably at his four kings, to say nothing of the superfluous ace, had never seemed quite so good. The betting had just begun when the door was flung open and in walked the Senior Proctor. 'Whose rooms are these?' 'Mine, sir.' 'Very well. You can stay. Everybody not living in this house, out!' 'But I've got ——' 'Never mind that. Clear the house,' whereupon they all picked up their stakes and George, throwing down his four kings, retired, not unreasonably, to the Festival Theatre to drown his sorrows. Someone, it transpired, had thrown a firework from the window of the rooms next door and it had gone off between the Senior Proctor's feet.

There must be a whole saga of proctorial stories and one day some enthusiast ought to collect them. It was an Oxford proctor, I fancy, who, having quelled a riot in the quad, said, 'Let those who can put those who can't to bed'; and an Oxford undergraduate who, when challenged by the proctor one evening regarding a parcel he was carrying under his gown, which turned out to contain a giant cod that he was intending to throw onto the stage of the old East Oxford theatre, made the immortal reply, 'Well, sir, it seemed a very sound thing to have about me.'

As with the proctors, so there were innumerable stories of eccentric, irascible or ironic dons, drinkers of the college port to a man, not wholly of the same ilk, one suspects, as some of the dons one reads about today. Now, I see, Clare College are to admit women as members of the college, largely, it seems, in order to 'keep up the academic standard'. In my view such a step should be a matter of a vote by all past graduates but we were greeted with this gigantic change in the character of the college as a *fait accompli* – and for all I know it may be a very good idea. It would not, however, have done for a certain Oxford don before my day, when the great question was whether women should be admitted as members not of a college but of the university. The women won and not long afterwards this character to his intense distaste found himself delivering his lecture to an audience of one man and all the rest women. He began it with: 'Sir . . .'

In Christ's, opposite whose main gate I lodged for my second year, there was an elderly don, a pillar of the college and the common room and a enjoyer of all the good things of a monastic life, who suddenly and unaccountably got married, which meant, of course, leaving his college rooms and living 'out'. After a while someone ventured to ask how he was finding the married state. His reply will be appreciated by anyone who has ever dined at a college High Table. 'The breakfasts are infinitely better,' he said, 'but the dinners are nothing like so good.'

We used to play quite a bit of poker, though a number of my friends played bridge, obviously pretty well. I made a study of it and came to the perhaps erroneous conclusion that it was a game to be played well or not at all, well enough at any rate, when people said, 'Do you play bridge?' to reply with a reasonably confident, 'Yes, I do,' and that this would take more mental time than I was prepared to afford. I have now reached the age when I much regret this decision and pass the information on, for what it is worth, to any of the young who care to listen. One could easily in those days with a moderately agile mind and a little concentration have learnt to play bridge to a handicap, in golfing parlance, of, say, nine, and that is all you need. Now I find it too late to pick up these damned systems and point-counts and to remember that when a man says, 'One club,' he really means he has six hearts and the ace of spades, or whatever it is.

One thing, however, I did get right and, little knowing where my future life lay, did not appreciate just how right it was. I taught myself to type. I was dabbling with a system of shorthand known as speedwriting, which uses abbreviations in the ordinary letters of the alphabet, some of which I remember and use to this day – *ts*, for instance, for *these*, *z* for *was*, and simply a *j* for *-ation, -etion, -ition, -otion* or *-ution* at the end of a word. Lectures made excellent practice for becoming proficient in this art, even though I never really did, but it meant that the notes had to be transcribed when one got home, so I acquired a typewriter and, on the ground that you might as well start as you mean to go on, forced myself to play the machine with all ten fingers, which is by no means as difficult as tuition schools would like you to think. This has been of infinite use to me and I tend to look with an unworthily smug condescension upon some of my colleagues in the Press tent, still, after thirty years, pecking away with two fingers.

The subject of my transcribed notes was Economics. Despite what must be one of the most brilliant literary 'send-ups' ever written – Stephen Leacock's parody of Homer ('Homer and

Humbug', *Behind the Beyond*, 1913) – I never regretted my time with the Classics, but I had exhausted what my limited talents were likely to get out of them and it was time to move on to something nearer to the great world outside. Either you have sat up till midnight wrestling with the composition of Latin hexameters and pentameters and Greek iambics (my first Army number was a perfect hexameter – one-seven, three-seven, two-double, eight) or you haven't, and, if you have done it at an age when too young in any case to specialize in learning to be a doctor or scientist or whatever it may be, it seems to me that you can have wasted neither your time nor your mind. If it only teaches you that one word means one thing and another something very like it but not quite, you have at least learnt something.

Economics, for which the Cambridge School was world-famous, was a very different kettle of fish, a mundane study of everyday affairs and people and their business and political behaviour. Our bible was Marshall's *Principles of Economics*, but how it would read in the strange, unbalanced world of today I cannot say. Looking back, I think the subject as a whole offered a good mental exercise in deciding the probable result of one line of action as against another and in trying to remain unswayed by emotion in the process, but later experience of the realities of life showed that things simply did not turn out Marshall's way. It all seemed to be based on a false assumption and an escape clause. The false assumption was of the existence of the reasonable man and deductions arising therefrom (see A. P. Herbert, *Misleading Cases*, 'Fardell *v.* Potts: The Reasonable Man'). The reasonable man, for instance, when feeling the pinch, would, it was reasonable to assume, give up his luxuries first. The world, alas, proved to be populated as to about ninety per cent by unreasonable men, who would give up the family coal rather than the telly (not that they had it in those days). It was on the assumption of an electorate consisting of reasonable men that I later ventured into politics. Oh dear, oh dear!

The escape clause, of which I make adroit use to this day, consists of the magic words 'other things being equal'. It cannot be too clearly understood that in real life other things were not, are not, and never will be equal. One example will suffice. In the early thirties there were no fewer than three million men, out of a much smaller population than today, unemployed; hanging

about on street corners, living on the dole, their existence en-
livened only by an occasional hunger march to London. Unemployment was the dread scourge to be cured and then avoided for
ever more. Such at any rate was the economic philosophy on which
I was brought up and to which I still adhere. Other things, however, have not proved to be equal. At the moment of writing
(1971) there are three-quarters of a million unemployed, and in
the modest family business of which I have the honour to be
chairman we are taxed, believe it or not, four pounds a week for
every man we employ!

As an insurance against failure in one's principal subject it was
reckoned judicious to take a subsidiary, since this, it was held,
might in marginal cases influence the minds of the examiners.
In these circumstances a number of us, largely as a lark and in a
slightly patronizing spirit, decided to take, of all things, Polar
Exploration. It turned out to be sheer magic and much of it I
remember to this day. This was because the course was conducted
by Dr (now Sir) Raymond Priestley, a man of modest demeanour
destined later to become Principal of Birmingham University.
Polar Exploration proved a pleasing contrast to discussing the
possible consequences of a rise in bank rate (other things being
equal), especially when one found that Priestley had actually been
with Scott to the Antarctic, and it was not long before we were
all hanging on his words. At one time he and three others were
landed on a barren island to make some botanical study or other
and the ship was to come back and pick them up. The days drew
on, the ice closed in, and the ship never came. Furthermore it
might never come. For all they knew, it had foundered. In any
case, it would be many a long winter month before they found out
one way or the other – rescue or a lonely and certain death – always
assuming they managed to survive the winter. They dug themselves a hole in the snow in which they could sit or lie, but at no
point on the island was the snow deep enough for them to make a
home in which they could stand upright. Blizzards, the kind that
had killed, or were to kill, Scott, swept across the island, sometimes at 200 m.p.h. and for days on end they could not venture out.
More than this I do not remember, except that they had a small
mug of tea every third Wednesday and smoked the tea-leaves
afterwards.

Priestley illustrated his lecture with slides, and one little episode, concerning that most comical of creatures, the penguin, delights me to this day. The penguin's great enemy is the sea leopard, which likes to lurk under overhangs of ice where it cannot be seen by anyone wishing to dive in from the top. A series of pictures showed first of all the penguins peering anxiously over the top, none daring to be the first to dive in. By what method of selection I do not know but quite unanimously they pick upon one of their number and begin nudging him with their flippers, propelling him towards the edge. His squawks of protest and his expression are almost human, but he is surrounded and levered inexorably to the edge. He slithers over backwards, righting himself into a beautifully executed dive, and comes up again. There is an appreciable pause while the others crane their heads ludicrously over the edge to see what happens to poor Charlie. All, however, is well. There is no sea leopard, and a moment later a whole shower of penguins dive gracefully into the sea. Simple stuff perhaps but, when you come to think of it, very near home.

I shall always be grateful to Priestley for his humorous and pain-less introduction to the cruel world of the Antarctic and the men who braved its perils. He could fairly have said, as did one elderly don to an undergraduate who apologized for having missed his lecture, 'You missed a great deal. I am, if I may say so, always good, but this morning I surpassed myself. Good day to you!'

The motor Proctor in my time was the redoubtable and much respected Dr Donald Portway, assisted by his chief henchman, Mr Crack. One was not meant to have a car in one's first year, though many, including myself, did, but this meant finding some minor garage or hideaway on the outskirts of the town rather than keeping it in a 'respectable' garage like Marshall's in Jesus Lane. Later, when one's car had become legitimate, it was a question of not being observed and having one's number taken when approach-ing the town at such time of night as would obviously not enable one to be within the college walls or one's rooms by midnight. The little village of Melbourn on the London road was a favourite trap, being virtually un-bypassable, and when in doubt it was advisable to proceed next day to the Castle Hotel bar, which appeared to be Mr Crack's headquarters, and with great affability tender a 'dog's nose' – i.e. gin and beer – and, of all things, a few old gramo-phone records. It was all rather akin to oriental bargaining, so that only after a decent interval of general exchanges would there be mentioned, merely in passing, of course, the subject which both knew to be the only one which had prompted this casual meeting in the Castle bar. At the end, with any luck and maybe a third dog's nose, it would be a case of, 'I'll cross him off my list. He never will be missed.'

This was, I imagine it will be generally admitted, the Golden Age of motoring. A Golden Age presupposes very great motor cars, not too many in all, and roads fit to drive them on. Only the privileged few could have the very great motors and I, with the £25 Morris Cowley with the thermometer on the radiator cap, was not among their number. I dare say there were only ten or a dozen such motors in the whole university and these were not so much envied as admired. One was a Delage owned by Oscar Botero, whom I never met, until thirty years later on the *Queen Mary* somebody said, 'Do you know my friend Oscar Botero?' to which I was able at once to reply, 'Ah, the one with the Delage.' I think he was quite taken aback – though by this time he had acquired a wife whose beauty exceeded even that of the Delage.

I did, however, come to know well through the medium of golf a tough, wiry, fearless little character who owned what will ever to me be the greatest motor of them all, the $4\frac{1}{2}$ supercharged Bentley – green, of course, and with a strap across the bonnet, the supercharger sticking out in front below the radiator and a huge tank at the back. How many gallons it held I never knew, but I do remember Fiske replying to the petrol-pump attendant's query of how many he should put in, 'Make it forty-two': and that in the days when you pumped it by hand. Billy Fiske neither drank nor smoked, though he got on well with the girls, but he was the most wonderful driver of a vehicle, be it a 'skeleton' on the Cresta, a big four-man bob or the Bentley. He already held the world record on the Cresta and had captained the United States winning team in the Olympic games on the bob, both of which are in effect motoring without an engine and bear the same relationship to motoring that gliding does to flying, both an exact science in that a single error can never be made up.

Our usual run was the twenty-one-mile stretch to the Royal Worlington Golf Club at Mildenhall and sometimes the time would be around nineteen minutes, and without a tremor of apprehension to public or passenger. Day after day, sitting on Fiske's left, I would notice my own front wheel passing within an inch or two of its track of the day before. The supercharger came in with a shrill whine at about 80 m.p.h., generally at the beginning of the long straight where the Cambridge road goes eventually uphill through the beechwood to join the London road short of the racecourse at Newmarket. Soon the needle would creep up into the red, staying for a while at between 110 and 120 m.p.h., till at precisely the same spot just short of the slope Fiske would change down to third at exactly 86 m.p.h., and every time the gear would go through like butter. This was, of course, before the days of synchromesh and, if you got it wrong, you could break your wrist, let alone the gearbox.

Fiske was a good golfer, almost good enough for a place in the university team, but the greens at Mildenhall were fast as lightning, even in winter, and having got us there in his monster at an average speed of something like 65 m.p.h. for twenty minutes, he could never understand why he found it so difficult to hole out from five feet. When the war came, he joined the RAF, flying a Hurricane from Tangmere in the Battle of Britain. He was the first American to be killed in the service of Britain in the war, and here I am sure you will forgive me if I quote of him again something I have written once before.

> A little incident at a Birmingham gun site will always stick in my memory. Twice a week two kindly ladies used to appear in a YMCA van and hoot encouragingly at the foot of our tower – whereupon the monkeys would down tools and rush down for their bag of nuts. They sold us chocolate and cakes and razor blades and tea, and lent out books, and were a cheerful and highly acceptable link with the outside world . . . One day, as I sipped my tea at the counter, I noticed the crossed Union Jack and Stars and Stripes on the side of the van. Underneath were the words 'Fiske Memorial'.
>
> Billy Fiske! My mind raced back over the years to the time when we used to travel almost daily the twenty-one miles from Cambridge to Mildenhall in his monstrous supercharged green Bentley . . . and to the days when his father had helped to send a team of us to play golf in the United States . . . Now he lies buried in a little Sussex churchyard, and a plaque in St Paul's Cathedral commemorates our gratitude.
>
> I wondered what crisp comment this forthright little man would have come out with, if he could have seen me drinking a penn'orth of tea from the van that kept his memory alive.

As my third summer term passed on its leisurely way, the trips to

the golfcourse, the lazing in punts on the Backs, the evening out-
ings, the Victoria Cinema with Ginger, the commissionaire, and
his familiar cleft-palated cry of, 'Standing room only. Waiting
room in the café where Bessie will accommodate you,' all became
marred by the still, small voice of conscience muttering the one
word, 'Exams'. We did not, of course, have to keep our noses to
the grindstone in the same way that the young gentlemen appear
to have to do today, though that was no bad thing, for the object
of the university in those days was as much to turn out the gifted
amateur, touching life at many points, as the professional. In most
branches of Economics I was reasonably confident of 'breaking
80', so to speak. There was, however, one dangerous exception,
and really it is extraordinary what blank spots there can be in an
otherwise normal mind. Mine was 'Money, Credit and Prices',
for which I sat under none other than that colossus of financial
Economics, Professor A. C. Pigou. I suppose having a money
sense is like having a card sense. If you haven't got it, you will
never get it. I hadn't and haven't, and what it has cost me in lost
opportunities I shudder to think. Later I was to fall in with a
coterie of bookmakers, of whom I remember in particular Ted
Durling, who was the principal layer in the main ring every night
of the week at either the White City or Harringay, running a very
big business on the horses during the day and one of the principal
street-betting areas in the West End of London. Ted had none
of the scholastic advantages that I possessed. It was simply that he
had a different brain. Of course, it was razor-sharp with practice,
and so it had to be, taking on the sort of customers that he took on
every night. It wasn't that his brain was better than mine. It was
different. With everyone shouting at once he would glance over his
shoulder and tell in a second from the jottings of his clerk the
exact financial position of the moment, which I suppose every
bookmaker has to do, but he also carried an extraordinary multitude of figures in his head during the day. Money, Credit and
Prices was his life and Professor Pigou's lectures would have been
positive chicken-feed to him. To me a bill of exchange maturing in
three months was double-Dutch, and still is.

Nor were the figures wholly in Ted's mind. Much of it was in his
pocket. After a game of golf at Addington once he said, 'I owe you
ten bob, Henry.' He reached in the front pocket of his plus-fours –
the fraternity always have these frontal pockets: you never know

what's going on at the back – and drew out a vast wad of notes with innumerable white fivers and tenners opening out at the bottom. No ten-shilling note, so he tried the other pocket, with the same result. 'How much have you got there, then?' I said. 'Oh,' he said, 'about twelve hundred and fifty.'

When the day of reckoning at last came, I had a splendid bout of tonsilitis and a temperature of 102° and at the end of three days of exams crept out, not to celebrate with the others but to crawl to bed, stopping only to note that Blenheim had won the Derby, just as I thought it would but had not the energy to back it. As to the result I will say only that I am entitled to call myself BAEcon. Cantab., I will not say of what class, but, as a wise and talented man once observed, 'There are far more potential Firsts among the Thirds than there are among the Seconds.'

8
Playing for Cambridge

It would be doing myself an injustice to say that my only thought at Cambridge was to get a golf Blue, or more correctly a half-Blue – not that anyone cared a damn whether it was a whole Blue or three-eights of a Blue: the great thing was to get it. On the other hand, in spite of all the varied excitements of settling down to university life, I confess that golf was never long out of my mind. The secret was to put one's name down for the trials – and then catch the captain's eye by doing well in them. These were held at Mildenhall, or more correctly the Royal Worlington and Newmarket Golf Club, whose nine-hole course (the 'Sacred Nine of Worlington', Bernard Darwin once called it) must be incomparably the best of its kind in the world. It was twenty-one miles away, past Newmarket, and the problem of getting there was solved by finding that Michael Copeman had a motor-bicycle and sidecar. Copeman had been the Gownboy 'hash pro' the year before myself, and, if I was, let us say, 4 handicap at the Classics, which may be flattering things a bit, he was plus 2. One day Humfrey Grose-Hodge, of whom I have written with enthusiasm, set the under-sixth classical three verses of 'Omar Khayaám' to render overnight into Greek iambics. They included the familiar lines:

> Ah, make the most of what we yet may spend,
> Before we too into the Dust descend;
> Dust unto Dust, and under Dust to lie,
> Sans Wine, sans Song, sans Singer, and – sans End.

Even then this seemed a bit much, since I hardly understood them in English. I wrestled with them until a late hour and finally took them to Copeman. Almost without hesitation he produced a copy, retaining perhaps a quarter of my own, which was so brilliant that Grose-Hodge took it straight to my housemaster on the ground that it could not conceivably be mine. I just got away with it but, as the Duke said of Waterloo, 'It was a damned near-run thing.'

As usual, rumour had it that never had there been such a profusion of freshman golfers with handicaps of scratch and deeds of glory to their credit and, though this proved to be untrue, it did not lend courage to one's feelings on the first tee. Many university golfers who have gone on to great things will tell you that for sheer nerves Walker Cups and such like are as nothing by comparison with one's first University Trials, and in my own more humble sphere I can cheerfully confirm it. I took well over 80 and it was not even worth while looking to see who had been picked for the first club match of the season. It can only have been about three weeks later, however, that I had a monumental piece of luck. The first of the four cups for which undergraduate golfers play each year is the Linskill, and in none too good weather I managed a 78. This did not win: it did better. It tied – and with the captain at that, which meant that Geoffrey Illingworth and I had to play off together. I will not claim that, as a player, Geoff was one of the greatest of university captains, but never mind that. I managed to beat him, thus making myself a certainty for the next Saturday match at Worplesdon. Here I drew a mercifully indifferent player in the singles and beat him 7 and 6, and from then onwards for the best part of four years never missed a match for the university.

W. T. Linskill has gone down in history as the 'founder of Cambridge golf', and who am I to deny it? It appears that he acted as honorary secretary during the several years that he spent at the university and accompanied the team when they played Oxford at Royal Wimbledon. They travelled from King's Cross in a wagonette and according to Bernard Darwin, who played in the match from 1895–7, Linskill, who was no teetotaller, was invariably brought home in the boot. His chief claim to fame, however, is surely the fact that he was returning by train to his native St Andrews with some other cronies on the 4.10 train from Edinburgh one day and, looking out at Leuchars Junction and failing to see his carriage waiting, decided to go on with them to Dundee. The train was about to start when a porter cried out, 'Here's your carriage now, Mr Linskill,' whereupon he hopped smartly out. It was the day of the Tay Bridge disaster, and this very train which a few minutes later plunged to destruction.

Two of my Cambridge foursomes partners: Horton Martin Row (left) and Eric Martin Smith, at the annual cricket match against the village of Codicote, Hertfordshire.

1929: in a Gordon England Brooklands model Austin 7, a notable single-seater racing car. I never drove it in a race but sometimes took it out on the road.

It seems hard to credit it now but we travelled to our matches by train, the 7.47 from Cambridge, players in the not too distant colleges actually humping their clubs to the station in the half-light on foot. Then it was all across London from Liverpool Street, generally to Waterloo, and home again by the last train, known then, and I trust still, as the Fornicator. By the following year there were generally enough cars to go round – it was always said, not, I honestly believe, with more than a suspicion of truth, that, if it were a toss-up for the last place on a Saturday, anyone with a four-seater car was a certainty. (If it was a question of two players vying with each other for the last place in the university match, the pair of them were generally dispatched to Hunstanton and told not to come home till one of them was the winner.) Nevertheless, to motor ninety miles from Cambridge in a bull-nosed Morris, play foursomes in the morning and singles in the afternoon, and then find one's way back to Cambridge in a winter fog was a more strenuous, and certainly more hazardous, business than sitting in a series of trains. One who shall be nameless drove off the road in a snowstorm straight up onto Royston Heath and with visibility nil took some time to become reorientated. Having reached Cambridge at last, he drove into the deep gutter alongside Trumpington Street, bursting two tyres in the process, and finally, limping into Marshall's Garage, took down one of the doors. The outer journey, before some of the older stagers became a little more familiar with the route, became an exercise in map-reading. How, for instance, do you get from Cambridge to Woking, even given a map, and how, when you have got there, do you find the golf club? High as Woking ranks among clubs which are difficult to find, even when you are within a mile or two of them, the most skilfully concealed is undoubtedly Addington. Try that one from Cambridge!

Gradually the pattern formed. Marshall's Garage at 6.30 – often in light snow but too early to telephone the club and find out if the course is playable, so we had better start – and breakfast at the Peahen at St Albans. One morning our best player, who owned an ancient Bean motor car known as the Dungbarge, was late. It was observed that he was wearing a scarf instead of the regulation golfing tie and was looking, it was thought, far from his best. After a long silence he said quietly, 'Have any of you bastards got a spare collar and tie?' It turned out that he had been rusticating all night in the neighbourhood of Newmarket and, when all was over, had left his collar and tie at the scene of the crime. Others who were not so sure of their place in the team, nor indeed so experienced in the temptations of this wicked world, carried on in a more orthodox way. When we arrived at the course, our hosts and opponents – one of them, I distinctly remember, 'Khaki' Roberts, KC, a tough nut if ever there was one – would often say, 'You don't mean you have driven all the way from Cambridge this morning?' Equally distinctly I remember thinking, 'I suppose the day will come when one gets so old and decrepit as to think it anything remarkable to drive from Cambridge for a golf match, but I can hardly believe it.'

It was these matches that helped to make golf beyond doubt the best game, I will not say to play but to have played, for the university, never mind whether it was half a Blue or a whole Blue. This is not in any way to disparage other sports. To have played at Twickenham or Lord's or, above all, to have rowed in the Boat Race are single experiences which nothing in golf could presume to match. On the other hand, Saturday by Saturday and mostly on Sundays too, we did receive a golfing education which could be matched by young fellows of that age in no other way. Even at the end of one year we should have played such clubs as Sunningdale, Berkshire, Woking, Worplesdon, West Hill, Addington, Stoke Poges, Royal Wimbledon, St George's Hill and Walton Heath in the main Saturday fixtures and, having returned to clock, or climb, in that evening, would cheerfully set out again to play other clubs of possibly less eminence on the Sabbath. Towards the end there was a two-day match against St George's, Sandwich, which might without offence to other clubs be termed the St Andrews of the south, and here we would be guests of members of the club in their homes, while at the end of it all there would be a blissful week or ten days in March at the scene of the culmination of it all, the university match itself.

Nor was this all, for the sort of people who belonged to and played for these clubs were liable by this time to have made some sort of mark for themselves, or, if younger, to be among the top players in the country, and many is the undergraduate, including myself, who has found the course of his life changed by the contacts and friendships made in these matches. A natural conversational gambit would be for the older man to ask the younger what he was going to do when he went down and it would be interesting to know how many times the senior, if he liked the look of the younger, would say, 'Well, don't hesitate to come and see me if you think I can be of any help.' In one match I played in the four-somes against the Chairman of ICI and, so help me, did not appreciate what an enormously big shot he was. We were also helped, in a way that the undergraduate is not today, though through no fault of his own, by the fact that the golfing world was much smaller. Bobby Jones and Walter Hagen loomed large across the Atlantic and would descend upon our shores once a year to show us the Open Championship Jug and take it back to the States, and every four years their Walker Cup team would murder our own, but, apart from that, what I may describe, without being able quite to define it, as 'the world of golf' was a much closer knit affair, at any rate that part of it in which we were privileged to move. In fact, it might almost be defined as those people who knew that 'Our Golf Correspondent' in *The Times* meant Bernard Darwin. *The Times,* the *Telegraph* and the *Morning Post* would attend our matches, with either their senior or deputy correspondent, and on Monday would carry a whole column on our doings, with the result of every individual game set out in full. The fact that so-and-so had received his Blue was also duly recorded and the make-up of the team a matter of public specula-tion. Such notoriety, whether merited or not, was both welcome and useful.

All this, as I have said, was based on Mildenhall, which is a little triangle of dry, sandy, 'seaside' land in the flat heart of rural Suffolk, complete with gorse and fir trees, just big enough for nine holes. Who laid them out I do not know, even after all these years, but either he was a man of genius or he brought off a gigantic fluke, for Mildenhall in my own experience is comparable only with the Old Course at St Andrews. Like great masterpieces of art or music, which are not to be fully comprehended at first sight or hearing, they are often a disappointment to the stranger, after all he has heard about them. In both cases you need about twenty rounds before you begin to understand what people are talking about. When at last I hung up my clubs, I was still discovering bunkers on the Old Course that I had never in my life seen before, and I doubt whether there are two dozen people who, given an outline map of St Andrews, could fill in correctly all the bunkers. The charm of Mildenhall, both the course and the club, was the continuity. Day after day one went out from Cambridge and found it the same. Year after year one returned later, and still it was the same. The white railing, the little farmhouse clubhouse, Mrs Williams's apple pie, and cream in quart jugs. There was no bar: just a hatch beside which you pressed the bell. I like to think of my friend and predecessor by three or four years, N. C. Selway, who on his first visit somewhat timidly pressed this bell. The hatch went up and there appeared the genial, rounded countenance of Williams. It was the very first time that Selway had pressed the bell and the very first time that Williams, the new steward, had answered it. They went on pressing the bell and raising the hatch to each other for thirty-five years. When the war at last was over and nothing would ever be the same again, I was among those who went back to play against the university at Mildenhall in their first post-war match. What would be left of it now? We turned off the main Newmarket road and turned again down the little turning short of the railway bridge – and there it was, absolutely unchanged. We pressed the bell, up went the hatch, and there was Williams. I nearly burst into tears.

What a game golf is for discovering people! I had known Selway on congenial terms for many years, though as one who kept himself somewhat to himself. It was only when we drove down to Mildenhall together from London after the war via the Ware and Royston Road that I discovered him to be one of the foremost experts on the coaching days. Every ten miles or so we would pass some well known hostelry, each with the characteristic arched entrance to the yard, beginning with the Bull at Hoddesdon, and going on through the Red Lion at Royston; the Rutland Arms at Newmarket; the Bull at Barton Mills, just past the Mildenhall club; and, ten miles farther on, the Bell at Thetford. My companion, who later produced a most beautiful book of coaching prints called *The Regency Road*, even knew all the timetables, including the, to me, almost incredible fact that, leaving Cheapside at 6.00 a.m., you were actually on the Front at Brighton at 11.45 – last stop being the Plough at Pyecombe, which is one of my present 'locals'. Competition was such that, far from ye olde Christmas cards and 'Landlord, fill the flowing bowl', the perished passengers had scarcely time to go round the back and get their flybuttons undone before new horses were in and the coach was away.

Nor in the early days was it always Mildenhall. Sometimes, nearer home, we would play at the Gog Magog club, 'the Gogs', on the curiously out-of-place ridge of chalk hills that rise from the flat plain only three or four miles from Cambridge, where in winter one battled with an icy blast which had arrived unimpeded from the Steppes of Russia. At other times it was the charming little nine-hole course among the fir trees at Flempton or, farther afield, what could be one of the greatest heath courses in England, at Thetford, to which we once, including a stop at a level crossing and 30 m.p.h. through Newmarket, averaged 66 m.p.h. in Fiske's Bentley. We had a match too against Royston, where the Cambridge captain of the day was regularly annihilated by their champion, Mr Shepherd, known on account of his calling as 'the Demon Barber'. Once a number of us descended on an open meeting at Knebworth, which you see on the left beside the railway just short of Stevenage as you go north from King's Cross. I mention this in order to be able to add that not only did I win a handsome piece of plate, which is on my sideboard today; not only did I set a record of 70 (no doubt long since broken); but after my caddie on the 16th tee had gone down with a tremendous crash of clubs and had lain for several minutes on the ground thrashing about in an epileptic fit, I finished with three consecutive 3s.

Back in 1928 I settled down at Number 7 in the side and this meant that, barring some sudden run of ill luck or loss of form, all should be well. Nothing reminds one more surely of episodes or periods in one's life than tunes. (When invited by Roy Plomley to contribute to his evergreen *Desert Island Discs* programme, I took it literally and managed to unearth perfectly simple and often banal little tunes which on my desert island would enable me to live agreeable periods of my life over again, and music-lovers must have thought me a complete philistine, which musically I suppose I am.) Thus the long days of waiting to achieve the great ambition are associated with a song, of which I dare say not a single record exists today, called, aptly enough, 'Just another day wasted away, watching and waiting . . .' What one had been so long watching and waiting for arrived at last some time in February in the shape of a letter in Illingworth's neat handwriting – I have it still – formally inviting me to take part in the match against Oxford at Prince's, Sandwich, in March.

89

By the same post Number 6 in the team, W. C. ('Wash') Carr, also received the magic letter. He was one of identical twins, though his brother, Horace, did not arrive at Cambridge till a year later, and they were the sons of Sir Emsley Carr, the owner, or near enough, of the *News of the World*. The family home was a big house near Walton Heath, the club itself being unobtrusively owned by the paper, and after our matches there or nearby some of us would be invited back to dinner. Sir Emsley was small in stature but big in heart and I formed a great personal respect and, indeed, affection for him. He could so easily have played the big shot, complete with dictaphones, messengers on motor-bicycles and 'As I said to the Prime Minister', which seem indispensable to some of the colossi of Fleet Street, and perhaps during the week they were part of his life, but with us he was the true paterfamilias, delighted at being surrounded at his own table with his sons and their young friends. The *News of the World* was at that time, I suppose, as well informed as any newspaper in the country, and therefore so was he, but he joined in with us at our own level without the slightest hint of condescension and I lift my hat to his memory. After dinner we would be taken up to the offices of the *News of the World* by the chauffeur, of whom I remember over forty years that his name was Redstone and that he had only one eye, and there shown over the giant presses as they poured out their seven million copies or whatever it was at that time. This was my first sniff of printer's ink and perhaps it went to my head, for I must have turned out a couple of million words of my own since then. Finally Redstone would deposit us at Liverpool Street in time for the Fornicator and thus ended another Saturday match.

One of these matches in particular changed my fortunes, both financial and otherwise. When later I had the honour of captaining the side I received a letter from another very big shot indeed, almost as big as the Chairman of ICI, none other than Lord Ashfield, who was later the head of all London Transport. Considering the circumstances it seemed couched in most humble terms. It would appear that some years previously there had been some disagreement between the university and the Coombe Hill Club and Lord Ashfield on behalf of the club wondered whether it would be possible to resume the fixture – it being at that time something of a status symbol for a club to have a regular Saturday fixture with the universities. I replied that the year's list was naturally full but that I would pass the message on for next year and in the meantime could we perhaps play on a Sunday? Thus it was arranged, and I found myself down to play in the singles against a certain Brigadier General A. C. Critchley, of whom I had read in golfing reports. I looked around for some white-moustached soldierly figure but found instead an upright character, soldierly indeed but no more than forty-two or so, taking savage practice swings at the daisies. I holed a putt of about five yards to beat him on the last green, which turned out to be not at all the sort of thing that he was expecting or was used to, and thereby laid the foundation of one of the most worthwhile friendships of my life. We were destined to travel tens of thousands of miles together before, ten years or so ago, he died.

It was after this match that Archie Compston sat on the fender, I can see him now, and pronounced in his booming voice, 'You're a bunch of lousy golfers. I could beat any three of you!' Tall, gangling and handsome in a cowboy-hero sort of way, Compston in every way loomed large on the golfing scene. He could be extra-ordinarily brusque and rude at times and women either loved or loathed thim, though in the end he never married. Anyone who came to him for a lesson was liable to have his clubs picked up, surveyed with distaste and thrown into a corner, while Compston shouted to his faithful clubmaker in the back room, 'George, show this gentleman a set of clubs!' One day, on meeting a rather pompous little man with plus-fours, eyeglass, and what would now be termed a crew-cut, he rubbed his palm on top of the little fellow's head and said, 'Gee, what a lie for a brassie!' He finished his days at the Mid-Ocean club in Bermuda, where he continued to be as forthright with his American customers, mostly to their delight, as he had been at home. I would give much, however, to have been present when in the course of a lesson he infuriated Virginia, the then Marchioness of Northampton, to such a degree that she 'did' him on the shin with an 8-iron. 'What did he do?' I asked. 'He bellowed,' she replied. For myself I got on very well with Archie – we once did a short book together which reads none too badly today – and I confess to being deeply touched that in the little 'shrine' they erected to his memory at Mid-Ocean there should be, beside almost the most brilliant bas-relief I have ever seen, a copy of my obituary of him.

'Archie was indeed a good and valued friend of mine as well as a very great player and golf doctor', wrote the Duke of Windsor to the then Governor of Bermuda, Sir Julian Gascoigne, enclosing a contribution towards the memorial. '. . . I would not like my name to be absent from the list of subscribers.

'It may interest you to know that I was indirectly to some extent responsible for his getting the post of professional at Mid-Ocean. We were playing golf at Wentworth, where he was the pro, one cold foggy day around 1946. Suddenly he told me he had been offered the post at Mid-Ocean, and knowing I had visited Bermuda, asked me if he should accept. We were not too far from the clubhouse, and I made him go in and telephone his acceptance before we played another hole! Alas, I never saw him again.'

That, however, as we sat round the fire at Coombe Hill, was all in the future. For the moment we were a bunch of lousy golfers and he would play any three of us. Two we would understand, yes, but three, surely not! N. A, Keith and W. H. Bermingham, our longest hitter and the one, let it now be whispered, who had driven up Royston Heath in the snowstorm, decided to take him on. Substantial wagers, by our standards at any rate, were laid and a little later, taking a day off lectures and such like, we reported at Coombe Hill, to find press photographers and my friend-to-be, General Critchley, already in attendance. Compston had craftily seen to it that the tees were set as far back as possible, which meant that there were six holes which he could reach in two and we could not. I went round, if I remember, in 72, which for me was no mean feat; Keith improved on this score at one hole, though equalling it of course at many others, and Bermingham improved not at all. Our best-ball score was therefore 71. Compston beat us by one hole, and the poor old Morris Cowley had to go in order to pay the debts. An awful lesson had been learnt, namely that the only difference between the better ball of two players and the best ball of three is the number of holes at which the one who plays worst on that day beats both of the other two. As in our case, the answer may well be nil. The third player may play quite well but never in fact win a hole off both the other two at the same time. It took me quite a few years to find three simple souls from whom to get my money back.

Other valuable lessons for later life, though sometimes I fear forgotten, were to be learnt from our matches. Among them was, 'I expect you'd like a glass of port to keep the cold out,' from one's prospective opponent in the afternoon singles, followed by, 'There's quite a crowd on the tee, so we'll just have one more; then we can get off.' At Worplesdon in those days the port seems, in memory, to have come in tumblers. I had my two of them before setting out to knock off an elderly gent (I expect he was about fifty), feeling that at this rate I would cheerfully take on Compston single-handed. I started 4,4,4,2 and was three up, but that was as long as the magic lasted and in the end I was lucky to creep in with a half. At Royal Wimbledon I was 'done' on barley wine, which at the time seemed no bigger than half-pints of bitter anyway. For many years after I went down I played for a number of clubs or societies against university teams and not unnaturally felt it my duty to impart to them these valuable lessons, thus gaining many a useful point against manifestly superior players.

It was during one of the vacations from Cambridge that a number of us went over from Bedford for some reason or other to play at Letchworth, including Bill Moore, the professional, and Morton, the greenkeeper, and I did my first hole in one. This is a most commonplace occurrence in golf but I mention it for two reasons. No, as a matter of fact, three; the third being that many years later, when I had become a great expert on golf, Messrs Thresher and Glenny, the well-known haberdashers, asked me whether I thought a hole-in-one tie would be a profitable venture on their part. I consulted various equally expert sources and we came to the conclusion that so many people had done a hole in one that the currency, so to speak, would be almost worthless and no one in his senses would buy a tie simply to announce to the world that he had accomplished this fluke at golf. Messrs Thresher and Glenny thereupon went ahead with their tie and at the last count had sold something like fifty thousand, which at thirty bob a time is nice business. So much for the experts of this world. However, back to Letchworth, where I started 4,3,4,3,3 and then, having sliced my second shot to the long 6th, holed out from about eighty yards for another three. Without putting the club back in the bag I then holed out for a one at the 7th. For years, out of tens of thousands who have holed in one, I was able to maintain that I was the only one in the game's history who had holed out twice running with the same club. The second curious feature was this. When I came to play the second shot to the next hole with the same club, an old-fashioned mashie, from about 140 yards, such was the

93

effect of the past few minutes on my mind that I honestly thought that this one too would go in. We all have two small voices in the back of the mind and I remember as though it were yesterday the second of them saying, 'The time will come when you think it ridiculous that you should be thinking that this one will go in, from 140 yards, just because the others did,' to which the first one replied, 'I can't help it, but that is what I do feel.' It did not go in, of course, but one with the same club went very near at the 9th, so I was out in 30, and so frightened that I took 39 to come home. However, we celebrated in Letchworth, Luton, Hitchin, Baldock and Bedford, so, all things considered, it was a memorable day.

In those days we had a week or ten days in preparation for the university match and the first of the four in which I played was at Prince's, Sandwich, then a magnificent links, some said the best of all, but doomed, alas, to be used as a target-range in the war. Afterwards it was restored by the late Sir Aynsley Bridgland but in a different form. It was said of Sherlock Holmes after his escape from Professor Moriarty at the Reichenbach Falls that he was 'never quite the same again', and thus it may be said of Prince's. In 1928, however, it was superlative, right beside the beach and the shingly shore on which so many Pakistanis were later to make their first tentative and illicit steps upon what was to be their home. It was only, I suppose, about the third seaside links I had seen, although North Foreland, where I had first burst into a momentary limelight, was only just up the road. This, however, was what Bernard Darwin so nicely called 'inland-super-mare'. I won my single against Charles Mitchell, 'the man with the million-dollar eyes', largely because I chanced upon, as caddie, a tall member of the well known and prolific Sandwich family, the Gisbeys. When we had a pitch with which to try to get down in two from off the green, which was often, he would hand out the club appropriate to the sort of trajectory he had in mind, walk forward and indicate the exact spot on which the ball should be pitched, and stand aside. It was not terribly difficult for me to do the rest and I must say the result was impressive. We stayed at that incongruous pile, the Guilford Hotel, which stands beside the lonely shore today, four-square against the wind, just as it did forty years ago, though somewhat modified within. I never use the lift without thinking of the final evening after the dinner when some people were just pressing the button to ascend when through the three-ply roof there descended with a mighty crash the person of the Oxford player George Adams. Having opened the gates above – how he did it remains to this day a mystery – and seeing the lift below, he thought what a splendid idea it would be to hop down onto the roof and possibly ride up with it. There is indeed a divinity which shapes our ends, and George is with us still.

The following year we played Oxford at Rye, which is the spiritual home of the Oxford and Cambridge Golfing Society and the scene in early January of the competition for their celebrated President's Putter. Rye was, and mercifully remains, unique. Together with Mildenhall it is probably the best winter course in the country and, again, its clubhouse is so simple that many of our American friends would scarce credit the almost passionate affection it inspires in so many – almost, one might say, a tin shed with corrugated iron roof and, until well after the war, external eighteenth-century earth closets. The only hot dish for lunch is buttered eggs and sausages, accompanied by a supremely good help-yourself sidetable, which of course is precisely what a golf-club lunch should be.

When first I went there, the little railway by which earlier golfers used to ride to the club had already gone and we approached by a winding road, throwing out pennies first to a gangly girl who opened the first gate, probably a grandmother now, and finally to an old rascal in a bowler hat, who lived in the wheel-less remains of a horse cab. Now there is a metal road for the trippers to Camber and the course has retreated to the seaward side, but little else has changed. Surmounting the distant hill, the square tower of the church still presides over the ancient town and sometimes, looking across the marsh at almost precisely the same scene that has greeted the wayfarer these three or four hundred years, one can see the weathercock glinting in the pale wintry sun. The clock was put in by a man from Winchelsea in sixteen-something and has never, they will tell you, gone wrong. Even earlier than that, when the sea used to come right up to the town, the French came one night and stole the bells, and the men of Rye in due course sailed forth and brought them back.

My partner in the foursomes that year was my dear friend and travelling companion Eric Martin Smith, a case perhaps of opposites fitting in together, for he was a very superior Old Etonian, allied with the great banking family of Hambro, and I

95

assuredly was neither. I like to think that perhaps I kept him in check when he tended to become too outrageously Etonian, and in doing so rubbed a few rough edges off myself. The year after he went down, he proceeded through round after round of the Amateur Championship at Westward Ho! and when at last, miraculously, he reached the final, our Cambridge contemporary, W. E. S. Bond, sent him a telegram saying: RIDICULOUS BUT STICK TO IT. It appeared in the press as having come from me, and, though I have always given credit where credit was due, this particular credit has always stuck to me. Eric went on to win and on the plinth of the vast trophy you will see: 1930, R. T. Jones; 1931, E. Martin Smith. After the war he became Member of Parliament for Grantham and a year or two later suddenly fell dead in his own garden, only in his early forties – a case, if ever there was one, of 'Those whom the gods love die young'.

At most of the big London golf clubs in those days the regular caddies tended to be brigands in long overcoats, and Walton Heath was no exception. After I had won my single there, my caddie, a man named Wilson, suggested that, as we were evidently so well matched a combination, it would be a good thing if he accompanied me to Rye for the university match, and thus it was arranged. (It was at Walton Heath that there occurred the basis of one of my favourite golfing stories, when Wash Carr hit a drive right up the middle, only to find the ball deep in a divot mark. 'That'd be a nice one to get in the Medal,' he said to his caddie. 'You'd never 'ave 'ad it in the Medal,' said the man darkly.) I mention Wilson because at the critical moment in the singles he put in on my behalf a supreme stroke of gamesmanship. My opponent happened to be an old friend with whom I had often played at Charterhouse, Pat Jackson, and in the morning I was four up at the 16th, well short of the green in three, while Jackson had a five-footer for a four. At this point I holed my chip. I only wish that the Master Gamesman himself, Stephen Potter, had been there to admire the timing by which, not a moment too soon nor a moment too late, Wilson, on picking the ball out of the hole, remarked to the world in general, 'Yuss. I thought we should 'ave one of *them* before long.' Jackson stood staring for a moment and then, having said simply, 'You little worm!' missed the putt. One of the many charms of golf and its infinite variety is that you accumulate over the years a whole host of personal memories – *this* happened here and *that* happened there – and thus in all the times I have played at Rye since, I have never passed the 16th green without thinking, 'It was exactly from *there* that I holed that chip.'

So far in two university matches my slate had remained clean but Hoylake next year, more properly the Royal Liverpool Golf Club, saw a sad reverse. For the team, and for myself in particular, everything seemed to go wrong. I spent my twenty-first birthday sitting over the fire with a sore throat, while outside the heavens opened and filled almost every one of the bunkers with water. The Hoylake fire brigade, aided by the green staff, did their best, but all to no avail. There was some question, I believe, of playing at Wallasey, but in the end the two captains, Eric Prain for Cambridge and Bob Baugh, a diminutive American from Alabama, for Oxford, decided upon a complicated set of local rules whereby in some bunkers you picked out for nothing, from others you picked out with the loss of a stroke, while in the rest you played the Rules of Golf. All this was done for the best and my own only criticism was that it was too late for the rank and file to become acquainted with which category of bunker they were in. The luckless captains, however, who had acted with the best of intentions, brought down on themselves an absolute barrage of hostile comment on the lines of: 'Who do they think they are to tamper with the sacred Rules of Golf?'

Prain and I played in the top foursome, one of our opponents being Charles Sweeny, who not long afterwards married the staggeringly beautiful Margaret Whigham, now the immediate past Duchess of Argyll, and had the mortification of lunching eight down and being finally beaten 10 and 8, the only double-figure clobbering I sustained in my golfing career. In the singles I was always going to lose to Alec Marples – 5 and 4 I think it was in the end – but the turning point came at the 17th in the morning, when I was on the green in three, sure of a five, and he was to the left in two, with a deep water-filled bunker between him and the hole. He lifted his head and fluffed into it – hooray! Alas, it proved to be one of those from which you could pick out for nothing. He did so, lifted his head again, and fluffed it back into the bunker. Picking it out again, he took an angry carefree blow at it, and holed out. Years later he was one of the Clerks of the House of Commons, among whose duties it is to mark off the names of the Members as they file through on a Division. Very often it befell me, during my brief sojourn therein, to come upon him in this capacity. 'Long-hurst,' I would say, but to the end I could never restrain a slight upward curling of the lip as I said it.

Some time after the match at Hoylake, by which time I had been elected captain for the following year, some bright fellow suggested that in the long summer vacation we ought to band ourselves together and venture across to the land of prohibition and plenty, the United States. We thought first in terms of a combined Oxford and Cambridge team, say half a dozen of each, but Oxford proved unforthcoming, so ten of us, having borrowed £150 from our fathers or wherever we could find it, set out from Cambridge on the good ship *Caronia* on our own – a voyage made memorable by a telegram announcing that I was now entitled to style myself BAEcon.Cantab. and by being realistically dressed up for the fancy dress ball by a forty-year-old widow. The way men automatically look women up and down, I found, is really disgusting, though I dare say that, if you are a woman, you may like it. My bust consisted of two glass pint tankards and I bear to this day the honourable inch-long scar caused by clanking them together with undue exuberance and shattering my right breast.

We played against about twenty clubs, first in Philadelphia, then in Boston, and then around New York, and two universities, including Harvard, by whom we were not too badly beaten; and only last year I stayed with a friend, Jim Baldwin, first encountered in that match forty-one years ago. Our second port of call was the great Pine Valley, perhaps the greatest inland course in the world and a golf club pure and simple, which is unusual in a land of lavish country clubs (women may, I believe, play after four o'clock on Sundays, especially in the winter) and here I played and was defeated by the President of the club, thus laying the foundations of a lifelong friendship with and admiration for Mr John Arthur Brown, who still comes over for the Medal at St Andrews and whom I met only recently playing round a new course near Palm Beach, still at the age of eighty-eight driving his own electric cart and bashing away with youthful vigour.

The first big moment in our tour came in the locker-room after our first match, at Huntington Valley, Pa, when our hosts said, 'I guess you boys would like a little drink?' On this subject the most awful warnings had been sounded before we left, It would be all right for *them*: they were used to it. Others talked of 'delayed action' and people dropping as though poleaxed. Many, it was said, were rendered instantly blind from wood alcohol, I opted for gin and queue-nine water, as tonic water was then called, and raised the glass with a lively surmise. It tasted just like gin and tonic, which in fact was what it was. Not always, however, were we to come out unscathed. Looking back, it was all rather pathetic. Adult and successful men were reduced to keeping their 'liquor' in the locker-room and in public even drinking whiskey poured from teapots. For the speakeasy – and what a splendid word! – it was a question of 'Knock three times and ask for Charlie', and this I remember actually doing. They were the days of 'Buddy, can you spare a dime?' and Al Capone and the Bearcat Stutz and raccoon coats and the hip flask and Rah, Rah, Rah!

We were duly noticed by the press, which we felt added to our stature, and I still have references to us as the 'invading British collegiate linksmen' and even, let me tell you, 'famed stars from the dear old country'. We were guests in Philadelphia at an enormous banquet given in honour of Commander Byrd, lately returned from remarkable exploits in the Antarctic, but I am afraid my principal memory is of the master of ceremonies announcing that only two pieces of music had ever been written for twelve women harpists and that the twelve women harpists he was about to introduce would play both of them. The ladies came on in long classical robes and started to pluck their strings but, alas, the clatter of knives and plates and the incessant chatter were such that eventually they rose in a body and swept out. I have thought ever since in terms of a 'sweep' of women harpists.

At Boston we played at the Country Club, at Brookline, where I had the honour of playing Francis Ouimet, who became another lifelong friend, one of the gentlest men who ever swung a club. As quite a poor boy from the 'wrong side of the tracks', as they say in America, he tied for the US Open Championship on this very course in 1913 with the British giants Vardon and Ray, which is equivalent to tieing with Nicklaus and Palmer today, and beat them on the play-off. He was only nineteen at the time and when, fifty years later, the championship was played at the Country Club again in his honour, I had the pleasure of sharing with Joe Loony, of the *Boston Herald*, the privilege of making a presentation to him.

Around New York W. E. S. Bond and I were entertained at Mt Kisco at the home of Mr and Mrs Donald Carr, where our host announced that he had managed to obtain a bottle of port in our honour. This tasted like rather ordinary cheap port, but what the bootlegger had done with it no one will ever know. In the morning neither of us was able to raise his head from the pillow, or indeed to move, let alone get up. Mrs Carr, after her husband's death – not before he had gone round the long Number 2 course at Pinehurst in his age, seventy-one – retired here to be near her son at Wentworth, where she died a few years ago at the age of eighty, her own distinction having been to write a charmingly simple little life of Jesus called *The Beloved Son*, which sold no fewer than four million copies.

These were rough days in America, though in a different way they are getting rough again now. There was a good deal of shooting and bumping off, but at least it was mostly each other that the gangsters were bumping off. In Camden, NJ, for instance, through which we passed on the day of our arrival – it made us feel almost at home to be in a place called Camden – a character had been warned by certain other characters that a 'pineapple' was liable to be tossed through his window. He speculated as to where he should have his dinner and decided that he might be safest in a crowded public restaurant. I have often imagined the spinning-out of his meal and his feelings as eventually there was nothing for it but to send for the bill. At any rate, as he ventured out into the street, a black sedan motor car drove slowly by and a moment later he was lying on the sidewalk riddled with machine-gun bullets and very dead indeed. What was most emblematic of the times, however, was that the local newspaper account, after lurid pictures and a long obituary of the deceased, ended with the simple words: 'A bystander was also killed.' He never even got his name in the paper.

Altogether we spent five weeks in the States on our £150, including the return fare in the *Caronia*, and what a lot of friends we made and what a lot we learnt in the process! For me it was the first of what must be coming up to something like fifty visits to those hospitable shores and the day after tomorrow, as I write, I am off again. I wish, though, it were on the old *Caronia* instead of one of these flying cinemas.

Back home in the familiar, happy world of university golf I

am afraid I was not really a great success as captain, though not, I like to think, a total failure. In football, let us say, a captain can inspire his men by actually running about among them on the field of play and by his shining example rally them to great deeds, but golf, even team golf, is essentially a lonely and still in a way a selfish game, for all you can do is to get on with your own match and do your best to add a point to your side's total. If you can do that, you come out with a hundred per cent, even though every other match be lost. Also, perhaps, the fact of being an only child and therefore essentially a loner does not help in the task of jollying other people on. At any rate it was, and remains, my view that what clothes a fellow wore, what clubs he played with, how much he played and how much he practised and what time he went to bed, were essentially his own affair. We were all within a year of so of the same age and it might be presumed that every man was doing his damnedest according to his own lights. What business was it of the captain's, therefore, to interfere? I did, it is true, arrange for a number of us to go over and take a little instruction from my boyhood hero Abe Mitchell, who was then private professional to old Sam Ryder, the seedsman and founder of the Ryder Cup, at the Verulam Club at St Albans – the one you see from the train on the left going north from St Pancras – but he all but ruined us in the process. Abe used to stand with his right foot square to the hole and then, after a very short backswing, give the ball the most almighty thump with his wrists and arms, the muscles of which, like those of the blacksmith, stood out like iron bands. Ours, however, did not, and the result was liable to be a feeble flailing motion resulting in a high slice.

Our match against Oxford took place at Royal St George's, Sandwich, but this time we stayed at the Bell, which, again, though modernized a bit inside, remains much the same friendly hostelry today, just beside the toll bridge, in what must be one of the least spoilt little towns of its kind in the country. Our preparation was not helped by a sudden summons for Bermingham and myself to attend an inquest at Hertford. Returning one Sunday evening after a match at Oxhey I had almost reached the bottom of the long hill leading down to Welwyn, and was beginning to bear right towards the by-pass leading to Stevenage, when the figure of an old man stumbled suddenly into the headlights from the left. I swerved and actually missed him with the front of the car but the poor fellow, who turned out to be a tramp and very, very much under the influence, stumbled on and ran into the back of the car. We got him to the side of the road, summoned the police, and eventually got him to hospital. It transpired that he had died of these self-inflicted injuries. I mention the matter because certain aspects would assuredly seem remarkable today, at any rate to me. Since I had invited the policeman at the time to satisfy himself that there was no question of drink involved, on my side at any rate, and he had done so, and since the accident had been manifestly unavoidable even by the most skilful of drivers, it never occurred to me, such was my automatic faith in 'British Justice', to exercise my mind for one moment as to the result of the inquest. Indeed, I had not thought even to inform either the college authorities or my parents, though the latter got to hear of it and in high anxiety sent a solicitor with a watching brief. A courteous hearing was given us by a coroner and jury and it did not surprise me for one moment when I was absolved from all blame – which, if you are an undergraduate driving back to Cambridge at night, means you really *cannot* be guilty – but I sometimes think with a shudder what a ghastly affair it would all have been today.

Back in Sandwich we got down to business again and at last on a bitterly cold morning I set out in the foursomes with my lifelong friend – and stock-broker – Horton Martin Row, who at breakfast, what with the cold and the natural feelings of one about to play in his first university match, had ordered grapefruit and, though securing a number of segments in the spoon, had failed to get any as far as their objective, some merely dropping off, others going over the shoulder, as with a man dropping a provisional ball. We were at one time, I think, three down but we managed to rally and from the Canal Hole, the 14th, went 4,4,3,4 to win on the 17th, which anyone who knows Sandwich will agree to be not bad on a cold windy day in March. It fell to me to have the more spectacular shots, while my partner filled in the equally worthy but less dramatic background, and so it was I who received the battle honours in next morning's papers.

In the singles it was my lot to play the opposite captain, Pat Marston, who had not long before, I believe, had jaundice. At any rate I finished my career as a university golfer at the 11th hole in the afternoon with a drive, a brassie and a putt for a three, and we shook hands and walked away towards the club. Instead of pleasure at my own success a huge wave of depression came over me. This then was the end; the end of the halcyon days; the end, it seemed, of the only life I had ever known. The future seemed to stretch out bleak and unpaid. I had no job. Indeed, I had hardly given it a thought. I knew neither trade nor profession, and such was the anticlimax that I lay on my bed in the Bell and wept, before getting up to dress for the dinner. Let not so many happy days be allowed, however, to end on so sad a note. In 1970 they played the match at St George's again and Pat Marston and I walked round together. Much water, and a certain amount of other fluids, had passed under the bridge in the intervening thirty-nine years.

9
Golfing Scribe

After walking sadly off the 11th green at Sandwich, realizing, as I have said, that the only life I had ever really known was suddenly over and that, 'BAEcon.Cantab.' or no, I had taken no thought for the future, I returned instinctively to Bedford and, my father having by this time retired to the little Somerset town of Clevedon, settled down in a rambling old hotel-cum-guesthouse called St Mary's Abbey. From here I embarked on a number of false but in the end not unvaluable starts, beginning with the family business, where my father's partner, a difficult man at the best of times, was now in charge. He used to do the buying, while my father, so to speak, 'looked after the shop'. On one celebrated occasion Fred Skinner had returned from one of his forays in London with a bargain lot of a gross of punt-poles, one of the most unlikely purchases perhaps of all time, since the only possible buyer would have been Mr Chetham, who hired out the boats on the river, and he had not a gross of punts, let alone the need for a gross of poles. When I was in the business, Mr Skinner brought back in similar circumstances a gross of the most frightful dental forceps, calculated to extract any tooth from any angle – relics, I fancy, of the First World War. He had secured them for a shilling each and had a green baize wrap-around hold-all made specially for them. 'If I only get a florin apiece for them, it will be a useful profit,' he said. The market in Bedford for a gross of dental forceps proved, however, to be limited, and it would never surprise me if, somewhere among the stuff stored on our upper floors today, they turned up once again. Though it was soon apparent that I was not cut out for a retail house furnisher, the experience was a useful one. After all, you are going to deal with shopkeepers all your life and it is a salutary experience to know what life is like on the other side of the counter.

The next experience was a correspondence course in company law and kindred subjects, and it remains my impression that it was an extremely good one. The most valuable lesson it proved, however, was that, just as Mr Colman made his fortune from that part of his mustard left on the plate, so the purveyors of this form of learning made their fortune from the unexpired portions of their courses. This, incidentally, was confirmed by a fellow-cadet in the war, who had been engaged in that line. They would devise courses on any subject under the sun, he said, and often the time would come when the next lesson had never so much as been written and someone had hastily to concoct it. If a particularly obstinate pupil looked like staying the course, they sent him a lesson calculated to knock him out for good and all, and it was a fact that no customer had ever been known to go the full distance.

The fun and stimulation of the 1931 election had turned my thoughts to politics, and I was much attracted by the writings of Sir Ernest Benn, founder of the Individualist Society and a writer of extreme clarity. I joined the society and attended a number of their meetings in London, as a result of which I found myself in an even less likely occupation than that of retail house furnisher, namely seller – or rather offerer – of advertising space in one of the Benn group of magazines, the *Hardware Trade Journal*. Every morning I would report in best black hat, overcoat and umbrella at the office in Fleet Street (No. 15 bus, 4d., from Westbourne Terrace, where six of us from Cambridge shared a flat under the rafters) and be issued with a list of prospective customers on which to call.

Three factors militated against success in this line. One, that all the prospects had already been thoroughly 'worked over' several times before; two, that practically none of them were directly connected with the hardware trade – the great American company of Westinghouse in Bush House still comes to mind in this connection; and three, that no reputable firm is induced to spend money on advertising by a young fellow who comes unannounced to their door. At first I used to tramp the streets of London, acquiring in the process an intimate knowledge of parts of the City I should never otherwise have known, but later, when it became apparent that this was no line for door-to-door work, I took to telephoning in advance and occasionally securing appointments, but it was soon borne in on me, as I lifted the receiver, that in a moment or two I should be saying, 'No? Well, never mind. I rather thought you wouldn't.' Some of them, though not many, were downright rude. A Mr Screeton, for instance, who made paint in Bermondsey – and I cheerfully get my own back on him after forty years – replied, 'There's not a customer of mine who reads your *Journal* and I wouldn't want his business if he did.' Still, it taught me another lesson I like to think I have always remembered. With hand on heart I can say that never in my life have I been rude to a commercial traveller.

After a few months of this there occurred to me a fantastic piece of good fortune and I am ashamed to admit that I cannot for the life of me remember how it came about or to whom to lift my hat in retrospect. Somebody introduced me to an amiable, easy-going character called George Philpot, who later had the irrelevant distinction of being in the only carriage in the London underground to be involved in a serious accident in forty or fifty years. George edited a little monthly golf magazine called *Tee Topics*, of blessed memory, and, as a result of our meeting, the light of good fortune shone upon us both. George, who was by that time old enough to look upon work rather as I do now, was enabled to stay for most of the afternoon playing billiards with his cronies in the Press Club, while I, a square peg in an absolutely cut-to-measure square hole at last, settled down to what every instinct told me was the kind of life I was going to love. Not yet, perhaps, the kind of living, for the arrangement was that I should be on probation for three months, after which, having practised at editing the paper while George was playing billiards or lunching with a potential advertiser, it would be ascertained what salary I should command, if any. In the meantime I had a family allowance of £4 a week and this, unbelievably, enabled me to move to the Connaught Club near Marble Arch and to dine as often as desired at the Praed Street premises of 'William No. 1 Harris, the Sausage King, also at Brighton' – sausages, chips, and extra shovel of onions, 1s. 2d. I was back in the world of golf where there was still so much to be seen and learnt, and so many people to be met, and where at least I knew basically what I was talking about and people still knew my name. As for this new world of writing and printing and editing and seeing the glossy result at the end of the month, I felt rather as a woman must feel when she picks up a dress and says, 'This is *me*.' Furthermore, it turned out that it *was* me, whereas the woman so often takes the dress back with, 'I knew the moment I bought it that it wasn't me.' The fact that elementary insight into the finances of *Tee Topics* showed that, however much the amiable George might wish to pay me, there was nothing with which to do it, did not seem to matter. This at last was my world and somewhere there would be a niche for me in it.

Writing now in the later stages of the more than agreeable life into which I had at that time just been initiated, I marvel at the good fortune which continued to dog my unworthy footsteps. The Depression was still very much with us and there had not, of course, been the golfing 'explosion' which is such a feature of the sporting scene today. The *Sunday Times*, then sister paper to the *Daily Telegraph* in the *Telegraph*'s present Fleet Street building, carried, broadly speaking, no golf other than agency reports. Someone suggested that a modest outlay on a man of their own might be justified: Sir Herbert Morgan, who had something to do with the *Sunday Times*, mentioned the matter to James Braid one day at Walton Heath: Braid said he did not know of anyone suitable but a young fellow who used to be captain of Cambridge had, he understood, taken to writing about golf in some magazine: from these simple circumstances came the turning-point of my life.

It was the last week of my three probationary months with *Tee Topics*, and there was arising between George Philpot and myself a certain unease, not impairing what had become a delightful and informal camaraderie between us but stemming from the awareness that the day of reckoning was approaching and he knew I knew there was nothing in the kitty and I knew he knew I knew, and indeed that he must have known all along, and neither anxious to broach the subject, though I was in the stronger position of the two since I knew, and he didn't, that I should be only too happy to go on in this new life, Micawber-like, until something turned up. The problem was solved by the arrival of a courteous little note from what proved to be an exceptionally courteous little man who signed himself, on the headed paper of the *Sunday Times*, W. W. Hadley. I was not to know, though I like to think I immediately appreciated, that here was one of the great, almost legendary, editors of Fleet Street. He sat dwarfed behind a large and rather untidy desk and revealed that the *Sunday Times* was considering including on the sporting pages a short regular piece about golf and that my name had been mentioned. Was I, he wondered, with that curious humility characteristic of men of his stature, and I shall always remember his words, available for further work? I revealed pretty rapidly that I was, and a few days later there began at six guineas a week a relationship which is now, as I write, in its fortieth year.

In those days there were three 'glossies', each costing as much as a shilling, the *Tatler*, the *Bystander* and the *Sketch*. Each of the last two carried a page about golf every week, but the *Tatler*, a little more 'social' perhaps than the other two, had not yet attained that level of progress – a position which was rectified by my being introduced by a friend to the editor. The friend was that same General Critchley whom I had met and defeated at Coombe Hill and who appeared to have already convinced the busy editor that he should have a golf page and that he, Critch, knew just the man, with the result that I emerged from a very short interview having painlessly extracted another six guineas a week. I think I only saw the editor a couple of times again – I have always held that what an editor seeks from a contributor is not his company but his contribution – but three bound volumes on my bottom shelf bear witness to my contribution to the *Tatler* having arrived on time for the next three hundred and fifty weeks.

It cannot have been very long afterwards that Eric Lobb, whose family firm make those wonderful shoes in St James's Street, pointed out to me an advertisement in the personal column of *The Times* saying: *Prominent London Daily requires Golf Correspondent. Sound knowledge of the game essential.* He wondered whether I would be interested, but who on earth would be, already sitting on the best part of £17 a week, unmarried and aged twenty-three? On the other hand it would be amusing, we thought, to find out who it was. The only Prominent London Daily we could think of with no resident golf correspondent was the *Daily Herald* and it seemed hardly likely in those days that their mainly trade-union readers would be interested. With an air of financially independent bravado I took out a sheet of the *Sunday Times*'s paper, wrote on it: DEAR SIRS, *I am interested in your advertisement in The Times*, sent it off, and forgot about it.

Next morning I received a call from the *Evening Standard*, which of course had never entered our heads, though when you came to think of it no journal could more properly be described as a Prominent London Daily. It is extraordinary how slowly the penny sometimes drops in this life. Even now it took some time for this one to drop but, when it did, I was round to Shoe Lane as rapidly as I had previously shot up Bouverie Street. I should need to carry on my two present commitments, I said. No difficulty about that, they replied, and how much would I want? I took a deep breath and said, 'What about £750 a year?' and the alacrity with which they replied, 'Of course, and can you start next week?' made me kick myself for not having said, 'What about £1000?' What matter? I now had three square pegs securely fitted into three square holes, to say nothing of what I deemed a fabulous income.

For one as work-shy as myself I look back appalled at the amount I had cheerfully undertaken and in fact cheerfully accomplished – but really it was a marvellous life for a young man and I do honestly like to think I appreciated at the time, and not merely later, how lucky I was. For one thing newspapers are not liable to ask how old you are; all they want to know is whether you can deliver the goods. Thus you can step straight onto a rung of the ladder which a barrister, say, or even a doctor, of much greater talent might not attain till his middle thirties. I have always had a sneaking sympathy for the chap in the Bible who got the most frightful stick for thanking God that he was not as other men are, but at the risk of incurring the divine displeasure I must reveal that from this time onwards I never went to a regular place of work and even now I am either entirely at home or entirely away, probably in some far distant sunnier clime, in pleasant places among mostly pleasant people who are anyway at their pleasantest in the circumstances in which I meet them, and all this almost certainly at someone else's expense. Furthermore I have never in my life, never, worked late during the afternoon. So it may be forgiven if sometimes, when I go down to see friends in the City and observe these hideous glass-box buildings and reflect that it falls to thousands of people to spend their whole working life therein, and in the same few square feet at that, I tend to feel, 'There but for the grace of God . . .' and a sort of guilty shiver comes over me in case providence gives me the same sort of stick as the Pharisee. Still, nothing can take it away now and all one can do is to be duly thankful.

The reporting press, as against the essayist type like Bernard Darwin, were less highly regarded then, it is fair to say, than now, but the newcomer takes it all as it comes. An evening paper requires about five telephoned reports a day to catch the various editions, to say nothing of incessant paragraphs for the Sports Diary and in the case of the *Evening Standard* the Londoner's Diary. My first assignment was an English Championship at a Yorkshire club and the accommodation for the entire press, which, knowing no better, I did not find strange, was a small potting-shed filled with flower-pots and empty beer-bottles. On the wall hung one telephone for the lot of us. Senior members of the fraternity, notably George Greenwood, who wrote for thirty-two years for the *Daily Telegraph*, had evidently complained, and it happened that when the secretary and some official came round to investigate, I was the only person in the potting-shed. 'There you are,' I heard the secretary say, 'There's one of 'em in there now.' Later, however, we began to have our own telephones installed, and I even had the luxury of a boy-telephonist from the office, or rather a succession of boys, who, no sooner had I trained them up to know the difference between a tee and a green, would become too old by union rules or some such, and I had to start on another. Eventually I had a young fellow called John Webb, whose father was on the *Daily Herald*, and, since he knew about golf and the needs of a newspaper, and actually wrote shorthand, he made life blissful indeed – which, alas, can be only a posthumous tribute since he was killed, with the rank of captain, in the war.

Sometimes, though not as often as I should have liked, I was able to cover something other than golf, and indeed at one time I am not sure that I was not the polo correspondent, in which capacity I attended a small meeting in the flat of Lord Mountbatten, by whom I was suitably impressed. He treated us with extraordinarily non-condescending civility. On another occasion I was one of the 'trained observers' dispatched to cover the coronation route in 1937 in case any misguided citizen should cause an incident. My own perch was just a plank balanced across two girders on the top of Grand Buildings, Trafalgar Square, not attached to them in any way, and I and a number of office boys sat with our feet dangling over the roofs, between which we could see the crowds like ants down below. The more the boys wriggled, the more the plank bounced about and the very thought of it makes me shudder today. I sat at the far end and under my right elbow the minute hand of a vast clock – I should say it was twenty feet long – heaved its way spasmodically round, jerking about a foot at a time.

I mention all this largely as an excuse to recall the story of the boy and the orange, which I find pleasing even to this day. We all had to bring our rations against the long hours of waiting and this boy had brought an orange. Every so often he would produce this orange from his pocket, eye it fondly, inspect it from various angles, and polish it till it glowed. Often, as the hours passed, I thought he was going to eat it but he always managed somehow to get it back in his pocket. I suppose he must have had this orange out a dozen times or more. Then at last came the Moment. The irrevocable decision was made and he dug his thumb into the peel. Casually he cast the pieces of peel down into the abyss and we all peered over to watch them bounce merrily down among the roof-tops and with luck fall through onto the people in the square. Suddenly there was a disturbance over by the National Gallery – it turned out later that a stand had collapsed – and this welcome distraction claimed everyone's attention, the boy's included. Idly he went on peeling his orange, but suddenly there was a choked cry of anguish. I turned to see him clutching a small piece of peel in his hand. He had thrown away the orange and kept the peel.

At the very early stages of the war, before I 'went for a soldier', I was sent to report a football match, taking my place as one of a row of journalists in the stand. There was a scrimmage around the goal, as a result of which the ball shot out and entered the net (and how well I knew the feelings of the goalkeeper!). 'Who do you reckon scored that one?' I said to the man beside me. Believe it or not, he wouldn't say. He even shielded his little bit of paper like a schoolboy fearful of cribbing by the boy next door. I was completely taken aback, but it taught me in a few seconds to appreciate one aspect of my working life for which I had not been sufficiently grateful before, if only because it had never occurred to me, namely the co-operation and general goodwill that prevails among our small, I will not say select, crew whose life consists in writing about golf. Nobody can be in ten places at once and, since a hundred or more golfers may be performing at the same time over several square miles of course, information was always, and still is, cheerfully shared. And if sometimes its accuracy leaves a little to be desired, well, one wrong all wrong.

This was a time of life of which it is difficult even now to write without a tinge of jealousy at the young fellow that once was me. Everything was new, or nearly new, and in the evening, having downed tools at about half-past three, when my 'daily' colleagues were just beginning to warm up to their work, and leaving the efficient Webb to add the necessary few lines later, I would depart and play some neighbouring course of which I had heard but not yet seen. It was largely as a result of this that I developed subconsciously the philosophy of what I have come to think of as 'gap-filling'; in other words going anywhere once and doing anything once if you have not been there, or done it, before.

The base for these operations was now 8 King's Bench Walk in the Temple, whose exterior was as exquisitely beautiful as its interior was antiquated. It was occupied by three birds of an almost identical feather: E. W. Swanton, now I suppose the doyen of practising cricket correspondents; Ian Peebles, the crafty Test bowler, who has just retired, alas, from writing for the *Sunday Times*; and myself. Why this trio should have been permitted the privilege of occupying rooms in perhaps the most beautiful part of the Temple I cannot say, but we were; and never mind the fact that the hot water was directed by an ancient piece of garden hose from an even more ancient gas geyser into a copper-stained bath. We were looked after by the admirable Mrs Smallbone, who came across from Battersea each day. That was more than thirty-five years ago; the other day Swanton somehow rediscovered her, now aged seventy-five: we gave her a suitably inscribed clock as a rather belated memento. The letter I received from her is one of the most touching documents I have ever seen.

The three of us became involved from its beginning in what must be almost the most comical episode in the history of the London stage, a play called *Young England* by an eighty-three-year-old author named Walter Reynolds, who wrote it with the utmost seriousness in the sermonizing vein of Hughes in *Tom Brown's Schooldays*. It was all about Boy Scouts and Girl Guides and the wicked Scoutmaster robbing the safe in the Scouts' Hut and the even more wicked Mayor evicting the widow, and somehow the Duchess came into it too. What the presumably sophisticated first-night audience must have thought of it I do not know, but the play could hardly have survived half a dozen performances if some unknown wag had not called out some ribald comment on the second night. Others followed, and by next day it had got round the clubs of London that there was going on at the Victoria Palace something that must be instantly seen before they took it off. Peebles was in, I think, on the third night and in the end became so word-perfect that he could conduct a whole conversation exclusively in quotations from the play. The plot was melodramatic rubbish of a high order but its success – it ran for months – was due to the splendid way in which the principals, John Oxford as Jabez Hawke the wicked Mayor, Guy Middleton as the Scoutmaster, and the beautiful Sylvia Allen as the Girl Guide mistress, night after night played it 'straight'. Having robbed the safe in the Scout's Hut, Guy Middleton had to come back, take out his handkerchief and wipe the handle against fingerprints. On the second or third night as he was preparing to slink away someone cried, 'Wipe the handle!' and later on, when the original wit had been exhausted and the rugger types had taken over, the noise of 'Wipe the handle!' would be almost like that of a football crowd. At first, however, the wit was extremely subtle and often one would think of some line one night, too late to get it in, and return on the following night for the sole purpose of trying it on. If it succeeded, it would probably go into the saga and be picked up by someone or other, night after night. Often the aged author would himself attend, striving vainly to keep order from his box. 'Order, order!' he cried one night. 'Large whisky and soda,' was the instant reply from the back. Some people picked up lines which particularly pleased them and would utter them just before the player did so, and really it could be very comical. If, for instance, as the Mayor discovered the footprints of the fleeing widow, you heard a voice from the auditorium saying in deep, theatrical tones, 'Footprints on the soggy ground,' you could be sure that Swanton was in the house. 'Ha!' John Oxford would say, without turning a hair. 'Footprints on the soggy ground.' My own line came when the beautiful Girl Guide mistress arrived to camp with her troop in the ancestral park: 'Drinking water must be our first consideration.' Not the least amusing aspect of this farce was the reaction of people who had come to see it in all seriousness, little suspecting that if it had been taken that way it would not have lasted more than three or four days. 'Don't you *want* to hear the play?' I remember an angry lady saying one day. 'Good God, no, madam! Do you?' said the fellow beside her. The show became known as 'the Club' – 'Going down to the Club tonight?' people would say – and I suppose I saw it thirty or forty times, without ever seeing the curtain go up or once paying to go in. It went from one theatre to the

other and once at the end of a week at the Piccadilly, the inde-
fatigable John Oxford came forward in his mayoral robes to make
a speech. Having thanked everyone for their support, he said, 'I
am afraid, ladies and gentlemen, I am a little hoarse.' 'But how
can a Mayor be a little hoarse?' said a voice from the back. Loud
cheers, but once again I can only resort to saying that it all appeared to be very funny at the time.

This particular voice was that of a very singular character,
Leonard Gullick, one-time classical scholar at Cambridge and
contributor of more than a hundred articles to *Punch*. On the way
back from the 1929 Walker Cup match at Royal St George's,
Sandwich, where he was a member, he and some companions
were deploring the fact that they had nowhere 'special' to go –
something between one of the more heavy and respectable clubs
perhaps and the less reputable variety. Whereupon Gullick threw
up his lucrative job in advertising and founded the Nineteenth
Club, first in Brick Street; then in Cork Street, where it was burnt
out during the war, though not by enemy action; and finally in
Old Burlington Street. He was christened, I think by me, 'the
Landlord' and the name stuck, to such an extent that he was rarely
known as anything else. He was dapper, suave, flawlessly turned
out and true child of the Mayfair that now belongs to the past. 'I
was always brought up,' he used to say, 'on the principle that no
gentleman was ever seen east of Romano's,' so that when two
members, attired in tails and with a couple of dazzling women on
their arms, revealed that they were going to supper at the Savoy,
his immediate reaction was, 'I never can understand why it is that
you have to go out into the country for your food.' In the war he
deplored all the curious people that had 'invaded our little village',
and his own farthest foray would be a visit to Brighton on the
Sunday morning Belle, a bottle of champagne with Harry Preston
at the Albion, a little lunch at the Metropole, an hour in one of the
shelters on the front, and back on the afternoon Belle, having
become to the great envy of his friends as brown as a berry. I
suppose the success of the Nineteenth lay in his never not being
there. Thus women could always go in unaccompanied and feel
at home and it became in this sense the only truly mixed club I
have ever known. The Landlord was no Adonis but for most
women, though not all, he had an enviably powerful attraction.
When I asked one of them why, she said after a while, 'I think it

is because he has such perfect manners.' By this time it was too late for an only child from darkest Bedfordshire to change his spots, but I pass on the Landlord's secret for the benefit of the young. He and his first wife were divorced and his second died in rather tragic circumstances. He then married one of the most beautiful girls any of us ever knew and despite the disparity in their ages they were as happy as could be. I remember going in one night during the war when some Canadian officers were in the club and she went on with them to the Café de Paris, leaving the Landlord to follow later. When he got there, the bomb had already dropped through the glass roof and not a single trace of any one of the party, including dear Norma, was ever seen again. Later in the war, in Dover Street, the very heart of his Mayfair village, a day-raider sent a six-storey building crashing to the ground. A few minutes later there emerged into the sunshine through a small gap in the vast heap of rubble the Landlord, attired in a flowered silk dressing-gown. After the war, when he had remarried his first wife as his fourth, it fell to me to act as best man for an old friend, whose bride to be had been married before, thus indicating a registry office. I asked the Landlord the form about this and without a moment's hesitation he said, 'Well, I always use Caxton Hall. They know me there.'

The Nineteenth Club was perhaps no Athenaeum but I am not too proud to confess that for fifteen or twenty years it afforded me and many a better man a more congenial base for operations than I can detect today, though I dare say that gin at a shilling, brandy and crème de menthe at two shillings, and income-tax at five shillings in the pound may have had something to do with it. For the whole of the war, apart from a week or two after the unfortunate fire in Cork Street, the club never closed, and men on leave from all parts of the world made a beeline for it, sure of a greeting from the Landlord and sure that he would be there. His was one of many of the unsung contributions to the war, and I shall not lightly forget the night, soon after all was over, when he was sitting at the top of the stairs, dressed, as it happened, for the first time for many a day in black tie and red carnation. A man whom I vaguely recognized came up the stairs. 'Well, well,' said the Landlord, 'I haven't seen you for years. Where have you been?' The man gazed at him and then gradually and uncontrollably burst into tears. He had been a prisoner-of-war for just over five years.

10

Some
Modest Successes

'Rational, industrious, useful beings are divided into two classes,' Churchill once wrote. 'Those whose work is work and whose pleasure pleasure, and those whose work and pleasure are one. Fortune has favoured the children who belong to the second class.' With which thought in mind I have to admit that it was a happy day when I started writing about the game of golf. Indeed, there were times when you could hardly call it work, since it offered unlimited opportunities of playing, even if not in the championships – which was perhaps fortunate since it also gave me a cast-iron reason for never winning one. My record as a championship golfer, in this country at any rate, was not, I am afraid, an impressive one. I played once in the English Championship and was beaten by the eventual winner in the second round, and once in the Amateur at Muirfield, where I was beaten by a dour but unknown Scotsman in the first. The Muirfield championship, incidentally, was won by John de Forest, now Count de Bendern, and was remarkable for the fact that every time he tried to take the club back to hit the ball he got 'stuck'. You could see him trying to will himself to move the club but it stayed as though stapled to the ground, and it was no wonder that the thirty-six-hole final took some time to play. Some people have even been known to get stuck at the top of the swing, which must be almost the most ridiculous complaint in all sport, but in view of my own ignominious departure from the game through the 'twitch' on the putting-green it would ill become me to pour scorn upon others.

Working for an evening paper, with five telephone calls a day, prevented me playing in championships at home but did not prevent my doing so on the Continent and, indeed, once in America, when after the 1936 Walker Cup match – a totally point-less affair, I fear, so far as the British were concerned – the team moved on for the US Amateur at Garden City. I had the temerity to enter as well and in fact came near to altering the course of golfing history. Our man, Jack McLean, reached the final, where he was virtually beaten by a diabolical stymie on the 34th hole by Johnnie Fischer, now a pillar of the US Golf Association. Fischer holed for a 2 on the 36th to square the match and finally won on the 37th, but his opponent in the final might never have been Jack McLean at all, since in the second round I was two up on him at the turn. I had not seen the last nine holes in practice and lost by 2 and 1, and a very good thing too, for it is just possible that I should not have survived to the final as McLean did! Only a year or two ago I was sitting up a TV tower at the US Open at Baltusrol with a very personable young fellow beside me assisting with the scoring, when he said, 'Didn't you play in the US Amateur in 1936, sir?' to which I replied that I did. 'Do you remember who you beat in the first round?' 'No.' 'My father,' he said. It made me feel a bit ancient – but not everyone has got through even one round in the US Amateur.

Against the less formidable opposition encountered on the continent I had rather more success, to say nothing of enjoying innumerable forays at an age when one had the stamina to do justice not only to the golf but to the pleasures of the evening. The first was when Eric Martin Smith and I, for some reason which for the life of me I cannot remember, though it may have been connected with my own happy memories of Lausanne, went off in 1928 to play in the Swiss Championship at Geneva. He got beaten, but I survived to the final, where my enthusiastic young caddie, alas, picked up my first drive after lunch under the impression that I was still practising and I lost not only the hole but also the general momentum and was beaten by 4 and 2. This was a bitter disappointment but it whetted the appetite for these continental excursions in the thirties, travelling sometimes like a gentleman by the Golden Arrow and Channel steamer, followed perhaps by the Blue Train or even the Simplon Orient – and who can fail to be thrilled by a board under the sleeper window saying: Paris–Strasbourg–München–Wien–Budapest–Beograd–Sofia–Istanbul – and sometimes by that most splendid flying machine with engines seemingly stuck all over it, the old Imperial Airways 'Hannibal'.

Early in 1936 I fell in with an extraordinarily nice German called

Schertel von Burtenbach, a fellow of about my own age, and I do
hope he survived the war, who had been sent over to London by
the German golf 'Führer', Karl Henkel, to explore the possibilities
of widening the opportunities for people to play golf in Germany.
This had led him to me and as a result I went over to survey the
scene and at the same time play in the German Championship at
Wannsee, the delightful country club outside Berlin at which
Percy Alliss was for many years professional. Having endured
some forceful coaching at the hands of Archie Compston I may
say that I won the championship, though my principal memory is
of the presentation of the massive trophy by the golf Führer.
Henkel was a big, handsome, slightly pompous, generous man,
head of the great Henkeltrocken 'German champagne' firm and
uncle-in-law of von Ribbentrop, and the presentation involved
standing for what seemed to be several minutes having one's hand
pump-handled up and down by him with only an occasional
'Herr Longhurst' in his speech to assure one that we were still on
the same track. All the same I was very proud to have won. I was
also intrigued to meet in the locker-room and have a long chat with
a character once known all over the world, the Kaiser's son, 'Little
Willie'. He would have been, I dare say, in his middle fifties at the
time and struck me as a particularly gentle and courteous man.

In the following year I had yet another attempt at the French
Championship, on what I still regard as the most attractive course
in France, at Morfontaine outside Paris. It was laid out by the
controversial English architect Tom Simpson, who did not care
a damn for anyone, particularly golf-club committees. When he
turned up at Morfontaine for some event after the war and said
rather grandly, 'Where's the first tee at this place?' I was able to
become one up on him by replying, 'Just where you put it twenty-
five years ago.' I managed again to reach the final and had visions
of becoming champion, geographically at least, of about half
Europe, but it was not to be. On the other hand I did have played
against me almost the best single shot, considering the circumstances, that I remember. My opponent was Jacques Léglise, at
that time a very competent golfer indeed, and on the short 17th
in the morning, when he was four up, he socketed his tee-shot into
some impenetrable bracken beside the tee, where it was not worth
even venturing in to look for the ball. Furthermore, he had done
the same thing in two previous rounds. 'My God,' he said, 'I

shouldn't like to have to play that shot if we were all square here this afternoon.' I went into lunch three or four down, got them all back, lost two again with four to play, won two back, and stood on the 17th tee all square. I put my shot on the green and stood back in a silence you could almost hear, both of us recollecting the event of the morning and what he had said. He hit it right onto the middle of the green and anyone who knows the psychology of golf will appreciate just how brave a shot it was. He won on the last green and we talk about it still.

Later that year the German Championship was played at Bad Ems where the atmosphere was still happy and gay and talk of war unthinkable. Four of us flew to Cologne, to be met with General Critchley's trailing caravan, in which we drove down beside the Rhine to the astonishment of the natives. We were staying in one of those grand old, tall-ceilinged Edwardian hotels still to be found occasionally on the continent. It had a very slow lift, worked by a rope, and I remember to this day the exchanges with a gigantic night porter who was hauling me up, alone, rather late at night.

'You comm from England?' 'Yes.' 'I haff *been* in England.' 'Oh, yes. Where was that?' 'Teeverton, Sommerset.' 'Ah, a very nice part. I hope you, er, enjoyed . . .' 'Ja! *Preesoner-of-war!*'

In the evenings we would drive down to Coblenz and dine beside the Rhine, on caviare and vodka, perhaps, Rhine salmon and Moselle, and peaches in champagne – and I only in my twenties. No wonder that, when the war had apparently destroyed this life for ever, I entitled a little book of reminiscences *It Was Good While it Lasted*! (Incidentally, the Forces Book Guild printed 53,000 in paperback form at a guinea a thousand, less tax, and they proved ideal for prisoners-of-war and those posted to Iceland, Baghdad, or the Orkneys, but when I asked for a dozen copies they would not give me any. When I offered to buy them, they said certainly not, they were intended for His Majesty's Forces; and when I replied that I was already one of His Majesty's faithful soldiers, at three-farthings an hour, a colonel in Finsbury barracks referred me to ACI Something-or-Other, after which I should have a better understanding of the work of that department and appreciate that he could neither sell nor issue service books free to the author or anyone else. I have the letter still and it still rankles. Eventually the publisher slipped me a few copies.)

You will be anxious to know, of course, whether I retained my title at Bad Ems, whither no fewer than forty-four entrants had come from Britain on the unfounded assumption that, if I could win, anyone could. The *Evening Standard* were also keen to keep their readers up to date on their correspondent's progress and sought a special report from Reuter. All went well until the round before the semi-finals, when I encountered a young German called Leonard von Beckerath, possibly their best amateur up to that time, who I am glad to say survived the war on the Russian Front. I found myself three down with seven to play, accomplished the next four holes in 3,3,5,3 – and got nothing back. Three down and three to play. The par of the last three was 4,3,4 and I swear I did them in 3,2,3 and won the lot, including the 18th with a putt of about ten yards. Von Beckerath beat me at the 20th, but my finish was the topic of the day: 3,3,5,3,3,2,3! At least I had hauled down my colours in a modest blaze of glory and could look forward to something pretty heart-warming in the *Evening Standard*. 'Longhurst,' said the Reuter man's special report, 'was three up on von Beckerath with seven to play, but *cracked*'!

Among those present at Bad Ems was Henry Cotton, who, in addition to winning the German Open, gave a fantastic exhibition of strength and accuracy by knocking a shooting-stick out of the ground with a 1-iron shot at a range of about twenty yards. Though he had won the British Open in 1934 (and had been presented with the trophy wearing my overcoat – which I still possess), this year, 1937, really represented his prime. There had been no Americans when he won at Sandwich in 1934. In 1937 at Carnoustie there had been the whole American Ryder Cup team and with a stupendous final 71 in driving rain, almost the best individual round I ever saw, he beat them all. We all tend to inflate the heroes of our early days but I have seen them all since that time and cannot believe that any of them, Hogan included, hit the ball better than Cotton. Nor do I know anybody who did not himself automatically hit the ball better when playing with him, though this is no place in which to be tempted into the technicalities of golf. It was a great advantage in my own line of life, however, to be his contemporary and to be good enough to play occasionally in his company, albeit not on level terms. He won his third Open after the war, fourteen years after his first, and, when King George VI came to Muirfield to watch, he put on a 66 for his benefit.

I myself have basked in Cotton's reflected glory and still do. On coming off the last green at St Andrews not long after the war I was surrounded by autograph-hunting children and, making the elementary mistake of thinking they knew who I was – whereas all they do is to rush up to all and sundry, thrust their books under his nose and then see who they have got – I signed a good many books. I was cut down to size by hearing a freckled, fang-toothed, ginger-headed boy round at the back exclaiming, on seeing my signature, 'Och, he's no' anyone!' All right, I thought, but he bloody well will be in future. Since that day I must have signed *Henry Cotton* in at least a couple of hundred books, thereby giving much innocent satisfaction to both parties. Furthermore, I still produce the most excellent specimens, whereas the Maestro himself has been getting a little slack in latter years.

He also won the German Open the following year at Frankfurt, but now the pre-war unease was setting in, though in fact there proved to be one more year to go. Nevertheless, the Germans, or the sort of Germans with whom we came into contact, extended to us the most astonishing hospitality. The Burgomaster gave us a banquet in the town hall; they took us to see the *Graf Zeppelin*; they took us on pleasure trips up the River Main, and gave us tickets for an open-air performance of *Hamlet*, played in the main square against a background of floodlit buildings that could have come straight out of Hans Andersen. We were entertained by Karl Henkel at his cellars in Wiesbaden, in itself an extraordinary experience, since they were forty yards underground and you walked down a ramp like a very long tube escalator, the air getting cooler every moment, until you came upon row after row of three million bottles of wine. They stayed there for three years, during the course of which one per cent, or about ten a day, burst. Down some distant aisle you would hear a muffled boom followed by a silvery tinkle of glass, and it was almost comical to gaze at a bottle and wonder whether it was just on the point of not being able to take it any more. It remains inconceivable to me that the people whose company we used to enjoy, and they, I like to think, ours, wanted war any more than we did and in that spirit I report with sincere regret that Karl Henkel was killed in a bombing attack on Wiesbaden.

Experience in all these championships convinced me that, while stroke-play at golf is held to be the more certain test of skill, knock-out play is the real test of moral fibre. If you finish fourth in the Open, you do not say, 'I was beaten by Smith, Jones and Robinson': you say with some pride, 'I finished fourth.' In match-play you have to admit that you were beaten by So-and-so, and maybe had to pack your bag after the first round at that. For this reason I always maintained, and still do, that match-play is the true essence of golf and that these 'round and round and round again tournaments', as Bernard Darwin called them, are but a substitute for the real thing. You never have the Great Fear in stroke-play: 'What am I going to say if this fellow beats me?' I once finished sixth in the Dutch Open at The Hague, but can remember the name of only one of the five who beat me, though certainly I remember that of the great Alfred Padgham, who didn't. I had a chance of even greater things but at the short 15th took about nineteen shots over the four rounds, thus reducing my young caddie almost to tears. It was only years later that he revealed himself to have become the almost permanent Dutch professional champion, Jerry de Wit. He had been too shy to mention it before, he said.

Prices were such in those days that other outgoings took us to such places as Noordwyk in Holland; to Ostend, Spa and Waterloo in Belgium, where Henry Cotton was professional when he made the break-through in 1934; to an annual match at Deauville, where Dale Bourn reported on the 1st tee in his dinner jacket on the way back from the Casino and was forced to concede the first nine holes while he went to change; to Dieppe and Wimereux, which is on the cliffs outside Boulogne, coming home from which I was permitted to steer the Channel packet – and, judging by the cross-hazards even then, no wonder they keep running into each other in the Channel now; and, of course, le Touquet, never quite my cup of tea but worth mentioning because in the French Open, from the very back tees of the magnificent New Course, I once did four rounds under 80, each one lower than the one before – 79, 78, 76, 75 – and, though the total may be comparatively modest, research reveals not only that only three men (Jack White 1904, Ben Hogan 1953 and Gary Player 1959) have won the British Open with four scores each lower than the one before but that practically no one else, however low down the list, has ever achieved this feat. I also, for the record, had a 66 in the Italian Open at San Remo; still, there is nothing for it but to admit that I never really made anything better than the second eleven.

Still, being a second-eleven golfer is much more fun than being a bad one, for all that the golfing rabbit, whistling in the dark, may tell you to the contrary, and to write about it and be able to play at the same time – constantly 'gap-filling', not only with new courses but new travels, new places and new faces – was an enviable life, a fact which I can honestly say I appreciated at the time. Almost every free week-end a number of us, probably based on the Nineteenth Club, would descend on some course and play seventy-two holes, a day's golf being then automatically reckoned to be two rounds, whereas nowadays, perhaps under American influence, it tends to be only one. Often our choice was the Dormy House at Bramshot, whose course beside the railway line just short of Fleet, scarcely detectable today, was perhaps the outstanding golfing casualty of the war. In the evening a boy would be stationed on the railway bridge, to which a bell had been connected. If he rang this the moment he saw or heard the train leaving Fleet, everyone knew that a good sharp run, and no question of 'one more for the road', would get them over the bridge and down the steps just in time to leap into the last carriage as the train pulled out of Bramshot Halt.

I suppose my most nostalgic memories must relate to that most remarkable of all golf tournaments, the Halford Hewitt, for which teams of ten a side from fifty or sixty schools, together with innumerable camp-followers, converge every April upon the little town of Deal. I am assured, and can only hope it is true, that a small group of people, including John Beck (later to become the only winning British Walker Cup captain) and Sir Harold Gillies, 'the well-known plastic surgeon', were discussing at lunch at Addington the desirability of founding an annual competition for teams of public school old boys, and that, the details having been agreed, somebody, almost certainly Beck, said, 'Now all we need is some bloody fool to present a cup.' At this moment Halford Hewitt walked in, to find himself almost at once immortalized as the founder of the best-loved tournament in golf. I myself was fortunate indeed. In the six years before the war during which I played for the Carthusian team we won five times and reached the semifinal in the other year, so that every year we saw it right through to the end. I am afraid we gained the reputation of being a far from teetotal lot and tended to make too much noise at the hotel, but it was all good schoolboy stuff. Hal, himself a Carthusian, presided in theory over the party. *De mortuis nil nisi bonum*, but it cannot be denied that at this time of his life he was not particularly 'with it' and did indeed make the perfect butt. In our sitting-room, when he picked up a paper, the nearest man automatically put a match to it – time and time and time again, and every time producing the same reactions of outraged dignity, so that it makes me smile even as I write it down. Every night he insisted on playing bridge and this time it was the nearest man's job, since he was rather deaf, to inform the other of the contents of his hand, so that I dare say some of the most preposterous bids in the history of the game were made late in the evening in order to get him out somewhere near all square. Harrow shared the same hotel, the old South Eastern at the end of the front, next to the Marine depot, and one night it was revealed to Hal that one of the Harrovians, George Henriques, later a president of the English Golf Union, was plotting to come in and pull his leg dressed up as a policeman. Henriques then went out and got a real policeman and the ensuing scene during dinner was not unmemorable.

Hal had the most beautiful house not far from Mildenhall, in which our team used to stay for an autumn match against the club. It was somehow rather typical of this much-persecuted but well-loved man that he should also possess a collection of flowering shrubs and trees hardly matched except at Kew – and not know the name of a single one of them. One night I saw a local stalwart, Boxer Cannon, creeping out after dinner and instinct told me to follow him. He had brought an elephant gun and, slipping an enormous cartridge into the breech, he stood against the drawing-room window and fired it off into the silent moonlit night. The explosion was such as must have reverberated through Bury St Edmunds and we returned to observe the effects of this splendid, if again rather schoolboyish, practical joke. The answer was that Hal had not heard it. He had been listening to the wireless – for an account of Pam Barton's great victory that day in the American women's championship.

On joining the Carthusian team I shared a bedroom with that gay cavalier of golf, Dale Bourn, and played in the bottom foursome with John Morrison, and thus it remained for six hilarious years. As well as John Beck, we also had such characters as J-a-a-ck Thompson, a prosperous Lincolnshire farmer and noted shot, who would come straight back from ski-ing and hit No. 1 irons dead straight through a cold east wind; Lionel Burdon-Sanderson, never heard of in competitive golf, who had often just come back from shooting lions; Pat White and Cecil Middleton, whose single in the university match of 1933 at Prince's, Sandwich, is still remembered; and, above all, as Trainer, the one and only Ben Travers, still tremendous company today at the age of eighty-four. It was characteristic of this humble and very 'human' man that, while still at the height of his fame as creator of the immortal Aldwych farces, recently revived on television, he should take with serious delight his duties of bringing the Eno's round on a silver tray each morning – always a wise insurance in the strong air of the south-east coast – and purveying the gin-and-kummel behind the 7th and 14th greens. Ben, it need hardly be said, is something of a raconteur and, should you ever get the chance, extract from him the story of his attempt in the First War to bomb the town hall of Reims, casting bombs over the side like bottles of Guinness. One of them, he still maintains, actually hit the town. They knight the most extraordinary people these days, but how they missed Sir Benjamin Travers I do not know. Or, better still, Lord Aldwych.

My partner, known inevitably in the press as the 'ex-Cambridge Triple Blue' – he played cricket and soccer for the university before the First War and golf and cricket after it – was a 'character' if ever there was one, and if our partnership gained something of a Halford Hewitt notoriety it was due almost entirely to his eccentricities, both on and off the course. So, I suspect, was our continued success – beaten only once in six years and then when the main match was over. I was strictly the 'straight' man. Morrison, however, carried seven or eight clubs sprouting from a torn canvas bag and bearing little or no relation to each other, mostly with hickory shafts and some with handles 'as thick as cricket bats'. He tended to appear in a deerstalker hat and a huge teddy-bear coat done up with string round the middle, which reduced him to about a quarter-swing, and, when it rained, he produced a vast waterproof skirt instead of trousers. By the time our opponents had recovered from the impact of his clothing, his clubs and his methods – it was nothing for him to take a putter from sixty yards – they were liable to be three down.

He became, of course, a legend, and I was perhaps the middle-man that helped to sustain it. It would not, I think, be uncharitable to say that my old friend tended, like so many of us, to be 'better after lunch', and it was with some foreboding, therefore, that I set out with him one morning at the ungodly hour of 7.20, still dark enough for the Goodwins Lightship to be still flashing rather than hooting in the Channel. At the 2nd hole he hit our second shot, with an evil-looking brassie, straight through a perishing cold headwind to within ten feet of the flag. Neither Cotton, Hogan nor Palmer could have done it better. Before anyone could find the appropriate comment for this extraordinary and unexpected stroke, Morrison had looked at his watch and cried, 'Seven forty!' It was at the same hole that in an after-lunch final I drove our ball into a bird's-nest lie in the rough. When I reached the scene, I found him and his caddie tugging one at each end of his brassie, like two chickens with a worm. 'No, no, sir!' the caddie was saying, to which Morrison was replying, "'s all right. 's all right. It's teed up.' He hit it about four yards.

I am often asked if the story of Morrison and the taxi is true, and the answer is that it is. On the morning that he hit the brassie shot at 7.40, we won our match very easily and were knocking on the door of the Chequers, the small incongruous pub beside the 14th green, by 9.20. Old Mr Marsh, who was born and lived all his seventy-five years in the Chequers, declared that he was not open, to which Morrison replied that it was all right, as he, Morrison, was a magistrate. Duly admitted through this remarkable assertion, my partner held court till such time as we could never walk all the way back to the clubhouse in time for lunch and the afternoon round. He therefore not only summoned a taxi from Deal but, fortified by a three-hour sojourn in the Chequers, ordered it again for the afternoon, on the natural assumption that we should again win by at least 5 and 4. We were duly five up with five to play and I have always thought it to be poetic justice that our opponents holed a long, fluky putt across the newly laid green and we had to go on. One of the caddies was sent surreptitiously round behind the Chequers to warn the taxi and, unbeknownst to our opponents, it followed slowly alongside the course, until such time as the match had gone to the 17th and it was not worth taking it at all.

I doubt whether they make all-rounders like Morrison today. Younger people these days may be forgiven for being unable to imagine the impact made upon soccer in the twenties by that happy band of brothers known as the Corinthians. To any soccer-playing boy like myself their names were household words – Chadder, Knight, Hegan, Ashton, Doggart, Creek and, especially, that unsurpassed defensive trio, Bower and Morrison at back and Howard Baker in goal. I remember vividly waiting for the result of their great cup-tie with Blackburn Rovers and the jubilation when we learnt of their victory. Little did I suspect that I should spend so many a memorable hour with the man who had been their captain on that historic day.

II

The Last Double-Twelve

It was in 1929, in the big black and white gabled house on the left of the 1st and 2nd holes at Hoylake – the home of the hospitable Little family, two of whose three fine sons were killed flying in the war, while the third, my own contemporary, after surviving Russian convoys, died suddenly a few years later – that I met one who is now my oldest friend and, incidentally, partner in our family business in Bedford, Lewis Byrom. The Byrom family were cotton and wool spinners, with dark, satanic mills at Stalybridge and Delph, and it must have been during the first of eight successive Christmases that I spent with them at Hollingworth that I made my first contact with the strange, all-by-itself world of motor racing. The car on which I found them working was a tiny Gordon England Brooklands model Austin 7, which they had raced with a certain amount of success on Southport Sands but only too often to be beaten by a similar car. I remember the awe, knowing little or nothing of the internals of a motor car, with which I watched Byrom and his younger brother, Jim, drawing graphs on the back of an envelope to show the ratio in which they intended to insert an extra gear, and this was in fact done by the elder brother, Rob, and the mechanic from the mill. They also inserted a super-charger and designed a new body nine inches lower with a slanting radiator like that of the front-wheel-drive Alvis. The end product was painted the traditional British racing green to match the Le Mans Bentleys driven by Birkin, Barnato, Dr Benjafield and the other heroes of the day and can honestly be said to have been a really notable single-seater racing car. I never drove it in a race, though I more than once watched it win, accelerating off the starting-line as though fired from a catapult, but I sometimes took it out on the road, and the exhilaration of driving this little open perambulator at nearer ninety miles an hour than eighty may well be imagined.

Henry Cotton at my wedding before the war. He was able to come to my daughter's and my son's wedding in the same coat.

On the Bob Run at St Moritz. 'Get off Sunny Corner as quickly as you can,' they said. Unfortunately we did.

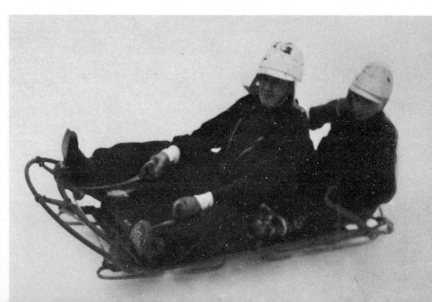

The Austin was eventually sold to R. O. Shuttleworth whose family owned the picturesque Bedfordshire village of Old Warden and who founded there the museum of ancient aeroplanes still in flying order. Brother Jim then achieved a lifelong ambition of owning a Bugatti ('Type 35 8-cyl. Grand Prix modifié') and with this we, if a mere passenger may so presume, had a number of successes at Southport, where you raced a mile course along the golden sands, then churned your way round a barrel with a good deal of shouting and cursing, and raced back again to repeat the process. Both Eric Martin Smith and I scored successes as passengers, he in the ten-mile race and I in the twenty, even though he unfortunately sat in some petrol and had to remove his underwear in the sandhills.

All this was but a prelude to the great event, the Double-Twelve at Brooklands, in which everyone when the flag dropped had to start their engines, dash off from the pits, and drive for twelve hours. The cars were then wheeled, not driven, into an aircraft hangar and once again in the morning you had to start them from scratch and be off – if they started, which many, after their exertions of the previous twelve hours, didn't. You may imagine the frustration of those who, as other cars roared past on the first and second laps, were still tinkering with their carburettors. No one, of course, could drive for twelve hours at a stretch and so each car had two teams consisting of driver and mechanic. I was mechanic to Lewis Byrom and with Jim we had none other than the redoubtable Billy Fiske, the one who had held the world's record on the Cresta and owned the $4\frac{1}{2}$ supercharged Bentley at Cambridge. The car this time was a 6-cyl. double-overhead-camshaft supercharged Amilcar, of which only a few had been made in the factory at St Denis near Paris. This particular one had been raced in a 200-mile race at Brooklands by Vernon Balls, the UK Amilcar expert, and had finished third to another Amilcar and Malcolm Campbell's Bugatti.

I suppose Brooklands was the best-known track in the world; the very name stood for motor racing; but not one in a hundred thousand of those who have looked down on it from the train between Woking and Byfleet can ever have been round it. Nowadays it is completely overgrown with trees and the modern commuter may be excused for passing by without ever knowing it was there. In its day, however, the very sight of its steeply banked grey concrete walls thrilled the spirit and with luck you might see some flying taking place in the open centre of the four-mile track as well. In fact, an old friend of mine, Raymond Quilter, having started his own career by jumping off haystacks with an umbrella, to say nothing of lying on his back between the rails for the thrill of hearing the Scotch Express run over him, ran a parachute school there. When a reluctant novice, standing on the wing, hesitated to jump, he once told me, you simply seized his wrist and flung him clear. If he 'knew it all already', on the other hand, you told him when to jump making sure that he floated inexorably down into the adjacent sewage farm.

The Double-Twelve, though a long-drawn-out affair, was to me a thrilling initiation into the strange world of motor racing. We stayed at the Oatlands Park Hotel near Weybridge, which I only discovered the other day to have been the home of the Duke of York, under whose 'protection' lived Daphne du Maurier's great-great-great-grandmother, Mary Anne. In our day it was inhabited mainly by elderly ladies. I am afraid we became known as the 'motor men' and, if the episode of the clockwork mouse which one of the party brought home from the Stock Exchange one evening was not in the best of taste, one may take refuge in the words of the undergraduate to the magistrate: 'I can only say, sir, that it appeared to be very funny at the time.' Nothing could have been more serious, however, than our preparation for the big occasion. Brother Rob ran the pit, complete with a time clock upon which normally those who worked at the mill stamped their cards on arriving for work, and a number of milk churns were provided for the petrol, which the crew of the moment, since no one else was allowed to touch the car, had to heave off the counter and pour through great funnels. The time clock which checked us lap by lap did in fact get an honourable mention as an example of efficiency from the public address system.

Looking down at Brooklands from the train, and even from attending meetings there, one had imagined whizzing smoothly, if noisily, round and round the track. Experience at once proved otherwise. The track was in fact diabolical. The concrete seemed to be corrugated, interspersed with great potholes and bumps, and one hardly ever seemed to feel all four wheels on the ground at the same time. One of my jobs was to depress a lever beside me once per lap to inject oil into the engine, and the only time the car was steady enough to do it was during a short smooth stretch of three or four hundred yards on the opposite side from the railway. All this was, I am sure, good for the liver, but it was murder on the spine and during our final three hours off on the first day I slipped out and bought myself, much to the general ridicule, a gent's corset. Honour was served, however, when later I found that most of the great men wore them too. Three hours is a long time to be bumping and buffeting at 100 m.p.h. round what feels like a stone-furrowed ploughed field, and I found myself anxiously looking at Pit No. 33 as we flashed by to see if they had put the milk churns on the counter, thus signifying that within a few laps we should be called in to hand over to Jim and Billy Fiske.

Between us we finished our twelve-hour stint on the first day, though many had by now fallen by the wayside, including an MG which had been a persistent nuisance to us throughout and eventually went up in a most satisfying puff of black smoke, and one had already learnt two of the very earliest lessons of motor racing: namely that, if you have been going very fast for a long time, the car, as you nip hastily out on pulling up at the pit, may still be going twenty miles an hour; and that it is no wonder if after a day's work at this essentially masculine activity the real men of motor racing like to be sure of something soft and blonde at the end of it. I once appeared on the television programme *Call My Bluff* with Graham Hill, and the way he looked across at our three fair opponents made them positively wriggle in their chairs, with the result that they got all the answers wrong and we won hands down.

On the second day of the Double-Twelve our Amilcar started at the first touch, despite having bumped its way round, flat out, for 1,200-odd miles the day before, and we duly did our three-hour stint before handing over. In our time off it was a great thrill to wander round the pits and the enclosure and mix casually with the élite of the motor-racing world, hoping to be taken, or mistaken, for one of their number. Time came to return to Pit 33 for our final spell and Jim and Billy Fiske were duly waved in to refuel and hand over. We knew from the time clock almost to the very second when they were due but, alas, they never came. We listened anxiously for a report of an accident but mercifully that did not come either, and a good deal later two weary-looking figures in once-white overalls were to be seen trudging back like jockeys at the Grand National who have lost their horses. Our particular horse was stationary at the bottom of the railway embankment with a con-rod sticking out through the sump. Thus ended my humble experience of motor racing, but it was enough to give one a tiny, very tiny, insight into what manner of men were the heroes of Le Mans and what qualities enabled Stirling Moss and his brilliant navigator, Denis Jenkinson, to win the 1955 Mille Miglia by driving a thousand miles at an average of 93.08 m.p.h. over ordinary public roads!

Yet when all was done, what was my outstanding memory of the Double-Twelve? Not the speed or the bumping or the manoeuvring or the noise or the novelty – but the moorhen that sat sedately on its nest at the edge of a pond only a few yards from the track. Not a lap passed but that I looked over my shoulder to see that it was still there. The bird took not the slightest notice of these lunatics and their infernal machines and seemed somehow to reduce us to size. I only hope she successfully hatched out the family and that the fortieth generation are nesting in the same pond this year.

12
Down the Cresta

On the principle that you don't miss what you have had but only what you might have had and never did, and now it's too late, the only sport I really miss is ski-ing – to say nothing of the delicious insinuations of what is nowadays politely known as the 'après-ski'. This I really could have had, and clearly it is the greatest sport in the world. I could even have started at St Cyprians but instead of starting I stopped. The Wilkeses took a party of boys every Christmas holidays but in the Easter term there would be much talk of So-and-so not having been any good and such-and-such didn't even pass his third class – I think it was Mürren they used to go to: always a 'test-conscious' resort – so, being an undersized little chap, I always opted out. One did not want 'tests' and almost certain ridicule in the holidays. It wasn't until the year before the war that I joined a party at St Moritz, partly because the company was so congenial, partly because I looked forward to having a go at the Cresta and the Bob, and certainly with the mental reservation that nothing would induce me to ski. They talked me into giving it a trial, of course, and three or four of us suffered daily on the nursery slopes from an unbelievably handsome instructor called Mingo Boz, pronounced Botz, whom we christened the Abominable Snowman. Botz would pick a particularly steep smooth patch and with his legs wide apart and his skis in an inverted V would turn with infinite slowness and control. 'I poosh with my right and I turn . . . I poosh with my left and I turn.' When later we graduated to loftier slopes, one of the girls twisted her ankle, whereupon Botz picked her up and zigzagged down to the bottom at great speed carrying her in his arms, much to the chagrin of the other instructors present. Once, when lying recumbent on the slope, I watched six men in cloth caps, the hallmark of the local experts, pass by at immense speed from some much greater height, graceful as swallows on the wing and just about as fast, and learnt later that the leading figure was none other than the Swiss Olympic skier, Rominger. In the all too short fortnight that we were there I did manage once or twice to achieve a modest *schuss*, or direct downhill dash, and it needed only this tiniest sample to tell one that ski-ing was in a nobler category than all other sports, sublime, all on its own. When I took off my skis on the final day, instinct told me it would be for the last time, and so it proved. The war came and after it everything was too difficult and I was too old and fat to start again. If only someone had told me in time!

Now I come to think of it, this was not quite the last time. In the earlier days of the war I found myself in Eastbourne with Alan Garrow (he was my best man and I was his) and his younger brother Peter (killed, alas, on a make-do wartime aircraft-carrier). Both were considerable skiers, though nothing like so considerable as the other brother, Dr Donald Garrow, who captained an Oxford team in Norway and over a course of a mile and a quarter averaged forty-eight miles an hour – and finished tenth! Sussex was covered with snow, but we managed to get the car up to Beachy Head, where it was proposed that we should make a *schuss* down the steep slope known as Cow Gap, from the top down to the edge of the cliff. To one who did not know whether, if he got going, he ever could stop, this was an intimidating prospect and it took a couple of good-sized brandies in the old Beachy Head Hotel to get me to the edge. I launched forth and had already reached such speed as to set me thinking that, if I did reach the cliff, I should make the Olympic ski-jumpers at St Moritz look like beginners, when my left ski caught in a submerged molehill and eighty yards farther on, still upside down, my ski-ing career really did conclude. Yet, again, not quite, for Peter Garrow towed the other two of us on skis behind the car down from Beachy Head to the Grand Hotel – so I may share one record after all.

At St Moritz, I did, however, run the Cresta each morning and on a good many days the Bob, and they support to this day the principle of 'not missing what you have had'. Once you become an habitué and the original thrill has worn off, you tend to become blasé and not much is added in successive years, so that what counts to the regulars is not the sensation of riding what must surely be the greatest toboggan run in the world but how long did you take to get down? For the purist, though, the fascination never ceases, for, however well you may have done, there must have been one or two tiny mistakes, involving perhaps a tenth of a second, and these can never be recovered. However well you do afterwards, you could have done that well without the mistakes.

Again, the 'nos morituri' aspect of the helmeted gladiators as they prepare for their turn helps to sustain the Cresta's carefully nurtured reputation for danger, as does the fact that they won't let the weaker sex go down at all, even one who, like Amy Johnson, had flown a single-engined aeroplane all the way to Australia. The real reason is, of course, that you can only ride the Cresta from half-past eight till the sun comes over the mountains at about eleven and softens the ice, and the men want it for themselves. Lord Brabazon, in fact, went down at the age of seventy-four. The truth is, as a passenger of mine was later to find out, that the Bob is far the more dangerous of the two and, if you go over the edge into the forest and hit a tree, sitting up and facing forwards, all four may be slit up like bananas, and this has indeed happened.

Nevertheless, anyone who declared that he stood at the top of the Cresta for the first time, waiting for his name to be called, without a few butterflies in the stomach would certainly be no candidate for a lie-detector test. As I recalled at the time of my own baptism. . . . You join the little knot of silent folk at the top of the run, write your name down on the list of starters, and set about equipping yourself for the fray. The equipment consists of special boots with metal 'rakes' sprouting from the toes, for retarding progress where necessary, metal knee-, elbow-, and knuckle-protectors, and compulsory crash-helmet. You finish looking like an ice hockey goal-minder.

Your toboggan has a little sliding seat to lie on and steel runners, which are smooth except for a few inches at the back where they are grooved. The idea is that at the corners you slide the seat back, clasping the front of the toboggan with the top hand and the back with the lower hand. The weight is thus thrust back on to the grooves at the back of the runners, enabling you to get a grip on the ice and push the nose of the machine down with the top hand. Or not, as the case may be.

The run itself is about the width of a narrow-gauge railway and the straight stretches are enclosed by two-foot walls of solid frozen snow. The corners are, of course, banked almost to the vertical and each has its name – Bank, Stream, Battledore,

Shuttlecock, and so on. The length in all is 1,320 yards, and the all-time record was at that time still held by Billy Fiske, who shot down in 56.7 seconds. At the time of my own inauguration we were on a course of about 1,000 yards, starting from the point known as Junction, as the full track had not yet been completed, and the record was 47.9 seconds.

The weird outfit, emphasizing the need for protection against violent injury or even death; the sight of successive riders flashing out of sight round Shuttlecock half a dozen inches from the rim of the banking, and the cries of: 'He's over! . . . No, he's not!'; the experienced hands reminiscing of the time when old So-and-so went over the top at such-and-such a corner and broke five ribs; the kindly advice to take especial care first time down or you've only yourself to blame . . . these and the chill of the sunless early morning must fill the least imaginative novice with a certain apprehension. 'The next rider,' I remember the voice of Colonel Hodgson at the microphone saying, 'is Mr Longhurst.'

I cast myself on to my little steel craft and made off down the ice, wondering where I should be in a minute's time. For the first hundred yards or so it was difficult to keep the thing from ricocheting from one wall to the other. Then we really got going, and the next few seconds remain a confused memory of wrestling with a toboggan that seemed to have come to life with only one ambition, to wriggle away from under me. We shot together up the first banking and round, right-handed, onto Battledore. I shot off it, down into the gully, and was tossed, like a cork on the ocean wave, onto the left-handed banking of Shuttlecock. Raking desperately with the left foot I managed somehow to get round, and after one more bend found myself emerging into the long straight that leads down under the main road and the railway.

This time I was able to avoid bumping the walls and the speed increased, I suppose, to sixty or seventy miles an hour. A wild, exhilarating sensation and I found myself actually singing aloud. I shouldn't have cared if it had reached a hundred. I wondered if I ought to be raking in readiness for the big banking I could see at the bottom, but decided to let it rip. I got round the bend, too high to be comfortable, and retain a confused impression of rounding a series of others before diving into the finishing straight where the experts touch eighty miles per hour. Yet of all the crowded sensation experienced on that first run, I remember most clearly the one that came immediately after the finish. The rider has no hope, of course, of pulling up for himself at that speed, so they construct a vast embankment to assist him, so steep that it would be quite impossible to remain on it stationary. As you hit this embankment it is as though some invisible giant had put his hand beneath your stomach and heaved you into the air. And even after eighty yards of it you have to rake hard to pull up.

I had come down with no serious hitch and waited anxiously for the voice to announce my time. 'Fifty-seven seconds.' Congratulations all round. Best time of the year for a novice. The next run was better, fifty-four seconds, and, inflated by this minor triumph, I was taken in hand by the then president, Harry Hays Morgan. 'I'm going to find you a faster toboggan,' he said. 'Believe me, it will make all the difference.'

Determined to do credit to my mentor and at the same time break all known records, I waited my turn and set off again; but, alas, the new craft took unkindly to its new master – if 'master' is the word – and bucked and slithered and wriggled and ducked to get rid of me. We remained together round Battledore and were bumping and rattling our way round Shuttlecock, when all of a sudden a strange unearthly silence held the air. Gracefully and with the greatest of ease, the Cresta, I, and Mr Hays Morgan's beautiful toboggan parted company.

At the starter's box the bell tolled twice to signify disaster and the voice announced: 'Mr Longhurst has gone over the top at Shuttlecock.' After flying through the air for what seemed eternity I pitched on my back, in a shower of snow, ice, small stones and straw and, remembering the secretary's instructions, stood up in the straw, like Ruth amid the alien corn, and waved my arms to signify that I was unhurt. Handing the toboggan to one of the numerous small boys who assemble in readiness to act as 'caddies' for those cast off at Shuttlecock, I trudged back to the summit.

A similar fate, I regret to reveal, overtook my first venture on the Bob when my passenger on a two-man bob was Colonel in the First War, Wing Commander in the Second, Walter Wilson. They had just opened the run from the top, and it included, for the first time that season, the famous Sunny Corner. Men had been at work for the past week or so, building up this great bowl-shaped hairpin bend (both the Bob and the Cresta, of course, have to be built afresh each year), but something had gone wrong with their calculations. Everyone was complaining of Sunny Corner. Even a couple of world aces, with Olympic flags on their crash helmets, had almost come to grief thereon, and had returned on the lorry to the top, full of indignant protest.

'Get down off the banking as quickly as you can,' was the general advice still ringing in our ears as Walter and I launched ourselves on our maiden voyage. Sunny Corner whisked into view in the forest below us, lined with gaping spectators thirsting for a crash. We rattled our way round it, horizontal on the banking, and all would have been well had I not recalled the kindly advice of the folk at the top and twisted the wheel to bring us prematurely off the banking. We hit the inside wall of the narrow outlet and the whole outfit capsized like an errand-boy's bicycle clattering from the kerb and discharging the groceries in the gutter.

Walter pitched on pretty well the only unprotected part of his person – his chin – and was stunned. I was thrown off on my back and slid forty frictionless yards down the track with my legs in the air. I recovered myself just in time to prevent the bob running over my unconscious passenger.

We drove home together in a sleigh and the next half-hour was a nightmare.

'What happened?' said Walter vaguely. 'Oh,' I replied in the mock-hearty manner one adopts to persons who are not quite themselves, 'we had a bit of an accident. Came off at Sunny Corner, you know.'

'Was anybody with us?'

'No. Only you and me.'

'Oh. Well, what happened?'

'We had an accident. Came off at Sunny Corner.'

'Did we? Was anybody with us?'

'No. Just you and me.'

'Who was steering?'

'I was.'

'What was I doing?'

'You were braking.'

'Oh, I see. And who else was with us?'

I had visions of Walter losing his memory, never being the same man again and so on, though mercifully, like concussed rugger players who go through the second half of a match without knowing what they are doing, he made a complete recovery and even said he would entrust himself to me again. Looking back on it reminds me of a truism invented by my friend Alan Garrow, which will appeal to all non-teetotallers, namely that sometimes you are drinking *with* the gin (or whatever it may be) and sometimes you are drinking *against* the gin. In other words sometimes the world gets rosier and rosier and the company more and more witty: at others no amount makes the world any better. This was one of those times. I poured myself a stiff whisky to try to overcome the thought that this might be the end of Walter's mental life: then, pacing up and down the room, another, and then another. For all the good it did it might have been water.

Though I missed ski-ing by mistake, so to speak, there were two other pursuits that I deliberately delayed till opportunity offered. These were fly-fishing and gliding. It was in New Zealand in the early 1950s that, on picking up a little book *Flyfishing for Duffers* by R. D. Peck,* it came over me that I was now 'senior' enough to join the fly-fishing community and I did so, with consequent hour upon hour of happiness, immediately on my return. For the gliding I had to wait rather longer, till, having moved to Clayton Windmills (of which more to come), I found there was a gliding club on the Downs beside Firle Beacon. Along we went, one Sunday afternoon, and it was not long before I found myself strapped in an open two-seater beside a congenial and extremely competent instructor. The machine appeared to be made of balsa wood no more substantial than the 'kits' you buy for the children, and I could only trust that it would bear my fifteen stone in addition to the instructor. We waited while a fellow glided down, perspex-enclosed in a single-seater, having kept himself aloft over the Channel for an hour and a half. The signal was given to the man on the distant winch and you could see the steel hawser snaking in the grass as it tightened ahead of the glider. Then it connected with a thump and away we went as though hurled from a sling, up at an angle of about forty-five degrees. Here was a most memorable sensation, just like the end of the Cresta, and I was astonished at the speed generated by the winch. After a while we levelled off and at a suitable height my companion pulled the little handle to let the cable fall to the ground. The long-awaited moment.

Lord Brabazon maintained that the 'only gentleman's way of taking to the air' was ballooning. He used to go up from the

* Black, 1934.

Battersea Gas Works (45,000 cubic feet £4.10s.0d. 'including labour and bags of sand: holders-down extra') and must have been the only undergraduate in Cambridge history to offer to his tutor as an excuse for being late the fact that he had been ballooning; but by this time most people, I think, inspired by those who had done it and by the writings of such as Terence Horsley and Peter Scott, would have acknowledged gliding to be flying in its purest and most 'gentlemanly' form. It was this belief that was now to be put to the test.

Was it really, as they said, silent? Apart from the sighing of the wind on the wings, yes, it was. Marvellous! We banked to the left and I looked over the instructor's shoulder across the Downs to Newhaven and the Channel. Here was everything I had ever hoped for and I had time to wonder how long it would take me to get my pilot's certificate, or whatever it might be. Since I never had to go to an office and could come almost every afternoon, I ought to pass and go solo in almost record time. By now we had levelled out and I turned to survey the landward scene on my own side. There was Ashdown Forest and Crowborough and the whole of the Weald and the North Downs. At this point I lifted my elbow and looked directly down over the side.

I gave what the thrillers would call a strangled cry. A-a-a-ah! Between me and a direct drop equivalent now to about three Beachy Heads lay only a layer or two of this pathetic balsa wood. Only half of me seemed to be inside the contraption anyway and, if we banked to the right, it must surely tip me out, harness or no harness. Probably the whole seat would come away, altogether. The silence was indeed wonderful and so was the view and so was Newhaven, but get out of here and do it quick!

Back on the grass in the summer sun, watching others soar into the air on the cable and come back smiling, I reproached myself with my timidity and determined, after a stiffener or two, to put it to the test again. I strapped myself in so tightly that I could hardly breathe. The cable duly snaked through the grass and seconds later the plug was pulled and once again we were on our own. I had been gazing steadily at the interior of the machine but now the moment of truth had come and I must look once again over the edge.

Thus ended my career in gliding.

13
Dad's Army

Dad's Army, the brilliant television skit on the Home Guard, to which I was glued once a week for most of 1970, never failed to remind me of what I look back upon as my finest hour, when I was undoubtedly the best-armed man in Bayswater. Immediately after the massive defeat of Dunkirk, which in a rather splendidly English way we still celebrate as a victory, the average citizen began to ask what, if anything, he could do to assist. The only answer appeared in my own case to be to report to the Town Hall at Hammersmith. This I duly did and was issued with an armband with LDV, for Local Defence Volunteers, and a three-figure number, which proves me to have at least been moderately quick off the mark. We were entirely unarmed, of course, as at the beginning of every war, but rumour had it that we were to be issued with pikes, presumably to hold underneath the German parachutists as they landed. My own headquarters turned out to be the St John's School in Clarendon Road, Notting Hill, and there, very gradually, we assembled that fine, miscellaneous body of men known as the Notting Hill Home Guard.

The early days, though, were really rather wonderful and it is difficult to write about them without false heroics creeping into the picture. We were in the final, people were saying, and playing at home. The Battle of Britain was on, much of it over London for all to see, and the day's results appeared on the newspaper placards like cricket scores – 186 for 10, and so on. One felt that they might be a little optimistic (though not so grotesquely optimistic as they finally turned out to have been) but they did us good. Everything conspired to lift one's spirit. It proved to be a heavenly summer and, if ever there was a land worth defending, this was it. Pubs went silent and streets almost emptied as men stopped to listen to the Old Man's defiant speech of 18 June 1940, the end of which ought to be learnt by heart by every child today – 'Let us therefore brace ourselves to our duties, and so bear ourselves that, if the British Empire and its Commonwealth last for a thousand years, men will still say, "This was their finest hour".' England, our England, was to be invaded for the first time for nine hundred years. The prospect was unbelievably stirring and the sense of unity almost impossible to describe. It might be tonight. It might be tomorrow night. It might be next week but – they are coming!

To receive them I possessed personally a .22 rifle with 300 rounds, a twelve-bore with 400, and a magnificent Mauser pistol, sighted up to 1,200 yards, whose wooden case fitted into the butt and served as a stock. It had been 'acquired' during the First War by a fish-frying-fat salesman in my section, and he presented it to me for the duration of the second. By kind permission of the Chief Constable of Sussex I have it still, and it is widely admired. I took it down to the range at Wormwood Scrubs, where it caused a minor sensation by making a louder crack than a service rifle. These three weapons, so far as I can remember, formed almost the total conventional armament for the defence of Bayswater. A glimpse of the possibilities of less conventional activity was furnished, during a course at Osterley Park, by a mild-looking little man called Crisp, who proved to be a brilliant instructor and the most calculatedly bloodthirsty character I still have ever met.

I think he had picked up his act in the practice round between the Germans and Russians in the Spanish Civil War, when it was learnt that, if you were short of rifles and ammunition and the rest of it, there were other ways of dispatching an enemy in your midst. The first thing one did, according to Mr Crisp, was to get rid of those bloody great boots and turn out in darkened 'sneakers', and with darkened hands and face. One's main personal weapon was a two-foot length of wire with little wooden handles at each end, like they use for cutting cheese, and it was not long before one became remarkably adept at the motions required to creep up behind the visiting German, slip the cheese-wire over his head, cross the handles, and pull. I suppose that, if I told my children that their portly and, I trust, respected father had for several weeks carried a cheese-wire for this purpose, and with every intention of having a go with it if occasion offered, they would give the standard reply, 'You must be joking!' but it was no joke at the time.

Mr Crisp taught us the ingredients of the Molotov Cocktail,

preferably in quart beer-bottles, which could be thrown most effectively at armoured vehicles when they came unexpectedly upon a road-block just round the corner. Or you could merely put up a barricade of canvas or household sheets across the road: it would be a brave driver who dashed straight through without finding out what was on the other side, and, while he stopped to investigate, you did him with a Molotov Cocktail from behind the hedge. Crisp's most devilish trick was reserved for the motor-cyclists by whom the Germans had been preceded in their blitz across France. You lay in wait round a bend with a thin steel wire, which lay across the road but was tied to a tree on the other side. At the appropriate moment you raised the wire and, if the wretched motor-cyclist was going fast enough, sliced him in half.

In the end, of course, they never came, but from the safety of one's fireside thirty years later one cannot wholly repress a sneaking wish that they had. The nearest I got was one night when the noise of the aerial activity was broken by the telephone.

'Notting Hill Home Guard?'

'Yes.'

'Notting Hill Police here. Parachutists reported descending in your area. Have you your men ready?'

I surveyed the recumbent figures on the schoolroom floor. The fish-frying-fat salesman, the retired colonel, the elderly taxi-driver and, mingled with them, a sprinkling of descendants of the original 'Notting Hill boys'. Had I my men ready? Well, as ready, I supposed, as they were likely to be in the foreseeable future. 'Everybody out!' I cried. 'This is it!'

It wasn't, of course. The parachutists were puffs of anti-aircraft fire in the moonlight, but it might have been 'it', and authority, learning the lesson that, if it had been, we should hardly have been able to return to normal home life in the morning, decreed that every man must provide himself with, and exhibit for inspection, rations sufficient to enable him to fight in the streets for three days.

In due course every man was lined up to exhibit his ration and I passed down the ranks inspecting a remarkable variety of pro-vender – till I came to the elderly taxi-driver, who held out a single lead container.

'What's this, then?' I said.

It was his iron ration from the Boer War.

14
A Night to Remember

My best friends could never, I think, have called me a brave man. It would have taken at least half a gallon of rum to get me 'over the top' in the First War, and as for spending weeks and months in the bowels of unarmed merchantmen in Atlantic convoys, or in any part of any ship in a Russian convoy, the very thought almost sends me reaching for the bottle. On the other hand, though I took two more of my 'nine lives' during it, possibly even three, I was somehow never afraid of the Blitz. There is no merit, of course, in putting on a bold front in face of something of which you are not afraid, or at any rate of which you take the cheerfully fatalistic 'if it has my number on it' view, as I must have done. The real merit lay with those who carried on when they were terrified.

We lived in a top flat in a four-storey block called Pembridge Mansions in Moscow Road, Bayswater, our opposite numbers, till war broke out, being a Mr and Mrs Redgrave with a little daughter called Vanessa. As the war drew near, my wife and I took a civil defence course, complete with how to detect the presence of mustard-gas, etcetera, as a result of which we became members of that almost infinitesimal body of people who have actually put on gas-masks in earnest. We listened, of course, to Chamberlain's broadcast and, when the siren went immediately afterwards, descended as instructed to the basement, thinking, 'This is it, then.' Overhead a man came running along the pavement, rattling a rattle and shouting, 'Gas!' We put on our masks and stood staring at each other, till about a quarter of an hour later, feeling rather foolish, we took them off and went on with our daily life.

Our second child was born in Welbeck Street on 9 August during the height of one of the few Battle of Britain dogfights that took place over London, on the day when my pre-war friend, Douglas Bader, not then the world-famous character that he is today, shot down the one that pitched – poor fellow – beside Victoria Station. My wife accompanied the children to the country, joining me from time to time in London, where I was working in Fleet Street till I 'went for a soldier'. On Saturday nights members of the staff would take it in turn to fire-watch in pairs on the roof, where, if we thought things were hotting up too much, we would press the alarm bell, whereupon the people hard at work below were meant to take shelter, which they rarely, if ever, did. Two interesting experiences arose from these spells of fire-watching: one the fantastic spectacle of the whole of St Paul's silhouetted against the fires raging in the city behind; the other to share on this lonely rooftop the wrestlings of conscience which eventually turned Peter Howard from a virulent political columnist into the leader of Moral Rearmament.

On Saturdays, when my services were no longer required, I would walk up Shoe Lane to take the last tube from Chancery Lane to Queensway, every station thick with slumbering bodies, the early comers luxuriating in wooden bunks, others wrapped in blankets on the platform. I had reached one night the corner of Shoe Lane and Little New Street with the sky lit up and the usual steady droning overhead (everybody knew that when you heard the double *Wrrr-err, wrrr-err* it was 'one of theirs', though I believe there was nothing in it), when there was a most almighty banging and clattering all around me. This turned out to be a cluster of incendiaries, some of which bounced off the wall while others jumped frenziedly about the pavement like Chinese crackers. Each weighed about ten pounds and, dropped from perhaps ten thousand feet, would have gone through one's skull like a bullet through an egg. My main reaction at the time was, 'Would you *mind*!' but I knew I had taken another of the nine lives. I often wonder whether the fellow that dropped them survived the war. If so, he ought to come to London and survey the handsome new office block in Farringdon Avenue, for the destruction of whose rather dingy predecessor, quite apart from endangering my person, his incendiaries were entirely responsible.

Next door to Pembridge Mansions was, and remains, a much bigger block, Windsor Court, in the basement of which an elderly Welshwoman lived alone in a rambling flat with five or six rooms. One of these, after a good deal of the 'if it has your number on it' argument from myself, together with 'better to come down with it than have it come down on top of you', my wife rented for us to sleep in. On the night of 16 April 1941, we returned in a taxi at about half-past eleven, the sky south of the river already aglow and the usual noises overhead. Fires were raging round Paddington; it was obviously going to be a thick night, and I remember to this day having given the taxi-driver an inadequate tip, which at least is not one of my normal failings. A certain amount of tension developed in our lowly bedroom, since I wished to go to sleep – after all, we could not get any lower underground now – while my wife jumped every time a bomb whistled down in the distance (to add whistling-devices to bombs was an intimidating stroke of genius on the Germans' part) or when the guns went off – not that they ever hit anything, but they afforded great comfort to the populace. Eventually my wife got up and dressed and joined two young women who also had a refuge in the flat.

At about three in the morning I was woken by the building rocking and a sort of *woomph*, followed by a jumble of other noises, glass tinkling down everywhere, rubble falling, people shouting. I sat up in bed to find it full of glass, big bits, little bits and bits no bigger than dust. A great many were embedded in the plaster wall behind my head, like the knives men throw in circuses, and I actually found a couple of sizeable pieces inside the back of my pyjama coat, kept up by the trouser cord. Later I discovered bits in my hair, through drawing blood when I went to scratch my head – this proving to be the only war wound about which I can boast to my grandchildren. Our single window opened into the bottom of the inside well of the eight-storey block, but we had covered it with a thick blanket in case of blast. In fact the blanket had shot across the room at about the speed of light and had as much effect as a pocket handkerchief. Glass had penetrated to every corner of the room, into the wardrobe, under the bed, everywhere, and for weeks afterwards it glistened in the carpet like silver dust. If I had not been lying down, I must have been slashed into a thousand pieces. Another life gone.

Meanwhile, the women in the adjacent room had brewed a cup of tea and my wife had been holding a cup and saucer in her hand. The blast did not shatter their windows, which faced outwards on the far side, but it did remove the cup and saucer, and no one ever found a piece of either of them again. One moment she had them, the next they had vanished, and the theory remains that, as a sort of clattering was heard up the chimney, that is where they must have gone. On the inner part of the building, however, the position was reversed and the blast proved to be the most efficient chimney-sweeper of all time. I found the night porter and his wife and daughter bleeding and completely black, the soot of eight storeys having been blown under immense pressure into their little sitting-room. I never in my life saw a mess to equal this room in the morning; windows shattered, furniture up-ended and a three-inch layer of soot over everything.

The two women were brought into our flat and revived and then came another girl who said that she was a nurse herself and that her leg was broken. She was calm and matter-of-fact about it, though she was only in her nightclothes, and sat wrapped in a blanket, refusing assistance till more urgent cases had been dealt with. Next came two boys from the ground floor of Pembridge Mansions, the smaller one with pants, vest, gas-mask and nothing else. He had walked barefoot through the whole cascade of glass and not scratched himself. He was grinning cheerfully and re-marked, 'They couldn't blow the pants off me anyway.' I gave him some slippers and put on my ski-boots, trousers, jacket and tin hat and went out to see what had happened and what was to be done.

The near corner of Pembridge Mansions was standing starkly against the night sky, the rest had disappeared – or had been reduced, rather, to one gigantic heap of rubble. I looked up instinctively for our flat and saw only stars. The land mine must have touched off on the back roof only a few yards from our kitchen and everyone in the block – except, as it turned out, one – must be buried in the ruins. There might, however, be a chance for the caretaker, an ex-naval man of uneven temper called Thomas, and his wife, who used to take shelter in a small room down a narrow stairway in the basement, together with a plump and rather simple girl called Miss Young. Being the only person who knew its whereabouts, I managed to burrow through the rubble near the still-standing end of the block and wriggle head-first down the remains of the stairway. The tiny passage at the bottom was still clear and there my torch disclosed Mrs Thomas, half lying, half sitting in the rubble, blackened, with blood all over her. Her throat had been badly cut and she had done her best to bind it up with a handkerchief. She was in a pathetic state but refused to move. 'I'm all right,' she said, 'but they've got me 'usband.'

All the gas-meters were blown sideways and there was a strong smell of gas down there. A jet had caught at the end of the passage about ten feet away and was steadily setting fire to the wood in the debris, casting an eerie but ominous light. The door to Thomas's room had been open, but the room itself was now crammed full of beams, blocks of concrete, shattered furniture, knick-knacks, everything, including the thirty or forty clocks he used to keep down there as a hobby, all ticking at once. In a tiny space near the door, the only space in sight, protruded the top half of Miss Young. She too was covered with blood and quite black – a feature of being bombed that you don't reckon upon till you see it.

Reading accounts of people being rescued from under debris, you feel that it must be largely a question of hard, continuous work, burrowing down like a mole and pulling the wreckage away. Experience soon showed otherwise. Miss Young was saying pathetically, 'Oh, get me out of here. I know you'll never get me out.' Her legs were pinned and she kept crying, 'It's me legs. Oh, get it off me legs. Please get it off me legs.' I lay sideways in the hole and began pulling pieces away. Soon the loose bits had gone. After that, nothing would move. I got my shoulder under and heaved. Nothing happened. It was plain that nothing ever would happen either. All the time the girl was repeating, 'Oh, I know you'll never get me out,' while I was trying to pass it off with an uneasy jocularity – 'Any minute now.' It was horrible to be near enough to hold the girl's grimy hand and yet be completely unable to do anything for her. I even got hold of her under the arms and heaved as hard as I could, reckoning that if she broke a leg or an ankle in the process it was worth it. Meanwhile the gas-jet was still burning and any minute one might be forced to abandon the hole altogether. The prospect of leaving the girl down there to burn alive hardly bore thinking about. It was clear that farther back in the room Thomas must be dead.

At long last the heavy rescue squad arrived and I crawled out of the hole and left them to it. I emerged to find that the far end of Pembridge Mansions was now an absolute furnace. At about eight next morning, however, they got Miss Young safely out, bruised black and blue and suffering, not unnaturally, from severe shock but miraculously nothing worse, and later they reached the bodies of the wife and child of a warden, decomposed already by fire and water. Poor devil, he knew they were under there and had to spend the night doing his job at the telephone. What a lot of unrecorded heroism there is in this world!

As always, the night was not without its lighter moments, including two fantastic escapes, one by Captain Melsome, RN, from the flat next door to ours, the one previously occupied by the Redgraves and now the only one on the roof left standing. He always maintained that you were as safe on the roof as anywhere, though when I met him in the early hours of the morning his views may by then have changed. He had simply walked down the crumbling stairs in his pyjamas, and moments after he reached sea-level the whole four storeys fell to the ground.

The other escape was that of the porter who was fire-watching on the roof of Windsor Court. The scene, had its consequences not been so tragic, would have done for one of the early comic films. He saw this awful engine of destruction floating inexorably down, swinging gently from side to side on its parachute – and he, eight storeys up, protected only by a few chimney-pots. He stood rooted to the spot till a colossal explosion rendered him momentarily senseless. He recovered to find that by some extraordinary chance he was still on the roof. His eyes were still popping out of his head when he got down, looking like a black and white minstrel. 'What did you do?' I asked him. 'I blew me whistle,' he said. Considering that 'our' bomb blew a huge piece of coping-stone off a building 350 yards away as the blast flies and broke nearly every window in Queensway, the fact that the porter was not blown off the roof at a range of forty or fifty yards was nothing short of a miracle. He might well have pitched a quarter of a mile away. Furthermore, he must have been the only man in the whole of the war to blow his whistle at a land-mine!

Other fortunate escapes were by two budgerigars and a canary, and Mr Bennett, of the Moscow Arms. I personally rescued the budgerigars and the canary when in search of bodies in the wreckage of a small house opposite. I took them across to Windsor Court and put them in the hall. The budgerigars were soon rubbing their beaks together with small noises, but the canary sat on the bottom of its cage with its wings spread out in a comically bedraggled way. It recovered and next morning, when I found its tearful owners, a busman and his wife who had been down the tube for the night on account of a premonition on the part of the woman, it was hopping merrily about on its perch. The woman seemed to love it like a child, and was afraid it would starve now that she had lost its hoard of birdseed.

Mr Bennett, it turned out, had taken overnight precisely that quantity of refreshment calculated to cause him to be down the passage answering the call of nature at the moment when the mine went off. One pint more or one pint less and all would have been lost, for it brought down on his side of the bed not only enough roof and ceiling as must surely have killed him but a mass so shaped as to miss the recumbent Mrs Bennett, even down to the curve, as I later confirmed, required to avoid her ample posterior.

Gradually it appeared that there was nothing more to be done that night. The smoke billowing up towards the east turned dark as the morning light began to overcome the red glow of the fires. In any other circumstances a heavenly morning, crisp and sharp, with a blue sky coming up and the moon still shining, with its familiar attendant star, and the dawn glinting on the barrage balloons. At about five the All Clear sounded, but it was something of a mockery with the fire still raging and people still under the wreckage – no one knowing quite how many. Actually the death toll proved to be twenty-eight. Two days later the demolition men, working in shifts at great speed and with a fine heart, were still hacking away at the ruins, hauling down the remaining walls with ropes attached to their lorries. Ten more people, they reckoned, were still there, including two old ladies called Miss Pollock in a flat below us, of whom my wife was fond. We could see our dining-room carpet on top of the debris and soon my books began to appear out of the dust. It is a fact that the first one picked out by the demolition squad was entitled *Germany Speaks*!

15
Gone
for a Soldier

Having got myself fixed up with what would have been a most
stimulating job connected with the RAF, I was at once directed,
to my intense annoyance, to a driver-training regiment in Blackpool. From a personal point of view it turned out to be one of the
best things that ever happened, but it did mean that not until the
very end of my undistinguished military career was I ever really
at full stretch. Still, I did to the best of my ability everything that
was asked of me by His Majesty's Army and nobody can do more.
The truth is that I got a good deal more out of the Army than it
claimed from me. Blackpool turned out to be a complete rest cure
after being blown up in Moscow Road. In late summer it was no
hardship to parade on the lower esplanade on the North Shore,
looking out very often over miles of golden sands to the silvery
barrage balloons of Barrow-in-Furness and sometimes even to the
Isle of Man, and it took me no time at all to turn into the complete
'old soldier', which is of course where a boarding-school education,
be it St Cyprians or Borstal, gives you the edge over those who
have never left home. Even so, I made one elementary mistake
when really I ought to have known better. In the course of 'looking
after Number One' I got myself what must have been almost the
best billet in Cleveleys, with a most charming elderly lady and her
daughter, who 'didn't need to take in soldiers but thought it would
be helping'. The mistake was not, as might be supposed, that of
getting the daughter into trouble but of not keeping my mouth
shut. As a result I was shifted and an officer moved in.

To have all worry about food, clothing, transport and even
laundry taken off your mind in the days of rationing was a great
delight, and one came to realize what a horrible amount of time
one wastes in having to think about these things in civilian life.
We started at the beginning again, myself for the fourth time. I

had soon decided that, if you fall in the river by mistake, as I had, the thing to do is to float down with the current, at the same time keeping a sharp look-out for any branch or such like as will enable you to clutch it and clamber out. At St Cyprians, at Charterhouse and in Dad's Army I had been alternately the instructed and the instructor and had long reached the stage of not minding whether you taught me to slope arms or I taught you. On the whole it is less trouble to be instructed, since you can exercise your mind on more interesting topics while going through the motions by instinct. The first of many lessons I learnt may sound a little conceited but I shall set it down, if only because it was such a genuine surprise. Having fallen into the pleasant peacetime routine of travelling widely, first class at someone else's expense, staying at good hotels and never short of a bob or two, I reckoned that I should be somewhat shown up when thrown into competition with the horny-handed sons of toil, working youths who really worked, beside whom I should appear over-indulged and unhandy by comparison. To my astonishment, and real astonishment, I found that I could without the least trouble do almost everything at least as well as any of them, including running about Blackpool sands in little knickers waving a great bamboo pole. It was surprising, if one may be realistic without being 'superior', how many knew practically nothing about anything.

It seems hardly credible that this was thirty years ago, and I have been refreshing my memory of some of the miscellaneous characters with whom I was thrown into contact in this salutary period of my life. Maggie, for instance, the elderly dictator of the kitchen of a particularly loathsome boarding-house-cum-hotel in which fourteen of us were billeted below stairs but whose identity it would be churlish at this length of time to reveal. Maggie's directness of speech and action led to frequent shindies in the kitchen. 'You —— off!' she said to the kitchenmaid, receiving in reply a well-aimed kick upon her aged posterior. The kitchenmaid ducked neatly as a bar of soap flashed across the kitchen. On another occasion it was the kitchen boy who offended. 'Come here, you undersized little pisspot!' yelled Maggie, seizing the boy's hair and shaking his head like a coconut. I even fell foul of her myself, on the subject of washing-up, which fell to each of us one day a week. I maintained (and still so maintain) that the object of plate-racks is to enable you to put plates away without drying them.

Maggie held that they must first be dried with a cloth. Perhaps I should have known better, but I stuck to my point. Her final word was a swinging blow across the ear with a wet dishcloth.

A rich ore of comedy was to be mimed in the murky below-stairs depths of our boarding-house. The man Ledger, for instance. How they passed him for the Army, even in those days, is just one of those things. Ledger was not 'a bit wanting' or 'not all there'; he was stark, staring mad. (Incidentally in the same intake we had another man who was eventually carted off to a lunatic asylum; a man who had one leg an inch shorter than the other; two with double ruptures; one who had kept himself alive for years on milk and fish; and a host of other crocks, the details of whose obvious disabilities now escape me – all passed as A1 by medical boards.) Ledger was about twenty-five and had been a miner all his life. His speech was pretty well unintelligible. 'Thar say?' he would say for 'You see?' and 'tray' for 'three', When at last they discharged him, he pinched my greatcoat to hand in, to keep his own for Civvy Street – about the only spark of sanity he ever showed.

In charge of the miscellaneous gang in the boarding-house was Bombardier Hartley, another young miner, this time with his head screwed on very much the right way. Now everyone has heard of lunatics who say they are Napoleon, or Jesus Christ, and so on, but it does not fall to the lot of many of us to hear one seriously do so. It happened at tea one day when we sat down to half a tinned pilchard each, generously provided by the proprietor.

'Ah'm Jasus Christ. That's who Ah am,' said Ledger.

The man beside him intimated that he did not accept this proposition, whereupon Ledger, with foam slobbering horribly from between his teeth, seized the largest knife he could see, caught the man round the neck, and held the knife to his throat.

'Ah'm Jasus Christ!' he said. 'Thar say?'

The situation, time-honoured manifestation of lunacy though it might be, was saved by Bombardier Hartley. Looking calmly up from his miserable pilchard, he uttered the memorable words:

'In that case you can set about turning these few small fishes into food for fourteen men.'

Having been taught to drive by a ginger-haired young chap called Syd, who came from Poplar (I worked it out that when I had my first driving-licence Syd had been three years old) I duly graduated to become an instructor, spending hours every day

going round and round the Norbreck and Cleveleys Hydros, sometimes wrestling for control of the wheel to avoid running into a
stationary milk-float and at all times sitting with the right hand
casually upon the knee, thus disguising the fact that it was within
inches of the brake and the ignition key – all the more understand-
able when, as happened one day on a hairpin bend in the beautiful
Trough of Bowland, you have seen the learner and instructor in
front of you, to say nothing of four men in the back, shoot forward,
disappear over the edge and after three complete somersaults finish
wrong way up at the bottom.

It also fell to me to fetch a new intake from Blackpool Central
Station. These turned out to be a particularly wild type of young
Glaswegian, mostly with long canine teeth and unintelligible
dialect. It did not surprise me when I failed to understand a word
they were saying. It did take me aback a bit, however, to find that
they had not a clue as to what *I* was saying. They had a peculiar
aversion to fish. When served up with some very fine herrings-in-
tomato, which I would not turn down even today, they cried,
'Fush! ——ing fush!' and set about each other with their knives,
fighting over the jam ration. The army gave most of them their
first chance and many turned into tremendous soldiers.

For myself I could not at first have cared less whether I became
an officer and it was not until I wearied of finding it necessary to
fire on only two out of six cylinders, so to speak, that I applied for
a commission. At last there came the great day when a number of
us presented ourselves before a commissions board. It was headed
by an elderly full colonel, who might have come straight out of
Osbert Lancaster. He had a long drooping moustache and an
eyeglass and smoked a Turkish cigarette, which he held in his
teeth, pointing downwards. He was assisted by stooges on either
side in the shape of majors. The interview was rather depressing.

What had I done before the war? I am afraid that the mention
of newspapers caused the old gentleman's cigarette almost to drop
from his teeth. I felt that there was leeway to be made up here. I
told him I had chosen light anti-aircraft (as against heavies or
searchlights, with which you were liable to be kept up all night).

'Guns?' he said. 'Know anythin' about guns?'

I had to confess that I did not, at the same time muttering something about being anxious to learn, etcetera.

'He doesn't know anythin' *about* guns,' said the president.

'No, sir,' said the claque on either side.

'Better go and find out somethin' about 'em first, eh?'

'Yes, sir. Undoubtedly, sir,' they echoed.

'There you are, you see. Don't know anythin' *about* guns. Better go and find out somethin' about 'em.'

I felt a trifle offended. It was true that I did not know anythin' about guns and it was obviously desirable that I should go and find out somethin' about them but, well, it wasn't so much what the old boy said as the way he said it.

The place where I was to learn somethin' about guns turned out to be a bleak, if finely equipped, hutted camp, not unaptly named Saighton, outside Chester, not far from Lord Westminster's Eaton Hall, and, what was perhaps more important, handy for a pub called the Rake and Pikel. What with the cold and the snow and the grey skies and the sinking of the *Prince of Wales* and the *Repulse* and the long-drawn-out prospect ahead, this was a trying time. The gloom, however, was suddenly relieved by an almost blinding ray of sunshine. Out of the blue, or rather the grey, there arrived a letter, optimistically addressed to Sergeant Longhurst. It was from my old friend, and in many ways hero, Lord Brabazon (to be), who was then, having been Minister of Transport during the Blitz, Minister of Aircraft Production. Would I go and be his personal assistant at the Ministry? My heart leapt and for days I walked on air with my secret. What a Cinderella-like metamorphosis it would be, from this barren square and no known future to London and the very heart of the conduct of the war! You may believe it or not, and I can hardly do so to this day, but the Army found the services of Learner-Gunner 1737288 Temporary Acting Unpaid Supernumary Lance-Bombardier Longhurst too valuable to spare, and dear old Brab, whose only weakness was perhaps his dislike of 'trouble', failed to pursue the matter.

What a wonderful man, though, and how much richer was my life for the privilege of his friendship. He was about twenty-five years older than me, but I am myself reaching the age when one can appreciate that the friendship of a much younger man is also in its way a privilege. He was without doubt the most *interesting* man I ever knew and I shall permit myself the luxury of leaving the barren barrack square of Saighton for a moment in order to say more about him. He seemed to have been 'in at the birth' of almost all the inventions which so suddenly transformed life in the early twentieth century. The walls of his office told much of the story of his life. Here, for instance, was Aviator's Certificate No. 1 of the Fédération Aéronautique Internationale, dated 8 March 1910 – thirty years after which the holder started the craze for 'personal' car numbers by securing FLY 1.

Next to it a young man with gum-boots, Norfolk jacket, and rather prominent teeth is seen grasping the levers of a Heath-Robinson flying-machine – none other than the 'biplane pusher with bamboo and ash framework', which was the first all-English aeroplane to fly. With it Brab won £1,000 from the *Daily Mail* for a circular flight of one mile, average height forty feet.

Another picture, surely a unique galaxy of aeronautical pioneers, shows, under the heading *First English Aerodrome, Mussel Manor, Shellbeach, Sheppey, 4 May 1909*, a knickerbockered group including all three of the Short brothers, Wilbur and Orville Wright, young Moore-Brabazon, and the handsome, ill-fated Charlie Rolls, of Rolls-Royce, whom 'Brab', as everybody called him and I shall henceforth do in this narrative, was later to see killed in an air display. How many people, I wonder, realize that the familiar RR for Rolls-Royce was at first red? I learnt this sixty years later at a private museum of vintage cars in Dayton, Ohio, where in fact the Wright brothers came from. This museum had a vast Rolls which had been built for some Maharajah in the early 1900s, and the letters RR on the bonnet were red. It was on Charlie Rolls's death that they turned them to black. Brab used to tell of driving his great friend Rolls to some rather grand function, I think it was Ascot, to which he, as a mere chauffeur, was refused admittance. He thereupon went off, obtained a bucket of water and carried it straight in through the main gate. 'Believe me,' he used to say, 'there is absolutely nowhere you cannot go so long as you are carrying a bucket of water.' 'What if they ask you where you are going?' I said. 'Oh,' he replied, 'you simply say, "I'm taking this bucket of water in".'

Other pictures reveal him, in chauffeur's cap, waiting to crank the first Rolls-Royce, with the Duke of Connaught sitting bolt upright as passenger; and at the huge high steering-wheel of the Minerva with which he won the Circuit des Ardennes in 1907. Beside one of the most remarkable pictures ever taken of the Cresta toboggan run are, curiously enough, two of a main-line railway station. Only very close inspection reveals it to be a model –

Mahoney's Point, Killarney,
one of the great short holes in the
world. I spent much time on the
course with Viscount Castlerosse,
and fell in love with Kerry.

Lord Brabazon of Tara,
an example of that rare, invaluable
and almost extinct species,
the universal amateur. He went down
the Cresta Run at the age
of seventy-four.

a reminder of younger days when Brab had the best model railway in England. He *would* have! He ran it with his brother-in-law, Clarence Krabbe, and when they had an accident they stopped and held an 'inquiry'. He would never travel by train without first inspecting the engine. 'Have you ever driven one of these?' he asked, as we were about to embark on a journey to Belgium. 'Ah,' he said, 'I'll tell you what it's like. It's like driving a very powerful sports car, with two big ends gone *and* a puncture.'

With his booming, unmistakable voice he could hold an audience anywhere, whether in the Commons, the Lords, after dinner or, particularly, in the United States. Proposing the toast of the Open Champion at a dinner, he opened with: 'It is only appropriate that a Member of Parliament whose constituency borders upon Liverpool and Merseyside should be asked to get up on his hind legs and propose the toast of Cotton.' It was he who in the Commons likened the Opposition to a 'lot of inverted Micawbers waiting for something to turn down'. Even his own side caught it when he referred to the 'snores of the Front Bench reverberating throughout the land'. It was certainly the then Archbishop of Canterbury whom he accused, when His Grace had made a speech on finance, of 'talking through his mitre'.

When Prince's, Sandwich, was used as a target range in the war, Brab declared that it was 'like throwing darts at a Rembrandt'. When Royal St George's was waterlogged and too little, he thought, was being done about it, he put a suggestion in the book 'that the water in the bunkers at the 13th be changed'.

Among the many 'firsts' in Brab's life was that, as a boy at Harrow, he was walking down Grove Hill when a few yards away from him a motorist put on the brakes too hard, ripped the spokes from his wheels and became the first man ever to be killed in a motor accident. While others stood back, waiting for the infernal machine to blow up, Brab stepped forward and turned off the ignition burners. He was the only person who knew what they were. Afterwards he gave a lecture to the school scientific society on 'The Motor Car' – 'a treasure,' he said, 'now lost to the world.'

People who worked with him were always astonished at the variety of subjects on which he could truly be described as expert. Yet in many ways he was an example of that rare, invaluable, and almost extinct species, the Universal Amateur. For those who pursue the humble game of golf, however, it is nice to think that a man of so many parts and of such immense distinction should have written in his autobiography, 'When I look back on my life and try to decide out of what I have got most actual pleasure, I have no doubt at all that I have got more out of golf than anything else.'*

After which diversion we may return to the barrack square and the endless embarrassing gun drill, which I never grasped, till one night I stayed in and learnt the whole damned book by heart. Another night I sat for about two hours in silence in a Chester pub in that lovely old terrace they call the 'Rows', 'appreciating the situation', as the Army has it, and decided that the only thing was to make a book about it, the result being, just after the war, a volume called *I Wouldn't Have Missed It*† – and nor I would.

All bad things come to an end and Saighton ended with the arrival of a commissions board and my subsequent dispatch as an officer-cadet, complete with white hatband, to Shrivenham, where life after a month or two of being chivvied about began to blossom forth and my personal philosophy of it to be consolidated. Shrivenham is a little Berkshire village between Faringdon and Swindon and, if you look out from the train a few miles short of Swindon, you will see the super-magnificent barracks away over in a park on the right. I never flash through the little station at Shrivenham on the way west from Paddington without thinking of the evening we arrived there and the sergeant who met us said, 'I can give you just ten minutes for a drink, gentlemen.' Gentlemen, indeed! This was a nice change and we trooped into the station pub feeling an inch higher. Better still do I remember the very first comment of old Major Willett, whom I came to respect so much. 'Well, gentlemen,' he said, 'until it pleases the Almighty to make all men equal, some will have to be officers.' It seemed to say everything. Shrivenham had a fearsome reputation for spit and polish and it was even hinted that the cadets had actually to scrape the unnecessarily luxurious parquet floors with razor-blades and un-screw the window-catches in order to clean them. Some indeed did, but not, after I had worked out that each man's quota came to about ten thousand square inches, your humble servant. The light dawned suddenly one dark Friday in the blacked-out barrack room stinking of Brasso. 'Bollocks!' I said, and so from that moment it was. Of course, it was easier for me, being around thirty and with a certain experience of life and people, than for the nineteen- and

* *The Brabazon Story* (Heinemann, 1956).   † Dent, 1945.

twenty-year-olds, and perhaps their aged colleague in a way had a good influence on them. They were liable to worry about things, especially the dreaded letters RTU, or Returned to Unit, so I appointed one of them my official worrier and when they came to say, 'Have you seen the notice? Everybody's got to [whatever it was],' I would say to my man, 'Get that well worried out by Thursday, will you? I have got to go out.' Strangely enough I think it helped, even if some of it did savour of whistling in the dark.

As April came and the preliminary chivvying-about was over, the Vale of the White Horse – we looked directly across to the White Horse itself on the Hill – emerged in all the glory of spring and I fell deeply in love with it. My senses quickened and I came to believe that the only real religion lay in the appreciation of beauty. We saw the Vale as it will never be seen by human eye again, without motor cars, and Sheet 104 of the Ordnance Survey became one's bible, as gradually, by bicycle, one began to bring it to life on the ground. One day, during a lecture on carburettors if I remember rightly, I began filling in on the back of the drillbook the names of all the golf courses I had played on and it came to something over three hundred. I turned it into an article and sent it to *Men Only*, founded by Reginald Arkell of *Green Fingers* fame and at that time one of the best little magazines ever published. He used it, and his letter revealed that he had a cottage at Marston Meysey, so I bicycled over to see him, and thus began another valued friendship. His thatched cottage could have come straight out of the picture-books, even down to the flycatcher nesting in the plum tree. Now with the march of civilization it will have been rendered hideous with the noise of the Concorde at Fairford.

Suddenly, with the arrival of the Americans, we were shifted from Shrivenham to make way for them and moved to Tonfanau, a little firing camp on the Merionethshire coast just north of Towyn. (This did not, however, completely sever my connection with Shrivenham. After the war, when it had become the Royal College of Military Science, they extended the small but admirable golf-course in the grounds and invited me not only to captain the Students' team in the annual match against the Staff but to drive the first ball to celebrate the opening of the new holes. The drive finished where everyone, including the striker, knew it would finish – a high slice behind an elm tree – but for several years now I have attended this delightful match, nowadays as non-playing captain, ever mindful of the less portly figure who paraded on that barrack square and 'bumped' those parquet floors, can it really be thirty years ago?) We went to Towyn by train, a journey of which Bernard Darwin wrote so charmingly in *The World that Fred Made*, for it takes you along beside the Dovey river past the links of Aberdovey that his uncle laid out with flower-pots for holes and the little station beside the clubhouse. At Tonfanau, which seemed, as near as we could get to it, to be pronounced 'Tonfanno', there were no more parquet floors, thank God, but scenery on a grander and more rugged scale than the dreamy beauty of the villages of the Vale. It was August, we were the only ones who had petrol, and away up into the hills we would go on 'schemes', trailing our Bofors guns, and gradually another sheet of the Ordnance Survey came to life. Barmouth, Dolgellau, Snowdonia, the Cross Foxes Inn, Lake Bala, beside which I slept one memorable night under a full moon, Machynlleth, the Devil's Bridge, even Aberystwyth. Meanwhile I had found as a 'mate', so indispensable in service life, a past colleague in the world of golf, and sometimes we would put the bicycles and golf clubs on the train at the little Tonfanau halt, get out at the clubhouse to play at Aberdovey, and ride home in the dark across the Towyn course where, if we fell off, the only way to start again, my mate having no light at all, was for me to point my front wheel in approximately the right direction, rotate it rapidly by hand to get a glimmer of light out of the automatic light, jump on, and hope for the best.

I think I was a cadet for seven months, including the month's leave between being ousted by the Americans and posted to Tonfanau, and it was about three months too long, but at long last, having been judged fit to be an officer, if not a gentleman, I found myself posted to what proved to be a splendid regiment stationed at the little town of Haltwhistle, of which I am afraid I had never heard. It turned out to be in Northumberland, under the lee of Hadrian's Wall, midway between Newcastle and Carlisle. This was autumn and one could see the purple moors stretching away into the distant south. One could also see the white posts beside the roads indicating their whereabouts when the snow came, and the prospect was not an inviting one.

The luck, however, held. Northumberland people, perhaps because of their rugged climate, are fine folk, and I found a wonderful billet with Mr and Mrs Bennett, with whom I corresponded for several years and whose married daughter I meet when I go to golf events at Lytham. Our 'schemes' took us high over the moors, sometimes to Alston, which is said to be the highest market town in Britain, and it was the first winter almost in living memory when not a single flake of snow fell. One day we put all the guns on a special train and meandered off cross-country to a firing camp at Clacton and in the course of the long journey a curious thing happened. I was sitting looking idly out of the window when a sort of sixth sense told me suddenly where we were. We must be on that little line that you cross on the way to play golf at Mildenhall, at the far end of Newmarket Heath. There was nothing by which visually to identify it nor had I ever travelled on the line in my life, but in a minute or two there we were, passing under the bridge.

At Clacton we lived in Billy Butlin's camp and very comfortable it was too, except when I came under enemy fire for the first and only time in the war and damn nearly lost my life. I was walking quietly back to my chalet after breakfast one Sunday morning, when there was a resounding thump and a hole suddenly appeared in a fire bucket full of sand just beside me. This was followed by a roar of aeroplanes, and I looked up to see four of them in line astern at about two hundred feet, all with black crosses on. They also dropped a bomb on the laundry and I lost a shirt and two pairs of socks. Still, better those than your life. The object in the fire bucket proved to be a cannon shell and a foot or two to the right would have done me no good at all. Being a firing camp, the place was bristling with Bofors guns for which these hit-and-run raiders were just the very target. Not a single shot was fired.

Later we moved from Haltwhistle to guard the training airfield at Hamble, on the Solent, and this too turned out to be most agreeable, until one day a message arrived from our battery headquarters to the effect that Mr Longhurst was to report to MGGS at Anti-Aircraft Command Headquarters. Nobody knew what MGGS stood for and nobody knew where AA Command Headquarters were, but it was eventually found that MGGS stood for Major General, General Staff (Cor!) and AA Command turned out to be a comfortable old house called Glenthorn, at Bushey, Middlesex, a stone's throw from Fighter Command at Bentley Priory. Having been interviewed by the burly MGGS, General Whitaker, I was ushered in to the more diminutive figure of the Commander-in-Chief, General 'Tim' Pile, probably one of the most popular generals in the war, and certainly the only one to keep his command for the entire war – even, as he called it in his book, 'within earshot of the House of Commons'. It turned out that after the First War all trace of anti-aircraft methods and their advancement appeared to have been lost and in this war they had had virtually to start again: not quite as simple as that, of course, but what he wanted was to record the stage to which we had now progressed, the steps by which it was reached, and how people in the future could lay hands on the relevant details. My name had been mentioned to him as one possibly suitable for such a task.

So I bade farewell to my comrades at Hamble with most genuine regret and moved into the spacious comfort of a large house at Bushey Heath which was where King Edward VII had entertained his lady friends and which had thereafter become, till requisitioned, the home of the Hartsbourne Golf Club. Physically I had fallen on my feet again. The mess was extraordinarily well run, incidentally by Guy Thompson, who had been a very accomplished golfer, and there was plenty of intelligent company, including Humphry Ellis (H.F.E. of *Punch*) and my lifelong friend Brian Ambler, who had been on the same staircase at Clare. The garden, complete with a huge and very productive mulberry tree, was a great delight and so was the twice-daily walk through the woods to Glenthorn; but the job with which I felt so privileged to have been entrusted was beyond the work of one man, even if ten times as gifted and industrious as I could ever claim to be. It would have needed a department. If the war had stopped at that moment and I had carried on with the job, I doubt whether I should have finished it even now.

As they seemed to be the newest and possibly most interesting part of anti-aircraft science at that time, I started off to trace the background of rockets, or Z batteries as they were known. I was able to go anywhere, ask and be told anything, and be received hospitably by officers much senior to myself; and very stimulating the work turned out to be, apart from the increasing awareness that it could never be done. I should still have been plodding on till the end of the war, had I not, one Saturday night in December 1943, been called from a game of snooker in the mess to take a telephone-call from Acton which immediately and completely altered the pattern of my life.

16
Every Inch
a Lord

Viscount Castlerosse was the most completely unique character I ever came to know reasonably well, unique in the sense that there was no one else with whom I or anyone else would even begin to compare him. There was only, so to speak, one entrant in that particular class. His monumental frame; his excesses, financial and otherwise; his follies and fortunes and misfortunes; his spats, lavender waistcoats and astrakhan coat; his conversational wit and outrageous goings-on, and behind it all an immense natural talent in the end almost to be thrown away, all these made it remarkable that I should have come to know him at all. I could easily write a book about him, and indeed would once have done so, had not some misunderstanding crept in at the last moment. Instead, since no narrative of my own life could possibly omit some reference to this remarkable man, I will, with the reader's indulgence, quote what I wrote in a series called 'My Hero' in *Punch*.

It is difficult, since he has no counterpart today, to do justice to the unique reputation enjoyed in the 1930s by the monumental figure of Valentine Viscount Castlerosse, later 6th Earl of Kenmare, not only among the more sophisticated society of London but in the minds of millions who never met him. To call him a 'columnist' would be almost *lèse-majesté*, since the younger reader might fall into the error of comparing him with the 'Paul Slickey' type of contributed column today. Castlerosse, in fact, every week for the best part of fifteen years, wrote under the title of 'A Londoner's Log' the whole of Page 2 of the *Sunday Express*. He wrote it all out in longhand with a battery of specially sharpened pencils – a mixture of people, places, philosophy, wisdom, satire and wit, interspersed with barbed allusions to the fickleness of women. Eventually he married the most beautiful woman in London and the rows they had have hardly been surpassed in the love-hate history of matrimony.

Castlerosse not only was, but looked, 'every inch a Lord'. He talked, wrote, ate, drank and had his being on the grand scale. His weight varied between eighteen and twenty stone and it seemed only proper for him to be attired in white waistcoat and spats and, in winter, a vast astrakhan-collared fur-lined coat. Low, the cartoonist, once drew an enormous cigar all by itself in mid-air; even the man in the street knew it meant Castlerosse. Wherever he appeared, he stopped the show – and never more completely than when he attended a huge fancy-dress ball made up as Holbein's portrait of Henry VIII, whom in any case he almost exactly resembled.

He was the only columnist, though I still hesitate to use the word, who wrote from above his subjects. He was not to be summoned by some public relations man to wait upon visiting actresses, notebook in hand, at inconvenient hours. With Castlerosse it was he who was the celebrity. As a result, the first question asked by visiting notorieties of either sex tended to be, 'Can anyone get me an introduction to Castlerosse?' It may seem incredible today, but there it was. 'Everyone' read his Sunday page, and anyone who figured in it was made for the day.

I suppose one's 'hero' is almost bound to be older than oneself, and this was so in my own case by nearly twenty years. You may imagine my feelings, therefore, on receiving a few years before the war a long handwritten summons from the great man. Having made a modest mark in writing about golf, I was now to proceed to his ancestral home at Killarney, where he had ideas about making not only a golf course but, on account of the temperate climate and the adjacent Gulf Stream, a golf course in colour. His dream, I like to think, came at least partly true.

After an all-day journey across Ireland I arrived at the little station in darkness but it was clear that something was afoot. This turned out to be His Lordship in person, complete with purple smoking-jacket and slippers with the crossed Cs monogram. In the morning I looked out with a lively surmise and found framed in the window a scene which I can exactly recall to this day – the tall avenue of beeches, the white horse in the paddock, the meadows leading down to a glimpse of the lake and, behind it all, the purple mountains of Kerry. An air of total peace prevailed and you could almost *feel* it. No noise, no aeroplanes, no radio, no newspapers till teatime, by which time they were meaning-less. Despite the differences in age and background my hero-to-be and I hit it off together from the start, mainly, I fancy, because I fell so manifestly in love with the place, and the life, for which he would willingly have exchanged the fleshpots from which, alas, he had to earn the money to keep them up. Later he was to lend me the house for my honeymoon – and we were shown up by old Dennis, the butler, into separate rooms. It could only happen in Kerry!

His life in Killarney was still semi-feudal. The lakes 'and all the fish therein' belonged to the family, and the ruined Ross Castle and the woods and desmesnes as far as the eye could see; and his predecessors, as was the custom of the day, had thrown a seven-mile wall round the lot. At the farthest end we spent much time on the golf course and I began to understand the general spirit of the place when the estate foreman said that in a certain part there had been a road there before but it hadn't been used for some time. 'How long ago would that be?' I asked. 'Oh,' he said, 't'would be about four hundred years.'

In the intervals we fished in the lake, or shot duck, His Lordship weighing down the stern of his boat so that the boatman could scarce get his oars to the water, and I think it pleased him to think of me tramping down before dawn to get a shot at the geese while he lay in bed. One day he announced that on the morrow we should go stalking. We drove as far as we could and then set off in single file up the mountain, Castlerosse leading the way, followed by myself, two retainers carrying rifles and telescopes, and in the rear another man carrying only a pail. I did not like to display my ignorance by asking the significance of the pail. Later it turned out to be the ice for His Lordship's whiskey and soda.

He drank on a scale in keeping with his person. In the First War, when he served in the trenches as an officer in the Irish Guards, photographs show him to have been as slim as a flagpole. He was shot through the elbow at the battle of Loos. It stiffened his right arm, so that he could never again extend it or hold it above his head – but it fitted perfectly for lifting a glass. It was nothing for him to pour half a pint of whiskey into a pint tumbler, fill it to the top with soda, and then down it in a single draught. One day after we had played golf at Ballybunion he downed seven bottles of Guinness and five half-lobsters and spent the journey home erupting like a minor volcano and cursing his long-suffering chauffeur, Godfrey, whenever the car hit a bump in the road.

He had once been a scratch golfer but now his arm limited his game. We played together at Walton Heath one day and he topped shot after shot. 'Pick it up,' he would say to his caddie in a lordly tone. At the last hole he tried a final stroke, with the same result. He tossed the club disdainfully to the ground and stalked towards the clubhouse, uttering the memorable instructions, 'Pick that up. Have the clubs destroyed, and leave the course.'

Castlerosse, like royalty, never carried money and could go for long periods under the impression that he wasn't spending any. Towards the end of his life he lived at Claridge's, and sometimes I used to lunch with him. A waiter would bring the preliminary drinks, for which of course no money changed hands. We would then proceed to the St James Club, where he instructed the porter to pay the taxi. Lunch consisted of almost anything which was out of season, or vastly expensive, or both, He signed the bill, returned to Claridge's, instructed the top-hatted lackey at the door to see to the taxi ('Of course, me lord; certainly, me lord!') and went to sleep – happy in the knowledge that he had not spent a penny.

One day in the absence of his equally long-suffering valet, Welsh, he had decided, quite erroneously, that he was short of shirts. He had summoned the shirt-maker and I happened to be there when the man arrived, fawning and rubbing his hands at the prospect of a substantial order. Valentine chose the most expensive pattern of pure silk, making sure, of course, that each shirt would have his monogram embroidered on the breast pocket. How many? Oh, make it three dozen. At pre-war prices perhaps two hundred pounds. The shirt problem, now solved, no longer existed.

Perhaps his most lordly gesture was when he tossed the entire morning mail into the waste-paper basket unopened. 'But you *can't* do that!' I said, with reluctant admiration, 'Oh,' he said, 'if there's anything, they'll write again.' Perhaps the shirtmaker was among them.

He left all his silk shirts and pyjamas, believe it or not, to the Convent of the Presentation in Killarney, and in the late fifties the nuns were still wearing apparel which they had made from them. The Mother Superior used to wear a pair of his monogrammed slippers. 'What little feet he had!' she said.

Relations between Lords Castlerosse and Beaverbrook, bosom friends, yet each, perhaps, envying the other for something which he himself did not possess, were sometimes strained – Castlerosse sweeping majestically through life, spending prodigiously and acclaimed wherever he went; Beaverbrook, his millionaire employer, knowing well enough who was eventually going to pay. One day when they were in Cannes together, there was a water shortage. Later Beaverbrook was taken aback to find on the hotel bill an item for twelve dozen bottles of mineral water. 'Quite in order,' said Castlerosse. He had had them sent up for his bath.

Eventually the debts and the creditors and the worry would catch up on him to such an extent as to be no longer concealable from Beaverbrook's suspecting eye. Rows and recriminations would be followed by the usual promise of reform, but the result was always the same. Beaverbrook had to put his hand in his pocket once more, generally to the tune of several thousands. There are those who suspect that secretly in his heart, like a parent bailing out a profligate but well loved son, he was happy in doing it.

'I see my moneylender has gone off to the war,' wrote Castlerosse in 1939, 'I only hope he charges the enemy with the same enthusiasm that he charges me.' By now, however, rich living, the best of everything ('I never cared for the second class'), and burning the candle at both ends, even though it gave a lovely light – all this, and sadness at the thought of yet another ghastly war, were taking their toll, and Castlerosse fell into an illness as melodramatic as London had known for many a long year.

Telephone calls poured in from all over the world and Claridge's had to instal a special operator to handle them. Flowers, get-well presents, messenger boys and actresses packed the corridors. His doctor, the present Lord Moran, prescribed 'absolute quiet, no food, no drink, no books, no thoughts about women, and no eroticism in your dreams'. Castlerosse, 'lying like a pink whale across the silken ocean of his great bed', as his biographer, Leonard Mosley, put it,* received his visitors with caviare and champagne, while Beaverbrook, to relieve the patient's mind, slipped the more urgent creditors £1,500.

In the end Castlerosse pulled through, but the world in which he had been so conspicuous a figure was gone for ever. He retreated to his beloved Killarney and from here began in 1942 to bombard me with fictitious telegrams, such as: YOUR AUNT WHO LIVES HERE IS DYING STOP WILL LEAVE YOU HER FORTUNE STOP COME AT ONCE. Army Council Instructions, however, were only too clear. Nothing but the illness of a parent or 'urgent business reasons' qualified one for leave in Ireland. Eventually Castlerosse wrote airily that he was 'proposing to spend another £40,000 on the golf course', in which I happened to possess one £1 share. 'This, sir,' said I to an understanding Irish General who knew Killarney, 'is urgent business reasons.'

September in Killarney! Fishing and shooting duck on the lake; the new golf course; scenery out of this world ('See what the Almighty can do when he is in a good mood'); and Castlerosse in his own home, the best company in the world. What a prospect to exchange for Anti-Aircraft Headquarters, the blackout and the Blitz! With a high heart I reached the bright lights of Dublin. I rang up a friend. Where was I going? he asked. Why, to Killarney, to spend my leave with Castlerosse.

There was a long pause. 'Alas,' said the voice, 'he died this morning.'

* *Castlerosse* (Barker, 1956).

17
Venture
in Politics

Three and a half years of economics, combined with an argumentative disposition, made it a certainty that I should take an interest in the General Election of 1931. In the days when you were 'either a little Liberal or else a little Conserva-tive' my father, I believe, was a Liberal. By 1931 you were either Conservative or Labour, though the Liberal interest did survive longer in Bedford than most places, and I think I should always have been anti-socialism (as against anti-Labour). However, in 1931 itself the question hardly arose. Political history has no part in a modest personal narrative such as this, but I should perhaps say that the Labour Party had been in office (not in power, as they were to remind us for years to come, since they were maintained only by the Liberals) and had, as the historians I imagine will now agree, made the most frightful mess of things. The hideous unemployment which in 1929 they had been voted in to cure had soared to above the three million mark and the nation was, so the May Committee roundly declared, financially bankrupt. A few of the leading socialists agreed to join in a National Government, for which patriotic act they were never forgiven, so that when I first entered the political arena with a resounding speech in the school hall at Bromham there was really little or no doubt which side one ought to be on. I was full of facts and figures and theories of what had precipitated the present crisis, even down to a mention of the bankruptcy of the Kreditanstalt in Austria, which was alleged to have set it all going, and the resounding speech was just getting into full flow when the entry of the member-candidate, Mr Richard Wells, on his rounds of the villages, put paid to it. There being no television in those days, there seemed nothing much to do when Mr Wells left for the next village and I was flattered when a voice at the back said, 'What about a bit more from Mr Longhurst?'

All this, combined with some cheerful heckling in the market square and a tour round the constituency in a procession of cars carrying banners and huge rosettes, formed a heady introduction to politics, and once you have been bitten by the bug it is almost impossible, as in golf, to throw it off. Indeed, I doubt whether I am completely immune now.

The result of the 1931 election was, of course, a super-colossal landslide for the National Party and many were the heart-rending tales of men with no previous political affiliations who had been persuaded to stand and were then heard to protest, having been elected by 20,000-odd, that they hadn't time to attend the House of Commons and it would ruin their business.

For myself politics began to stir again, and in earnest, during my time in the army when eventually I had become an officer and had seen the insidious rubbish fed compulsorily to the soldiers by ABCA, the left-wing Army Bureau of Current Affairs – of whom it was afterwards wittily said, I think by Lord Mancroft, that their principal victory was the General Election of 1945. Such men as could be mustered were lectured by people sent down from ABCA and I remember in particular, when I was in charge of the modest defences of the airfield at Hamble, a sinister long-haired character coming along to one of our gun-sites and giving a harangue to three or four bored gunners on the days after the war when social justice would prevail. I was all in favour of social justice prevailing, but when he brought in something about 'manning the barricades' I thought we had had enough. He said he was connected in some way, I forget what, with Southampton University and, if so, no wonder the universities enjoy the reputation they do today. I even heard that he was rewarded with a seat in Parliament in the famous victory of '45.

I was also lured towards the idea of taking an eventual part in politics by Lord Brabazon (to give him his later title). He was twenty-eight years in the House of Commons before being 'kicked upstairs', as a result of an atrocious breach of confidence by a fellow guest at a private luncheon, and more than anyone I have known before or since brought the House of Commons to life. I remember his description of the arrival of Black Rod to summon the faithful Commons to the Lords to hear the monarch's assent to bills (*Le Roi le veult*) and of the great doors being slammed in his face while the Commons went through the motions of debating

'Shall we let him in?' so that never again, after Charles I, should the King's man enter the Commons without permission: and I have always remembered, too, his telling me how incredibly well informed you could be as a Member, not through learning State secrets but because, whatever the subject might be, among the six hundred of them there was always one Member who knew all about it and would be only too happy to tell you over a pink gin in the smoking-room. I determined to put my name down as a potential candidate and Brab was one of my three sponsors.

As I have more than once mentioned, the pattern of one's life is liable to depend on being in the right place at the right time. Thus it happened that my wife had taken some job in the office of Eric Hooper (later, as Sir Frederic, a considerable figure in the business world), who was adviser and energizer behind a group of middle-of-the-road Tories known as Tory Reformers, among them such persons as Quintin Hogg, Peter Thorneycroft, Hugh Molson, Thelma Cazalet, Lord Hinchingbrooke (who later relinquished his titles to become plain Mr Victor Montagu, which was perhaps a pity) and even the peppery and much senior Lord Winterton. Occasional contact with some of these whetted the appetite and the hope that I too might one day be 'in' and I sensed that, if the miracle ever happened, I should wish to become one of their number.

In the autumn of 1943, when I was in Anti-Aircraft Command Headquarters, the untimely death of Captain Hubert Duggan caused a by-election at Acton, which is that part of London to the left of the White City and before you come to Ealing, and on the principle that, if you did not throw your hat into the ring, you would never learn how quickly it would be thrown out, I applied to be among those considered.

About forty others, I later gathered, did the same, and you may imagine how gratified I was, and indeed surprised, to get a letter from W. J. Twidell (to rhyme with 'idle'), the agent for Harrow, who had been appointed to handle the by-election since Acton were far from being able to afford one of their own, requesting me to present myself, 'with your wife if you are married', before the selection committee on the following Thursday.

Five candidates were to be given half an hour apiece on the Thursday and another four on the Friday. We were the last on Thursday evening, and I remember feeling that this might be something of a disadvantage in that the selection committee, being but human, might have one half of their minds on the business in hand and the other half on their suppers!

My wife and I duly presented ourselves at the headquarters of the Acton Conservative Party, a blacked-out little shop in the High Street opposite the police station, and spent a few nervous minutes in conversation with Twidell, while the inquisition upon the previous candidate was concluded in the inner sanctum. He emerged at last – looking a little pale, I thought – and we found ourselves confronting a committee of four men and four women and, behind the desk, John Kent.

John Kent, as I soon came to learn, was a local 'character'. Everyone knew him. He was chairman of the Willesden bench of magistrates and the best, the police said, they ever had. He was short and bespectacled and wore a black hat perched defiantly on the back of his head. He had a ve-ry . . . er . . . de-liberate way of . . . er . . . speaking. 'And now perhaps,' he was saying, 'you will be so good as to in-form us why it is that you seek to be the Member of Parl-i-ay-ment for Acton.' This was not too formidable a problem since in Walter Mitty fashion I had already made the speech many dozens of times, little crediting that it would ever come to be delivered. I made, perhaps, a telling point in saying that it was not so much this election that mattered, since whoever they chose could only do his best in the time available, but the next one, when the full weight of the left-wing political machine would be turned upon us, and that it was for this that we must prepare. At any rate I had my say and answered their questions and felt that we had had a fair and friendly hearing. So the committee went off to their suppers and my wife and I crossed to the King's Head to bolster morale and celebrate the fact that, come what might, we had achieved the short list and a number of eminent gentlemen had not. We could hardly expect to be at the top of the list. But on the other hand I did not see why we should be completely at the bottom. We went our respective ways, my wife back to the night shift at the BBC and I to Anti-Aircraft Command, trying to keep my mind from day-dreaming on what might happen if the chance in a thousand turned up. I had not, of course, told a soul what I was up to.

It was late on Saturday evening and I had just potted the last black in a game of snooker when I was called to the mess telephone to speak to a caller who gave no name. It was Twidell.

'Congratulations,' he said. 'Unanimous.'

In the little telephone box the world suddenly seemed to stand still. There was a long pause.

'Why, didn't you expect it?' said Twidell. 'When can you start? Can you come over on Monday morning?'

The implications of what I had undertaken began to dawn on me and, as people do at points of crisis in their own little affairs, I wanted to be alone. I wandered out into the rose garden and gazed across the fields lying peaceful in the moonlight below. Even today I can remember how awed I felt. It was no good passing it off in the good old English way with: 'Oh, it's nothing.' It was tremendous. Gradually the mood passed and a certain confidence took its place. If the selection committee had made a blunder, let them take the blame. *Caveat emptor!* Meanwhile, by God, I would show them they hadn't. I returned to the mess to reveal my strange secret and order drinks all round, while a small nagging voice in the back of the head kept asking, 'Who's going to tell which General in the morning?'

Fortunately there were experts in our headquarters who had these things at their fingertips and within two days permission had reached us by special messenger that the Army Council were agreeable to this comparatively lowly employee standing for Parliament, and on Monday I duly reported for duty.

The little shop had been transformed into an office and a tremendous air of hustle and bustle – I will not say confusion – prevailed. Envelopes had appeared by the thousand and volunteers, mostly women, were busy at trestle tables addressing them from pages torn from the voting register. I was introduced to innumerable folk who wished me well, and whose names I did my best to memorize. I was the object of much critical, though I am sure friendly, scrutiny, and felt rather like the 'condemned man'.

It does not take you long, when you are a parliamentary candidate for the first time, to realize that, though you may technically be the central figure in the picture, you are, in fact, small fry beside the agent. He is the real master of ceremonies. He alone knows the tricks of the trade, the organization, the cost, the procedure. There are many pitfalls into which the candidate may unwittingly fall, from casually buying a beer for a voter in a pub (which is sufficient to disqualify him) to failing to produce various documents at the right time at the Town Hall. The agent is not only the candidate's guide, philosopher, and friend, but a combination of bodyguard, nursemaid, and manager as well. When disaster seems to threaten, he encourages his man with tales of hideous things which occurred at previous elections within his experience – and yet his man got in. If his man appears to be verging on the over-confident, he applies the corresponding antidote. He stands between his man and a stream of visitors and deputations, advising him which to see and which are no good to him.

I am not sure it is not merely sentimental gratitude that makes me feel to this day that Twidell, who, alas, died some years ago, must have been one of the best agents in the country. It was his twenty-second election and it was comforting to think that he had lost only two. His comfortable figure and walrus moustache, surmounted by a villainous felt hat, gave him a wonderful air of solidity and confidence. Whatever went wrong, he had always known worse.

There were at first ten candidates in the field. Though it was obvious that many of them would not eventually, in racing parlance, come under the starter's orders, this fact was very useful in attracting the notice of the press to the election. One candidate was a Mr Owen. I forget what he stood for – I am not sure that he did not claim to represent the old-age pensioners – but he was a curious and entertaining figure and added much to the gaiety of the proceedings by walking about with a crate-like affair on his head, plastered with bills. With a faithful hound at his heels he marched rapidly about the streets, handing out tracts. In the local press he inserted odd advertisements advising the people of Acton to: *Store Potatoes Now. Under the Bed is a Good Place.*

In the end, the field resolved itself into four: Walter Padley, a twenty-seven-year-old 'political organizer' of the Independent Labour Party, which held that we were fighting a 'capitalist-imperialist' war and it was therefore no concern of theirs; Miss Dorothy Crisp, whose vigorous articles in the *Sunday Dispatch* had been attracting notice (though not, perhaps, so much as she had banked upon); Edward Godfrey, who proclaimed himself a 'British Nationalist'; and myself.

Miss Crisp, a lady with a ready pen and a lively intelligence, had been one of the unsuccessful applicants for the honour that had eventually fallen to me and it seemed to be accepting defeat with a rather ill grace when she decided to stand as an 'Independent Conservative'. We felt rather badly about this at the time, and, as she lived in the May Fair Hotel, I permitted myself to refer to her, ungallantly but with a certain degree of wit, as 'the nightingale from Berkeley Square who wants to sing in Acton'. In the *Star* she had said: 'I have very definite ideas on how this country should be run, and I must put them over or burst.' We determined that it should be the latter.

These were the four who turned up at the town hall on nomination day, accompanied by their agents and armed with their nomination papers and their £150 deposits. No cheques are accepted, and you have to bring the money in cash – though I noticed that it was returned by cheque! To get it back you have to poll one-eighth of the total votes cast.

We held meetings, of course, and various eminent personages came down to address themselves to virtually empty halls in the blackout, but the main weapon was the election address, with myself on the front, my wife and two children on the back and the text in the middle, the latter being described by Beverley Baxter, MP, I am glad to recall, as a 'brisk and vigorous Tory document'. The local press gave everyone a fair crack of the whip and, it being a by-election all on its own and not too far from Fleet Street, we got quite a show in the London papers too. One of them made all sorts of speculation on who had been my 'backer', which was irritating, seeing that I had done it all on my own, and Padley went so far as to circulate pamphlets revealing that I was the 'nominee of the anti-Russian Fascist, Lord Brabazon'. Later I arrived to see that he had plastered the constituency with posters informing the voters that: *Longhurst feasted with the Nazis. Millions of bottles of champagne, etc* . . . Good Lord, I thought. When was that? It turned out that he had got hold of my inoffensive book of reminiscences *It Was Good While It Lasted* – and I bet he got it from the public library – and lifted some stuff about my having been taken to see Karl Henkel's cellars at Wiesbaden while defending my golf title at Bad Ems. All this shook me at the time, but William Barkley wrote a good lampoon in the *Daily Express* on the theme 'Oh that mine enemy might write a book', and perhaps it did no great harm. A ——'s trick, though, all the same. They always say

politics is a dirty game but I never saw, and still don't see, why it
has to be.

We had some rather splendid posters, with such slogans as
Churchill has been to Persia for you. What will you do for him?, the
answer being of course to vote for Longhurst, and we also, at first
to my great embarrassment, toured the constituency with a
suitably decorated loudspeaker van, which at first I thought a
gross invasion of privacy. Twidell, setting me down at the Western
Avenue roundabout, told me to get out and get on with it, and I
never to this day pass the fruit shop at whose queue I delivered my
first harangue without a vaguely guilty conscience. Last time I did
so it was in company with none other than Arnold Palmer, who
seemed suitably amused. Soon, however, the heart hardened and
I needed no prodding from Twidell to 'give them a last shout
before we go home'. What we liked best was to catch them in a
queue. The technique was to stop up-wind and deliver at a range
of about fifty yards. They could not fail to hear. They could not
answer back, and they could not, it being wartime, afford to lose
their place in the queue. They might shuffle a bit and pretend not
to notice, but there was nothing they could do. We came to know
what time of day the most profitable queues were liable to form and
where, and shamelessly acted accordingly. For years afterwards
if I saw a nice long queue it seemed a pity not to get up-wind and
give it a few of the well chosen.

Many of our posters had the doubtful advantage of bearing a
large reproduction of the candidate's photograph. We were pasting
the first one up proudly outside the office when a lady passed by
with a perambulator. She stopped and gazed.

'Bin all right if they'd left the face orf!' she said, and passed on.

Then there were window cards and what the agents, in their
hardhearted way, call 'throw-away cards'. The former are hung
in the front window by supporters, and a warming sight it is to
see a road nicely 'hung' with your own cards. It is, however, a
short-lived satisfaction, as the next road is almost certain to be
festooned with those of your opponents. The 'throw-aways' are
about the size of playing-cards and carry the candidate's photograph, together with a simple exhortation to the recipient to vote
for him. They are handed to all and sundry at all times.

Children were particularly keen on these cards and crowded
round to receive them. We were gratified at their early interest in

the government of their country and used to tell them to take the cards home to Mum and Dad. One evening a most respectable citizen appeared and asked for me. He was flourishing a throw-away card.

'Are you aware, sir,' he said, 'that this card was brought by a boy to 44 — — Gardens this evening?'

I said that I was not, but that it was more than likely. He had taken the card, it seemed, and the following had ensued.

'Penny, please.'

The gentleman handed over the penny (they say there is one born every minute!).

'By the way, where does the money go?'

'Oh, it goes to 'Enry Long'urst.'

'Oh, and what does he do with it?'

'Er . . . he takes it to the bank.'

I wonder where that boy is now. A millionaire property tycoon, I dare say, or in some maximum-security wing.

One evening there was the little matter of our bills being pasted over with those of one of our rivals. Our bill-poster, a man with only one arm but a wide vocabulary, was almost speechless with fury. 'There won't be one there tomorrow,' he kept muttering, 'there won't be one there tomorrow!' Late that night he reappeared. 'Come outside,' he said. In the back of his van was a four-foot heap of bills, still limp and sticky. When dawn came, we held the field again.

An election is, for the candidate, like a horse race, in that he must time himself to run strongly right through to the end, after which it does not matter if he almost drops dead, and this I certainly did. At long last, at nine o'clock, the last ballot-paper was in, the ballot-boxes were sealed and carted away, and we retired for refreshment, satisfied that no further efforts on anyone's part could alter our fate.

Next morning we all presented ourselves – candidates, wives, agents, supporters, officials, and hangers-on – at the Central Hall to witness the counting of the votes. The black ballot-boxes with their pink ribbons and seals were stacked on one side of the hall, and round the edges, horseshoe fashion, was a line of trestle tables. Admission is by ticket only, and, once you are in, you are not allowed to leave. The counters of the votes sit on the inside of the horseshoe, and the 'scrutinizers', to see fair play, watch them from the other side. The candidates, avoiding each other at first, peer over the shoulders of the counters with an air of disinterested confidence to see how their respective piles are growing. They come to know how the prisoner feels as he waits in his cell when the jury have retired to consider their verdict!

A really close count must be a nightmare: a recount sheer mental murder. For myself I missed a certain amount of thrill because I developed the symptoms of incipient 'flu – the dullness of mind, the general apathy, and what they call in the north a 'thrutched-up' feeling in the head. Even so, it was exciting enough. Peering over the shoulders of a counter as he sorts the papers, you see *Longhurst, Longhurst, Longhurst, Longhurst,* and make a mental note how satisfactory it is to stand in a constituency of such enlightened citizens. Wandering further, you see *Padley, Crisp, Padley, Padley, Godfrey, Padley,* and wonder what can be the future of England under a democracy composed, it would appear, wholly of illiterates.

As the piles grow, they are sorted into bundles of fifty and placed on a table in the centre, and here is the real weather-gauge of the candidates' fortunes. They have the right to go through the piles, searching for papers wrongly inserted, but the chances are just as strong that you will find one of somebody else's in your pile as one of yours in somebody else's, and it is on the whole a profitless business. Both Twidell, however, and Padley's bearded agent appeared to think it worth while and spent much time in ferreting about among each other's piles with ill-veiled sneers upon their faces. The only major success, let it be conceded, went to Padley's agent, but it was a two-edged triumph. He found a batch of fifty wrongly included in our quota. Unfortunately they were Crisp's.

I fell into conversation with Godfrey and spent much time with him. For myself I knew nothing about him, though much play had been made (not by me) of his alleged 'Fascist background'. I can only say that he expressed opinions of a strongly forthright English character and we got on well together, linked by a common dislike of Padley and all he stood for, and have in fact from time to time corresponded since. Eventually the ice was broken with Miss Crisp, too, and even my wife was soon talking in an animated and amiable way with her. Godfrey, Crisp, and Longhurst, for all their political differences, at least had it in common that they believed it to be 'their' war.

As the piles began to mass on the centre table, we gradually took the lead. There were checks and set-backs, but we kept ahead and with a furlong to go, so to speak, it was pretty clear that only some hideous disaster could keep us out. Twidell, bustling round and making extraordinary and inaccurate calculations on the backs of envelopes, reached the stage of forecasting not the result but the majority, while I disappeared periodically behind a curtain to fortify myself with a swig from a bottle of influenza mixture. Padley was running a clear second, but Miss Crisp was upsetting the book of form by amassing a very small total beside what we, and indeed she herself, had had cause to forecast. Godfrey was clearly due to forfeit his deposit.

The instructions to voters in every polling-booth were plain, one would have thought, beyond the powers of a lunatic to misunderstand. You put one cross on your paper, and only one. Yet a steady flow of spoiled or doubtful papers was trickling along to the town clerk's table, a hundred or more. Some had two crosses against one name. Some had crosses against different names. One or two had crosses against three names, while others had no mark whatever. One wondered what was the mentality of the individual who traipsed all the way to a polling-station on a miserable December day to insert a blank paper in a ballot-box.

Not all were disqualified. We assembled to watch the town clerk, as recording officer, adjudicate upon 'doubtfuls'. He allowed the ones with two crosses against one name, disqualified others. 'Good for Padley,' he would say. 'Bad. Good for Longhurst. Good for Crisp. Bad . . .'

The result had become virtually a certainty, though the count was by no means over (I reckoned that we were 'dormy'), when a reporter from one of the news agencies came and asked for a 'message' on my victory. 'Not on your life!' I said, touching wood hastily. He argued and cajoled, and, knowing his problem from personal experience, I eventually agreed, pledging him under all manner of forfeits not only to hold the message till the result was announced but, in the event of my losing, never to reveal to a soul that I had issued a message at all. I dictated in a quiet corner a message about 'this splendid majority being Acton's Christmas present to Mr Churchill. . . .'

At last it was all over. I shook hands with the sheriff, Sir John Catlow, who was to announce the result.

'Delighted to come along,' he said. 'As a matter of fact, it has got me off a hanging!'

He mounted the platform, followed by the town clerk and the candidates, and rather as one in a dream I took the winner's traditional place, amid some friendly cheers, on his right hand. Padley, as runner-up, sat on his left, and beyond him Miss Crisp and Godfrey, each of whom had lost their £150. I recall the unworthy thought passing through my head that it was a pity these affairs were not run on the basis of 'winner take all!'

Sir John Catlow announced that there had been an election in the Acton Division of Middlesex and that the following was the result:

Longhurst	5,014
Padley	2,336
Crisp	707
Godfrey	258
Majority	2,678

I made a short speech, thanking the various folk who had done the work of organizing the election – not forgetting the police who had stood guarding the polling-booths with a purely impartial air in the perishing cold – and Padley said he was glad there was such a good minority in Acton in favour of 'international Socialism'. We came down from the platform, and there was much hand-shaking and patting on the back for my wife and myself from well-wishers, whose congratulations were all the more acceptable for the fact that they had only known us for three weeks. Twidell said he had 'never had a moment's doubt', and John Kent wore a suitably truculent air as though challenging any man to question the result. For myself, I felt I could sleep for twenty-four hours.

As we left the hall, Miss Crisp and I cordially shook hands, while Padley and a group of young gentlemen with long hair and coloured scarves were engaged in singing 'The Red Flag'. Even in the hour of triumph, I fear that my heart did not warm to them and, though in a later Socialist administration Padley became one of Her Majesty's ministers, he never quite succeeded in becoming one of my favourite characters.

18
Hon. and Gallant

On the morning of 16 December 1943, I presented myself at the St Stephen's entrance of the Palace of Westminster, accompanied by my wife in her best flowered hat, to be greeted by a policeman and photographer. On my remarking to the former that he must be getting used to this sort of thing, he said, 'Oh yes, sir. Must have done it a couple of hundred times by now.' We marched along St Stephen's Hall, under which Guy Fawkes manipulated his unsuccessful gunpowder treason and plot, and with a hasty glance at the statues of Charles James Fox, Pitt and others I fortified myself with the thought that they too were new boys in their day. I was directed to the Whips' Office, where there awaited the usual kindly welcome and my Writ. The Writ to the new Member is what the ring is to the best man at a wedding. It was only a document showing that there had been a by-election at Acton and that Henry Carpenter Longhurst had been elected – which would have shaken Uncle James Carpenter! – but it was impressed upon me by everyone I met that I was as nothing without it. Like the best man with the ring, I put it for safety's sake in a pocket I do not habitually use and then every few minutes clutched feverishly at the ones I did, found that it wasn't there, concluded I had lost it, found it in the special pocket, transferred it to another one, and so on.

My sponsors were the Chief Whip, James Stuart, who later became Lord Stuart of Findhorn, and Peter Thorneycroft, now also ennobled, and soon we were duly assembled on the big red settee at the end of the chamber, which is technically outside the House, waiting for our cue. Mr Attlee got up and said, 'I have a statement to make to the House,' and read out the dramatic news of Churchill's illness, and then, as something of an anti-climax, I fear, the Speaker, a remote figure in long grey wig at the far end of the chamber, rose and said, 'Members wishing to take their seats will now come to the table.' We advanced to the bar and formed ourselves up, 'Bow,' whispered the Chief Whip out of the corner of his mouth. We bowed, took a smart pace forward with the left foot and, I like to think, performed the drill in true military fashion. Two sets of seven paces and three bows got us duly to the table, where the sponsors fade away and you are left all alone in the world, trying to take in all at once a series of pictures and emotions that can only come once in a lifetime. The clerk at the table, taking my precious Writ, proferred a Testament and a rather frayed copy of the Oath and, holding one in each hand, I remember reading – I don't really, but have looked it up – 'I, Henry Carpenter Longhurst, do swear, That I will be faithful and bear true Allegiance to His Majesty King George, His Heirs and Successors, according to the Law.' I do, however, remember stepping over a series of distinguished ankles protruding from the front bench, including Mr Eden's, and signing a big vellum book at the top of a new page, accompanied by the traditional welcoming cries of 'Hear, hear' from both sides, together with a few muttered undertones of 'Who is it?', and a moment later Speaker Clifton Brown leaning down from his high chair to shake hands with another smile of welcome. I made my way out into the lobby and another world.

To a gregarious person like myself life in the House of Commons in those days was heaven. I should never have made a good minister but I should, I like to think, have made what they call a 'good House of Commons man'. Of course, the humblest Member, the newest new-boy, is at once made to realize that he is something of a fellow, from the moment when the policeman, by some extraordinary sense recognizing him at first sight, holds up the traffic to let him cross the road, and constant repetition of 'We are privileged to have with us here tonight . . .' is liable to go to anyone's head, though I can honestly say I do not think it went to mine. The danger is not so much of becoming swollen-headed as of becoming something much worse, namely a bore to one's friends outside, to whom the mystique and the business of the day mean less than nothing, and this I regret to confess that to a certain extent I did.

One of Lord Brabazor's sayings was 'Always try and get it on the file *going down*', and herein lies another of the great privileges of a Member of Parliament, that of direct access, of getting it on the file going down instead of on an obscure file fighting to make its way up. Matters raised by a Member of Parliament, however stupid – the matter, I mean, not the Member, though the latter may also qualify from time to time – have a special tag attached to them and go down through a ministry like the proverbial dose of salts. Other and more important things can wait, but get this one out of this office *now*! To anyone who has been messed about by the faceless ones and feels strongly about it the privilege of getting it on the file going down is supremely satisfying. There was also a nice unspoken slant to it, in that you could hint, without being able to be taken up on it, that, if nothing were able to be done by the ministry in this particular matter, you would understand and nothing further would be heard about it. On the other hand it was equally possible to make it plain in the most honeyed terms that, if they didn't bloody well do something about this one, and quick, you would never let it drop. In most cases the Man in the Ministry, who, of course, had never heard of the matter, was grateful to you for drawing it to his attention and only too anxious to help.

Perhaps I may quote one case of the 'never let it drop' category because it gives me so much satisfaction even to this day. One of my constituents, of what would then have been known as a working-class family, wrote me a pathetic letter, as a result of which I went down to see him and his wife that same day. They were a most worthy couple and the wife was still red-eyed with weeping. It was their son. Ever since he was old enough he had been in the sea cadets. He had done well and had long been promised a place in the Fleet Air Arm. When the time of his call-up arrived, he found himself directed to the coal mines. He protested, but of course he could only get it on the file going up. Impersonal answers came back redirecting him to the mines. Not unnaturally he refused. So now, believe it or not, they had actually clapped him in Wormwood Scrubs. In a respectable working-class home these things count for more than in some of those higher in the social scale, many of whose members have seen, and many more ought to have seen, the interior of the Scrubs. The parents were heartbroken, would never be able to lift their heads up in front of the neighbours again, and so on. I was deeply affected by all this. The lad may have been technically in the wrong, but to clap him in the Scrubs, no! I returned to London, telephoned the Home Office, intimated the 'never let it drop' character of the case – and the boy was out by nightfall. I had got it on the file going down. And if by chance he should read this, let him write and let me know what has happened to him over the ensuing twenty-five years.

When the House of Commons chamber was destroyed in the Blitz, the Commons moved to the Lords, which is exactly similar. There was some talk of rebuilding the Commons in a 'lecture theatre' form but this was firmly stamped on by Churchill, a 'good House of Commons man' if ever there was one, so that one of the first impressions of the new boy is of sitting directly opposite one's opponents, open to every jibe, snigger and hostile glare, and with nowhere to put your papers. A lecture theatre with a desk for each of six-hundred-odd members would have killed this stone dead. Again the 'ye olde' Gothic architecture, the rabbit warren of passages and committee rooms, the impossibility for a week or two of finding any one of the skilfully concealed lavatories, the sudden emergence through some dingy door onto the terrace and the breath-taking view over the water to Westminster Bridge – what would the Palace of Westminster be if they had put it, say, in Piccadilly? – all gave life therein a quality completely unique. When the flying bombs came, we were moved almost overnight to Church House, a modern building round the corner, and in an instant the atmosphere was gone.

I suppose the basis of the much quoted 'best club in London' theme is the Smoking Room, to which, as what Dr Johnson described as a 'clubable' man, I found myself at once attracted. Here, overlooking the Thames, our wants were attended to by Mr Collins and Mr Wright and here were to be found not only birds of my own feather but many of more glorious plumage, including from time to time for a nourishing brandy the Great Man himself. It being an inflexible tradition that comment in the Smoking Room is sacrosanct, I resist only with the greatest difficulty quoting what he said one morning about people who come down to the House to make an apology. Many of the less 'clubable' members affected to despise the Smoking Room, and what they called the 'Smoking Room vote', though I never knew quite what this meant, and I used sometimes to feel guilty qualms about enjoying it and the company so much, but my conscience has at last been completely relieved by the opinions expressed in his auto-biography by my hero among 'ordinary' members, A. P. Herbert. Hardly a man, perhaps, to call 'ordinary'. Poet, writer, dramatist,

humanist, wit and a great Member of Parliament, beloved, and as
an opponent feared, by all, he slipped in for Oxford University in
1935 by means of a brilliant election address, of which, until a
grandchild recently destroyed it, I possessed a copy. It contained
such gems as '*Agriculture*: I know nothing of Agriculture', and is
now very much a collector's piece. I can still never quite forgive
the Socialists for spitefully abolishing the university seats, thus
depriving the House of Commons of A. P. Herbert and, in effect,
of all independent members. Still, it has served them right in the
end, for, though in those days no university ever returned a
Socialist, nowadays none of them would return anything else.

I am afraid I cannot claim to have made any great impact in
parliamentary life, but then one was not really meant to. In the
wartime coalition all that was required was one's support of the
Churchill Government, which I rendered with regularity and
enthusiasm. I did at least surmount the hurdle of making my
maiden speech, when I managed to 'get in' in a two-day debate on
foreign affairs. It was all about the inadequate manner in which we
let the rest of the world, particularly the United States, know what
Britain and the Empire were doing in the war, a subject on which
I felt patriotically earnest at the time. For your maiden speech
you get due warning – and never again – as to when the Speaker
hopes to call you; nobody interrupts; and the next speaker has by
tradition to say that rarely have they listened to a more promising
oration, etcetera, all of which is very comforting and civilized but
does not alter the fact that, if anyone tells you he sat there wholly
at ease, looking forward to the moment when the Speaker would
call upon him to make his maiden speech, he is a liar of the deepest
dye. My time was to be 'about two o'clock', so that a couple of
cautious pink gins and no lunch seemed indicated. I found a seat
on the third bench below the gangway and almost at once my mind
became a total blank. I had forgotten not only what I was going to
say but what it was going to be about. Something about the
Americans, or something. Another pink gin perhaps? No, no.
The Speaker's eagle eye would detect me. Somebody sat down,
and in a haze I rose, together with numerous others. To my horror
I heard the Speaker utter the fateful words: 'Captain Longhurst.'
Perhaps the shock cleared the brain. At any rate it suddenly all
came back and I remembered what it was that I had wanted to say
and then, for what it was worth, said it. Having just re-read

ACTON DIVISION of THE COUNTY of MIDDLESEX

PARLIAMENTARY ELECTION

Admit *Capt H. C. Longhurst*

to the Counting of Votes

in the Central Hall, Acton Lane, Acton

on 15th DECEMBER, 1943, at 10.30 a.m.

H. C. LOCKYER,
Deputy Acting Returning Officer.

The Declaration of Secrecy must also be produced.

*In the autumn of 1943 I stood as
Conservative candidate for Acton.
In December I went to Central
Hall to witness the count and,
as it turned out, to be elected.*

Hansard of 22 February 1944, I can appreciate why it failed to alter the course of history, nor did our foreign affairs take a sudden upward turn as a result of it. All the same, while it may not have had the distinction of Lord Birkenhead's, at least it was not as big a flop as Disraeli's. Perhaps the best thing about it was that it was over.

There was in those days virtually a one-man opposition in the person of Aneurin Bevan, a born agitator if ever there was one but with whom I had many an amicable drink in the Smoking Room. To get up and oppose Churchill in person ensured that Bevan received fantastically disproportionate publicity and this in the end turned him almost into a legend. It also needed the skin of a rhinoceros. One day Bevan was ranting at Churchill in his high-pitched Welsh voice: 'Is it not a *fact* . . . is it not a *fact* that [whatever it was] . . .' The Old Man let him finish, then slowly rose and, peering across at him over the top of his spectacles, said slowly, 'I should have, ah, conceived it impossible to state the opposite to the truth with, ah, greater precision.' The boys in the lower school cheered as though to say, 'Well done, sir. That's done him, sir.' Most people would have cringed with embarrassment and made some excuse to withdraw. On Bevan it had no effect whatsoever.

I once ventured to challenge the Old Man myself. The real 'forgotten army' was not that in Burma but what was known as 'Paiforce' or PAIC – Persia and Iraq Command – who were serving in the most appalling conditions: one bottle of beer a month; no hope of leave; sandfly fever, which is so depressing that a guard had to be mounted over the victims in case they laid hands on a rifle and did away with themselves; the lot. There was a joke about a general inspecting a troop of men, including one with straw sticking out of his ears and a pith helmet on his head upside down, and saying, 'Which of you men has been two and three-quarter years in Paiforce?' This made a splendid cartoon in a Sunday paper for whom I wrote an article about these forgotten men, having just toured round Persia and Iraq and seen the conditions under which they were serving. When the medals (on which a great many people set much store) were being dished out after the war, I discovered that Paiforce were to receive the same recognition as a home-based firewatcher. The only person to whom a Question could properly be put down was the Prime Minister, so I made so bold as to do so. The real sting of such a Question lies, of course, not in the Question itself but in the Supplementary with which the questioner proposes to follow it and, when the original Question had been duly brushed off, I came back with: 'Is it not grotesque that men whose conditions of service have ranged from temperatures of 120 degrees in the shade to being dug out of the snow, dead, should receive the same reward as a lady firewatcher in Blackpool?' The old man turned round to where the voice had come from, with a fierce 'Who the devil are you?' glare, but there were a few encouraging 'Hear, hears' and I felt, so help me, that I might almost be one up. Whereupon he got up and said, 'I don't think we need, ah, bring Blackpool into it.' Mingled cheers and laughter; collapse of junior Member. And why? Because the Labour party had just finished their conference in Blackpool. Crafty old ——! Of course, had I been Bevan I should have stood my ground and said, 'And now, sir, could we perhaps have a serious answer to a serious question?' which would at once have put even Churchill on the defensive. My nerve failed, however, and so, come to that, might yours have done. And now I cannot even remember whether Paiforce got their medal.

I did once have rather better luck with Aneurin Bevan, though not without a few hours of acute embarrassment. He was ranting and raving about something or other, I forget exactly what but it was clearly a load of rubbish, when, almost before I knew it, I found myself standing up and saying, 'Perhaps that was when the hon. gentleman said the Russians could win the war in a week?' He stopped in his tracks but, being one of the most practised debaters in Parliamentary history, rallied immediately and declared that he had never said any such thing or, if he had, when was it? And was he not entitled to demand that the hon. and gallant gentleman should either furnish proof or apologize? One or two of his Clydeside allies also jumped up and rubbed in the 'Apologize or else'. I felt acutely embarrassed and it was not long before I was wishing I had kept my mouth shut. The fact of the matter was that some time previously I had been sitting in the Library opposite Quintin Hogg when he had looked up and said, 'Listen to this.' 'This' proved to be a quotation from Hansard, in which Bevan, criticizing, as usual, the higher direction of the war, had sneered, 'The Russians would win the war in a week.' This sort of thing was among his less endearing characteristics and it had stuck in my mind, so that, before I knew what I was doing, I had blurted

it out. Now I had to slink out and search through *Hansard* to see
if I could find it. If not, I should have to go back and make a public
apology. Quintin Hogg, it appeared, was somewhere in his Oxford
constituency and I rang all round the county to try and find him.
No luck, so there was nothing for it but a search in five years' back
numbers of *Hansard*. The clock ticked on and there was hardly
half an hour left before the House rose when I found it. I forget
the year but I know the date was Guy Fawkes' Day, so I was able
to make something of the 'damp squib' theme. The Speaker duly
called 'Captain Longhurst' and I succeeded, I like to think, in
putting a suitably apologetic face on it for a while before extracting
the evidence from my pocket and reading it out, with appropriate
emphasis on the date. Bevan leapt to his feet and cried that he never
said the Russians *would* win the war in a week, he said the Russians
could win the war in a week, etcetera, etcetera. Or maybe it was the
other way round: not that it made any difference. I got a sympathetic cheer and walked an inch or two higher as I made my way
to the Smoking Room.

Looking back, I find that the comparison between being a
Member and being back at school remains as true in the memory
as it seemed at the time: sometimes the Lower Third on a particularly bad day under a timid master; at others rising to emotional
heights which you know will be with you for ever. I never cease
to be thankful that my own brief sojourn included what must
surely be the greatest single Parliamentary occasion in the past
fifty years, and I would not sell the memory for anything you
cared to offer. I wonder indeed what one would have been offered
for a seat on 8 May 1945, when Churchill was due to come in and
announce that the war with Germany was over? It was a brilliant
summer's day, just like those golden days which had made England
seem so worth defending when we had awaited invasion five years
before. The House holds, I believe, about three hundred of its
six-hundred-odd members, though you can squat in the gangways
or even sit one on top of the other, as members have been known
to do, like broody hens, when disputing each other's right to a
particular place, or you can stand behind the Speaker's Chair or
behind the Bar, technically outside the Chamber. On the great
day I managed to squash into one of the gangways, gazing round
with awe and imprinting the scene on my mind. When he arrives,
I thought to myself, I shall stand and cheer myself hoarse. It was

not for nearly half an hour, however, that he did so and in the meantime someone had to keep the pot boiling. This was brilliantly done by my hero, A. P. Herbert, who, in addition to his other accomplishments, had acquired a complete mastery over the incredibly complicated Procedure of Parliament.

At long last there came a stir among the crowd behind the Speaker's chair, the crowd parted, and through it emerged the architect of victory, looking strangely solemn, emotionally moved no doubt by the stupendous welcome he had just received in Parliament Square, which was the cause of the delay. We all stood up (except, believe it or not, Aneurin Bevan, who remained obstinately seated) and a great cheer went up. Not, however, from me. I waved my order paper but being, like the great man himself, easily moved to tears, I now could hardly see, let alone cheer.

The Prime Minister advanced slowly to the Table, made the announcement that the war against Germany was over, and then in the very words used by Lloyd George in 1919, moved: 'That this House do now attend at the Church of St Margaret, Westminster, to give humble and reverent thanks to Almighty God for our deliverance from the threat of German domination.'

So after a while we all filed out into the sunshine, the comparison with school being even at this historic moment irresistible, the Speaker leading the way, followed by the headmaster and the deputy headmaster and the senior masters and the junior masters, followed in turn by the prefects and the senior boys and then, among them my lowly self, the junior boys. How fortunate that none suspected at this supreme moment how many of them were within a month or two to be expelled!

The sun blazed down as we filed slowly through the huge crowd and into the dim interior of St Margaret's, where we made our way into pews appropriate to our standing. I have before me, as I write, the Order of Service and I can see it clearly. At the time, however, I could not begin to read the words, let alone trust myself to sing. Up in the front pew, however, one could distinctly hear Churchill letting himself go with 'Land of Hope and Glory'. We were duly blessed by the House of Commons chaplain, Canon Don, and emerged again into the sunshine and for many of us, including my humble self, political oblivion. Never mind, I was there once, and many a better man would give much to be able to say the same.

19
Farewell
to Westminster

The General Election of 1945 remains one of the most extraordinary, I suppose, in Parliamentary history, if only because of
the Service vote. I naturally thought it a pity, and still do, that
the Labour Party did not have the grace to leave it to the Churchill
Government to finish off the war, but there it was. What made the
election unique was the fact that the ballot at home was held in the
ordinary way but the ballot-boxes were then sealed away not
overnight but for three weeks, while the votes of men serving in
distant parts of the world were collected and brought home. There
was, therefore, a three-week period when now, if ever, the opinion
polls and the forecasters could assess the result, since everyone
knew not merely how they would vote but how they actually had
voted. The service votes, even if every one were returned, which
of course they weren't, could not come to more than ten per cent
of the whole. The fact is that the forecasters got it even more
wildly wrong than in 1970 and no one had the slightest inkling of
the result. Sometimes, surrounded by supporters and fortified by
a little refreshment, I thought that we might be in by perhaps a
couple of thousand. At others I thought we might be out by as
many, and the Labour Party thought just about the same.

The election itself had its lighter moments. I enjoyed the lively
meetings, as against the dismal by-election affairs in the black-out,
with 'the boys' gathered at the back, barracking and putting the
set-piece questions about Mrs Churchill's gardener, who was
alleged to be underpaid, and tied cottages – the latter a long-hop
to leg since one simply replied, 'No, no. I think that if Mr Attlee
wins this election he must go into No. 10' – but the underlying
bitterness and hate, engendered particularly by the shop-stewards
of the great engineering works of Napier's, whom even at a range
of twenty-five years I look cheerfully back upon, with two

honourable exceptions, as the biggest lot of so-and-sos I ever came across in my life, was a little hard to bear. Nothing that one could do would convince workers in this and other factories that the ballot really was secret or persuade them to risk victimization by exhibiting a picture of Churchill in their window, let alone of the notorious imperialist-fascist Longhurst. Having secured Acton's fine town hall for the eve-of-the-poll meeting we had a memorable final flourish, with 1,200 packed inside and late-comers beating on the doors a quarter of an hour before we were due to start. Douglas Bader, just released from a prisoner-of-war camp, came down to speak and even the ranks of Tuscany could scarce forbear to listen for a minute or two, but, after that, babel was let loose and it became what elections must have been like in the 'good old days'. A couple of men took their coats off to each other for a punch-up in the gallery (one of them actually introduced himself to me only a month or two ago!), an elderly and irate lady supporter in the third row hooked a young hooligan round the neck with her umbrella, the din was unceasing, and a good time was had by all, including, truth to tell, the candidate. Even then no one on either side really suspected the result. When the votes at last were counted, however, it was the socialist-communist candidate who appeared on the right of the returning officer on the balcony of the town hall with 19,000, and the imperialist-fascist on the left with 12,500. There seemed little malice in the triumphant cries from down below of 'It was good while it lasted' and 'What's it feel like to be redundant, 'Enry?', but I must say I was sad at heart. It would be idle to deny that a certain unworthy satisfaction came to mind when we heard that an even richer imperialist-fascist in the person of Colonel Mitchell, a vice-chairman of the Conservative party, was 'out' in the neighbouring constituency of Brentford and Chiswick by even more, and finally that we were only one small piece of jetsam cast out on a national tidal wave. Still, I like to think even to this day that, though we left 19,000-odd political enemies, I left very few personal ones and my wife left none at all.

They say that politics make you cynical. Let us rather say realistic. I went in with an almost starry-eyed, crusading sincerity, but the hard truth is that to be effective, within your own modest limits, you have got not only to get in, which I did, but also to stay in, which I didn't. Everything, therefore, spoken, written or performed, has to be judged partly by 'How will it affect the vote?'

You may be forgiven for imagining yourself, before you learn better, addressing great numbers of constituents and putting your intellectually unchallengeable point of view before them for their adult consideration. 'The case I put before you tonight . . .' – to which some reply, 'No, it isn't,' and others, 'You're a ——' Out of perhaps thirty thousand or more the vast majority never meet or see you. A third, perhaps, are committed against you and a third, if you are lucky, for you. By the rest you are swept in or swept out according to the tide of any particular election. I worked extremely hard in Acton, which I could reach in a quarter of an hour from our house in Chelsea, and was incessantly there, if only because I enjoyed it so much. I wrote a column called 'BRASS TACKS by Acton's MP' every week in the local paper and never refused an invitation to meet any society or group of constituents. Better still, my wife became incredibly popular and it would be difficult to estimate how many votes she must have been worth. And, after all that, we were swept out by nearly 7,000. My own estimate is that a hardworking member and a popular wife may between them make a difference of perhaps 3,000 or 4,000 votes and that we should otherwise have been swept out by 10,000 or 12,000. Public meetings as an influence in politics are a thing of the past and you are judged less by the case you put forward than by your leader's appearance on the telly. As to the internal politics of constituency associations, I made the mistake of thinking that these were nothing to do with the Member, or prospective candidate, and that he should steer conscientiously clear of them. The truth proved otherwise. He should keep a close ear to the ground, for the truth is that some sections of the committee are certain to be 'anti' if only to be against the others who are 'pro'.

Still, I did have one little piece of luck. On getting into the House of Commons, I had relinquished my army pay and been temporarily released for civilian employment – I forget the official term. No sooner had I lost my place than within a matter of days I was summoned to report for duty at Woolwich, reverting from captain to second lieutenant. The temporary acting supernumerary unpaid lance-bombardier who was too valuable to release to become a cabinet minister's personal assistant was still much too valuable to release as a second lieutenant now that the war was over. Somewhere in the back of the mind, however, something struck a chord. Had there not been a Question to Ernest Bevin as to whether those released from the services for civilian employment would be called up again after the war, and had he not answered in the negative? I am sure that in doing so he had not ex-Members of Parliament in mind, but never mind. I happened to see Lord Burnham, who was a big shot in matters of this order in the War Office, coming out of the headquarters at the bottom of Grosvenor Gardens, which is now the National Steel Board. I mentioned it to him and thus, for the last time, 'got it on the file going down'. A few days later I had jumped what might have been a very long queue and was reporting at Olympia for my demob. suit – beside a man whom I have just met for the first time since in the Salisbury Club, Rhodesia! Even so, there was a sting in the tail, which still serves to amuse my friends. A little East End tailor, without bothering to measure my manly, military chest, took one look at me, turned over his shoulder to his assistant and said, '42, short, portly'.

Meanwhile in Bedford they had lost the seat to Labour in the person of T. C. Skeffington-Lodge, soon to become known as Spiffington-Dodge but, let me at once say, an extremely nice and cultured man. The margin was 288 and you could find that number any morning in the High Street who had not even troubled to vote. Some friends of mine in the town suggested that I should put my name forward and, having ascertained that the defeated member, Sir Richard Wells, did not intend to carry on, I did so and I think I was justifiably proud in eventually being selected to carry the banner in the next election, whenever it might be. I could not help feeling, too, how proud my father would have been.

Thus, having got in too easily in the first place, I now started all over again at the bottom to serve my political apprenticeship and to do it the hard way. Bedford was both a town and country constituency. The town had a population of more than fifty thousand and there were heaven knows how many villages, still 'truly rural' and not yet become little dormitory towns. As in Acton, the Tory organization had lapsed during the war, whereas the Socialists had kept theirs going, and we had to start pretty well from scratch. Sir Richard Wells, of Charles Wells, the brewers, had been able in more peaceful parliamentary times to enjoy not only the best club in London but a nice old house in the riverside village of Pavenham, but with a living to earn and travels to be undertaken I had to remain in London and keep going down to

Bedford whenever I could. I shudder to think how many dark winter nights we spent in remote villages, trying to find the school and, very often, the caretaker who had not even opened it up. In each village we aimed to raise a chairman, a secretary, a treasurer, and someone to distribute our monthly magazine, the *Gazette*, for which I wrote a powerful piece every month. I have some of them still and really they are not at all bad. In fact, they were circularized by Central Office to quite a number of other constituency magazines. Within a year we had a branch in every village, with an encouraging array of flags on the big wall map in the agent's office, each signifying a village properly 'manned'. Almost every month we had a meeting in the Shire Hall, addressed by some prominent figure who had survived the previous election, to say nothing of the present Lord Hill, not then a Member but known to millions as the Radio Doctor. He drew the biggest crowd I ever saw at a political meeting.

I made the usual speeches myself and had much simple fun with a statistic which I like to think I worked out for myself and which never failed to be greeted with a stunned and incredulous silence. It ran something like this. 'Ladies and gentlemen, I would ask you to imagine a steadily accumulating pile of money, starting with fifty pounds on the day that Christ was born. Every day we put into it another fifty pounds. Every *day*. Every day for a *thousand years*, and we are still sixty-six years short of William the Conqueror. Fifty pounds for every *day* for another five hundred years, till the great and glorious Elizabeth I, when the spirit of Englishmen, etcetera, etcetera . . . Fifty pounds for every day for another three *centuries*, and fifty pounds for every day for sixty years of Queen Victoria, when the spirit of Englishmen once again, etcetera, etcetera . . . Fifty pounds for every day for another fifty years and for good value, ladies and gentlemen, fifty pounds for this very day. And now with this colossal, stupendous pyramid of money, we still have . . . [*pause for effect*] . . . *substantially less than the Socialists lost on groundnuts*.'

This was true. They lost £37,000,000, and I have little doubt that they, and the Tories too, have lost even more in even less probable schemes. It always, however, stopped the show and gentlemen would be seen to be doing hasty sums on the back of an envelope. Nineteen hundred and whatever the year might be, multiplied by 365. And the answer is that, whatever the year, there have not yet been anything like three-quarters of *one* million days since the birth of Christ. At the end of 1970, for instance, ignoring leap years, there had still only been 719,050. So when next you read of the Government of the day having spent or tossed away *x* millions on this or that, just add two noughts and divide by 72 and you have the number of pounds for every day since Christ was born that we have to find for that project this year. It makes you think. Or, if it doesn't, it ought to!

The lot of the prospective candidate, especially if you have once been a Member, is not an easy one. You cannot *do* anything for anyone: you cannot get anything on the file going down. However often you are there, there are always people to say, 'Quite a decent chap, I believe. Such a pity he is never here.' Nor did I ever solve the one about mixing with people, which I enjoy, at, say, the Swan or the Bridge. If you don't, they say you are too full of your own importance to mix with ordinary people. If you do, they say, 'Such a pity he is never out of the pubs.' Nor was the position helped by an item in the *Sunday Express*'s political irritant column signed Crossbencher. Someone had warned me, though I could scarce believe it, that a young fellow had been going round the town asking if anyone knew anything about me and they gathered that he had been sent down by the *Sunday Express* for this specific purpose. Why, I do not to this day know. The item which speaks for itself, reads:

> Who else is in trouble? There is Mr Thomas Cecil Skeffington-Lodge, 44-year-old Socialist who sits for Bedford.
>
> Mr Skeffington-Lodge is concerned about the smallness of the 288 majority with which he won Bedford in 1945. And he is said to be on the scrounge for a safer seat.
>
> I counsel Mr Skeffington-Lodge to stay put. He has good friends in Bedford.
>
> And one of them is his prospective Tory opponent, Mr Henry Longhurst, top rank amateur golfer.
>
> Mr Longhurst is a Tory refugee. He scuttled from Acton after he had lost that seat in 1945.
>
> Now he is active in Bedford. And Bedford socialists say that every time he speaks he wins fresh supporters for Mr Skeffington-Lodge.
>
> Many local Tories agree with him. For they say that their candidate is a bad mixer and has a poor platform manner.

And they say also that while in golf Mr Longhurst's handicap is plus one, in politics it is Mr Henry Longhurst.

Such comment, passed eagerly from one to another all round the constituency, can hardly fail to do harm. It saddened me – especially the 'bad mixer' bit! – and I wondered what manner of man would stoop to find material for his column in such a way.

Meanwhile the Labour party – 'We are the masters now' – had hardly been rising in popularity and soon it became clear that with all the work we had done we were not only likely but virtually certain to reverse a majority of a mere 288. It must have been about three years before it dawned upon me by one of those infinitely slow mental processes that I really was going to be the Member of Parliament for Bedford and I began asking myself, which I might have asked before, what was I going to do when I got in and on what was I going to live? I had taken up with the *Sunday Times* again and was doing a great deal of travelling, regularly to America and twice to the Far East, but a Member of Parliament can hardly remain a golf correspondent. Presumably it would mean joining the business of one of my friends to whom parliamentary contacts would be useful, a not wholly engaging prospect. Furthermore, what had happened once could happen again. I might duly get in and then once again be swept out by forces beyond my control. At long last after months of heart-searching I went down and, out of the blue, resigned. Some, I am sure, were sorry to see me go, and indeed I have their letters still. Others may have sensed that a prophet is not without honour save in his own country. I drove back to London thinking. 'A safe Conservative seat for life and you have thrown it away. You must be the biggest bloody fool in the whole of Britain!' Looking back over my life over the past twenty-odd years, I can see that I did choose a very agreeable road, but I often wonder what would have happened if I had stuck to the other one. I suppose I should be a knight by now, or even a life peer. Lord Wind of Mills, perhaps.

20
Golf
Gives Me Up

When the war was over I took up once more with the *Sunday Times* and in the end it became the main work of my life. Perhaps the best thing that could happen to any writer was the shortage of paper during the years immediately following the war. Indeed, it was this more than anything that made me try to become a 'real' writer at all. Previously it had been a question of stretching it out to twelve hundred words or so. Now it was a case of saying what you had to say in four hundred. 'Taken by and large,' one might once have written, 'it may well be that Oxford will prove to have a slight advantage if the wind blows,' and this would be good for filling out three or four lines. Now one was forced to learn better. 'Taken by and large,' whatever it might mean – and, come to think of it, what does it mean? – could go for a start, and so could 'it may well be'. Further pruning then reduced it to 'Oxford seems better in the wind' and then, as there might be no wind anyway, why not leave it out altogether? Every little counted, even saving half a dozen letters, as in 'try' for 'endeavour', and any bureaucratic type of verbiage and jargon automatically went by the board. The prime example remains, perhaps, 'accommodation units' for 'homes', which Churchill so splendidly shot down with 'accommodation unit, sweet accommodation unit', but I do not think I should ever have been guilty of that. I took to reading the great man with care, for the writing rather than the substance, especially *My Early Life*, which became a constant travelling companion to be read half aloud in aeroplanes. One came to realize that when he wrote: 'Short words are the best and the old words, when short, are the best of all,' not only was he right but he was also making life infinitely easier for anyone who was trying to write decent, clean English. This is a point which I gratefully try to rub in when occasionally invited to present the prizes at a school and therefore to 'oblige with a few words'. I soon came to realize that, like the sentence I have just quoted, nearly all the memorable Churchill 'quotations' are wholly or mainly monosyllabic. 'Never in the whole field of human conflict has so much been owed by so many to so few.' . . . 'Blood, toil, tears and sweat.' . . . 'Give us the tools and we will finish the job.' . . . 'What kind of a people do they think we are?' Of Lord Jellicoe he wrote: 'He was the only man on either side who could lose the war in an afternoon.' Perhaps my favourite, though not of course so well known, has forty-four words, every one of which is a monosyllable, except four of two syllables and one short one of three. It concerned Lord Charles Beresford, of whom Churchill said, 'He was one of those orators who, before they get up, do not know what they are going to say; when they are speaking, do not know what they are saying; and when they have sat down, do not know what they have said.' A notable example of plain, pungent English and a great encouragement to the aspiring essayist, who tends to think that to write well you must inflict the reader with long words and purple passages.

Thus economy of words became quite an art in itself and I am sure that it improved the writing of all upon whom it was forced. I myself came to enjoy this constant lonely battle with words, lonely because no one can help you. You can have ten secretaries, electric typewriters, pens, pencils, pencil-sharpeners, rubber bands, peace and quiet, anything you fancy, and at the end of it all you are still faced with is a blank sheet of paper which you alone can fill and, having done so, have got to admit it was the best you could do. The artist with his blank canvas has at least got something to paint. Another great writer of English, as I see it, is P. G. Wodehouse, and from him I learnt two things, one of them particularly comforting, namely that to write well you did not have to write on a serious subject, so there was no reason why I should not try hard just because I only did little pieces about golf. The other was that good writing *flows*, in other words you may well have the right words but not have them in the right order. Although it is poetry, not prose, the classic example is, of course, 'The ploughman homeward plods his weary way.' There are, I believe, dozens of orders in which the words can be put – but only one right one. However trivial or hilarious the subject, Wodehouse's writing always flows. He used to go over it again and again until it emerged as though he had just tossed it lightly off the pen.

I also came to think of writing as resembling a steak-and-kidney pudding, which, however fine the ingredients, is useless without a dash of salt and mustard, and it seems to me that it may be lack of this salt and mustard which makes the leading articles in the 'heavy' newspapers so sparsely read and practically never quoted. It was this that brought home to me with sudden clarity the blindingly obvious fact that, if it isn't *readable*, people won't read it – at any rate those who, like newspaper readers, don't have to. Instinctively I tried to live up to one of my heroes, the Rev. Sydney Smith, who said, 'I think I never wrote anything very dull in my life.' He was amusing enough company, incidentally, to have caused the great Mrs Sarah Siddons to fall off her chair at dinner with laughing. I have written one or two very dull things and learnt from bitter experience that people will pass one dull paragraph and will probably pass a second but with the third you have lost them. I spent two years of my life battling with a book for British Petroleum and on the first interview said to the then Chairman, the late Sir Neville Gass, one of the nicest and gentlest men who ever drew breath, 'Do you want people actually to read this book?' – bearing in mind that most company histories are distributed to the right quarters but not in fact read. 'Oh yes,' he said, 'we certainly do.' Would he agree, then, before we started, that, if it were not readable, people would not read it? Thus it was most amicably agreed and I set out to render readable what turned out to be in many parts a thrilling story. Alas, when the galley proofs came back, rats in the office had been at the manuscript. I restored my version and sent it back, but the rats must have got at it again, and so the tug of war went on. I mostly won in the end but I mention it largely as an excuse to quote as fine a piece of execrable jargon as ever came my way. I found in a galley proof, proposed to be published under my name, the words: 'It was then decided that the time was ripe for construction to be commenced.' And I had written, 'They decided to begin.' I felt sure that Churchill himself would have been on my side!

At any rate the *Sunday Times* became the mainstay of my life, though I was fortunate enough to have other arrows to my bow, which is a valuable insurance in the precarious world of news-papers, where you never know when you are going to wake up one morning and find you have been taken over. A curious sensa-tion it is, too. 'I wonder how much *I* fetched?' you think to yourself. Your mind goes back to army quartermasters and your old owner and the new haggling over the inventory. Vans, motor, 150; bulbs, electric, 3,200; correspondents, football, association, one; football, rugby, one; cricket, one; golf, one, and so on. 'Oh, don't let's waste time arguing. Give you fifteen million the lot.' In the days after the war, however, when one was owned by Lord Kemsley, all was at peace and those with whom I was brought into contact were quite a little band of brothers, devoted to keeping ahead of the *Observer*. On my rare visits to the office, generally to get free paper, I knew where to find them (I should have to ask the commissionaire now) and they always had time to put down what they were doing and stroll across to the Blue Lion. One week we were overtaken by the *Observer*, a fact which I believe was kept from his lordship, since the figures were only published monthly. Then at the crucial moment came Suez, our rival's attitude cost them 68,000 readers overnight, the month's figures came out right, and the day was saved. However, I know little of these things and have never by the mercy of God been involved in 'office politics'. Nor have I ever been much of a 'journalist' as such, though I was for twenty-six years a member of their union till resigning on purely a matter of principle. I did for a year produce a whole page of strictly non-golfing comment on life in general for the sister paper, the *Daily Sketch*, so perhaps this qualified me as a journalist, but somehow I think not. I still think of myself as an amateur. Nor would I wish ever to be a whole-page columnist again. I used to be cynical at the expense of regular columnists whose attitude to life and people tended to be: 'Is he or she or it worth a paragraph?' If not, they had no time for you. Now I learnt better. No sooner is one page published than you start getting in a panic for the next. The *Sunday Times* flowed on in its own calm way but even then I will admit to the unworthy thought, when some well known golfer passed on to the next world, 'Will he do for Sunday?'

A milestone came up on 19 October 1947, when I wrote a piece about the American-sized ball and the smaller British one (I am doing it still and the controversy will easily outlast me) and referred somewhere to the latter as 'this miserable pellet'. Why not, I said, use this as the heading to the article? No one, golfer or not, could refrain from starting an article headed *This Miserable Pellet*. Then once we had got them started it was my job to get them through to the end. The sports editor, Pat Murphy, a life-long friend as well as colleague, who has now escaped, lucky devil, to the South of France, not only concurred but put the little article in a 'box' in the middle of the back page and there it stayed for a quarter of a century. Week after week I churned it out, passing it off lightly but in fact trying hard with every word, and especially the headlines, often the most difficult part of all, and only a year or two ago it was discovered that I had done twenty-one years without missing a single Sunday, which I believe is a record. Compliments were exchanged, and a lunch was laid on, but per-haps the nicest thing was that the *Observer* allowed their corres-pondent, Peter Dobereiner, to write a very handsome piece, quoting not only my name but that of their principal rival. I am sure it did not lose them a single reader to the *Sunday Times* but so generous a gesture is rare in the jealous world of journalism.

It would be stupidly over-modest to say that the continuity of 'see you same time same place next Sunday' did not manage to collect a goodly company of 'regulars', so regular in their reading habits, in fact, that, when occasionally for technical reasons a report, say, of the Open Championship would occupy a couple of columns with a large headline along the top and my name under it, people would come up and say, 'I see you didn't have anything in on Sunday.' They had got so used to seeing it in its box in the middle that they could not see it anywhere else on the same page. Indeed, I claimed, and still claim, to have been more widely read in the lavatory of a Sunday morning than any other writer on any subject, the reason being not that it was so brilliant but that it was just the right length and did not need folding! Many people, therefore, had already read it when they got to the golf club, so the great object was to give them some anecdote, some little bit of 'salt and mustard', or some absolutely lunatic golfing tip, which they could quote at the bar, thus drawing our efforts to the attention of such philistines as still adhered to other papers.

The *Sunday Times* were always very tolerant with me and I like to think I gave them good value in return. I was permitted, for instance, to put off doing my piece till Saturday, sometimes at a loss for a subject till the early hours of the morning, and then to telephone it – hence some of the rather splendid misprints, though I can say with the utmost honesty, having known them by voice for so many years, 'I think our telephonists are wonderful.' Each

Saturday when I have finished dictating my imperishable piece, one of them habitually says, 'That's it, then. Another one for the shelf!' The best misprint occurred when on account of Easter I had to produce my invaluable contribution by Thursday, which I did this time in my own handwriting. Thus we had, instead of 'the immortal Bobby Jones', 'the immortal Bobby Imes', as a result of which I had by return of post a note from 'Stinker' Murdoch saying, 'I do so enjoy your articles in the *Sunday Tones.*' For myself, I have always enjoyed the correspondence which a regular column brings in from readers. It is flattering that they should trouble to write, and I like to think that I have never let one go unanswered. I have even kept some letters for twenty years before finding an apt moment to quote them. Others, it is true, incline to try the patience – as when, for instance, that venerable figure of the early days of golf Old Tom Morris came out through an obvious telephonic error (on my part, through not spelling it out) as Old Tom Maurice. I hesitate to say how many people wrote to correct this one and it irked me that after all these years they should think I could not spell the old boy's name. The greatest corrective postbag, though, came when I had made reference to places where certain players had fallen upon golfing disasters – Compston at Hoylake, Jurado at Carnoustie, Macdonald Smith at Prestwick, and so on – and suggested that they would be found to have these names written on their hearts 'as Mary Queen of Scots had Calais'. Oh dear, oh dear! When the postman delivered a huge pile of letters on Tuesday, the first one told the common story. It was not, of course, Mary Queen of Scots but Mary Tudor, the Bloody Mary after whom presumably the vodka and tomato juice is named. One letter in particular cut me to the quick. It was from a fellow with whom I had been at St Cyprians. 'What,' he would like to know, 'would Mum Wilkes have said?' I had a pretty good idea, and did not like the sound of it.

The *Sunday Times* made one very sound investment in me which brought dividends to both parties. This was in sending me to America, and sometimes a good deal farther afield, before any of the other papers, daily or Sunday, thought of sending their own correspondents. It was soon obvious that golfing supremacy was going to lie with the Americans and, though one did not want to be always writing about how much money Palmer and Co. were making, interest always lies in the best, wherever it may be. So over I used to go, at a cost of only a few hundred pounds, and each trip could not only be stretched to three Sunday pieces but would furnish background comment later on. There is nothing personal in it if I say that this gave me, and therefore the *Sunday Times*, the edge over all our rivals, who were reduced to writing: 'Judging by all accounts . . .' 'All accounts' was me. For years I had it all to myself, never able to think why the others did not cotton on. For purely golfing events I went not only to many cities in America but to Canada, Buenos Aires, Mexico City, Singapore, and Australia, where I thought that, having got that far, I might as well go the whole way round, taking in New Zealand and visiting my friend George Francis, the one who had the 'four kings and a bloody ace' at Cambridge. I took sixty-eight days going round the world, faithfully sending in my piece each week, and turned it into quite a readable book called *Round in Sixty-Eight*. In America I can look back on events not only around New York but at Boston, Philadelphia, Baltimore, Atlanta, Buffalo, Detroit, Dayton, Chicago, Oklahoma City, Tulsa, Houston, San Francisco and doubtless others that escape the memory. San Francisco is every Englishman's favourite but I am not sure that mine is not Oklahoma City, upon whose background I became, through an inborn fascination with 'the early days', reasonably expert. My mother, for instance, was already aged twelve when they had the famous 'Run' from the Kansas border in 1889, all lined up in a row, some with waggons, some alone, with the sheriff in wide black hat and long black coat starting them off with a pistol. The ones who made the first fortunes, of course, were those who waited and came up in their own time with the beer and the women. Later, however, they discovered that they had put their capital plumb, bang, slam on top of one of the biggest oilfields in the Western hemisphere. Colossal fortunes were made and everyone had a 'nodding donkey' pumping away in his backyard – 'seven times up and down for the oil company, and the eighth for me'. 'Come orn now,' I remember one chap saying to another in the club, 'how many wells yew got? Yew don' *know* how many wells yew got, do yew?' It turned out to be rather more than three hundred. The only trouble was that, having shifted into barren reserves, in the best apartheid fashion, what Indians they did not kill, the white settlers found that they had not reserved to themselves the mineral rights, so the Indians were sitting on oil too. Perhaps the best part was that Oklahoma was still a dry state, with the result that, though I have attended the 'six o'clock swill' in Sydney before the Australian licensing laws began to become civilized, I have never seen so much hard liquor drunk as in Oklahoma. Some people never learn.

We had come on to Oklahoma for the Amateur Championship from a Walker Cup match at a place called Kittansett, with the accent on the middle syllable. The course was right out on a point, leading out from the little New England harbour of Marion, Mass., the home of Tabor Academy, who come over and row at Henley each year. There were no hotels, no tourists, and very few spectators, and we were billeted in members' homes around the course, from which it was possible to step out directly onto the beach and into warm sea water. Nothing, anywhere, offended the eye and the New England architecture made one continually want to stop and do a watercolour. The members turned out to be as nice as their surroundings and I am only one of many out of the British party who have kept in touch with their hosts of eighteen years ago. People often ask me if I could live in America, to which I give a polite negative. I would settle in Marion, however, tomorrow. What other games, I wonder, would let one enjoy an experience like this and call it work?

After the war I continued to play golf myself and quite well at that. Joan Pemberton (as was) and I reached the final of the Worplesdon Foursomes and with Bill Shankland of Potter's Bar, later to be Tony Jacklin's first mentor, I managed to reach the semi-final of the *Daily Telegraph* Foursomes, which was a good performance since neither of us would claim to be at the top of our respective trees. I suppose I must have been scratch for about twenty years and I have no doubt whatever that in my line of country it helped if one got one's name in the paper occasionally as a player. It was also extremely good fun to combine business and pleasure in this way. What I enjoyed most of all, and still do, were the spring and autumn meetings of the Royal and Ancient at St Andrews, and I would as soon have won the King William IV Medal as the English Championship, not that I was ever good enough to win either. People often ask me which is my favourite course and I have no hesitation in saying the Old Course at St Andrews, though anyone who makes the pilgrimage to this golfing Mecca and plays only one round or two, probably among a lot of holiday fourballs taking four hours, is justified in wondering whether those who dote upon it are not either 'saying the right thing' or mad. The Old Course is unique, so far as I know, in that it has no separate fairway for each hole but merely a strip of golfing ground which you share going out with those coming in, even to the extent of having two flags on each green. You thus have all the world to drive into but, unless you take into consideration the wind and the position of the flag and such like, you can find yourself tee-ed up on the fairway with a quite impossible shot to follow, so before every stroke you have to stop and say to yourself, 'Now what exactly is it that I am trying to do?' The more sensitive golfers, not necessarily of any great ability, get the most frightful attacks of nerves before setting forth in the Medal and the situation is not improved by the array of faces staring out through the windows of the Big Room just behind the tee and the certainty, as you try to get your second or third shot over the Swilcan Burn, that you are being observed through the binoculars. I myself have taken 90 – off a then handicap of 5 – which would have been unthinkable on any other occasion. The sense of continuity is a great characteristic of the Medal and one reason why I should so much like to have added my name to the 130-odd people who have won it since His Majesty presented it to the Club. I like to think of them all, for instance, on Medal day, 1861, gazing out of the windows of what was then the Union Parlour and cursing the rain and gale in which they were soon to set out. In those days the life-boat was kept at the mouth of the Swilcan Burn. A rocket announced that a ship was in distress and Maitland Dougall, member of a great naval family and later himself to become an admiral, went down, found them a man short, took the stroke oar, rowed for five hours in the bay, came back, inserted some buckshot in his ball to keep it down against the wind, and won the Medal with a score of 112. How proud one would have been to follow a man like that!

As my travels, writings and broadcasting increased, to say nothing of my age, my golf fell away and it became less and less fun to do progressively more badly something that one had once done reasonably well. I had had every reason to believe that I should turn out in middle age, and even later, to be an accurate and crafty player, always liable to beat an undergraduate, but it was not to be. My swing disintegrated and I became quite pathetically bad. I kept meaning to take myself in hand and go in for a fortnight's serious practice, which I knew was all that was needed, but somehow, with all the travelling about, I never got down to it. If I played on Sunday mornings, I did not enjoy it, and, if I didn't, I had it on my conscience that somehow I ought to be. What settled the problem for me was what we call the twitch and the Americans the 'yips'. This is so ridiculous a disease that non-sufferers can scarcely credit it. It attacks the victim almost always on short putts, though one great professional who might otherwise have beaten the world had it on short pitches. It does not come on all short putts, but you always know in advance when it is coming. You then become totally incapable of moving a piece of ironmongery to and fro without giving at the critical moment a convulsive twitch. Some people simply stab the ground and move the ball a few inches. Others catch it on the twitch and send it shooting past the hole. Bobby Jones has recounted how he was playing with an American professional called Wild Bill Melhorn, who suffered from it, and on one green Melhorn, trying to hole a yard putt, actually putted it off the green and into a bunker. I was reminded only the other day of an occasion I had forgotten when a caddie had said to me, 'I think it would be better if you stroked the ball a bit more, sir,' and I had replied, 'Dammit, you don't think I *mean* to do it like that, do you?' I am, however, in good company. Jones himself got it – he described the sensation as of the ball 'apparently vanishing from sight just as the club was about to strike it'. The great Harry Vardon got it. Sam Snead, still at fifty-seven one of the finest swingers in the game, actually had to take to putting croquet-fashion between the legs. Ben Hogan, the most determined golfer of all time, not excluding Palmer, wanted two par fours for a record fifth US Open and not only missed a yard putt on the 17th but 'yipped' it. 'Once you've had 'em, you've got 'em,' they say, and he was never the same again. The Americans tend rather unkindly to call the affliction 'whiskey fingers', and so it may be with some, but Snead is a lifelong tee-totaller and Vardon was a most abstemious man – though I particularly like his reply to the lady who asked him to sign the pledge: 'Moderation is essential in all things, madam, but never in my life have I been beaten by a teetotaller.'

I am afraid that by constantly writing about it I may have served to spread the disease, in which context I am reminded of my friend and neighbour Tubby Ionides, who incidentally won the Grand National Irish Sweep on Sundew. Some people have only to read about that other ridiculous golf shot, the socket, in which the ball shoots off, knee high, almost at right-angles, to start doing it themselves, yet quite unable to do it on purpose. Confessing to be one such, my friend added, 'I am worse. I am a *carrier.*' So perhaps am I with the twitch. After one piece I had written about it an old Austrian doctor wrote to me from London saying that he knew the answer, so I naturally hurried to see him. The answer, he said, lay in the angle of the right elbow, i.e. neither stretched straight nor fully bent, as in putting, and there may be something in this, for if you stretch your right arm out as far and as stiffly as possible, you can make some sort of stroke at a putt even when the curse is upon you. What really shook me, however, was when he added casually, 'Violinists sometimes get it.' Here we may imagine the twitch in all its full horror. The hushed Albert Hall and the master, as his elbow bends to the fatal angle, giving a sudden and convulsive jerk and nearly sawing the instrument in half, never to play in public again. I was thoughtless enough to tell this to Hogan in Mexico City once and I have an awful fear that it hastened his downfall.

In the end I think they will find it akin to vertigo, or the case of the rabbit and the stoat. The rabbit can do twenty-five miles an hour and the stoat, I suppose, about four, but the rabbit stands paralysed like a man with a four-foot putt. Similarly you could guarantee, drunk or sober, to walk down a road without touching either side, but put the same road, unfenced, over Niagara and you would be on your hands and knees within a few paces. Thus I came one day to the last green in the Medal needing a four for a net 69 and a faint chance of defeating at last one of the most tight-fisted bodies in the world, the handicapping committee of the R and A. My second got on the green, only to roll back into the Valley of Sin, in which one stands at about eye level with the flag. I pitched up and the ball ran so straight that I had time to think, 'By God, it's in! 68!' It stopped just short, a few inches perhaps – but when I got up onto the green the eye had been deceived from down below and it was a yard short. I was standing idly thinking of nothing while my partner holed out when suddenly it came over me. *I can't do it.* I looked at this hideous thing – just like the one you may have seen poor Doug Sanders missing to win, or rather not to win, the 1970 Open on the same green. I stood over it and remember with the utmost clarity thinking that I would willingly lay down a five-pound note on the green not to have to make this putt. Suddenly I found that the putter had shot to and fro and the ball was as far away the other side. I scuttled round and a moment later it had shot by again and we were back where we started. I doubled back, jerked at it again and this time by sheer good fortune it hit the back of the hole, jumped in the air and went in – but even as it disappeared I knew that my golfing days were numbered.

I forget where it happened but in the middle of a round, which I was regarding with the usual distaste, a small voice within me said, 'You don't *have* to do this,' and I thought, 'No, by God, I don't.' A great wave of relief came over me and on D-Day, 1968, I put the clubs up in the loft with the water tanks, closed the hatch, removed the steps and walked away. Nor have I for one second regretted it. I had travelled a long and happy road since we had cut the holes with our penknives on the Common at Yelverton, but now it was rather like having sucked a very good orange dry and realizing that you were eating the peel. Why not chuck it away and try an apple instead? Which is what I did.

21
East of Suez

It is a familiar theme of mine, I am afraid, how one's life is governed by just happening to be standing in a given place at a given moment. Looking back, I suppose I can consider myself a widely travelled fellow, and indeed people often say, 'Where have you just come back from?' or, 'Where are you off to next?' Before the war I had managed a couple of trips to America and a good many to the continent, but wider travels began through my happening to be standing by a window in the House of Commons library, gazing out on the unforgettable prospect of the Thames and Westminster Bridge and thinking of nothing in particular, when a voice beside me said, 'I say. You don't want to go to Persia, do you?' This turned out to be the assistant librarian, Hilary St George Saunders, author of some very fine wartime pamphlets on Bomber Command and such subjects. He had been engaged, it appeared, by the then Anglo-Iranian Oil Company, previously the Anglo-Persian and now BP, to write a book on their wartime activities, which were, as I was to discover, as remarkable as they were unknown. It would require a good deal of rigorous travel, which he had neither the time, nor at that moment the health, to undertake and he was therefore looking for a collaborator. 'It would mean you would have to go to the Persian oilfields, Tehran, Baghdad, Haifa and so on,' he added. I think it was Baghdad, City of a Thousand and One Nights, that settled it, and the result was that I found myself one steel-grey December day in 1944 rolling out from dismal Greenock to join the one-time Cunarder *Nea Hellas*, bound in convoy for Port Said.

It was Churchill, I believe, who said that troopship life was not to be considered as a sea voyage but as a 'form of trench warfare', and indeed hundreds of men live, eat, sleep, and have their being in a low-ceilinged mess deck no bigger than a decent-sized parish hall. Having learnt just in time that the ship would be 'dry', I had prudently concealed a 'bottle of each' and, by strict rationing of one tot morning and evening concealed in mineral water, managed to make it not only last the journey but sustain me in writing, in our crowded mess, 30,000-odd words of *I Wouldn't Have Missed It*. Most writers will confirm, I think, that good work can be done to a constant background buzz of talk and movement, while with two people conversing in the same room nothing can be done at all.

The convoy passed safely and sedately through and it was impossible not to be thrilled with the first sight of Cape Trafalgar and the thought that it might be on this very patch of water that Nelson fought; or with the Rock of Gibraltar; or to have pointed out by some Eighth Army veteran the whereabouts of such historic spots as Benghazi, Derna and Tobruk. The ship at last hove to at the entrance to the Canal, not far from the vast statue of de Lesseps, which bears so little resemblance to Tyrone Power, who took the part in the film, and Port Said, I must say, lived up to its name. I had certainly not been ashore five minutes before an unsavoury individual plucked at my arm with: 'Feelthy pictures?'

I must be one of thousands for whom the railway journey from Port Said to Cairo represents their first glimpse of the Middle East, and it took me some time to identify the chord which it immediately struck in my mind, namely that the whole thing was the illustrations in a child's Bible come to life. Square mud-walled villages, black-veiled women carrying pots on their heads, men belabouring tiny donkeys with loads so big as to obscure the wretched beasts altogether, women drawing water from the wells beneath the palm trees. On the road one observed within a mile or two a petrol truck doing a steady fifty, a string of camels, some water buffalo and, miles from anywhere, a man for no apparent reason rolling a large barrel.

It would be idle to pretend that being, or even, later having once been, a Member of Parliament, however humble, does not bear stimulating dividends by way of entré to eminent personages such as ambassadors and generals, who, once satisfied that you do not propose to go home and write startling reports about their parish, are liable to make you a good deal better informed than the next man, and this of course adds much interest to one's travels. In Cairo, for instance, I found myself lunching beside the impressive figure of the Ambassador, Lord Killearn, formerly Sir Miles Lampson, and, if it were possible, an even bigger man in the person of General Betts of the US Air Force, of whom I remember only his graphic tale of a snowed-up Russian airfield and how the Russians simply forced every woman from the neighbouring town to march out with a shovel and work till the snow was cleared. I also at a private party had half an hour with King Farouk, who would have been about twenty-five and whom I found a most amiable and personable fellow, far removed from the pathetic figure of fun he later became. Like any good tourist I 'did' the Pyramids and, however squalid the activities of man around their base, one could not but stand in awe at the thought of all the vanity and misery that must have gone into making these supremely useless monuments to long-deceased human potentates – seven million tons of stone on a base the size of Lincoln's Inn Fields and almost as high as Beachy Head.

I am delighted too to have sampled the legendary Shepheard's in its heyday.

The leavetaker, the base wallah, the holiday maker, the traveller to India and the Far East [I wrote at the time] all gravitate sooner or later towards Shepheard's, where they mount the half-dozen steps from the pavement to the veranda, there to endure the scrutiny, as they pass through to the interior, of one of the most cosmopolitan gatherings in the world – Arab sheiks (much too portly to ride horses and gallop away with young ladies into the desert, though one cannot help thinking the world was rather more fun when everyone thought this was how Arab sheikhs did carry on); British brass-hats and subalterns; tarbooshed Egyptian contractors; Greek merchants with oval-countenanced, raven-haired daughters of an indescribable loveliness (the Greeks no doubt have a word for these damsels and it may not be daughter); and Jewish gentlemen with half-inch diamonds, ten-inch cigars, and no intention of going to Israel. Inside, Shepheard's is a sheer Victorian period piece, and I hope they will never change it. Red plush, ornate gilt carvings, palms in pots, conservatory, solid-looking men's bar with tiled floor, string orchestra at tea-time, and, in most parts of the interior, almost too dark to read. All just as it should be, and the moment they alter it Shepheard's is no more.

Alas, the Egyptians did alter it and it is no more. They simply burnt it down.

As to the City of a Thousand and One Nights my impression after spending the One was that anyone who liked could spend the other Thousand, though I did later have cause slightly to moderate this uncharitable assessment. When they put on for British troops in Baghdad an American 'Arabian Nights' film, complete with Douglas Fairbanks as the 'Sheek of Araby', I believe there was almost a riot. Baghdad in winter, however, has a benign climate and you can grow, as though weeds, the most beautiful violets in the world. Both then and later I had the pleasure of meeting the Regent for young King Feisal, as gentle and cultured a man as you could wish to meet. Ten years or so ago the mob dragged him and the young king out, and, having butchered them, tied them to the back of cars and dragged them through the streets. They also, as usual, besieged the British Embassy, where my friend Wreford-Brown was military attaché. Luckily he was on leave at the time, so all they did was to get out his car, hack it to pieces with hatchets and set the remains on fire. Both these people and the Egyptians, it may be noted, were able to vote in the United Nations to impose sanctions on Rhodesia.

As to Anglo-Iranian, its wartime story for some reason was never written and not long afterwards Hilary Saunders, alas, died, but my travels over the company's territory and respect for its tremendous unsung achievements made me, perhaps, an obvious choice when the time came to celebrate its fiftieth anniversary in print, and this I did – after a couple of years with the rather splendid assignment 'Don't trouble to ask. Go anywhere in the world you like and draw whatever money you need' – with a book called *Adventure in Oil*.* This I am happy to say is still handed out to newcomers to the company, if only to show them that the pioneers did not have it so good, and the writing of it gave me such varied experiences as eating a sheep with the comedian Terry-Thomas in an obscure outpost in the Persian Gulf; walking through the Eternal Fires, much subdued since they were the 'blazing fiery furnace' of that imperishable trio Shadrach, Meshach and Abednego but still stinking as abominably of rotten eggs; and flying round the Rockies in a helicopter. As usual, I found the early days the most fascinating, though I will not enlarge on them here, save to say that the name G. B. Reynolds and the date 26 May 1908 ought to be in every schoolboy's history book and assuredly will be found in none. Reynolds, in his mid-fifties and strangely enough very much the English gentleman, had been slaving away

* Sidgwick & Jackson, 1959.

in the most appalling conditions in Persia for seven years when a coded cable from home told him that funds were exhausted and he was to sell anything he could and 'pack it in'. With him to guard the drillers were Lieutenant Arnold Wilson, later Sir Arnold Wilson, MP for Hitchin, and a detachment of the Indian Army. Reynolds played for time by saying he must wait for confirmation by letter; the work went feverishly on; and at 4.00 a.m. Wilson, asleep in his tent beside the rig, was awoken by frantic shouting. Emerging from his tent, he saw oil spurting fifty feet above the derrick, smothering the drillers and their Persian crew as they danced wildly round the rig, yelling and choking, partly with excitement and partly from the escaping gas. On this morning of 26 May 1908, with just ten days to spare, they had penetrated what proved to be the biggest oilfield then known to man, the forerunner of all the oil in the Middle East. As to Abadan, at that time a desert island, whose name in Persian means roughly and rightly 'damn all', they had now turned it into a city the size of Sheffield, but here again, having written one book about it, I must not be tempted into starting another, though I may perhaps pause for what was to me a highly entertaining interlude.

One of the 'characters' of Abadan was a large, imperturbable Liverpudlian known to everyone as Diver Jones, who was responsible for some quite astonishing underwater feats, such as, with his mate, J. W. Q. Costain, refloating a 250-ton tanker which had been sunk just below the junction of Tigris and Euphrates beside what is supposed to have been the Garden of Eden, though with a river temperature of 102 degrees and continuous work for a month it may well have seemed otherwise. Diving, as I see that I recalled soon afterwards, is 'like baling out with a parachute, driving a railway engine, standing for Parliament, walking Niagara on a tightrope, or being hanged – a thing which every man has imagined himself doing but few in fact have done' – though I can now lay claim to having done three. On the old principle of 'try anything once' I managed to get them to let me have a go at diving and a memorable experience it proved to be. We repaired to an offshoot of the Shatt-al-Arab river called Braim Creek, where the water is so muddy that you cannot see your hand in front of your face, and it was in this opaque and rather smelly font that I received my underwater baptism.

We climbed aboard a kind of flat barge, manned by a number of

The famous tightrope walker, Blondin, and his manager, Harry Colcord of Chicago, over the Niagara in 1860. Colcord had never stepped on a tightrope in his life and had to dismount halfway across to allow Blondin to recover his strength.

Abadan in the late 1950s : diving in Braim Creek of the Shatt-al-Arab. I qualified as 'Hon. Member of the Society of Underwater Workers'.

Persians, complete with donkey engine, ropes, lengths of what looked like hosepipe, and three diving-suits. The first move was to take off our coats and put on great woollen trousers, leggings and sweaters. Sometimes, Jones and Costain said, they put on seven pairs of these leggings and still could not feel their feet when they came up. The woollen outfit is followed by a thick gaberdine suit into which you have to be shaken, like something that will not quite go into a sack. Then you soap your hands and slide them through tough rubber wristlets. The suit, needless to say, has no openings at the bottom of the trouser legs: your feet fit into the ends, rather after the style of the 'frogmen'. So, with the wristlets in position, you are now sealed up except for the neck. The next step is to put your head through an iron ring like a horse collar, which is then bolted, with wing nuts and a special spanner, to iron plates inside the suit. Somebody forces your feet, which look like flippers in the stiff gaberdine, into a grotesque pair of boots done up with straps and ropes, and someone else pulls a strap tight round your middle. You make as though to take a step across the deck, only to find the boots so heavy as to be apparently nailed thereto. In fact, you now weigh some two hundred pounds in addition to your own weight, and I confess to a certain amount of apprehension at this point, for the deck was slippery and sloped downwards to the water, there was no rail, and I reckoned that, if I did slip, I should sink like a stone and no power on earth could save me. I was relieved when they slipped a rope under my arms. One pull, they said, meant 'OK' and four 'Pull me up'.

At this point I paused to watch Costain descend the ladder and vanish slowly from human sight, till his existence and whereabouts were marked only by rings of bubbles. I lumbered across to the ladder and stood half-way down for them to lower the helmet over my head and bolt it to the horse collar. It was making a wheezing sound and emitting a faintly rubbery air reminiscent of the moment before the gas comes through at the dentist's. Finally they screwed the round, thick glass facepiece into place and there was nothing for it but 'Going down now, sir!'

Whatever else it may be, diving is no job for anyone who suffers from claustrophobia, especially in muddy water where you can see nothing at all and only changes of light tell you how deep you are. By pressing our helmets together, Costain and I could just see each other well enough to give the victory sign, but after that

I never caught another glimpse of him. You live in a little world of your own, smaller and more constricted, perhaps, than anything your mind had ever dwelt upon: a little room, as it were, hardly bigger than an outsize football. It has a window in front and a window at each side and, when you turn your head, you feel that the windows ought to turn with it. But although you can raise your hand to your head, you cannot touch it and this enhances the sense of constriction. If you have something in your eye or want to scratch your nose, you can get within an inch of either but by no power on earth can you touch them. So of course you want to, desperately.

In this opaque water there is no means, other than an instinct which of course I did not possess, of telling where you are. The boots are so heavy and solid that you cannot tell whether you are standing on a firm surface or not, though the bottom of Braim Creek was too slimy to tell anyway. What is worse, you cannot tell which way you are facing, nor even which way up you are. Theoretically, all this is controlled by a valve in the helmet which regulates the outflow of air. Close it and you inflate yourself and rise to the surface, flat on your back and distended like a long-deceased fish. Open it out and you sink firmly to the bottom. The knack is to open it just enough to take the weight off your shoulders.

Costain and I floundered across to the slimy piles of the jetty, which we could feel but could not see, and I came to realize something of the measure of these men's achievement in staying under water for hours, hacking away at a steel hawser with hand-saws or crawling into the interior of sunken vessels, all as though completely blind.

After a while I began to pant, as one does at high altitudes without oxygen. It got worse to the point of being alarming. I was going to pass out. I had no idea whether I was deep or shallow; facing north, east, west, or south, or lying face downwards. The muddy waters swirled across the window of my tiny world, closer, as it seemed, and closer, and there was no one to tell. Nothing for it but four pulls on the rope, and pretty unmistakable ones they were. The rope tightened and I inflated myself to help Diver Jones, who was holding it, to haul me like some inert porpoise to the surface. And never was a man more happy to see the light of day. As I sat casting off the cumbersome equipment, I deplored my lack of staying power.

'You don't want to worry about that,' they said, 'we didn't like to tell you, but everyone passes out first time!'

And here is a curious thing. Had I been asked to give evidence on oath as to how long Costain and I had been underwater, I should have said, 'Two and a half minutes.' If pressed, I might have said, 'Three.' I should have been certain beyond the point of reasonable human doubt that three was the maximum. The answer was twelve and a half. Very strange.

Later they sent me a fine illuminated scroll to certify that I had 'qualified for admission as an Hon. Member of the Society of Underwater Workers, having been underwater for a period of twelve and a half minutes at Braim Creek, Abadan, Persia . . .' It hangs framed on my wall. I am very proud of my union.

From Abadan I went up to Tehran with schoolboy delight by what must be one of the most remarkable railways in the world. It starts from an appalling place called Andimeshk, in summer one of the hottest in the world, and the wartime running of it by an international set-up, as part of the great Aid to Russia campaign, sounded crazy but had the merit that it appeared to work. On the flat patch of sand which served as a platform were British Red-caps, trousers immaculately creased, boots gleaming, hats squarely on the head; American 'Snowballs' with polished pistols; Persian gendarmes in light blue; and the Russian police with their flat caps and soft shiny boots, all strolling up and down in pairs, while the local black market squatted on its haunches offering packets of Camels and Lucky Strike stamped 'For sale only to US Forces in Alaska'. The engine driver, or rather the locomotive engineer, was an American with rimless glasses, a long-peaked ski-ing cap and large cigar. The guard was Persian, the ticket-collectors British and Iraqi, but somehow or other, as I have said, it worked. I found it a thrilling journey and remember it well. The line climbs up through the foothills and, as you look ahead and see barrier after barrier rising against you, the last defences indistinguishable from the average picture of the Himalayas, you would deem it impossible for any railway to thread and burrow its way through to the other side. It does so by snaking along the valleys, popping into more than a hundred tunnels, often out of one and straight over a gorge and into another, and the engine panting along at a steady twenty becomes a familiar companion as the frequent curves bring it into the passenger's view. At one point we overtook a train of cattle trucks, each containing fourteen Russian ex-prisoners-of-war, being repatriated under armed guard to their happy homeland. It had been said at Andimeshk that we were due in at eight next morning and, as we came to a halt in Tehran, the station clock was striking eight. Full marks for the locomotive engineer!

Tehran in those days was a singular place. The public water supply was still obtained as it ran down the public gutters, but some of the scenes in the minor streets might have come straight out of Utrillo. I lunched with the rather taciturn ambassador, Sir Reader Bullard, and wandered with him round the embassy gardens, just as Churchill had done the year before during the meeting with Stalin and Roosevelt. Almost completely inaccessible at this time, Tehran was the scene of fantastic inflation and one fellow I met, deterred by constant thieving, had jacked up his car, removed the tyres, and sold them in the bazaar for £1,250. Meanwhile the price of demonstrators, which the Russians used actually to drive in lease-lend vehicles to whatever Allied embassy was the target for the day, had risen with inflation, as doubtless it is doing in England today, and had reached the unprecedented price of a shilling a day, with cheerleaders, who told them what to shout and often got it wrong, actually claiming lunch money as well.

'There's something about Tehran,' a friend said to me. 'A man will do things in Tehran he would not dream of doing anywhere else in the world.' Alas, I was not there long enough to put this engaging theory to the test before it was time to start the long drive, with four spare tyres, down through the Paitak Pass to the refinery of Kermanshah, which had the literally thankless task of fuelling and maintaining all the Aid to Russia vehicles. A single moment of this journey stays vividly in my mind. After passing through the Russian-occupied town of Quasvin the road climbed to a vast snow-covered plateau, where it crossed diagonally the railway leading up to Tabriz. The scene was one of infinite desolation and a silence almost as absolute, one imagined, as the Antarctic – until a tyre burst. A train had passed up just in front of us and, as it faded into the distance on its way up to Russia, there occurred an unforgettable optical illusion. The line rose slightly but the snow and the sky blended into each other, as they so often do from the air, and no horizon was visible to the human eye. We might have been specimens in some vast grey bowl. And so, as the train, vanishing, gradually absorbed itself into the grey landscape, it seemed quite distinctly to be climbing into the distant sky.

Days later I found myself in Damascus, which still at that time retained an authentically biblical air, and thence by a beautiful drive down through little white villages with cypress trees and heaps of oranges at the roadside, to the too much Promised and still un-Holy Land of Palestine. Our way took us past Acre, whose ancient battlements are chipped by the assorted missiles of a thousand years, to Haifa, and thence to Jerusalem, where I had the good luck to stay with the High Commissioner, Lord Gort, vc. Being concerned in politics, I naturally became involved, I hope impartially, in that most tedious of all running feuds, Jews v. Arabs, with the British as usual being blamed and shot at by both, but will recall only a lighter side of my stay, namely that in his living-room Gort had a patent apparatus of which I still have not seen the like – a round log of wood, lying on its side, with a board see-saw fashion, on top. You stood with one foot on each end of the board and tried to balance yourself on the log or even make it roll from side to side beneath you. The finest indoor exercise for stomach muscles, said the High Commissioner, who decided many affairs of State from this log-rolling posture. We all took turns on it after breakfast.

Government House, which of course governs no more, was on a hill and every morning one could walk round the terrace in the spring sunshine, looking across to the indescribable beauty of the Old City and on the right the Mount of Olives. Nowadays the Old City is divided up between the warring factions of Israel and Jordan but then you could wander through it at will, and on foot at that, since the streets are mercifully not wide enough for motor cars. In the centre is the Church of the Holy Sepulchre, a little 'touristy', perhaps, with little stalls offering images, candles, crosses and souvenirs with many a holy text strewn before the visitor's eye, but I seemed all the same to catch the spirit of the place, whereas the equally beautiful Church of the Nativity in Bethlehem, a grand enough old Crusader church with its tiny door so that no man could enter carrying weapons, struck no chord of reverence or solemnity in my mind. Somehow as I stood beside the railed-off grotto and saw the names of the sightseers scrawled all over the walls, it never really struck me that this *was* the birthplace of Jesus.

22

Nightmare
over Niagara

Many years ago the women held their Curtis Cup golf match against the Americans at Buffalo and in the course of it, like any good tourist, I went to see the Niagara Falls, to become at once intrigued not so much by the Falls themselves, which, as Oscar Wilde said, would be much more impressive if they flowed upwards, as by the extraordinary antics of folly, nerve and self-destruction performed by mankind under, in and over them. Of those who went over the Falls in barrels, rubber balls, and the rest of it, and even the boy who recently went over by mistake with nothing and still lived, I will mention in passing only two, because I wish to come to the Awful Moment. The first was one of the most unlikely figures, perhaps, of all time, a tight-waisted, corseted, thoroughly Victorian, middle-aged schoolmistress, Mrs Annie Taylor. Having inserted a kitten in her barrel, she sent it over the Falls in a trial run. When she opened the barrel, the kitten was dead. Next morning, 4 October 1901, sharply reminding would-be dissuaders to mind their own business, she eased herself into her barrel and in front of a crowd of several thousands was cast off. Meanwhile her manager retired to a bar and averted his eyes. Three hours later, bruised, battered but by no means bewildered, and with the bun on her head still neatly in place, she was hauled alive from the barrel. Having sacked the manager for dereliction of duty in retiring to the bar, she set herself up as the Queen of the Mist and, posing beside her barrel, made a living by signing autographs. The second case I will mention was our own Captain Webb, the greatest swimmer of his day, who, having conquered the Channel, poor fellow, but not his own financial affairs, stepped in to swim the Rapids and within seconds was swept to extinction.

We come now to the tightrope walkers and the Awful Moment

and my excuse for including them is the fact that I have dined out successfully on this particular episode for years without a suspicion of failure and that I have at last laid hands on a picture. The greatest of all tightrope walkers was a thin, cadaverous man with matted hair and beard, Jean François Gravelet, son of one of the heroes of Napoleon's army, otherwise known as Blondin. He first walked Niagara in 1859. A year later he was back, his name a household word all over the world, with the Prince of Wales (later Edward VII) and former President Millard Fillmore among the spectators. He put on such a show as made women tear handkerchiefs to shreds and strong men bite their nails to the quick. He ran to and fro, slipping deliberately in a swirl of legs and arms and recovering himself. He walked across backwards; with baskets on his feet; and on stilts. He lowered a mug, and, hauling it up, drank the waters he defied. He held out his hat at arm's length and the local sharpshooter from the Maid of the Mist put a bullet through it. Finally he took out a portable stove, squatting on the rope, and cooked and ate an omelet. At last it seemed there was nothing more for him to do. At this moment there steps into the picture a man who to me is one of the unsung heroes of all time – Blondin's manager, Harry Colcord of Chicago.

It was the manager's idea. Somehow they had to go on attracting the crowds. What about taking a man across on his back? Splendid, said Blondin – and we may imagine the scenes that followed. 'What about you, sir? Nice chance to achieve fame and fortune . . . All over in a few minutes . . . No? Well, you, sir? Come along, sir . . . No?'

At what point the dreadful inspiration entered Colcord's head we do not know. We may surmise, without doing him posthumous injustice, that he had been drinking at the time.

'I suppose,' he said, 'I shall have to do it myself.'

Now Colcord had never in his life stepped on a tightrope. So, while we may never envisage ourselves in Blondin's position, we can without the least stretch of imagination see ourselves in the manager's.

When the great day came, 100,000 people assembled on the banks. Betting was fast and furious. The odds were even money.

The manager, as big a man as Blondin, took off his coat and mounted the maestro's back, and a moment later the pair embarked on their frightful expedition. On the downward journey all went well, but, as they mounted the slope on the other side, their pace was seen gradually to slacken. Amid a muttered rumbling of speculation among the watchers on the cliffs they came to a full stop.

Let us leave the watchers and focus our attention upon the nightmare predicament of the two figures balancing over the abyss. This is the Awful Moment.

'It is no good,' Blondin is saying, 'I am exhausted. You will have to get down!'

The reader may be left to imagine for himself what surged through the manager's head; the appeals to the Almighty to spare him but this once, and never again; the urging-on of his exhausted steed; the dread realization; the frantic groping of his shiny shoes for the rope invisible behind and below.

Somehow he made it, and for minutes they stood upon their awful perch, the maestro panting to recover his strength, Colcord clutching his hips from behind, and speculators on the bank advancing the odds to even money Blondin, 6–1 the manager.

The latter, of course, had no chance of walking up the steeply inclined rope. How was he to remount? A sort of creeping, furtive, one-knee-at-a-time action suggests itself, though whether you can climb on a man's back that way with the remaining foot balanced only on a swaying steel hawser is open to doubt. Yet the full-blooded leap – 'Allez, oop!' – with its attendant probability of the whole ensemble disappearing in a flurry of arms, legs, and twenty-foot pole, gyrating slowly as they fell and vanishing with a scarcely visible splash in the swirling torrent below . . . no, I cannot think they would have decided on that.

The lonely, desperate conference has never, alas, been recorded, nor the method by which the manager at last climbed back, but get back he did, and the picture shows the pair of them with ten yards left to go. Colcord's eyes have vanished into their sockets; his mouth is agape; his cheekbones stand out like a skeleton's.

'I break out into a cold sweat,' he recorded later in life, 'whenever I think of it.'

So, for that matter, do I.

23
Farther East
of Suez

Long-distance travel has for most people become a question of
'air or not at all' but I am glad to have sampled it in the days when
there was still a certain sense of adventure to it and at any rate you
did not fly so high that you could not see the ground. The other
day I realized that I had reached the final absurdity of air travel,
almost the negation of the word travel itself, when I was flown
to San Antonio and back and, on returning, realized that I had no
idea where I had been. All I knew was that it was somewhere in
Texas and it took me quite a time to find on the map. All I had
seen in the course of this five-thousand-mile penetration 'deep
in the heart of Texas' was a piece of concrete at each end.

Far different was the voyage of the George King Able, a humble
Dakota so-called because of its identification letters, in which,
only a month or two after the war, I was to accompany the then
Director-General of BOAC, my old friend and Coombe Hill golf
opponent General Critchley, on a proving flight down to the Far
East. At the last moment he could not come, on account of the
publication of some White Paper, but I carried on in order to meet
the staff in remote parts for whom I was to do a weekly news-
magazine from home. The George King Able was fitted out rather
as an 'executive' (ghastly word!) aeroplane would be today, with
chairs, table, desk, bar and so on, the principal occupants now
being General Sir Drummond Inglis, who had joined the Cor-
poration as No. 2 and was coming to inspect his new sphere of
activity; Harry Barman, who, if I remember, was No. 2 Admin;
and for a while D. F. Landale, who was returning to try and pick
up the threads of the great Far East firm of Jardine Matheson in
Shanghai. In command was Captain Ronald Ashley, a dark-haired,
dashing, determined character, for whom after his wartime exploits the leisurely trip of the George King Able must have been

the proverbial piece of cake. He had, in fact, spent most of the war at Leuchars, just across the Eden Estuary from St Andrews, flying unarmed to and from Stockholm ferrying escaped prisoners-of-war, ball-bearings or maybe a VIP strapped with his Thermos and sandwiches in the bomb-bay of a Mosquito. He did it more than a hundred times, once six nights running, six hours there and eight hours back.

Malta, Cairo, Bahrein, Sharjah, Jiwani (just a runway and some tents in a howling wilderness) and Karachi. It was only on the last lap to Karachi that we finished what was then a sensational innovation, our pre-cooked frozen food. Later there occurred to me the thought that many cities, though perhaps not London, are identifiable in the mind by colours. Hong Kong, for instance, is bright blue and yellow, Singapore is green and chocolate. Rangoon is red and grey and Calcutta green and white, but clearest of all is Karachi. It is brown.

Next day we droned on and on at our modest 160 m.p.h. over the dusty plains of middle India, having now fallen into a daily routine of catching up with our work until 11.30 a.m. at which hour precisely the George King Able 'opened'. Work was put away, refreshment was produced from the cupboard, Ashley came back from the front and the morning session of 'liar dice' began – a game at which General Inglis proved a master hand, passing on a pair of nines as four queens with a benign smile that would have done credit to a bishop. At last the desert began to give way to a green patchwork of cultivation and eventually there hove in view the fantastic capital city of Delhi. We only spent a couple of days there but I am glad to have set eyes on Gilbert Scott's, as I thought, immensely imposing Government Buildings and on the ancient forts little changed since the 1400s, and to have spent a night in the legendary Cecil Hotel with its suites of rooms opening out to lovely gardens and, even in wartime, dinner for sixteen a mere matter of course – with our hostess making desperate efforts to find out whether I was Anybody or not, so as to assign me an appropriate place in the batting order for going in to dinner. Next day on and on again with the occasional muddy river winding its way for fifty miles on either side (from the air it is quite impossible, incidentally, unless there are waterfalls, to tell which way a river is flowing) and then suddenly in the far, far distance on the left, separated from the horizon by a greyish haze, the snowline of the

Himalayas. I must have sat gazing at it for an hour, but in an instant one's mind could transfer itself across the intervening two hundred miles. Somewhere up in that white line was Everest and somewhere on it lay the body of Mallory, who just before my time had been a master at Charterhouse.

Soon the earth turned watery in the sunlight and here was Bengal in the rice season, and finally the overpopulated squalor of Calcutta. At the hideous airfield so aptly named Dum Dum, I don't know why, brigadiers and unshaven French parachutists side by side were dumping baggage into trucks to take it to the aircraft; anything to get away, and who should blame them? The new Government at home had just appointed as Governor of Bengal, a post second only, I believe, to that of the Viceroy, an ex-railway porter who lived in a little villa called 'The Thrush's Nest' near Bristol, an appointment which I mention only as an excuse to recall his absolutely splendid and historic remark, which endeared him to everyone, about being more used to hootin' and shuntin' than huntin' and shootin'.

Next stop Rangoon and the delta of a river familiar to every English schoolboy since almost his first geography lesson, the Irrawaddy. The great European-style buildings and fine avenues and the mass of shipping in the harbour looked highly impressive, till closer inspection revealed the buildings to be mere shells and the ships, 650 of them to be precise, to be not only in the harbour but resting on the bottom of it. You never saw such a shambles and it was almost a privilege to have witnessed it, especially when secure in the knowledge that you were shortly to be on your way. The Japs had begun it by pointlessly letting every public utility run down, even though they had unlimited local labour to keep things going, and, when they left, the Burmese moved in with a vengeance, looting not only every article of furniture but even the door handles, the electric light fittings and the wainscoting. The navy had taken over the remains of the Strand Hotel, which was to Rangoon what Raffles' was to Singapore and Shepheard's to Cairo, and five of us reckoned ourselves lucky to be allowed to share a room with no furniture. The new Governor, Sir Reginald Dorman-Smith, who bore a strong resemblance to Ronald Colman, had returned to the sumptuous palace and by now had a desk and a few chairs in his study, where the window was open to the night air, so that the usual winged visitors came in by battalions,

buzzing, hopping and crawling, according to their several capa-
cities. The Governor, meanwhile, nudged grasshoppers nonchalantly from his hair with the stem of his pipe, while in an
adjacent room a full colonel with red tabs sat at a trestle table on
an upturned crate. Amidst all the squalor and disintegration,
however, there towered unharmed the mighty golden spire of the
Schwedagon Pagoda, which, like the Pyramids, the Taj Mahal and,'
in its way, I suppose, the Empire State Building, is one of the
wonders of the world. If the Fourteenth claimed to be the Forgotten Army, Burma, the scene of their operations, remains the
Forgotten Country. Not long after our visit the British abandoned
the work of several generations (including that of Elephant Bill)
and sailed away, and in due course the new rulers of Burma were
welcomed in the garden of No. 10 Downing Street. A year later
a newspaper republished a picture of them. All but two had either
been assassinated by the others or had in turn been executed for
assassinating them.

So finally, hour after hour, down over the rubber plantations of
Malaya, to which so many of my generation of Bedfordians had
devoted their lives, and eventually Singapore, where we were the
first civilian aeroplane to land at Kallang. We duly inspected the
runways at Changi, where in a sort of tropical Dartmoor the Japs
had imprisoned six thousand men in a building built for six
hundred. These runways had been built by forced Australian
labour, who might be assumed to have incorporated as many
invisible flaws as possible, and it was a question of whether it would
be safe for BOAC to land on them. We also inspected the airfield
at Seletar, near the Johore Causeway, where a number of planes
not unlike our own were parked, with green and red crosses. They
were the ones in which the Japanese had come to surrender.

A queer people. The Commander-in-Chief, General Sir Miles
Dempsey, told us that the hill-top house in which he received us
had been the Japanese Admiral's headquarters. When he and his
staff arrived, they found notices on the door saying in five languages:
"Reserved for the Commander-in-Chief of the British Forces. Not
to be looted.' Inside, the house was beautifully furnished and
there was even ice in the fridge. Two years later a man told me in
Singapore that he had returned to one of the banks there and
found all the records intact, all totted up and sealed in waterproof
containers. After a number of visits, however, I still suspect that,

while there are many parts of the world in which I should probably run to seed, I should rot more quickly than anywhere in Singapore.

I do not think one could be accused of political partiality, or in my own case of sour grapes, if one suggested that the Socialist Government elected in 1945 was antagonistic to private enterprise to the extent of being positively spiteful. The desire to launch out on one's own, to be one's own master, to seek one's own fortune, still runs deep, however, and it soon became apparent to Ashley, who in old days would have been cut out for a privateer, that the shackles of a peacetime nationalized industry were not for him. Time and again on our journey in the George King Able he had held forth on the prospects of air charter. 'That's what it's going to be after the war, old boy. Air charter.' He therefore left BOAC and founded the air charter firm of Skyways, to which in due course Critch came in as chairman and General Inglis as chief administrator, and a formidable trio they made. A few months later I once again happened to be standing in the right place at the right time, when Critch turned suddenly to me and said, 'Look here. Can you go to China?' Not unnaturally the answer was 'Of course!' and within a matter of days I was once again being lofted on a January morning, just as the first flakes of snow fell, over the flooded gravel pits of Staines, bound for Hong Kong in a converted Lancaster bomber with Captain Brian Greensted and twelve fellow-passengers; a million and a quarter pounds' worth of gold; and, as air hostess, as they were called in those days, the shapely raven-haired daughter of an air marshal, Carol Pearce. Skyways was already becoming phenomenally successful, but in air charter you had continually to be looking for business and the present intention was for me to join Maurice Curtis, one-time traffic manager with BEA, and together investigate the possibilities of making a profitable intrusion into civil aviation in the Far East, which was still in a state of unresolved chaos.

We made our way down the now familiar route – Malta, Cairo, Abadan, Karachi, Calcutta – but this time we branched off, at half-past four in the morning, for the 1,650-mile hop over Burma and Indo-China and the mountains known as 'the Hump', over which Aid to China had been flown in the war. Dawn came up to reveal a limitless mountainous landscape of dark green jungle, broken only by winding paths and little clearings in which vast teak logs lay scattered about like matches. Nor was dawn the only thing that came up. To avoid some bad weather we climbed high enough to need oxygen, and what with the oxygen masks and the bumps and the feeling of being very, very far from home, our little company began to lose some of its composure. What finished it was the breakfast served up by Miss Pearce when the masks were removed, which I remember with smug satisfaction to this day since I was the only one to finish it: brawn, lovely shiny multi-coloured brawn, wrapped in shiny cellophane; shiny, hard-boiled egg; red tomatoes; green lettuce; and a profuse top dressing of rich yellow mayonnaise.

For two wonderful months Curtis and I, based on Hong Kong, travelled our potential parish, ranging out to Bangkok, Shanghai and Singapore, persuasively interviewing officials, occasionally slipping a fast one on our competitors, trying to master the new Civil Aviation Act, which seemed designed solely to obstruct private enterprise but with whose details I will not bore you now, and a new international agreement, which a good many nations appeared to have signed without having read it, whereby if country A ran a service to country B, then country B was entitled in turn to run a service to country A. The Chinese, knowing perfectly well what they had signed, continued to use Hong Kong while cheerfully denying us the right to run a service into China, though their own was in such parlous condition that the local paper, after reporting the crash of the day, featured a column headed 'Other Crash Reports'. I in turn learnt from Curtis some of the economics of running an aeroplane and the fantastic differ-ence between what it made for you when it was in the air full of passengers and what it lost you while sitting on the ground. Ashley, incidentally, once broke all known records by keeping two Yorks in the air for 2,400 hours in one year: not bad at 200 miles an hour and 14s. a mile.

Hong Kong itself was heaven as a relief from all the controls and political bitterness in England, more from a sense of being out on one's own, following however humbly in the footsteps of William Jardine and Matheson, who had opened up the coast of China to British trade and were virtually the founders of Hong Kong, than from the fact that you could buy in Hong Kong almost everything that was unavailable at home. The other airline operators advertised their flights with pictures of aeroplanes with four motors but, when you got down to it, it would be an old

Dakota. We flew in one of these to Bangkok. The air hostess, who had a figure so outstanding that she spent most of the time answering questions as to whether it was real (I understand it was), was leaning against the wing, chewing gum. 'Hey!' she said. 'Yew boys com'n' on our ship?' The ship in question had the old facing-inwards seating and it was not long before the girl was squatting on the floor with a Chinese film actor and two Malayans, playing cards.

Thus we became very proud of our Lancastrian and lost no opportunity of flying it over the little colony, making a tremendous din and showing the public not only the two big Union Jacks on its tail fins but also the fact that it indisputably had four motors. When later on Greensted was due out again from England, we assembled quite a distinguished welcoming party at Kaitak, which was then one of the most dangerous airfields, I suppose, in the world. Whenever anyone looked at his watch, we said, 'No, no. He's due at 12.25.' It was about 12.23 when we first heard him and a couple of minutes later, give or take thirty seconds, when he roared over Kaitak. Curtis and I cleared our throats nonchalantly, shot our cuffs, straightened our ties, did a knees-bend or two and, if the truth be told, felt very, very proud. We were much assisted, too, by our Miss Pearce, who, Hong Kong being confined in so small a space, did not fail to attract attention. We gave a prestige dinner party in our hotel one night to win friends and influence people and were much aided by her appearance in a tight-fitting black dress, long black gloves, black shoes, and black bag, the severity of the ensemble being admirably set off by a challenging pair of long black earings. 'Who's that?' the buzz went round. 'Oh, that?' we said. 'Oh, that's one of our air hostesses.'

We worked extremely hard, and in the end not wholly without success – and indeed the report, which was my responsibility, cost forty pounds to type – but, as with one's days at school or the university, it is the lighter side which survives the passage of time. We had thought, for instance, that, with the huge note issue in Hong Kong (there are no coins) and the millions of new notes needed to cope with the inflation in Shanghai, banknotes would make excellent air freight and that speed might make all the difference. We discussed this with the chief cashier of the Hong Kong and Shanghai Bank, whose massive building dominates the waterfront. (The American Club also had a few rooms in the building, and an American magazine captioned a picture of it with: 'The American Club in Hong Kong. The Hong Kong and Shanghai Bank also uses part of the building.') Unfortunately, however, only a day or two previously a Dakota, which I fancy Curtis and I were the last to set eyes on as it threaded its way through low cloud towards Kaitak, hit the top of Mount Parker, killing its unhappy crew and scattering over the mountain-top something like a million pounds' worth of gold, mostly in Mexican Eagles – thus setting in motion the biggest gold rush ever known in the Far East. The chief cashier, Mr Morrison, a Scotsman of course – no big British firm operates overseas without at least one Scotsman called Morrison – after some genial reminiscences about golf informed us politely that they had three months' reserve of notes and a fast ship therefore served their purpose perfectly well. He could not resist – and one can hardly blame him – suggesting that anyway, with the best will in the world, they would not wish to see their banknotes distributed about the summit of Mount Parker.

Next morning, right across the front page, a headline revealed that thirty cases of their banknotes sent by ship from Hong Kong to Shanghai had been found, when opened, to contain stones. I remember to this day with what childish satisfaction, and indeed I smirk at the recollection as I write it down, I took out a sheet of notepaper, pinned the cutting to it and wrote to Morrison: 'We respectfully beg to draw to your attention the fact that, when Skyways carry banknotes, they deliver banknotes. We can, however, quote a special rate for stones.'

When the Japs conquered Hong Kong (and how many people, I wonder, remember that we had signed a treaty with the little perishers agreeing not to fortify it?) they erected an enormous victory memorial on the top of the Peak, as big as one of the new tower blocks of council flats in London, and one day we had the pleasure of sitting in a friend's garden over a glass of refreshment and at a range of only about five hundred yards watching it blown up. This was to be done not with one great explosion but with hundreds of small plastic bombs timed to go off at once, and very impressive it was, to be sitting up there, when the preliminary beating of gongs had ceased, in absolutely dead silence, gazing at this huge ungainly white edifice, certain that for miles around hundreds of thousands of eyes were fixed upon it too. Suddenly innumerable puffs of white smoke spurted from the base; slowly, ponderously, the whole edifice crumbled to the ground and, when the smoke and dust cleared away, only a tangled pile of masonry remained to remind the world of the would-be master race of the East. A satisfying episode.

I am glad also to have sampled real Chinese food with one or two real Chinese experts and to have become adept enough at that supremely civilized art of eating, i.e. with chopsticks, not only to have balanced three peanuts on top of one another one evening but also to have lifted them up by the bottom one. Dinner consists of anything from twelve to twenty courses, for which you use the same little bowl, dipping each morsel into a series of sauces beside you and enduring with celestial calm, lest you offend your host, a few severe burns of the palate until you learn better. Perhaps the most pleasing aspect of dinner with the Chinese, though, is the service. A young girl, trim as a tulip, hands you a hot towel with which to wipe the manly brow. She places a flower in your button-hole and with great deftness refolds the handkerchief in your breast pocket. She stands behind you throughout dinner; doles out the dishes that require a spoon, competing with the other girls for the best bits on your behalf; fills your glass the moment you take a sip from it – a dangerous one, this, till you know the ropes, since at any moment there may be a cry of ' *Yam sing*', which means 'Bottoms up' – hands you your cigarette and lights it, and is very hurt if you attempt to peel your own orange. Just like home, in fact.

On a more serious level, each of us in turn had bright ideas in our role of twentieth-century merchant venturers, Curtis's more profitable, though less potentially sensational, than my own. His brainwave was to fly live fish fry from Hong Kong to stock the reservoirs in Singapore and he was successful enough in that ninety per cent arrived alive instead of five per cent in the days when they went by water in tanks periodically stirred by coolies, but the Chinese, as may be remembered, have difficulty with the letter *r* (we asked for grilled fish for breakfast in our room one day and it was not until we wrote it down that the waiter appreciated our desire. 'Ah,' he said, breaking into a vast gold-toothed grin, 'glilled fish!'), so whether Curtis, flying his live fish fry, was frying flying fish or flying fried fish or simply frying flied flish, the Chinese concerned in the operation did not to the end discover.

My own brainwave occurred on the way to Shanghai, whither we prudently proceeded on the good ship *Wing Sang*, owned of course by Jardine's, rather than risk figuring in 'Other Crash Reports'. Among our few fellow-passengers was the Russian commercial attaché in Chungking – also, as it happened, with a couple of gold teeth. Though he would come into the little saloon and read a book in English, he hardly spoke, and it was not until the last night that we got anything out of him. 'The English are too weak,' he said, 'You do not compel people. You are too weak in India, too weak in Palestine, always too weak.' He spoke the language well but it was strange to see how totally indocrinated so intelligent a man could have become. At any rate I steered the talk round to caviare, of which I used to be inordinately fond until some allergy turned it against me – which has been good for the pocket if nothing else. Could he, as commercial attaché, arrange for us to buy caviare? He seemed most enthusiastic. There was plenty of caviare, he said, all of the very best quality, in Vladi-vostok. They were pleased to sell it, but would only dispose of large quantities at a time, such as, for instance, a thousand kilos, or nearly a ton. The price was about 3s. 6d. a kilo and we should have to arrange the transport. He would be pleased to fix all the details.

I did some feverish calculations on the back of an envelope, revealing that here was the best caviare in the world at about 1s. 8d. a pound. It would be excellent freight, neatly packed and weighing heavy for its size (which was what made bullion the ideal air freight). We had a Lancastrian due in Hong Kong in a fortnight and it would carry six tons. In most cities outside Russia caviare was fetching up to £1 for a portion that would hardly cover a half-crown. Six tons of this, bought at 1s. 8d. a pound and flogged for £15 or £20 a pound at all the major stops on the way home and the remainder in still-rationed London – here was a proposition of which the pious founders themselves, Mr Jardine and Mr Matheson, might well be proud! I pursued the matter with energy, imagining how proud also our principals at home would be of this spectacular coup by one not previously connected with such ventures. Alas, alas! The Russians would indeed sell us the caviare at 3s. 8d. a kilo and it was indeed the very finest quality in the world – but try and get permission out of them to land a converted bomber at Vladivostok! All the same I dream of it still. *Six tons*!

The total disintegration of a great city like Shanghai was enough to make you weep, but there it was, and I am glad in a way to have seen it. Furthermore, most of us have a secret fascination for bribery and corruption on the really grand scale, and here was that too. By 1943 the hated red barbarians had been squeezed out – we think of ourselves as white but the Chinese logically enough see us as what we are, namely red, and, if you don't believe it, look around you at the next club dinner, where anyone who turned white would be at once helped from the room – and now the local Capones had taken over. One gang had secured the whole of what river transport remained, so that it cost more to ship a car across the river than to bring it from San Francisco. One man we met had been burgled sixteen times and the fire brigade, once the pride of the city, had let another man's house burn down through being unable to come to terms with his neighbours as to what it was worth to them to put the fire out.

The best rackets, however, were in their way rather pathetic. These were UNRRA (the United Nations Relief and Rehabilitation movement) and Lady Cripps's Aid to China. Most of the goods shipped in by the former were on sale on the black market almost before the vessel had docked. As for Lady Cripps's £2,000,000 fund, to which so many schoolchildren had contributed their pennies, it was first changed at the official rate of 80 dollars to the pound against the going rate of 8,000, thus squeezing it for 7,920 out of 8,000, and the remaining 80 was duly milked as it went down the line. I asked various people how much of it they thought had reached its intended destination, and the highest estimate came from a senior RAF officer. He reckoned about £10,000. Nevertheless, it is quite an experience to see a currency in disintegration. Before leaving, Curtis and I drew $1,000,000 apiece, or about £20, and, as I hope the average reader would also have done, spread them out on our stateroom table like a couple of schoolboys and solemnly photographed each other – and, if only I had got the apparatus in focus, I could have treated you to a picture of 'the Millionaire Author'. As it is, I have long claimed to be the only man who has actually paid $25,000 for a bottle of Eno's!

Our researches took us also to Bangkok, which I greatly enjoyed, though many don't. The landscape is as flat as Lincolnshire – though the north of Siam is a land of mountain and forest, dashing torrents, teak, exotic birds, beasts and flowers, and one day I hope to see it – and Bangkok itself has almost as many waterways as roads, these going by the delicious name of *klongs*. Thousands of people lived permanently on the *klongs*, in boats with thatched cabins or little wooden houses perched on stilts – a homely, unsophisticated and doubtless insanitary existence but of a pleasing simplicity beside our own – and to one brought up on the slow-moving waters of the Ouse it all had a strong appeal. The people had natural grace and good manners and nothing offended the eye, though things may be different now that the city appears to be one huge GI brothel and even has modern hotels for the flow of American tourists sampling the fabulous wonders of the Orient.

We were taken care of by friends in the Borneo Company, the founders of modern Sarawak, who also found Mrs Anna Leonowens, the original Anna, as 'mastress' for the children at the court of the King of Siam. I later wrote a book for their centenary and remember the thrill of handling the real King of Siam's original letter. One evening they took us to a party given by a young member of their Siamese staff to celebrate the birth of his firstborn. Better-class Siamese women do not, or did not, normally appear in public, but on this evening our host's friends had brought their wives and these young women with their gleaming black hair ornamented with flowers, their bronzed skin, delicate features, and exquisite figures made one feel extraordinarily red, hamhanded and European. We stayed at the home outside the city of one Bill Adams, of Shell, who was away at the time – he had been the oldest prisoner-of-war to work upon the Burma railway and survive – and I cannot help recalling even now breakfasting on his veranda in our dressing-gowns, basking in the February sunshine and reading in the *Bangkok Times* about 'parts of Derbyshire cut off for last ten days . . . people [including my wife in Chelsea] queuing at water hydrants in the middle of London . . . motors abandoned . . . factories shut . . . homes fireless . . .' and so on. 'Tst, tst,' we would say. 'It must be *terrible* for them. Boy, more eggs and bacon!'

On the more serious level we proposed, in view of the international agreement previously mentioned, that Skyways should found Siamese Airways and run it on their Government's behalf. We were much aided by the British Minister, Mr G. Harington

Thompson, and in due course found ourselves waiting upon the Director-General of Transport. Lively interest was shown and in the course of the next twenty-four hours, including sitting up half the night, we produced a vast and detailed plan, got it typed and copied, sent copies to the Director-General and the British Minister, cabled home, and sat back to await developments. In the meantime, there being ground to cover in Singapore, we went down in the flying-boat, which, for all Lord Brabazon's adage about ballooning – and my own observations on gliding – is perhaps the only 'gentleman's way to fly', calling at Penang, which I still think I might retire to, on the way. Eleven days later we were back in Bangkok, waiting keenly upon the Director-General and a colleague who was to succeed the recently deceased Minister of Transport – only to find that neither had even read our document. However, the Siamese are much too nice to be cross with for long.

The time came at last reluctantly to return home – on the day the last trace of snow melted in England – and make our report. We recommended that Skyways should 'get in' in the wide-open world of Far East aviation by running a direct service with a Lancastrian between Hong Kong and Singapore taking about five and a half hours, to compete with the BOAC flying-boat, which took two days with a night stop and no running water at Bangkok, and not long afterwards this was laid on. Brian Greensted took charge of the operations; Miss Pearce designed herself a saucy white uniform with gold buttons; and soon the Lancastrian was commuting to and fro twice weekly like clockwork, full for every flight, paying the whole of its costs, and making a profit.

Another inspiration in which I played a modest part was the 'Hong Kong Mail'. The mails between England and her most prosperous colony were carried by a once-weekly flying-boat service, which, if it was not delayed – and it often was – took eight days, so it was nothing for a business house to wait nearly a month for an answer. We found that a Lancastrian was ideal for the average mail between London and Hong Kong and that with a spare crew at Karachi we could do it in a day and a half going out and in two days, against the clock, coming home. The 'Hong Kong Mail' would be the finest, fastest mail service in the world, and one's chest did rather tend to swell at the thought of it.

The colony were delighted but not, alas, the nationalized institutions at home. The 'Hong Kong Mail' was still-born and people continued to wait a month for an answer. And in due course the Lancastrian to Singapore was stopped by influence from home; the flying-boat, heaving a sigh of relief, returned to her comfortable two-day schedule via Bangkok; and the State airline joined in a subsidiary called Hong Kong Airways – a title which, if they only knew it, had been registered by Curtis and myself in a fit of mischief months before.

24
Darkest Africa

It seems strange – or does it really? – that the happiest time of my life should have been spent farthest from civilization. This was the heart of the Sudan with my friend Peter Wreford-Brown, who was then commanding that part of the Western Arab Corps known as the Sudan Defence Force. It started with the most exhausting day I remember: an early morning flight from Khartoum in an eight-seater Dove, this being only a few years after the war, to El Obeid, and thence over nothing but bush, red sand, scrub, and grotesquely eroded hills to El Fasher. There I was met by a young lieutenant, Jake Sharpe, who collected the mails while I devoured bacon and eggs. At midday we left in two Commer trucks – made almost certainly, I could not help thinking, in Luton! – and bashed and bumped our way through the bush for eight and a half hours to Nyala; then after a meal with the District Commissioner, Ranhold Laurie, another three and a half hours in the light of the headlamps to a little village called Abu Sela, where, totally exhausted at the end of a nineteen-hour day, I stumbled to bed in a thatched hut.

This was in the province of Darfur, right in the centre of Africa, whose left-hand boundary, if you happen to find it on a map, resembles exactly the profile of the first Lord Oxford and Asquith. Here was, to me, a completely new life. There was not a single road apart from an occasional track, which might well have been washed away by morning. You simply drove at the bushes, knocking them down and running over them as you passed, and half a mile of smooth straight surface would be a tremendous 'bonus'. For trees you had to 'steer ahead', as in ski-ing, in other words you could turn the wheel before the tree and still hit it. Some of the huge tebeldi trees, forty feet round, were hollow and were used for storing water. For the rest the scrub looked rather like bright yellow hay, but you had only to set foot in it to be covered instantly with the most prickly and adhesive burrs in the world, which the soldiers used to scrape off with a bayonet, as though shaving one's trousers. This stuff and the camel thorn, they said, could stop an army.

Not only were there no roads, but no signposts, no radio, no newspapers, no printed word of any kind, no shop, no rest house, no tourists, no visitors of any kind; and the December climate, hot in the day, cool at evening, was absolute heaven. Abu Sela proved in the morning to be a camp of specially built huts, which go by the charming name of *tukls*, round a central square with the purple standard of the Sudan Defence Force standing bravely in the middle and two flags flying from the *tukl* of the Governor of Darfur, Mr K. D. D. Henderson, all of us being on the way to the great annual horse show farther down in the interior. A fire burned permanently in the square, while obscene vultures hopped around, dust-bathed, or sat like bundles of old sacking in the trees. As against that, there flew into the neighbouring marsh each evening whole skeins, if that is the right word, of what must surely be the most beautiful of the bigger birds, the golden crested crane, In charge of the camp was Nazir Ali el Ghali; a handsome fellow of the type dear to lady novelists as a 'sheek' – until he put on a European overcoat over his jellaba and at once became like something out of a Baghdad bazaar. He turned out to be, of all things, a noted expert on Sherlock Holmes in Arabic!

On trek, if you did not shoot for the pot as you went along, it was a question of army rations and another tin of M and V, as I soon learnt on the journey to Abu Sela, when Sharpe, who was an expert 'scrub driver', suddenly stopped and, seizing a .22 rifle 'acquired' in Germany, dashed into the scrub, through which an object like a black periscope was to be seen rapidly retreating. This was the head of a bustard, a bird like a miniature ostrich, but, alas for our dinner, he missed it, as would almost anyone with a .22 bullet. Later I succeeded in shooting one and it was bigger than a very big turkey. As passenger I soon learnt never to travel without a loaded twelve-bore beside me, the main target being the parties of guinea-fowl often to be found wandering in the bush. '*Gedad*!' the Sudanese soldiers would shout from the back of the vehicle, though I had probably seen them already. At first, but not for long, I thought it rather unsporting to shoot at a sitting bird but soon I was trying to manoeuvre the truck so as to get two or three *gedad* with one shot. No sooner had I done so than the soldiers would jump off to cut their throats with a knife, since they would be unclean unless their spirits were dispatched to Allah while they were still alive. The slightest movement of a small feather in the breeze was sufficient to indicate that the bird counted as alive. Sometimes the guinea-fowl – and even in England today I never see them without thinking of them as *gedad* – would scuttle off into the bush, whereupon the soldiers needed no word of instruction. The whole lot would jump down, run into the bush, form a semicircle and drive the birds back over the guns, the driver having by this time got out to join in the shooting. *Gedad*, though clumsy-looking on the ground, fly extremely well – but one's eye is wonderfully sharpened by the thought of M and V.

The soldiers themselves were magnificent men, huge fellows, some of them, and mostly coal black, with flashing white teeth when they smiled, which they were liable to do most of the time. They squatted cheerfully on sharp-cornered ammunition boxes as we bumped through the scrub and one of the very best jokes of the year had been when Abdul had been thrown off at 30 m.p.h. and broken his leg. When we stopped for lunch on the way down, the batman set up a table, chairs, and a spotless white cloth, with proper plates and cutlery. When I demurred and said surely it would do if we just had a sandwich or something, Sharpe at once put me right. All concerned would have felt deeply insulted if we had turned their efforts down. The cook would have been greatly distressed and we should have lost face with the men. This gave me much pleasure, since I have always held that there is nothing wrong with personal service, much as it is looked down on today. If things had gone differently with me, nothing would have induced me to go on a motor assembly line. I should have become a butler or gentleman's personal gentleman, preferably to His Grace but in any fine country establishment where the port that was good enough for them would be good enough for me. At any rate I soon formed the opinion that, for the conditions under which he works, the Sudanese army cook must be the best in the world.

I remember one idyllic night, miles, perhaps hundreds of miles, from anywhere, with just the three of us, the Governor, Wreford-Brown, and myself, sitting around the fire. There is dead wood all over the place, so you simply gather three miniature trees, spread them out with just the ends touching, and light the ends. When you want to stoke the fire, you merely push the ends together. In these circumstances, apart from the necessities to keep body and soul together, you would never guess, any more than I did, what is the most indispensable item in your equipment: the answer is – your chair. If you do not have your own chair or, to quote another of my half-dozen Sudanese words, your *kursi* with you, there is nowhere, not anywhere, to sit down. I can recall this particular evening as though it were yesterday. The total silence of the heart of Africa cast a spell over the scene and most of one's thoughts remained unspoken. Venus, deep down in the west, actually cast a shadow. You could tell the time by Orion's Belt coming up from the west, and the Plough appeared later in the north. They were accompanied by a spectacular display of shooting stars, as many as three at a time, and I enjoyed the tale of the man who was leading his men through the bush by a guiding star, when 'the bloody thing shot'. The impact of drink was quite extraordinary. At the end of a day's trek in this dry climate, starting perhaps at dawn, there had never been a moment when you wanted a drink more intensely, nor needed so little when you got it. The evening's quota might be half an inch of whisky in a big tumbler, then another, lasting perhaps an hour. Back in Khartoum both would have gone in ten minutes.

Near at hand, invisible in the darkness, would be the cook, and if some of the housewives at home were sent out for a few elementary lessons in the Sudan instead of wasting money on glossy magazines they never use, it would be much to the benefit of the English males. All the Sudanese cook carries with him is a few pots and a sort of flat grill. He has no idea when someone is going to clap their hands as a signal for dinner, but a cheerful voice answers immediately out of the darkness. We sat gossiping and ruminating till someone discovered it was 9.30. Hands were hastily clapped and in a matter of minutes each of us had his own table, white cloth, cutlery, and a bowl of soup. No sooner had we finished the soup than there appeared a teal apiece, shot that day and still at this late hour of a moisture and succulence difficult to credit with sauté potatoes and a tinned vegetable; followed by a sort of soufflé, and coffee.

Any sort of water-hole in this arid land was good for a quick inspection, with almost the certainty of a miniature stalk and a shot or two. The first that I remember was typical – a pool of perhaps an acre with taller trees standing out from the scrub, maybe half a mile from the track. As we approached we could see life on the water, so my host went round to the right, the driver to the left, and I to the middle. As I got near, a little too soon, up went three geese; perhaps a dozen teal; a number of ibis, birds with long black bills like outsize curlews; a heron; two cranes; and the inevitable party of waders, which I took to be stilts, flying with their long red legs trailing out behind. The geese looked wonderful as they wheeled away in the sunlit sky and any moment I thought to see one of them drop, but they were just too quick. The teal came over me and I dropped one in the water. The driver's puttees were off in a flash and a moment later it was duly knifed. Not long afterwards we came on another pond, with another three geese, perhaps the same birds, and dispatched two, one somewhat doubtfully with the .22 – but a dinner is a dinner and you cannot eat it in the air.

On other occasions we had more organized duck shoots, and these were a joy indeed, partly because, if you are so minded, the very prospect of wildfowl quickens the senses, and partly because of the tremendous variety of birdlife that crowds round patches of water in a dry country. I have vivid recollections of standing at the water's edge beneath some big trees in the early-morning sun. Across the narrow stretch of water the reeds and willows might have fringed a little bay at Killarney. The place was alive with geese and duck and the first shot sent them off, but they were driven to and fro by two guns at the other water a mile away. They presented a fine variety of shots (and incidentally my first right-and-left at geese) and some of the teal flew like jet-propelled plummets – but it was not only that. The birds one did not shoot at were an equal delight. A couple of golden-crested cranes, for instance, kept coming back to within a few yards – such exquisitely dainty creatures till (as so often happens!) they open their mouths, when their slow *honk! honk!* sounds like an aged London taxi-driver with a bulb horn. Innumerable doves flitted to and fro, cooing 'two-by-two, two-by-two' and sipping at the water's edge, and an old maribou stork with his huge bill trod fastidiously through the reeds and took off with a great flapping and creaking as though his joints needed oiling. On the other side of the lake the lowing of beasts indicated a village. And when, as we left, a couple of the women arrived carrying on their heads pitchers of fresh milk for us, merely as a gesture of welcome, the morning seemed complete.

Darfur was a man's country if ever there was one and not for a moment did sex rear its ugly, or according to how you see it, delectable head. No women of any desirability were ever on show and, unless you were grand enough to be a Commander-in-Chief or Provincial Governor and bring your own, you could reckon to lead a strictly bachelor existence, at any rate so far as white women were concerned. On the other hand, the locals did not think very highly of bachelors, and Henderson told how, when he was a DC, they urged him to marry. 'Take any girl you like,' they said. 'Then, after your three years are up, you can divorce her and go back and marry your own. Anyone would be proud to marry the first one.' 'And what about children?' Henderson had asked. 'Oh,' they said, 'the next husband could bring them up as interpreters.' We did attend one open-air dance, if you could call it that, with three drums under a tree and a number of dusky damsels of unfortunate appearance shuffling around, while the others stood in a ring round the edge. It is true that two males were lying on their side shuddering and two girls making complementary movements a few feet away, their meaning being reasonably obvious but not calculated on a hot afternoon in full daylight to send a European berserk – though they did tell me that a Sudanese spent five years in England studying medicine and, the moment he saw native women dancing on his return, turned immediately back into a complete savage. What he would have thought of London at the moment of my writing this, when only three major cinemas in the West End are showing films fit to take the family to, I hesitate to think. Perhaps he would have been like the natives at a party given for some VIPs in a French territory bordering on the Sudan. The French, according to a classic story, created a fine fountain, complete with coloured lights, and, to impress the VIPs further, added a few naked girls to splash about in the water. The VIPs were duly impressed, and so were the Africans. 'Ho, ho, ho!' they cried. 'Ho, ho, ho!' They were looking at the coloured lights.

The horse show and parade which was the object of our exercise was held at a little village called Sibdu, where again some splendid huts had been prepared for us. This was an annual event when the people assembled with their horses and the Government either

At the annual 'horse show' in Sibdu, Darfur. After the official ride-past of about two thousand men, all armed with nine-foot spears, pairs of riders performed duffas, *feats of flat-out riding and pulling up hard.*

Shooting snipe near the village of Ekiad in Egypt, accompanied by a guide, his assistants and a horde of uninvited juvenile assistants.

bought them or declined, according to the verdict of the Government vet, a Scotsman called Ian Gillespie. Any resemblance to a horse show in England would, however, be purely coincidental. The parade was led by the Governor and the head of the local Rizziegat tribe, Nazir Ibrahim Musa, riding side by side, with an escort of sixty horsemen, attired, astonishingly, in chain mail. Ibrahim Musa was a figure one could never forget: a tremendous old boy with jutting beard and one of the cruellest faces I have ever seen, a descendant of the savage slave-traders described in C. S. Forester's *The Sky and the Forest* and one who would, in the absence of outside authority, instantly have taken it up again, as doubtless his successor has already done. Both he and his horse were magnificently decked out in red robes with gold facings and, attached to his wrist, he carried a villainous four-foot whip. Here was a real *man*, with eleven sons and daughters too numerous to be worth counting.

Next came the District Commissioner, Laurie, in plumed hat, followed by the Sudan Defence Force with their standard of the Cross of Lorraine on a purple background and, somewhere among them, myself. There was, of course, no stadium, but something a great deal more impressive, an avenue of thorns laid out on either side and behind them perhaps two thousand mounted men, each holding aloft a nine-foot spear. As the procession passed, they lowered their spears, like sheaves of corn bowing in the wind, to signify their subservience to the leading figures and, my word, was it impressive! Behind the horsemen were a great number of spectators, a good many of them women who kept up a constant high *lu-lu-lu* sort of wailing which I believe is known as ululation, and at the far end two red-robed men on camels, each with one thick drumstick and one thin, beat out a persistent *oom-da*, *oom-da-da* rhythm, which after an hour or so made you want to start doing a dervish-dance yourself.

At the end of the avenue we duly dismounted, while the Nazir and his escort went back to the start. They then did a ride-past on their own, Ibrahim Musa dipping his sword to the Governor and then dismounting to stand beside him, whereupon all the horsemen, without a word of an order, much less the masses of 'operation orders' that would have been held necessary in more literate countries, began their own ride-past, or perhaps one should say 'gallop-past'. They flashed by, nine abreast, many leading a number of riderless horses, some with foals following their mothers. Some had stirrups, some not. Some had leather reins, some had rope. Some had bits, others just a noseband. All carried nine-foot spears. When all had gone by, they went back to their places along the line, while pairs of riders performed *duffas*, which means riding flat out to a certain point and then pulling up in a cloud of dust. Experience showed that you got the maximum acceleration out of a horse by lashing it as hard as possible with a four-foot whip, while the best braking was to be obtained with a bit that was just not quite as sharp as a razor-blade. If you had put forward an RSPCA type of line on this, they would have thought you off your head. Meanwhile one learnt an elementary lesson in crowd control, which might be useful in Australia, where crowds now wreck cricket matches by running onto the field of play. Some of the crowd, in their eagerness to see the riders coming, eased themselves too far forward for the Nazir's liking. He beckoned to a red-robed figure, a jet black fellow with slant eyes, flashing teeth and the inevitable whip on his wrist, and indicated his wishes with the merest gesture of a finger. It really is very simple. If you want people to move back, you simply go along slashing them in the balls with a whip as hard as you can. It's surprising how quickly they move. Meanwhile gales of ho-ho-ho laughter would sweep along the spectators on the other side as a whole line of white-gowned figures were seen to be doubled up, howling. The smiles were quickly removed from their faces, however, when a moment later they got the treatment themselves.

After leaving the horse show we had, somewhere on the way back to Fasher, the great lion hunt, of which I wrote soon afterwards in *Country Life*. Though I say it myself, my old classics master, A. L. ('Uncle') Irvine, wrote to say that he considered it a good piece of writing, so much so that he had cut it out and, at the age of eighty-four, pasted it into his commonplace book. What with that, and the fact that it was twenty years ago, I take the liberty of setting it out as I wrote it with the memory fresh in my mind.

Another striking event was the great lion hunt, which I had been promised before leaving England. Lions are vermin in Darfur, so that one had the prospect not only of a new experience and something to dine out upon for the next few weeks but also of doing one's good deed for the day. The inhabitants think highly of anyone who kills a lion, irrespective of how he does it. Thus, as much face is to be gained from potting a beast, unconscious, at a hundred yards as from the local procedure of cornering it, armed only with spears, and doing it to death by hand – or even, as did the brother of one of the men out with us, rushing in and stabbing it with a bayonet as it was leaping upon another man.

Early one morning we drove a dozen miles out from Abu Sela, where a very large, very black fellow stopped the party and conducted us through the scrub to a water-hole. Here we found the beaters, thirty of them, and a more splendidly bold and bloodthirsty crew you never did see. All were mounted and all carried long spears with heads as sharp as razor-blades. Some had stirrups, some had not. Of those who had, the majority preferred to insert only the big toe – for, of course, none boasted footwear of any kind. Their ancestors, many of whom fought with such fearless frenzy against the machine-guns of Omdurman, made no bones about it: their stirrups were often no more than a small metal ring for the big toe.

At the water-hole more horses were waiting – my own a fine white stallion with sheepskin saddle – and we rode for another twenty minutes, mostly through camel-thorn, to a wadi fringed with rushes and tall trees. A casual glance noted that many of these trees would, at a push, be climbable – especially when aided by that sudden charge of adrenalin which, the medical experts tell us, enables a man in an emergency to jump a ten-foot wall, and later not know how he did it.

The firing party, consisting of the Nazir Ali el Ghali, Captain K. Timbrell, Laurie and myself, disposed themselves strategically to cover the approach of the lion, which was to come 'padding up the wadi'. The Nazir and Timbrell squatted in the tall grass, while the not so intrepid white hunter, comforted by the thought that any animal which survived this barrage deserved anything it could get, concealed himself in the fork of a tree. With a good deal of glinting of knives members of the Sudan Defence Force squatted enthusiastically in the bushes around.

The beaters vanished and an air of utter peace descended on the scene – an atmosphere which all who shoot will understand, when the beaters have gone but not begun their task, when anything may happen in the end, but nothing assuredly will happen for half an hour, and the world around, provided you keep still, settles quietly down to its daily life again as though you did not exist.

Last-minute instructions were given to the novice: how, if there were two of them, he was to shoot the lioness – 'the one without the mane' – as the lion would in that event push off, while the lioness in similar circumstances would stay and become awkward (a singular reflection, one could not help thinking, upon the King of Beasts), and how, if it came to the last cartridge, he was to hold his fire till the lion was at a point about fifteen feet away – as likely, one thought, as the novice counting ten before opening his parachute.

Peace reigned and one was left alone in the sunshine with one up the spout and five in the magazine and a highly charged sense of anticipation. I do not know how many times I drew a bead on the imaginary tawny shape slipping silently round the end of the wadi. But, alas, it never appeared. A cry in the distance, then another, and another, meant that the beaters were converging on us, and soon they were riding in on all sides from the scrub. The head beater, a terrific fellow who made one glad that, for this generation at any rate, peace prevailed in the Sudan, explained the situation with many gestures and in a language that I did not understand, and off they all galloped again to drive the other end of the wadi. Here too, however, the result was a blank.

So the horses were whistled up from their refuge half a mile in the rear, and we all repaired to the water-hole there to lunch off ice-cold beer, hot soup, roast duck, and coffee, and so home to Abu Sela – only to be met by an urgent deputation as to what was to be done about the lion.

It had just killed a bull, right on the outskirts of the village!

So now, after an all too short spell of what had seemed at this time of year and by contrast with an English winter an almost idyllic existence, it was time to return to headquarters. As to the golf course at Fasher, I am conscious of having written about it before but will allow myself the luxury of mentioning it for positively the final time, since out of the 400-odd courses on which I have played, including some on which no blade of grass has ever grown or ever will, Fasher remains unique. There was no clubhouse and the members, it was said, could be counted on the fingers of two hands, or at any rate on those of the owner of the village adjoining the course, known as Abu Shoke, the 'father of thorns', who had seven on each. There was no clubhouse and no tees, but there were nine greens, each with a hole in, generally with the metal rim sticking up out of the sand, interspersed with a particularly vicious form of camel thorn, the spikes of which were sharp enough not only to penetrate a ball, let alone the seat of your trousers – another local rule said you could 'dethorn' a ball without penalty – but also to be habitually used in place of gramophone needles. Members of the SDF were riding all over the course, practising for their tattoo, jumping on and off at full gallop, riding two horses at once and so on, and the surface of one green was far from improved by the paw marks of a couple of hyenas. We teed off in the sand at the top of a bluff looking over a magnificent view and played down to the 1st hole, marked by a small boy in a nightshirt holding what turned out to be the club's only flag. No use having permanent flags, they said. If you had wooden ones, the ants would eat them and, if you had metal, the locals would melt them instantly down for spears. So when one had reached within a few yards of the green, the boy doubled off through the camel thorn to hold the flag in the 2nd hole, while a huge coal black caddie advanced in stately fashion to the hole and placed his feet at right angles behind it for the player to putt at. The 7th, I remember, was a short hole with the green surrounded by this ghastly camel thorn, but the Governor described it with a certain amount of local pride as being 'set in a sylvan setting'. The climax came fittingly enough at the 9th, when one of the caddies, distinguished by a blue diamond on the back of his jellaba, became noticeably restive. The blue diamond, it transpired, signified that he had been seconded for duty from the gaol and he feared he was going to be late for lock-up. He was therefore sent back in the Governor's car. One feels somehow that, though he and the Empire of which this was part had long since been dead, Kipling would have approved.

Certainly he would have approved of the Sudanese Band, who had only been learning three weeks, under the tuition of a Corporal Wilkes of the South West Borderers, and who that evening were to beat the Retreat for the first time, a ceremony I have witnessed in many parts of the Empire and never without a tear in the eye. The Band were a fine body of men, immaculately turned out in white with blue puttees and turban-like hats. They had bugles and pipes and a five-foot drum which had been presented to the 'Black Sultan', Ali Dinar, by Lord Cromer, and the drum major was learning to twiddle his staff in the best Guards fashion.

Ali Dinar had turned against the Allies in 1916 and had been hunted down and killed somewhere near Abu Sela and now the Governor lived in what had been his palace, and a pretty remarkable residence it was, at that. In the office was a picture of the dead Sultan and his magnificent red and gold velvet chair of State. The living-room had been his dining-room. All the doors were most beautifully inlaid with ivory and so were the window-doors, some of which were left open to form cupboards within the three-foot-thick walls. Big stone steps led up to a balcony, parts of which had been enclosed to make separate rooms, and at each of the four corners of the main room were the shelves on which the naked slave girls sat during dinner – and, one would imagine, without too much fidgeting either, since an elderly fellow who had worked for three years for Ali Dinar as a boy, when asked what he was like, replied, 'I never saw him. We were not allowed to look above our knees!' Over the main gate was still to be observed a sort of wickerwork cage in which offenders were made to sit and roast in the sun during the Sultan's pleasure. For more serious offences he simply had them thrown down the well. Retribution in this savage part of the world is simple and direct. Ibrahim Musa, for instance, would simply order the man to be taken a mile or so from the village and in the full heat of the midday sun cause his ankle to be attached to a large log, the size being nicely calculated to ensure that the victim might, or again might not, just succeed in dragging it back into the shade before perishing from thirst and the heat. In other parts of the Arab world it is common-place, when a man has been caught thieving, to bring forward a bucket of boiling tar and a stout chopper and cut off his right hand. There is a refreshing directness in this, as against our own, as I think, more barbaric methods, and I often wonder whether the train robbers would not have opted to lose a hand rather than spend thirty years without seeing a woman or a blade of grass.

The Sudan remains a savage, barbaric land, its surface scratched by civilization in the shape of the Sudan Civil Service, who tended to be 'outdoor' types, as against the classical scholars of the Indian Civil. Laurie was a case in point. Some time previously a fellow DC, John Wilson, was surprised, on emerging from his courtroom, to see a spear, plunged into his back by a dissatisfied litigant, come out through the front of his stomach. By some miracle it had missed the vital parts and not only did he recover but he and Laurie, neither having rowed for eight years, returned home on leave and together won the Coxwainless Pairs in the 1948 Olympic Games.

Already, though, the writing was on the wall, and I had noticed in Laurie's bungalow in Nyala a huge volume of Gray's *Anatomy*. He resigned and became in due course a successful doctor at home. What Darfur has reverted to I do not know. I do know, however, that I should want a very powerful escort before I ventured down there today.

25

Up the Tower

Life is a mixed bag – chances offered and taken, more often chances missed or not even noticed. Successes are sometimes to be scored by honest toil and solid worth, more often by happening to be standing somewhere, thinking of nothing, at exactly the right time. In the latter category may be placed my entry into broadcasting, which for about thirty-five years has been one of the most pleasurable activities of my life.

Television is, by comparison with radio, a push-over. In television – I am talking, of course, of golf – in times of local difficulty, which means quite often, you can always intersperse what Sydney Smith, referring to the loquacious Macaulay's conversation at dinner, called 'brilliant flashes of silence', and indeed, as I hope to show in due course, this may gain you much merit. In other words you can always sit back and let them look at the picture. In radio, if your mind goes blank for three seconds, they think the set has gone wrong. It is essential, therefore, in an emergency to possess the ability to 'waffle on', and with this from the first I never had any great difficulty – on the radio or anywhere else, come to that! Two other qualities are desirable, both of which I can claim to have possessed in those dim distant days when they started putting out golf reports on the radio and including it in sporting 'magazine' programmes. I think you should not only know but be able to 'feel' the game, in the sense of knowing exactly what is going on in the player's mind, especially in time of trouble, when it has so often gone on in your own. You should also on the radio be able to *talk*, from a few scattered notes, maybe, rather than read a piece written out beforehand – which presupposes that you can remember what you have seen; the scores, incidents, situations and so on. This, though I say it myself, I had no difficulty in doing and was even able to telephone reports five times a day to the

Evening Standard without writing anything down. A much senior colleague once remarked that I 'never appeared to make any notes'. I accepted the compliment with good grace, at the same time thinking, 'Does the time really come when you can go out on a golf course and not even remember what you have seen?' Alas, it does. I can follow the whole of a championship final these days and hardly remember a shot. Probably waffling too much on the way round.

I believe I can claim to have done the first 'live' outside broad-cast on golf when the BBC set up a glass box on stilts at some vantage point far out on the Little Aston course outside Birming-ham, overlooking two greens and three tees. In a way we were not unsuccessful. We saw plenty of play, chopping and changing from one hole to another, and had an added piece of good fortune when a past Open Champion, Arthur Havers, completely fluffed a short approach shot in front of our window. Perhaps he was unnerved by the thought of being on 'live' for the first time in history.

Then the BBC brought in a portable apparatus with which it was to be possible actually to follow the golf, and here the initiator, at the English Championship at Birkdale the year before the war, was the doyen of our profession, Bernard Darwin. He set off onto the course accompanied by two engineers, one carrying a portmanteau-shaped apparatus strapped to his back with a long aerial sticking up vertically behind his head, and the other lugging round the batteries. I naturally listened with professional interest, having been invited to carry out a similar venture at the Amateur Championship at Hoylake later on. It was soon pretty clear that the venerable scribe was finding it heavy going and it was no surprise when he declared, on returning to the clubhouse, that golf, so far as he was concerned, did not lend itself to this type of broadcasting.

At Hoylake on the morning of the quarter-finals we tried to follow the play but soon came up against the elementary stumbling-block that in order to describe the play you had to see it and in order to see it you had to be within range of the players and they could therefore hear what you were saying, which was not only extremely embarrassing but led to persistent cries of 'Shhh' from the silent spectators. For the afternoon semi-finals (as a result of which A. A. Duncan and Alex Kyle reached the final, completing the first round in two hours and twenty minutes, which is less than it takes Americans these days to play nine holes) we set ourselves up on a knoll beside the 5th fairway, well out of the way but with a reasonable view of the distant play. It seems incredible today but the signal for us to start was to be the lowering of a white handkerchief by an engineer perched on the roof of the Royal Liverpool clubhouse. The exact hour of the broadcast in those days had to be printed in advance, so there was no flexibility in time. The first semi-final came and passed, then so did the second.

At this point the engineer raised the white handkerchief and we were under starter's orders. He lowered it briskly, and we were 'off' – whereupon the second match vanished from sight, leaving our little trio silent upon a knoll in Hoylake, unable to move since our range was only a mile. I state with confidence that I gave an absolutely splendid and dramatic eyewitness account of the play, understandably interspersed with a good deal of the 'wish you were here . . . lovely view across the bay' sort of stuff, and I could not help feeling that not everyone could have waffled continuously or to such effect for ten whole minutes about non-existent play. I thus returned to the clubhouse feeling that a hand or two might well be extended. Instead we met the engineer. He was most apologetic. 'We had to fade you out after a minute or two,' he said, 'on account of a technical hitch.'

Much as I respect the club, Hoylake has never been my happy hunting-ground for either radio or television. In 1936, when golf on the radio was comparatively new, the engineer and I were stuck in a tiny glass-fronted box situated among the guy-ropes at the back of the refreshment tent, with barely room for ourselves and a suspended microphone. Firstly, one day's play in the Open was cancelled on account of a snowstorm – in July – and I had to do three ten-minute pieces on an Empire programme filling in for a whole day's play that had never taken place. Then a couple of friends espied me from afar and with schoolboy delight advanced upon our humble box. I hope I do them no injustice but I suspect them in memory to have been Andrew McNair, of Sunningdale, and another fine golfer and Olympic fencer, Francis Francis, who left the Guards to marry an actress and now grows pineapples on an island in the Bahamas. At any rate I was in full spate when they came and made rude two-fingered gestures outside the box, pressing their noses against the glass and generally carrying on as though provoking a monkey in a cage. Finally, when once again we were in full flow, a waitress came out behind the refreshment tent carrying an enormous pile of plates. The strange spectacle in our little box so distracted her attention that she tripped over a guy-rope and sank with a crash that reverberated throughout the Empire. I explained what it was and gather that it gave innocent pleasure as far away as New Zealand.

Whether I can claim to have done the first 'live' television of golf, I am not sure. I suspect that this distinction also fell to Bernard Darwin, in an experimental show at Coombe Hill. At any rate my own baptism was experimental enough in all conscience. It took place on the 14th fairway at Moor Park, and I fancy that the object was not so much to entertain the public, practically none of whom had television sets anyway, as to see whether the picture could be successfully transmitted to Alexandra Palace. As may be imagined, it was a splendid and most entertaining shambles, judged by the standards of today, but it is something to have been 'in at the birth'.

Several players of distinction were assembled to play chip shots to the green and I am not sure now, and wasn't then, that a few little matches were not devised. There was, as I remember, only one camera. However, spectators flocked up from everywhere, as when you have an accident in a deserted street, and an animated scene soon developed. I had a microphone attached to about twenty-five yards of cable, but the main interest lay in neither the players nor the commentator but the monitor, which was housed in a large box on the fairway. Unable to see the play from beside it, I adjourned to a neighbouring mound, descending from time to time, with my cable acting like a minesweeper, and trying to get through the crowd round the monitor, mostly women, all saying, 'Coo, look. There's a picture!'

The first serious attempts to televise live golf were directed by Antony Craxton, who used to do the Queen's Christmas broadcasts. Many were from Wentworth, which in summer, with the trees in full glory and a shirtsleeved crowd moving from hole to hole enjoying themselves in the sunshine, can present a magnificent picture. I remember Craxton saying how golf even then attracted quite a large 'rating' by comparison with what had been expected and how many housewives on housing estates said that they knew nothing about it but liked to watch because 'it seemed such a lovely place'. Nowadays, of course, this holds good to a much greater extent and some of the scenes in colour – so much superior to the American colour, for once – can be really heavenly. All this helped to create the so-called golf 'explosion', which has been one of the sporting phenomena of the times. When we started, hardly a cameraman knew anything about the game and had to be told each time, 'Now drop down. No, wider. Now relate the ball to the hole,' etcetera. Everything and, I like to think, everybody seemed so agreeable, however, that they began to ask, like tens of thousands of other people, 'Can anybody join in?' and, the answer being 'Yes', they took to bringing a single club with them, encouraged by my fellow-commentator Bill Cox, one of the leading teachers of the game, and I shall never forget the scene at the 16th hole at Wentworth one day when, the programme having finished, about a couple of dozen technicians poured out from the headquarters in the trees and lined up for a lesson. Now almost everyone concerned has taken to the game and few of the cameramen need to be told, in the golfing sense, what to do.

For myself I always thought the 'beauty shots' and the little irrelevancies, though we seem to have time for few of them these days, added to the appeal of golfing programmes: the 360-degree panorama of, say, Turnberry, with the Clyde and the Isle of Arran and the long encircling arm of the Mull of Kintyre and Ailsa Craig; or Muirfield, with the distant tracery of the two great Forth Bridges and the Kingdom of Fife on the other side of the Firth; or St Andrews and the bay and the snow-capped Cairngorms: or, again, the small boy at the 8th at Wentworth who, immediately the last match had passed by, emerged from the undergrowth and started fishing in the pond; or the lark's nest focused upon by an alert cameraman at Muirfield during the Open. The producer had to sacrifice this camera for quite a while before the mother lark returned to the nest to feed the young, and there were many afterwards who said that this was the best bit in the programme, never mind Jack Nicklaus. The same cameraman's roving eye and telephoto lens discerned a couple on the sandhills just outside the course and it was nip and tuck whether their subsequent union did not feature, live and in colour, for the first time on this or any other screen. If only the producer had been under notice from the BBC at the time, he might have risked his arm and given the world a most entertaining exposure – and I sometimes wonder what I should have made of the commentary.

What we put up with in the early days never ceases to surprise me. For the Walker Cup match at St Andrews I was stuck up on a tall tower out by the 'Loop', where the holes criss-cross each other at the far end of the course, making it almost impossible on a small monitor to detect who is playing which hole and who is crossing over playing a different hole. Once again the wind howled in, direct from the North Sea and twice as strongly at forty feet up as on the ground, and soon it was so cold that one became numbed. Nor were the senses quickened by the fact that the British team lost every match on both days. For the second sitting I borrowed a fine, fur-collared flying-coat from the barman at the Scores Hotel, but once again I gradually froze, to such an extent that I eventually found myself huddled over the blurred picture, thinking how poor it was and that there wasn't even a commentary. It was quite a time before the penny dropped. I suppose I can now claim the doubtful distinction of being the only BBC commentator who has actually forgotten to do the commentary.

Another time, at St Andrews, it was the picture that failed and I heard frantic voices from London saying, 'Tell him to do a sound commentary till we get the picture back.' This was really like old times and the 'lovely view across the bay' stuff came back as naturally as though it were yesterday. In fact, at St Andrews, there *is* a lovely view across the bay. I kept this up for about twenty-five minutes till eventually we got going again, and at the end of it all strolled back from my perch at the 17th to the Royal and Ancient for refreshment which I felt had been well earned. As I got inside the door, the porter handed me a telegram. It was from the Nore Golfing Society. FIRST RULE OF ELECTRONICS, it read, IF IT DOESN'T WORK, KICK IT.

What can be the mentality of the man who actually rings up the BBC during the course of a transmission as did a doctor during the play-off for the Open between Thomson and Thomas at Lytham? We were in full voice when the producer came in with: 'There's a doctor who has just rung the BBC in London with a message saying, "Tell Longhurst there is no p in Thomson".' This is a moment for instant decision. The answer comes immediately to mind, but do you give it? Do you say, 'I understand a doctor has just rung the BBC to say there is no p in Thomson, and if it is of any interest to him this is by no means the only thing in which the p is silent' – or don't you? I didn't, but I still have a sneaking wish that I had.

Another penny that dropped slowly was the realization that the commentators do not have to be at the same height and in the same place as the cameras. At Wentworth for years we had a colossal tower, sixty to seventy feet high, out by the 7th hole, often with ladders on the outside, inevitably with whippy shafts, so that after each step you took they came back at you and tried to throw you off. I used to stop half-way and pretend to admire the scenery. The fact was that my heart was by this time going at 142 and I was thinking, 'What a silly way to go.' One day we had, by a fine combination of muscular strength and bravado, none other than Douglas Bader, on a little platform only one level below our actual box, which for a man with no feet was no small feat. And for good measure we also had Sir Ian Jacob, Director-General of the BBC: high-level stuff, in fact, in every sense.

Even by this time, however, we still had no protection whatever from the elements and one day, through someone lifting up the binoculars, which were acting as a paperweight, the whole of the scores were blown instantly away, coming to earth many seconds later nearly a quarter of a mile distant. Luckily the broadcast was nearly over and I could remember the leading scores. Nor were we any luckier at Hoylake with the television than we had been with the radio. In 1955, when the art itself was making progress but before the days when commentators were held to be human, we were stuck up on a tall and precarious tower behind the 17th, open to all the elements. The wind howled, the rain lashed across the links, our scant piece of waterproof protection was whisked off and fetched up in Meols Drive, and the score-keeping apparatus, already mottled with the running ink of ball-point pens, eventually became so sodden that when you tried to turn the page it simply peeled off.

Gradually it came to be appreciated that, if you wanted to 'show the winner winning', the thing to do was to concentrate, as the Americans were already doing, on the last five holes, together with any 'bonus' holes that the same cameras might be able to cover elsewhere – as, for instance, at St Andrews, where the first five and the last five all share a common strip of ground. It was also realized, as was really known all along, that the commentator need not be able to see what he was talking about, since his first task is to watch the monitor, the cardinal sin being to talk about something the viewer cannot see, thus driving the latter into absolute frenzies of frustration. Thus at last we began to be pitched nearer the clubhouse rather than miles out on the course, and up only one ladder, and the hand of civilization was extended towards us in the shape of little glass boxes to sit in.

For years it fell to one person to introduce and close the programme and calculate the scores by glancing at the sheetful of figures so painstakingly kept by the scorer beside him, rather as a bookmaker glances over his shoulder at his clerk, the public scoreboards being in those days indifferent and there being no 'leader boards' at all, apart from the odd chalked blackboard from which the elements had almost certainly washed away any information it may once have given. The annual headache was the fear of giving a tremendous build-up to the final scene in the Open Championship, only to find that one had made a wrong calculation from the figures and that, far from being the winner, so-and-so was due to play off in the morning. Later we had the luxury of Harry Carpenter to keep our own scoreboard, in vision, in his own little box, and finally we graduated to quite a big, glass-fronted room, grandly known as the studio. This houses the numerous technicians; the 'captions' team, who are responsible for attaching magnetized names and figures and plans to a board to be super-imposed on the picture; the scoring system; anything up to four commentators, all sitting in a row and nudging each other to fix who is going to do the next hole, and finally Harry Carpenter, to whom in a moment I must pay tribute.

It will be appreciated that I have not the slightest idea how any of all this miraculous mass of gadgetry works. Indeed, the miracle is that it ever does. The producer sits in a dark van known as the scanner, hidden away in the trees and reminiscent of a wartime RAF ops-room, and is faced with as many pictures as he has cameras, all giving a picture at the same time. He selects one of these and it should appear on both of two extra screens below the others, thus making three pictures all the same. The left-hand one of the lower two is what he is sending out and the other is what, as a television viewer, he is receiving. If there is no picture on the left, there is naturally none on the right, since nothing is going out; and then there are cries, just as there used to be in Light Anti-Aircraft in the war, of 'It's the generator, sir'. If there is a picture on the left but not on the right, it is a case of 'Nothing to do with us, sir. It is leaving here all right'. Either is a case of 'Normal service will be resumed as soon as possible'. The Man in the Scanner controls all the cameramen and the sound units out on the course; tells the commentators when to go on and what is coming next, and controls the video-tape unit by which to record events to be shown later, at the same time conducting a spirited running battle with London for more time.

The biggest 'ops-room' type of scanner ever created was one in which Ray Lakeland was in charge as producer. This was at Aintree after the BBC had paid Mrs Topham some enormous sum for the television rights of the Grand National, following that formidable lady's somewhat unsuccessful attempt to do it off her own bat. Not only was every part of the four-and-a-half mile course covered by a camera, but also the winner's enclosure, interview points and Heaven knows what else, with the result that Lakeland in the end might have been conducting the Battle of Britain. At last the great moment came and they were 'off'. I need hardly describe the concentration required by the producer over the next half-hour, for which they had all been preparing and rehearsing for so long. It was broken in the middle for Lakeland by an enormous Liverpool policeman, who had somehow got in and was now nudging him on the arm. 'Are ye busy?' he said. If not, it transpired, 'Chief Constable would like you to come and 'ave a cup of tea.'

The babel going on in the scanner has to be heard to be believed and furthermore *is* heard, not only by the commentators, who can at least push their earphones back, lay their hand-microphones down on the table and let the customers look at the picture while they themselves take an aural breather, so to speak, but also by Harry Carpenter, who cannot remove his little earpiece and therefore has to take it all the time. Thus, while he is urbanely pointing to the board, indicating the fluctuation of events during the day and who was, or now is, leading, there is coming into his ear a cacophony of noise, interspersed by a bell-like feminine voice: 'Thirty seconds to the end of Harry . . . twenty seconds to the end of Harry . . . ten seconds to the end of Harry . . . nine, eight, seven, six, five, four, three, two, one – *Music!*' I sit in admiration while Harry not only goes smoothly on but sometimes even starts a new sentence on 'four'. This time, I think, they must surely have beaten him, but no. 'So we look forward [three] to seeing you here at [two] Wentworth at the [one] same time tomorrow' – and Harry, hats off to him, has done it again.

It was to Ray Lakeland, and to the fact of happening once again to be in the right place at the right moment with my mouth open – literally, and with the right elbow lifted, at that – that I owe another experience in television which has given me more delight than I can say and has turned out to be a compliment not only, if I may say so, to me but also to 'us'. Lakeland was for some reason at the 1965 Carling tournament at a course called Pleasant Valley outside Boston. I was also there but, having no work to do until the Friday, was idly sitting around having a drink, when he informed me that CBS (the Columbia Broadcasting System), who were televizing the event, wondered if it would interest me to go up one of their towers, it being their rehearsal day, and 'see how they did it'. I was naturally intrigued and did so, joining one of their announcers, as they call the commentators, John Derr. So far as I remember I only said a few words into their microphone, but to my astonishment I got a note from the producer, Frank Chirkinian, inviting me to do the 16th hole next day. This turned out to be a long short-hole of some 210-odd yards, where the players drove from an elevated tee down between two bunkers and onto a huge green, behind which we sat under a big parasol on a tower no more than twenty feet high.

'After all I've been through', as my mother is fond of saying, I soon discovered the luxury that is the lot of the American television announcer by comparison with home. Firstly, we ascended our little tower by a broad set of steps instead of a death-trap ladder. The next luxury was the thought of having only one hole to pay attention to, and this a short one at that, so one did not even have to watch drives as well as second shots. I gather that the same babel of anguish and frustration takes place in the scanner, or 'truck', as they rather mundanely call it, as at home but their communications system is such that the commentator is spared hearing it while trying to enlighten the world with his observations, so that in one's ears almost total peace reigns and one hears only one's fellow commentators, plus a quiet background voice saying, 'After this putt throw it to 18,' or simply, 'Throw it to 16.' This lack of chatter was at first disconcerting and I kept suspecting that I had done something wrong and that we had been cut off.

Another great luxury is that in almost all cases the golf 'telecasts' are limited, through the expense of sponsorship, to two hours on the final day and an hour and a half on the day before, covering in both cases, of course, only the concluding stages and therefore the best players. At home we may go on for the whole afternoon, 'shared with cricket' or some other sport, only to find that the cricket is washed out and we have to go on for hours. During the Open of 1970, on account of the racial prejudice against the white South African cricket team, we were on for the best part of six hours, with two relays of commentators but no respite for the producer, and, if he had been 'certifiable' at the end, one would have sympathized and understood. The real commentators' curse, however, is the miraculous videotape. In the old days we were 'not on again till 4.20', and one made off for well-earned nourishment till needed again. Nowadays it is: 'Stand by to record So-and-so and Such-and-such as they come in,' all this being to fill in a later transmission time when perhaps no figures of merit are within range. All very wonderful but it makes you sigh for the good old days!

At any rate at Pleasant Valley I did all I was called upon to do, which heaven knows did not seem very much, naming the players and their scores correctly as they came up to the tee, which one could hardly fail to do in view of the fact that a very efficient young fellow had already put a piece of paper in front of one's nose containing the information, and occasionally adding some commonplace comment before being told to 'throw it to 15'. It transpired, however, that completely unwittingly I had managed to cause two minor sensations in our limited little world. One was when towards the end a young Mexican called Homero Blancas came to the 16th hole with the prospect looming before him of picking up, if everything went right, the equivalent of some £12,000. It proved to be a little much for him and, taking a 2-iron, he hit the shot that a good many of us would have done in the circumstances; in other words he hit it right off the sole, half topped, and it must have stung like the devil. 'Oh, that's a terrible one,' I said instinctively. 'Right off the bottom of the club.' In fact, it scuttled down the hill and finished on the green, but that wasn't the point. I had said it was a bad shot – which of course it was – but no one, it transpired, had ever said such a thing before, at any rate in such downright terms. This, though it took some time for the penny to drop and

I can sometimes scarcely believe it still, was the first 'sensation'. The second took even longer to dawn on me. Golf being, like billiards, a 'silent' game, that is to say that silence is expected while a man is making his stroke – unlike, say, the Cup Final, when both viewer and commentator are conscious of being one of a vast vociferous crowd (though even so, compare the silence that comes over them when a man is to take a penalty and therefore to make a single individual stroke) – it had never occurred to me from the very beginning that one should do other than remain silent while the golfer was actually playing his shot, so that 'talking on the stroke' had always seemed to be one of the cardinal sins of golf commentating, even though, heaven knows, I have found myself often enough guilty of committing it. This had not been, up to that time, the accepted principle in America which it has since become and the 'brilliant flashes of silence' turned out to be the second 'sensation'.

Also, of course, the most commonplace little expressions in one man's country may seem strange and catch the attention in another's. Towards the end of this (for me) momentous day, for instance, I announced that the eventual winner, Tony Lema, later so tragically killed in a private plane accident, had a very 'missable' putt. This, I was told, was greeted with much applause by the crowd watching in the locker room. 'You hear what the old guy said? He said, "He's got a *missable putt*!"' For some extraordinary reason this commonplace and self-explanatory expression seemed never to have become part of golfing language in America.

Anyway, it was all good for trade and not only was I invited again by CBS, this time to the Masters at Augusta, which must have a separate mention of its own, but also by ABC (the American Broadcasting Company), who handle such 'prestigious' events as the US Open and the US PGA championships. This has meant not only a minimum of four visits to various parts of the States each year but also a whole host of new friendships among the general camaraderie of television, which, though I hope it does not sound pompous, is the team-game to end all team-games, since there are so many links in the chain between the original product and the viewer's screen that a single incompetent or bloody-minded link can ruin the whole enterprise. Most of the ABC people, including Roone Arledge, the big boss, and Chuck Howard, who produces the golf, are, I have to confess, younger than I, and it sometimes occurs to me that they look on me as more of a latter-day W. C. Fields than an up-to-date commentator, but so long as they employ me, what matter? The friendships I have made will last a lifetime.

In a modest way, too, my name has gone into the language of television, for by the time we all met in America I had already grown portly enough to wonder what I was doing, climbing these ladders at my weight and age, and made so bold as to wonder whether it would not be possible to somewhat civilize this mode of ascent. From that time onwards a form of staircase, complete with handrail, has been the order of the day, for which I and all my successors may be truly thankful. What I am really proud about, though, is the fact that, in the directions to the scaffolders who erect the towers, these staircases are ordered by ABC under the name of 'Longhurst Ladders'.

Such is immortality!

As a result of the pleasant episode at Pleasant Valley CBS, as I have said, invited me the following April to cover a hole at the Masters at Augusta, Georgia, and for the past five or six years I have had the honour, to say nothing of the aesthetic pleasure, of sitting on a little tower at the back of the 16th there too, once again a short hole and clearly, I should have thought, among the first half-dozen in American golf.

Augusta in April is heaven. The course itself was a nursery and many of the original trees and shrubs were left to grow on when in 1930 Clifford Roberts, a New York investment broker, persuaded the one and only Bobby Jones, who had completed his Grand Slam (the Open and Amateur Championships on both sides of the Atlantic in the same year) and was himself from Atlanta, to join him in creating a national golf course – 'a retreat of such nature and such excellence that men of some means and devoted to the game of golf might find the club an extra luxury where they might visit and play with kindred spirits from other parts of the nation'. This they certainly succeeded in doing.

> I shall never forget my first visit to the property [Jones later recorded]. The long lane of magnolias through which we approached was beautiful. The old manor house with its cupola and walls of masonry two feet thick was charming. The rare trees and shrubs of the old nursery were enchanting. But when I walked out on the grass terrace under the big trees behind the house and looked down over the property, the experience was unforgettable. It seemed that this land had been lying here

My first 'live' golf on television, on the 14th fairway at Moor Park : it was a splendid and most entertaining shambles.

An unforgettable moment. A surprise presentation by press colleagues to celebrate my twenty-one years without missing a Sunday : Jack Wood, Leonard Crawley and Ronald Heager.

for years just waiting for someone to lay a golf course upon it. Indeed, it even looked as though it were already a golf course, and I am sure that one standing today where I stood on this first visit, on the terrace overlooking the practice putting green, sees the property almost exactly as I saw it then.

Year by year I myself have sat in the same chair on the same little balcony, upstairs, looking through the wisteria down at the same scene, while the same coloured waiter comes out and says, 'You like the same as last year, sah? Beefeater on the rocks?' Everything, indeed, is the same and it is only by looking down at the huge scoreboard that you can tell which year it is – a Palmer year or a Nicklaus year or whatever it may be. The same people come, decked out in every colour of the rainbow – ridiculous under the grey skies of Britain but exactly right for the spring sunshine of Georgia. They bring the same folding chairs, take them to the same place as last year, and, many of them, sit there all day every day each year. One year we had a three-way play-off starting at one o'clock. This made it inconceivable that the game should reach the 16th hole before five, yet when I went down there to be 'taped' at about mid-day, many of the regulars, whom I had come to know by sight over the years, were already in their places, with no prospect of a shot being played before them for five hours.

The Masters, though it may have envious critics, is something special. A strong sense of traditional decorum is preserved, and woe betide the man or woman who did not observe it when Clifford Roberts's eye happened to be upon them. The spectators never run – would you mind! – but they do love to shout, and from time to time a colossal yell reverberates between the pines as someone holes a putt which, from the roar that greets it, might have been the winning goal in a Cup Final.

It all started in 1934 when the select gentlemen who had formed the Augusta National club, in a part of the world where the climate hardly permitted tournaments in the heat of summer, conceived the idea of inviting some of the leading players of the day to a tournament in the spring, when it was perfect in Georgia and the players were not engaged elsewhere. This was a great success and at once became an annual event. Who christened it 'the Masters' no one seems quite to know, nor is it certain that the pious founders would ever have started it at all if they had known what eventually they would be letting themselves in for. However that may be, the tournament they created remains unique. No advertisements are allowed to disfigure the scene either inside or outside the grounds – except when some supporter of Arnold Palmer (not, we may be sure, the great man himself) hired an aeroplane to fly noisily over the scene all day trailing a banner with the words GO ARNIE GO – nor is any mention of filthy lucre permitted, and this really is something when you consider that the 'leading money-winner' seems to be the chief focus of interest in American golf. All the television directors and commentators have to submit to a solemn lecture forbidding mention of any tournaments other than the US and British Open and Amateur championships and the American PGA (other tournaments on the professional tour simply do not exist) and especially forbidding them to mention money in any form. No prize money is announced beforehand and none presented at the time, it being held sufficient for the winner to have won the Masters and to have been invested with the traditional green blazer which thenceforward, even though he be a millionaire, he wears with justifiable pride. Only later is it revealed that the first prize this year came to $25,000 or whatever it may be.

From the side of the town on which I am usually billeted, one drives to the course through avenues of elegant houses whose gardens – open to the road, as always in America, not hedged in – are ablaze with azalea, rhododendron and dogwood. On the course itself two holes stand out and on a sunny afternoon they really take your breath away: the 13th and 'my' hole, the 16th, of which I will let the picture tell the story, except to add that on the 13th you may imagine the great Georgia pines a hundred feet high and the bank at the foot of them a solid mass of vivid scarlet, orange and yellow azaleas. At both holes the water is liable to remain an equally vivid blue, even on a cloudy day, due possibly to the fact that, if you get there early enough, you will see a gang of dusky workers, each with a watering-can full of blue dye! It was in this that I once said that Doug Sanders's ball had 'found a watery grave'. This appears to have given much innocent pleasure, since I am still reminded of it.

Augusta National, rare among the more prosperous clubs in America, is a golf club pure and simple, like Pine Valley and Cypress Point, with no swimming-pool nor gigantic locker room complete with barber, masseurs and the rest – an old porticoed plantation-style house with an unspoilt air of elegance and peace.

Among the pines on the left are a number of white cottages, or 'cabins', as they call them, in the same style, one of them a gift from the members to President Eisenhower, and behind these, discreetly secluded by a hedge, is what is probably the best 9-hole, par-3 course in the world, again enclosed by a background of spectacular colour. Here they hold a tournament on the day before the Masters, the record for which is held by Art Wall, who, believe it or not, had two 3s and seven 2s for a 20. So altogether, as you may gather, the Augusta National is not a bad place for us scribes and commentators to earn our living in, especially those of us who arrive, in April, fresh from an English winter.

Perhaps I may add one final comment on my own modest operations in television, namely that, whatever you may say, it is nice to be recognized, even if only by one's voice. This is not vanity. It adds much to the pleasure of a taxi ride, for instance (as well as to the tip!), if the driver says, 'I'd know your voice anywhere,' and starts talking about golf. Only the other day, hailing a cab opposite the American Embassy in Grosvenor Square, I said, 'I wonder if you could take me to Cricklewood Broadway?' to which the man at once replied, 'I'd take *you* anywhere.' Like so many London taxi-drivers he was an avid golfer – they have a golfing society of their own – and actually had a golf magazine beside him in the cab, open at a picture of Arnold Palmer, who once, he said, the biggest day of his golfing life, he had driven in this very cab. All this is not, however, the irrelevance to the subject of the Masters that it may seem, for my peak was reached, and you can hardly blame me for relating it, when, on handing in my baggage at Cape Town airport in South Africa, I had had time to say only, 'I wonder if you could check in this shooting-stick as well as the suitcase?' when a transatlantic voice behind me said, 'Hey! Aren't you the guy that does the 16th at the Masters?'

26

The Duck-egg Blue
and Others

Though my family were only, as I have indicated, in the middle echelons of the middle class, I do not remember a time when we did not have a motor car. Despite a certain staid correctness of behaviour my father was always one for the latest gadget, and I myself remember hearing the scratchy but miraculous sound of Dame Nellie Melba – or was it Clara Butt? – reaching us through the crystal of what must have been almost the first wireless set in Bedford. Long before that my father had taken at once to the horseless carriage and the fact that his first number was BY (for Bedfordshire) 71 showed how early he had joined forces with the internal-combustion engine which eventually was to ruin the England he knew.

Incidentally, the Lord Allington of the day declined to allow Dorset's letters to be BF, on the ground that he was damned if he was going to be BF 1. The beauty of which is, of course, that it never occurred to His Lordship that he would be assigned anything but No. 1.

Later we had the inevitable model T Ford – 'any colour you like so long as it is black' – and this I remember advancing on my mother as she cranked it and pinning her to the garage wall. Only the common sense of a woman from the village whom she was giving a lift into the town and who saw a lever marked B, presumably for Brake, and pulled it, saved the day.

There was still a great camaraderie of the road and you never passed a man tinkering with his car without stopping to ask if he needed any help. You carried a couple of cans of spare petrol, blew the tyres up with a foot-pump, and automatically asked anyone arriving after a sizeable journey whether he had had any punctures and how many times he had had to stop and change a plug. There were no roadsigns, even at crossroads, and the speed limit everywhere was 20 m.p.h. The AA man always saluted a member and, if he failed to do so, you stopped to ask the reason why, which was almost always that he had observed a posse of horny-handed constables with stop-watches concealed behind the hedge and operating a police trap on a particularly inviting stretch of road farther along. Chickens had not learnt the wariness of their successors of today and often, coming round the corner in the country, one drove into a flurry of fowls, leaving one or two fluttering on the road perhaps, and was faced with the quick decision between owning up and pretending not to notice. My mother still recalls with some bitterness having her number taken by the farmer's wife, who made her pay for the hen but would not give her the remains.

I took to the road on my fourteenth birthday with a New Hudson two-stroke motor-bike, graduating to a Raleigh and sidecar and finally to the immortal P and M Panther, which, though not so aristocratic as the Scott, put one 'one up' on most of one's friends and competitors. On my seventeenth birthday I had my first car, after a good many surreptitious drives in the family Wolseley – no L plates, driving tests, or rubbish of that kind: indeed my old Charterhouse friend, H. E. Weatherall, on positively his first outing alone in the driving seat, towed a caravan with an old Austin from the South Downs to Lewisham. My own first car was a boat-shaped two-seater Alvis and soon took one of my nine 'lives'. It must have been 1928, when the Midland Championship was played at Luffenham Heath. It was only my first year in the Cambridge team and this was my baptism in the broader world of adult competitive golf. I did rather well, I remember, starting with a 72 and finishing with a 74, though with a rather moderate round in between.

When all was over, I went across to Leicester to have dinner with my old friend and original teacher Jack Seager, then at the Rothley Park Club, and later set off on the fifty-mile drive back to Bromham. The moon was shining and the Alvis, with the hood down and the exhaust emitting that throaty noise so beloved of the young, was going wonderfully in the brisk night air. There was no hurry, as my parents were away, and I remember thinking that I really had done rather well, indeed might be said to have 'arrived' in golf, and that everything in my little world, so far as could be seen, was right. There was hardly a soul on the deserted road and I sat back to enjoy the drive.

The next thing I remember was turning over to get into a more comfortable position in which to sleep and a general sense of peace and contentment. This eventually was broken by a voice above me saying, 'Hi!' If you are driving late at night and you see beside the road an Alvis lying on its side with the headlights still on and shining across the road, and thirty yards farther on a corpse on the grass verge, you not unnaturally stop and investigate. You approach the corpse, I imagine, with mixed feelings. There it is, lying dead still in the moonlight, but what do you say? A lot of people, I suppose, would say to it, 'I say, are you all right?' which it manifestly isn't. My lone commercial-traveller friend and benefactor, as he turned out to be, came out with 'Hi!' and this is what woke me up. The car was quite a long way down the road and elementary reconstruction showed that it must have hit the verge and turned over three times, decanting me first time over and as near as a toucher breaking my neck, which was stiff for months, in the process. Had I and the Alvis not parted company it must surely have 'got' me second or third time over, and not long ago I had the pleasure of opening a speech to a gathering of road construction engineers attended by the then Minister of Transport, Mrs Barbara Castle, with: 'It is interesting to reflect, at any rate to me, that if only I had had a seat belt I should have been dead for thirty-seven years.'

'Where are you going?' said the commercial traveller. I looked blankly at him. 'I don't know,' I said. 'Well, where have you come from?' 'I don't know.' 'Well, who are you?' I had no idea. We wandered vaguely about the grass verge, which was strewn with golf clubs, not only mine, alas, but those of two county players who had entrusted theirs to my care, when suddenly I saw myself as clearly as anything in Stamford three days before. I was on my way to the Midland Golf Championship. It was at Luffenham. I played in it. I did rather well. I went to see dear old Jack Seager. That's it: my name is Longhurst, and I am on my way home to Bromham.

No one had ever told me of anyone going to sleep in a motor car but this is what I must have done. Less charitably minded readers may care to know that with Jack Seager I had had a steak, one pint of beer, and a black coffee. The poor old Alvis was a wreck and I incurred delayed concussion which set back my powers of concentration, especially on the golf course, for more than a year, but in the circumstances anyone would be happy to settle for that.

After the sad demise of the Alvis I graduated, as did most young fellows lucky enough to have a car, via the bull-nosed Morris and later the more aristocratic square-nosed variety, each with thermometer over the watercap, the needle of which nearly always seemed to point to red for Boiling. My father bought me a new one for £150 (no, not a misprint) and, just as only bad news is 'news' to a newspaper, so all that I remember of the Morris is creeping along in a blinding snowstorm one night past the Fox and Hounds at Goldington and striking the front of a bus emerging from a side turning on the left. I rather abused the driver for what was palpably his fault but my feelings may be imagined when it was revealed that he had in fact been stationary, having backed into the turning to start the return journey.

Having had the unbelievable good fortune to strike early in life a job that not only combined work with pleasure but also was paid as though I were a grown-up, I found myself in 1933, at the age of twenty-four, in a position to own a 'proper' car. I wish I could remember who put me onto it but the choice fell upon an open four-seater Hudson Terraplane 8, one of the first of the 'power—weight ratio' cars, with a vast American engine and an elegant, shell-like body. It had been driven in the Scottish Rally by a well-known woman driver, whose name escapes me, and so, I suppose, counted as second-hand, but at any rate the price was £225 (again not a misprint) and together with my lady friend, now a very celebrated columnist, I reported at the works on the Great West Road and prepared with great pride to start up the monster and drive it away. 'Excuse me, sir,' said the Hudson man, 'but the engine *is* running.'

One of the most splendidly 'snob' feelings in motoring is the virtual certainty that you will never see another car exactly like yours – nor is it wholly disagreeable to see a number of people admiring it as you come out of the pub! The Terraplane's acceleration was fantastic for those days – it once in second gear accelerated a couple of golf balls clean out of the cubby-hole and onto my lap – and friends who drove it had never driven anything like it before. The engine was so vast that you could start, if you cared, in top gear, in which it would also go at 2 or 3 m.p.h. A trick that never failed to impress was to work it up to about 90, take your foot off until it was down to the minimum, then get out, walk ahead, and let it follow you along like a dog. Little things please little minds, but it really was rather fun.

The Terraplane lasted three or four years and then the 'built-in obsolescence' typical of American cars began to show to such an extent that one day I left it at a Bedford garage and said, 'Send me what you like for it.' The answer was £27. A year or so later, damn me, there it was in the car park at Wentworth, unmistakable even apart from the familiar AMC 510 and looking like new. After admiring my old friend for a while with mixed feelings I left a note in it for its owner, asking how it was and, if it was not a rude question, how much did he pay for it? I was disappointed to receive no answer and forgot all about it, till after the war, many years later, I met a red-haired soldier of fortune in a bar in Honolulu. 'Oh,' he said, 'sorry I didn't answer your note. I was the fellow who bought your Terraplane.'

After a few years with an open four-seater Morris 8, probably one of the best small cars ever made – this one made no trouble of carrying four grown-ups, two children, two bicycles, two suitcases and the bull terrier up Watlington Hill, which is saying something – I decided, with my eyes open, to commit a deliberate act of folly and buy, second-hand, one of the last of the 'gentleman's motors', included in which definition were such makes as Bentley (pre-war), Delage, Delahaye, Lagonda, and suchlike.

Incidentally, on one of my rare expeditions to the office of the *Sunday Times*, probably to pick up some free paper, I had got as far as the very busy crossing of Theobalds Road and Gray's Inn Road when smoke began pouring from under the bonnet of the little Morris. I pulled up at the side and, if one person said, 'You're on fire,' a dozen did, till eventually I replied rather sharply, 'What the devil do you think I am on?' Finally one more sensible than the rest said 'Would you like me to ring for the fire brigade?' A few minutes later, by which time a vast crowd had collected, a distant clanging of bells heralded the arrival of the appliance and round the corner it dramatically came, the biggest in London, possibly in Europe. Its huge ladder projected over my miserable little burnt offering, a fireman stepped nonchalantly down and with a faintly perceptible hiss squirted an extinguisher onto the remains, and that was the end of an old and valued friend.

I consulted an expert regarding my 'gentleman's motor', but in the end it was an amateur who led to my undoing – none other than Patrick Campbell, whose diabolical stammer has brought him fame on the television, thus presenting to a wider audience a 'character' that had long convulsed a more intimate circle. My mother, when well into her eighties, once met him for a minute or two and for years afterwards continued to ask, 'Have you seen that fool Campbell lately?' At any rate it was he who revealed that he knew a man who had for sale a very fine 'd-d-duck-egg b-b-blue Lagonda'. Of course, it being Campbell, I should have known better but the Duck-egg Blue, as it came to be known, joined the stable and very fine indeed it was, especially with the hood down. It weighed, as I found when taking it to Ireland and had to discover the figure, just under a ton and used almost as much oil as petrol, but never mind: one did indeed feel one of the last of the 'gentle-man motorists' and the sight of a similar car invariably drew a wave from both parties.

Driving home from Guildford one night, once again in a blinding snowstorm, I was peering cautiously through the arc cleared by the windscreen wiper when the sharp left-hand corner at Alford crossroads took me by surprise, luckily at only about 25 m.p.h. I wrenched the wheel round, but the Duck-egg Blue continued majestically forwards, onto the little triangle of grass where stood the AA box. There was a sound as of several hundred matchboxes being crushed at once and the AA box, alas, was no more. It was late at night, you could hardly see fifteen yards through the snow and the whole scene was completely deserted, yet within minutes a sizeable crowd had collected, one of whom made the intelligent suggestion that maybe the telephone was still intact and we could alert the AA man, who lived not far away. Torches were flashed and the instrument located. I suppose it was the flattest in Post Office history, the back wheel having passed precisely over it. Meanwhile, the Duck-egg Blue was going quietly *P-rr-m*, *P-rr-m*, as though awaiting further instructions, and soon, aided by a few willing shoves, we were up the grass bank and away. Inspection in the morning revealed that this splendid machine had totally destroyed the Alfold AA box without so much as a scratch on the bumper.

I suspect that love of the Downs, on whose chalk anything blue, from flowers to butterflies, will thrive, may be the cause of my always having had light blue cars. At any rate the present incumbent, a Ford Mustang, is no exception, and with it I shall be happy to settle down for life, waiting to see whose built-in obsolescence causes us to break down first. I have always been a 'fresh-air fiend' and England, strangely enough, so long as you are not accompanied by a lady who has just had her hair done, is the finest climate in the world for an open car or, as they call it these days, a 'convertible'. In America or the Middle or Far East, it is nearly always either too hot or too cold. To me, to drive through what remains of our countryside in an open car on a crisp and sunny December's day – and we do get them – brings back the golden age of motoring. I ordered my Mustang in Detroit and, though the breed has a somewhat fearsome reputation, my own variety is a real old gentleman's motor car – huge engine, no gears, power steering, and a little button which causes the hood to go up and down by itself. As I went and fetched it from Lincoln Motors, my mind went back to an almost identical occasion. 'Every thirty-three years,' I said, 'I come down to the Great West Road and collect a light blue American motor with a huge V.8 engine.'

This one has a left-hand drive, as a result of which I find I am virtually the only person in the country who drives on the left-hand side of the road. The situation is a familiar one, Up in front the cement-mixer rumbles ponderously along the winding road. Six feet behind is the ancient family saloon and four feet behind him the souped-up Mini, ready, given one-eighth of a chance, to jump them both. Then, in echelon out towards the right – the last ones well over the white line – come an assortment of half a dozen others.

Finally there is myself, power-steering the beautiful Mustang along the left-hand gutter with the finger and thumb of one hand, the little finger delicately extended as though at the vicarage tea party. Having a left-hand drive I am the only one who can see what is coming in front of the cement-mixer. I alone know that, as the family saloon nerves himself at last to swing out and have a go he is going to miss by a hair's breadth the oncoming red Jaguar, and that, when he gets his nerve back to try again, he will miss equally narrowly the post office van – and now, a broken man, he is jumped by the Mini.

Soon after I got the Mustang, it occurred to me to see if it would do the same 'walking along with you' act that had so amused my friends with the Terraplane, so one day I made it 'do its ton', which is motoring jargon for 100 m.p.h., and took my foot off the accelerator. It slowed down and down and down – not to 3 m.p.h. but to a full stop. Luckily I was not showing off to anyone, but alone. I had forgotten it had no gears.

27
The Norfolkman

Ever since I collected my *Railway Wonders of the World* and used to be taken for a walk down to the railway bridge 'to watch the trains' I have taken a positive delight in travelling by train and almost alone among the travelling public, so it would seem, I think our trains are wonderful. Some of my friends willingly take their lives in their hands and drive by car, among the nine million others of their kind, even as far as Scotland. For myself, I tell them, I am driven by my chauffeur and accompanied by my chef, butler and assistant butler. I am served, as I sit in my armchair with my table and my light, with drinks and ridiculously cheap four-course meals. In other words I go by train. There used to be no more exquisite moment than when, somewhere near Newport Pagnell, one looked down on a stretch of the M1, with red Minis seeing desperately if they could beat the train, at almost the precise moment when one was asking one's butler for the second gin. This sport has unfortunately ceased, since the train now does something over 100 m.p.h. This is not always an improvement and arises only from the mistaken conception that half an hour one way or another really matters. The other day in Edinburgh, the aeroplane that was to take me home to Gatwick having been diverted to Glasgow, I boarded the Queen of Scots and settled down for a pleasant day's reading, eating, drinking, and watching the countryside roll by. Alas, in place of those wonderfully comfortable dining cars they now had separate four-legged movable chairs. Thus, having ordered my half-bottle, I found myself chasing it half-way to Newcastle, legs twisted round the chair to avoid being thrown off, clutching the bottle with one hand and the glass with the other, with the certain loss of either if one let go, the whole ensemble being shaken as a terrier shakes a rat. Indeed, the only quiet passage we had was through Morpeth Station, where the night sleeper lay on its side from the night before.

The real 'gentleman's way to travel' was, of course, by the old Pullmans, of which there used to be one on most of the main trains from Victoria, the 'midnight' being something of an institution as revellers arrived at 23.59 and 50 seconds to be hauled on board by the steward as the train began to draw out. One evening four of us in the coupé of the car *Peggy*, having heard awful rumours about the withdrawal of the Pullmans (the nationalized railways had always been jealous of them), formed the 'Pullman Protection Society', of which I was unanimously elected Honorary Secretary. The man on my right, who hasn't been seen since, said, a trifle indistinctly, 'We shall want a float,' and handed over two fivers – which I still possess. We had some fine stationery printed (at my expense) and after writing a few powerful letters to the press, who will print anything, however grotesque, if it comes on printed paper from the secretary of some society, thus making it 'official', we aspired higher and demanded the truth from the big boss in person, David McKenna. He replied that they were indeed taking off the Pullmans and were replacing them – and shame upon so educated a man for such abominable jargon! – by 'a new type of classless catering vehicle', and, by God, that's just about what they are. Now all we have left to defend is the Brighton Belle, and even that is doomed. All we shall have instead of a national institution is an ordinary train with, if we are lucky, one 'classless catering vehicle'.

I missed my first great railway experience at the age of six, and regret it bitterly to this day, when an engine-driver on Farnham Station asked me if I would like to climb up into his cab and, wanting nothing more in the world than to do so, I suddenly came all over shy and could not bring myself to do it. It must have been more than fifty years before I got another chance.

At the start of some golfing tour of Belgium, by train and boat, I accompanied Lord Brabazon, as was his wont, to 'inspect the engine'. I mentioned his love of trains to an old Clare friend, Geoffrey Coaker, who had by this time become a considerable 'railwayman' on the LNER, with the result that a few days later we found ourselves, attired in boiler suits, mounting the footplate of the steam engine *Robin Hood* to accompany, I will not say assist, Driver Peters – who, like almost all long-distance drivers, looked like a retired admiral – in hauling the Norfolkman from Liverpool Street to Norwich, 120 miles in 120 minutes with a stop at Ipswich. We started quietly enough with *Robin Hood* puffing and panting in a most human sort of way up the long 'bank' to Brentwood, but thereafter, as Driver Peters coaxed his iron steed up to 90 m.p.h. I soon realized that his lordship had understated the case. It was more like driving a very powerful sports car with all the big ends gone and four punctures. I retain a confused impression of a deafening din, steam, smoke, vibration, blasts of heat as the fireman opened the hatch to feed the inferno blazing within, and a scalding sensation round the ankles as he periodically hosed down the cabin with jets of boiling water.

The outstanding impression, however, came as a surprise. It was the feeling of superiority. As a passenger, you mount one step and then sit down. On the engine you climb up four steps and then stand up. Both literally and psychologically you look down on the rest of the world. I can see as though it were yesterday a little man waiting in his little motor car at some little crossing in rural Suffolk. 'Yes,' I thought, looking contemptuously down on him as we thundered by, '*and* you'd better!' As for the passengers, you hardly give them a thought. Out of sight, out of mind. You suppose they are coming along behind there somewhere, eating, drinking, sleeping, reading or whatever it is they are doing, but one thought, even if you are not the driver, monopolizes the mind, to urge this great monster to Norwich in time. I had forgotten about Ipswich and, as we swept into the station and had to pull up for a whole crowd of paying passengers, one resented the interruption and felt like pulling out while most of them were still messing about, trying to get in. When eventually at Norwich they all streamed past without a passing glance for Driver Peters or our fireman, who had shifted about a ton of coal, I felt like rattling a collecting box in front of their expressionless faces. I washed my hair in the stationmaster's office, but after the fourth immersion the water still came out like draught Guinness, so I gave it up.

How different was our return in the diesel! Padded armchair; sliding window out of which to lean a nonchalant elbow; uninterrupted, smokeless view of the road and the countryside; everything clean as a new pin and 2,000 horse-power throbbing behind the soundproof door – the Rolls-Royce of the rails.

'Yes,' said Driver Williams, 'but there's no *interest* in 'em. The old steamer's almost human. You've got to *get* something out of her.'

There was another surprise, namely the number of birds that apparently prefer the railway line to the surrounding meadows, heaths and woods. Crows, pigeons, partridges, pheasants and innumerable sparrows. There being no vegetation on the line, one can suppose them to be in search of grit. The crows, I noticed, are the wariest. They get up at a range of 200 yards. Pigeons step off with an offended air at the last moment – often, indeed, too late.

With merely a couple of levers, one in each hand, and a 'dead man's pedal' which begins to bring the train automatically to a halt if one takes one's foot off it for seven seconds, I formed the impression, doubtless erroneous, that on a clear day I could safely be entrusted with a diesel train myself.

In the open country one felt little impression of speed, but when it came to roaring between the narrow platforms of the suburban stations and over the points at 85 m.p.h. the feeling of superiority and 'Out of my way!' became more insufferable than ever, and the temptation to seize the knob and give the peculiar two-tone diesel tootle to passengers waiting for mere 'stopping' trains proved quite irresistible.

I retired to my bath in the Great Eastern Hotel with a smug satisfaction at having 'done it at last', and look back with the rather sad thought that, so far as the old 'steamer' is concerned, no one will ever do it again.

28
Ajax
Rings the Bell

I am among those millions of English people, though not I think of other nations, who have never known what it is to live without animals about the place. The first ten years of my childhood were dominated by a majestic half-Persian grey cat called Tim, who distinguished himself by catching the rat which was being released for the terrier to catch, before the terrier had so much as seen it. We always seemed to have rough-haired fox terriers, but the sense appears to have been bred out of them in order to produce idiotically long heads for show purposes and you hardly ever see one these days.

I will pass over the various owls, squirrels, white rabbits and the rest which shared my boyhood, pausing only to mention Polly, the old grey parrot, a bird of beady eye and evil disposition, who hated men and could bite your finger to the bone. He could whistle 'Pop Goes the Weasel'; could count up to six, saying 'Y' for five, as parrots can't pronounce the letter *f*, which is perhaps just as well; and would call out, 'Bring the trap round in 'alf an hour.' He died during church on Sunday morning *aetat* 68, and I had known him for my first twenty-five years.

I have enjoyed for the best part of a lifetime the friendship of John Beck, who in 1938 had the distinction of captaining the only British team ever to win the Walker Cup Golf match. This friendship was only once threatened – by a dastardly trick perpetrated by his wife upon mine, as a result of which the Siamese cat, Sapphire, entered our lives. Sapphire was lying in front of the fire in the Becks' home with what we later knew to be the usual quota of non-Siamese kittens. 'Oh,' said my wife ecstatically, 'it's a Siamese!' Mrs Beck's mind moved fast. 'Would you like to have her?' 'Oh no, I *couldn't*!' 'No, really. We should *love* you to.' And so it came about.

We lived at the time at No. 10 Markham Square, off the King's Road, Chelsea, one of that immensely elegant terrace of four-storey houses built in the 1830s by permission of His Majesty, as the deeds said, by William Evans Markham in the King's Private Road – and God knows what he would have thought of it now! We bought it for £3,500 at the end of the war and thought we were frightfully clever in selling it a few years later for nearly double. They tell me it is now worth about £37,000. Incidentally, with four floors one above the other it taught me that never again would I live 'vertical'. It also taught me at last a lesson that some house-buyers and house-builders never learn, namely that you live *inside* a house looking *out*, not *outside* looking *at* it.

No. 10 became Sapphire's new home. In the basement was the room in which I worked and the kitchen with the ancient geyser which once blew my wife clean across the room and up against the dresser. The kitchen window opened to a little back yard and, however tightly it was closed, Sapphire's admirers seemed to slip through and pervade the house with their hideous aroma. The idea was to wait till Sapphire started 'posturing and calling', as the cat-fanciers put it ('Yes,' said a north-country friend of ours, 'and there's a good deal of that goes on at the —— Country Club on Saturday nights, too') and then take her to one Ajax, who lived down the Fulham Road with a little old lady with a hearing-aid and a stick.

The time duly came and Sapphire was wrapped up in a scarf and taken off by taxi, the economics of the act being that, if you only got three male kittens at eight guineas and two female at six, that would be thirty-four guineas, and even allowing for two guineas for Ajax, half a crown for the maid, and the price of the cab both ways, you were still quids in – even though half had already been spent in advance at Peter Jones. Ajax, it turned out, lived in a little room on his own, sitting on a tall stool, from which on the releasing of Sapphire from the scarf he leapt down and started operations with gratifying dispatch. Indeed, he was attempting a second bite at the cherry, so to speak, when his owner, not wishing to dissipate one of her main sources of income, prodded him off with her stick, saying, 'That'll do, Ajax. That'll do' – a phrase which naturally entered our family life and has remained ever since.

At last the investment came to fruition and Sapphire retired to the airing cupboard, there to be delivered of six. Four black, two tabby. The dark stranger had got in first. I think she had twenty-seven altogether before finally the kitchen window was bolted and barred for days ahead and the Ajax procedure carried out once more. Success at last! Not six, however, but one: a pale pink, rat-like little object but indisputably Siamese. We christened him Ting-a-Ling, since Ajax had this time rung the bell, and he grew up into a rather ugly square-faced cat but destined all the same to become famous, for our next door neighbour at No. 11 was Warren Chetham-Strode, the playwright (*The Guinea Pig*, etcetera) and author. Siamese cats are born scroungers and on one of his forays down the back yards of Markham Square Ting-a-Ling, while Moira Chetham-Strode's back was momentarily turned, hooked a complete roast duck off the kitchen table and only his own growling gave him away. (Another time two maiden ladies who lived about ten doors down said, 'We had your little cat in yesterday.' 'Oh,' I said, 'I hope he didn't, er . . .' 'Well,' they replied, 'there wasn't very much on it.') At any rate after the duck episode the fare at No. 11 was obviously superior to that at No. 10, so Ting-a-Ling moved in with the Chetham-Strodes and with them moved away to Rye, where Warren wrote an enchanting book about him called *Three Men and a Girl*,* which I am sure would give you great delight.

My parents when I was an infant used to go in for bulldogs, a sloppy, slobbery breed but much feared by the innumerable tramps who were a feature of life in those days. For ourselves we have always lived with bull terriers, with which, it seems to me, man forms a closer affinity than with any other species of dog.

Incidentally, I was cutting up some meat for ours with the one old-fashioned really sharp knife that we possessed when I inadvertently and quite painlessly, it being so sharp, passed it half-way through my thumb. When I told my mother of this, she went one better, little suspecting what pleasure her macabre little story was to give my friends. 'I can remember the cook,' she said, 'cutting the end of her thumb right off and it fell on the floor. She went to pick it up, hoping she might be able somehow to stick it on again, but she was too late. The bulldog had had it.'

My wife had had bull terriers before we were married but the first jointly owned one joined us a year or so after the war while I

* Heinemann, 1958.

was away on some trip in the Far East. I had reached the front door on my return and my wife was just beginning to explain, when the legs were cut away from her by a bustling white whirlwind in the shape of Sally Something-or-other of Ormondy, from which I deduced her to be descended from the great Boris Something-or-other of Ormondy, who at that time was still to be seen waddling about the drawing-room of my old friend and golfing companion, Raymond Oppenheimer, possibly the world's greatest expert on the breed.

Dear Sally! I have written perhaps overmuch about bull terriers in the past, and especially about Sally. In Markham Square her abiding passion was cats and, when she lay apparently asleep but with half of one eye open, as immortalized in the picture by Cecil Alden, I had only to whisper, 'Was that a . . .' or, 'Did you hear . . ?' for her to dash into the hall and leap up against the front door turning full circles on the rebound. I suppose it was about eighty yards from our front steps to the high wooden fence surrounding the bombed church which used to preside with such grace over the end of the square. At any rate I swear that cats have been known to reach this sanctuary in about six seconds and the dog, thundering along like an express train, never caught one in a fair race, though she did manage to bowl an old ginger tom over in the open, only to return with her nose criss-crossed and covered in blood.

Sally, alas, went the way of all flesh – talk about 'giving your heart to a dog to tear'! – and Raymond Oppenheimer, knowing that once you have had a bull terrier about the house the place seems only half alive without one, at once came through with the offer of another. 'Do not close your minds,' I can hear him saying, 'to the idea of having a dog' – i.e. a male. 'Very well, if you say so,' we replied, and thus there entered our lives, never to be forgotten, Robert Something-or-other of Something, an amiable, rather oaf-like creature, as he turned out, with a jaw like an alligator. He was about six months old, which may have been a little late, but anyway bull terriers, probably the most obstinate creatures in the animal world, not excluding mules, need training by someone who has time, and I was constantly away. Often, however, the battle of minds would take its familiar course. 'You will,' you say to the dog. 'I won't.' You *will.*' 'I won't, you know.' 'I tell you you will, *and* I mean it.' 'Oh well, I might – but I don't say I will.' At this point the telephone rings and all is lost. 'Not that I ever meant to,' says the dog and you are back to Square One, with the dog now 'one up'.

Bobby never went for the postman or bit anyone. He just ought to have been in an Approved School. 'This is Lewes Police Station,' said a voice one day. 'Are you the owner of a white bull terrier? . . . Well, he's sitting under my desk.' Oh Lord, I thought, what's he done now? 'A lady found him drinking water out of a flower-pot on one of the graves in Lewes Cemetery and brought him in . . .' He must have wandered eight miles across the Downs.

It was at the time when one man, uninvited, brought the scourge of myxomatosis to Europe and the downland rabbits were wandering around, ghastly half-blind objects, and dying in hundreds. Bobby, the mighty hunter, brought in half a dozen a day and laid them on the lawn, where they lay till the next burial party was mustered. He also had a wooden pole, five feet long and the best part of three inches thick, which must have weighed several pounds. It was his great delight to get this pole by the point of balance in his massive jaws and run flat out with it, straight at an opening in the wall about three feet wide. The collision was frightful to behold and sometimes he would somersault clean over the pole at impact. With blood coming from his back teeth he would then collect the pole, retire and charge again.

It was natural that a love-hate relationship should grow up between Bobby and our seventy-year-old gardener, and one would see them occasionally, one at each end of a rake or hoe. This is a time-honoured game but is normally won in the end by man. Not so in this case. The dog's grip was so strong that Mansbridge would be forced to give up the tool and go and get another. One day he was planting out the sprouts, when the dog came along behind him, pulled them out one by one, and laid them at his feet.

Every woman has, secreted somewhere in her wardrobe, a feathered hat for weddings, Conservative fêtes, vicarage bazaars and the like, and my wife proved to be no exception. Bull terriers are easily bored and one day we left Bobby locked in the bedroom. When we came back, it looked as though a fox had got into a tropical aviary. First the brown cardboard box, then the tissue paper, and then the feathered hat. 'You *wretched* dog! Did *you* do this?' 'Oh, well . . . sorry!'

At last he went too far and started chasing the sheep. A home was found for him with a lifelong lover of the breed, who proved to be the unlikely combination of an ex-sergeant-major and Oppenheimer's hairdresser, and we delivered him one day to his new home in Mitcham, my wife shedding a few tears, rather as did Mrs Barrymore in *The Hound of the Baskervilles* on the disclosure that the convict on the moor was her younger brother. 'He went from crime to crime but to me, sir, he was always the curly-headed boy.'

After which we only once had news of Bobby. He had just wrecked the sitting-room.

Bobby was followed by Millie, one of whose rangy, illegitimate daughters, the result of an unfortunate and embarrassing liaison on the front lawn, still visits us from the neighbouring farm, and loves me, and only me; and now the present incumbent, Kerry, an almost all-black brindle, so christened because she was to go off for a year's tea planting with my daughter in Kerala in Southern India, sleeps her way peacefully towards the close of her allotted span. It must be ten years since my wife and daughter went to a nearby kennels to pick up a cat for a friend and there was Kerry, I forget if she had any other name, due to be killed next day because some wretched human could not be bothered. There was never, I like to think, a moment's hesitation in their taking her into our household. We dispatched her to Cochin on a cargo boat, on which she became the favourite of all, especially the captain and the cook, and in her year in India she achieved one, as I like to think, unique distinction. She nipped an elephant. It must have looked from the rear like a very old postman with baggy trousers.

'A dog,' said Sherlock Holmes, 'reflects the family life. Whoever saw a frisky dog in a gloomy family or a sad dog in a happy one?' As I look back on Sally and Millie and Kerry, and even on Bobby, I reflect that, if Holmes was right, we must be one of the nicest families in the world.

29
Huntin', Shootin'
and Fishin'

Of the above immortal trio, so ingrained in country life when I was a boy but now an object of unseemly mirth to the philistines, my experience of the first was very small, no more than a day's cubhunting on a frosty October morn with the Oakley, an occasion to which I had for days looked forward with feelings no less intense than those preceding the approach of the Christmas holidays at school. That hunting people were, and probably are, almighty snobs I have no doubt. In any case it is almost impossible, when mounted on a horse, not to feel 'superior' to those who are in the literal sense 'inferior' on the ground. Nevertheless, though fox-hunting in the more populated parts of the country is now becoming an anachronism, I am glad to have had my one taste of it and to have attended the meet at the Bromham Swan every Boxing Day and even, more recently, to have afforded a stirrup cup to the Southdown when they have met at the Windmills. When times were right, it must have been the greatest sport in the world, but, if you are to be pursued by little men with placards or students laying false scents – all amenable to seeing foxes 'humanely' destroyed by gassing, strychnine, or the gangrene resulting from being indiscriminately potted at by farmers with shotguns – it may well be time to pack it in.

I did, though, now I come to think of it, enjoy a day's hunting with the Yarram Park some two hundred miles inland from Melbourne, Australia, and, while it might not have done for the Quorn, it lingers as an experience not lightly to be forgotten. The Master was one Charlie Coffey, who was head rabbiter – every Australian sheep station has an official rabbiter – to John Baillieu, an old friend of mine and pre-war Oxford golfer, and was Master not only of the Rabbit Hounds but of the same pack in their capacity of Fox Hounds. They duly met in the back yard, nine of them all told, or, as a huntin' man, perhaps I should say four and a half couple, and they must between them have reflected the lineage of every breed known in Australia since Captain Cook. Three were specialists: Michael, quarter pointer, quarter retriever, half completely anonymous, was, as it were, the chief detective and head burrower; Sandy, a tall, bushy-tailed, yellowish-white animal, was the long-range expert; and Nip, close-cropped and short in the leg, undertook the role played in more aristocratic circles by the hunt terrier. The rest were strictly utility.

Shoving each other like tube passengers in the rush hour, they scrambled into the back of the station wagon, grinning all over their faces at the day's prospect, and away we went, up a long red-dust avenue between two rows of magnificent gum trees, for all the world like the approach to a stately home of England, then away across one paddock after another – some green and flourishing, some still awaiting the hand of man – down towards the lake, where a few days previously the MFH had discerned a family of foxes.

The scene here was strangely like an English park, open, but liberally sprinkled with venerable trees, many of them ring-barked by the early settlers and now dead, but still gauntly dignified. Here and there you could see a cloud of white birds circling round a tree-top, clearly visible at two or three miles' range in the virgin atmosphere, their raucous screeching floating back across the still air. These were the cockatoos so familiar at home a generation ago.

The scene of operations turned out to be an enlarged rabbit burrow on the banks of the lake, complete with the usual tell-tale evidence at the entrance. Incidentally, when we got to the lake, Baillieu gave a toot on the horn, whereupon about a hundred black umbrella-handles popped up from the reeds. They were black swans looking up to see what was going on. There had been four cubs, said Charlie, but they were getting on and might be gone by now. Michael took his official place at the head of the burrow, while the others stood aside in a comically deferential sort of way. 'He'll tell me if they're there,' Charlie said.

As plainly as if he had delivered the statement in writing Michael indicated that they were and a tremendous burrowing and scrabbling began, the Master weighing in with the long-handled spade, pausing only when the burrow was divided and further indication was required from Michael. For some minutes the work went on, interrupted by sharp 'chi-ikes' as some enthusiast took a glancing blow on the nose from the spade, and soon the burrow was open for eight or ten yards. Four yards back from the opening Sandy, the long-distance ace, for whom the penny dropped slowly at this sort of work, dug furiously on his own, receiving shower after shower of earth full in the face from the hind legs of the others. You can't be an expert at everything.

Over the next few minutes I could willingly draw a veil. Peeping out from the bottom of the burrow there appeared a furtive, frightened, and poignantly appealing little face. My heart melted. No such faint-hearted unorthodoxy, however, entered Charlie's head and a moment later he had yanked out the first of the four cubs and flung it high in the air, to be instantly dispatched in a howling scrimmage of dogs. As the third was pulled out, the fourth slipped away and made a bolt for it, but the wretched little creature was brought down.

So much for the family, which Charlie, with positively surgical skill, set about demasking with his jack-knife. The Australian Government paid 7s. 6d. per mask skin. (Why not brushes? 'God knows,' said Charlie.) He was delighted not only with the prospect of 30s. but also with the sport he had provided. He had taken out a friend from Tasmania who had never seen a fox, he said, and of course they never set eyes on one all day. 'So I got 'im one later and skun it.'

Now for the luckless parents. They were never with the cubs during the day, it appeared, but never more than a mile away. The master whistled up the pack, who were cooling themselves off in the lake with just their heads showing, like water buffalo, and away we went again, this time for something uncommonly like the real thing. With the pack fanned out on either side we ranged at 20 or 30 m.p.h. across what might have been Newmarket Heath, bestrewn with tussocks reminiscent of the Rushes at Westward Ho! and with a background of deep blue mountains.

I dare say we had gone a mile when someone detected a lithe, russet shape streaking through the tussocks some way ahead of the pack. Charlie let forth the Australian version of 'Tally-ho!' ('There 'e goes, the f——r!') and at the same time Sandy, picking up the scent, gave tongue to the rest. Outpaced before long, the fox doubled back, and the last sight I had of him was when he leapt four feet in the air among the tussocks, twisting and turning as he jumped. They brought him down in the open a hundred yards from the car, a huge dog fox, and Charlie got out his jack-knife. Alas, poor Father!

To my secret relief we failed to find Mother, who has doubtless raised many another family by now, and, as we jogged home, I got Charlie talking about his singular pack. A pointer-type was limping pathetically along beside the car, looking up at us, and if ever a dog was 'thumbing a lift' this one was. 'He's putting it on,' said Charlie. 'Always does that when he sees a car. He'll sit for an hour beside the road when he knows the foreman is due to drive by.' Another with quite a severe cut on its leg drew the comment: 'He won't hurt. Sew it up when we get back. What with? Bit o' wire. Put sixteen stitches in one of 'em the other day.'

His training methods, it seemed, were simple and direct. 'If they don't come, I give 'em a charge of No. 12 [i.e. 12-bore]. Reckon I shot that pointer twenty times before he learnt.' A dog's hunting days, he said, ran to five or six years. 'After which,' I said, 'I suppose you, er, sort of pension them off in honourable retirement?' 'Nah!' said Charlie. 'Shewt 'em.'

As I said, it would hardly have done for the Quorn.

My shootin' career, I suppose, began on the twenty-five yard range at St Cyprians under the guidance of Mr Sillar, where I can honestly say I turned into quite a proficient shot and in the holidays became, with a .22 and cartridges filled with shot instead of a single bullet, the scourge of the local sparrows. Later I graduated to a .410, with which at absolutely maximum range and to the astonishment of both I shot a mallard drake flying high over the river and was so proud that I had it stuffed. Every boy ought, if opportunity offers, to be taught to play golf, ride a horse and handle a gun, simply so that if some better-off citizen later says, 'Do you play golf?' or whatever it may be, he is able at least to reply, 'Yes, but I am afraid not terribly well.' This may open a surprising number of doors and certainly it has done for me. I claim it as no particular virtue but I have always enjoyed most those forms of shooting which involve a certain amount of effort, plus a reasonable chance for the quarry to survive, and this, of course, includes all forms of wildfowling. Much of mine was done in Kerry just before and after the war, and, if you want a cure for a hangover, try a day up to your knees in the bogs and peat hags, waiting for the sudden *zzt, zzt* of a startled snipe and the tiny zigzagging target.

I once had a day shooting snipe in balmy sunshine, though with one or two unusual hazards, near the village of Ekiad, some two and a half hours' drive down beside the Ismaelia Canal from Cairo, my companion being a splendid fellow called Nicholas Strekalovsky, a Russian artist whose pictures of bird life and of the fantastically coloured rocky coast of Sinai and the Red Sea once induced King Farouk to buy the contents of one of his exhibitions *en bloc*. Our guide was Mohammed, spit image of Field Marshal Montgomery in a darker shade, and we were instantly surrounded by a horde of uninvited juvenile assistants, which neither a long walk through the palm groves nor the threats of Monty and his adult assistants contrived to throw off. We splashed through the still, lifeless rushes and the mercifully warm water but the opening shot, when it came, was made no easier by a chorus of yells and shrieks from behind. One child clutched my arm, another prodded me in the back, the more experienced crouched like miniature wicket-keepers to catch the empties, while all jumped frenziedly up and down yelling, '*Abou, Abou!*' It sounded to me like, '*À vous, à vous!*' and the answer proved to be that it was a relic from the French Occupation, only they cannot pronounce the letter *v*. Discharging two barrels without effect, I made some irate comment and this was greeted with howls of glee and giggling and poking in the ribs. The snipe shot skywards, whereupon the children all squatted in the rushes making kissing noises which they believed, erroneously, would lure it down. After shooting about thirty snipe, and very nearly two children, we adjourned to Monty's little home for a glutinous feast of figs, dates and sweet tea, while the rest of the village, mingling among the assorted livestock, gazed in with awe from without.

In Killarney, where it is migratorily possible that some of the snipe we saw in Ekiad had actually at one time lodged, a great delight was to row silently round the little rushy bays beside Ross Castle in search of duck or, better, to lie in wait for the geese. My mind goes back to 4.42 on a December afternoon just after the war and a moment of which I had been dreaming for six years. Half an hour's hard rowing had brought myself and two companions to the fringe of some water meadows, where we had found for the boat the perfect hiding place, a cavern worn away in the rocks, and I can sense the scene as though it were a few days ago rather than some twenty-seven years. Away over the lake the sun had gone down in splendour over Carrantouil and McGillicuddy's Reeks and, secreted in various gorse bushes, we waited in silence in the afterglow, all thinking the same thoughts. Will they come tonight? As the light faded, a few duck flighted in on whistling wings and I remember a distant church clock chiming the quarter-hours. Soon it would be too late, but at last, far away but unmistakable, we heard the sound that sends such a shiver up the spine, sets every nerve on edge and remains completely indescribable, the cry of the wild geese – twenty or thirty of them in V-formation at perhaps three hundred feet. As they reached the lake, they came tumbling down, as rooks do at bedtime, and then, re-forming, passed over my companions' ambush. I thought they had been caught napping but in a moment a couple of vivid flashes stabbed up into the violet half-light and a goose 'poured' down from the sky like a barrage balloon hit in the war. Another fell further away and I heard the dog splashing his way to it. Ten minutes later the same distant cries, the wide cautious circling, the suspense, and then the air is suddenly black with them. After six long years, what if I miss them now? However, all was well and as we rowed back in the dark I reflected that no smugness in the world equals that of a fellow who returns home clutching the neck of a wild goose.

After a long dull drive from Dublin in a hired car which had to have a matchstick periodically replaced in the hole in its sump, I had wondered whether Killarney, after all my wartime talk, might not be about to let us down and whether I was not about to lose face with my aforementioned friends Little and Byrom. I should have had more faith. We arrived at the International Hotel at half-past four for the aftermath of what proved to have been the very first dog-racing meeting ever held in Killarney and the place was filled with not only the local sporting fraternity but also a lively contingent of bookmakers from Dingle and Tralee. I recall especially a character wearing two overcoats and a cap, who appeared to have only one phrase at his command, 'Small brandy quick!' At about four in the morning Miss McSweeny behind the bar declared herself open to no further business. 'No,' she said firmly, after piteous protestations. 'No, 'tis no good. This bar is closed. If you want another drink, go into the next room.'

Later on, escorted by the versatile and redoubtable Dr Billy O'Sullivan, known even now, though he is my age, as the 'Young Doctor', to distinguish him from the many other Doctors O'Sullivan in Killarney, we drove up into the hills in pursuit of the woodcock at Glencar, where they shelter in the holly bushes on the wild, rugged hillsides. We arrived to find about twenty beaters, all like the rural Irishmen of the caricatures, of whom one in particular remains in the memory. He had a battered hat, incredibly long arms, and a six-inch grin which revealed a solitary tooth sprouting from his lower jaw. We knew him as the Original Man. Really, no shooting man has lived till he has assisted at a 'cock' shoot in Kerry. We marshalled ourselves in U-formation for what must surely be among the most cheerfully dangerous operations in sport, some inside the holly, others on the outskirts, guns and beaters happily intermingled, each with little or no idea of the whereabouts of the other. 'Rattle dem bushes, bhoys,' the headman exhorted, 'rattle them bushes,' and the 'music' began, the Original Man contributing hoarse cries of '*Kerksh, Kerksh*'. The 'music', however, is nothing to what happens when the first 'cock' flits silently from the bushes. Everyone stops. 'Ma-a-ark!' they all yell, irrespective of whether they have seen it or not, and soon you find yourself yelling too. I once, without a word of a lie, found myself trying to shoot a swerving woodcock with two dozen people yelling 'Ma-a-ark!' and a donkey braying its head off a few yards behind. Fatigued by their exertions on our behalf, the beaters at the end of the day consumed between them one hundred and forty pints of porter.

At about the same period I enjoyed another strange day's shooting, with a member of the Army staff and P. B. Lucas, the one who had been second in the juvenile tournament at North Foreland so many years ago and was now commanding the RAF station at Bentwaters. This took place in the Deserted Village, a sleepy little hamlet on a remote fringe of the coast of Suffolk, upon which the army had descended six years before and, together with two thousand wild acres of gorse, heather and bracken, had swallowed whole. The Hall became headquarters; barbed wire and sentries enclosed the condemned area; and the inhabitants, sadly nailing boards over their windows and locking their back doors for the last time, moved away to the neighbouring towns. All day in pursuit of such pheasants as had not been scared away by flame-throwers, mine-destroying tanks and surreptitious rifle practice, we wandered at will and met not a living soul. Down past the silent churchyard, where the rude forefathers of the hamlet slept in their unkempt graves; past the church farm; through the dilapidated two-hundred-year-old cottages; and along past the Chequers. We had an excellent day. I will not enlarge on what Sherlock Holmes might have called 'The Singular Episode of the Captain, the No. 4 Cartridge and the Tame Goose', but we got a dozen pheasants, some duck, a hare or two, and as many rabbits as, standing up in the car on the way home, we cared to shoot in the glare of the headlights. A memorable day, but one we may hope that no one will be ever in a position to enjoy again.

Of the more formal forms of shooting I think I can honestly claim to have been more interested in the occasion, the scenery and the company than in the size of the bag, though if anyone says he enjoys a whole day with practically no result the truth is not in him. An exception, perhaps, was a day of indescribable beauty up above Lancaster, when from a wood which looked as though it must be teeming with pheasants only one old cock was eventually dislodged. Rather in keeping with Osbert Lancaster's wartime cartoon – 'I suppose you realize, Sir Henry, that to the pheasant you and I are just so much flak?' – it passed down the line unscathed and flew into a small copse. On emerging from here it was fired at by at least four of the guns, again unscathed, after which one of the party, my friend Byrom again, said to the keeper, 'Do you think we shall tire this pheasant out?'

On the other hand I have from time to time been invited to shoot with the 'nobs', though I will not embarrass my hosts by naming them. On one tremendous occasion I found myself, on scanning the printed list of guns, one of only two commoners – and the other was Mr J. Arthur Rank! Furthermore I was drawn next to him. At one stand we were in a deep Berkshire valley, facing a wood high enough to enclose a public road half-way up. A keeper, on learning that I had not shot there before, revealed that this was where they had set up the record before the war – 647 birds, I think it was, at this one stand. I felt rather like the incoming captain must when driving himself in at St Andrews and wished that I had drawn a place somewhere out of sight round the corner. In due course birds began to appear over the top of the wood, looking the size of starlings with long tails and going like the wind. As Mr Rank fired at them, there would be a pause of what seemed several seconds, after which the bird would throw back its head and pitch stone dead a quarter of a mile behind. My own miserable pellets seemed hardly to reach the bird, never mind bring it down, and the unworthy thought passed through my mind, as it does through the golfer's, that, being obviously plus-two at the game, he had a better set of clubs, so to speak, or specially wound balls or something. When it fell to my lot, many years later, to find myself at a charity golf occasion sitting next to the Duke of Edinburgh (I hope I have not been guilty of name-dropping in these pages, but you can hardly blame me for dropping this one) I ventured to ask him whether, since without flattery he is an extremely good shot, he thought Mr Rank had had a 'better set of clubs', or indeed whether he himself had. He obviously knew a great deal about it and convinced me, alas, that in neither case was it so. He himself used perfectly straightforward guns and standard No. 6 cartridges. So it must have been me.

Of all forms of shooting known to man nothing to my mind, for sheer elevation of spirit, for casting off the cares and frustrations of current life and generally recharging the human battery, comes near to equalling a fine August day on the moors, though I dare say I have had no more than half a dozen in my life. I see myself once again in the end butt, with the other nine out of sight over the brow of the hill. Alone in the silence and the sunshine, I have twenty minutes to let the scene sink in, before the sheep on the crest a mile away give warning by uneasy movement that the beaters are on their way. Down below, the River Wharfe winds its way through a rich valley dotted with sycamores. On the far side is Ilkley Moor, of music hall legend, where, my hosts assure me, half the population of the West Riding of Yorkshire walk at week-ends and still the grouse survive. Behind us the Blubber-houses Moor conjures up visions of the irate Lord Walsingham in '88 blazing furiously away on his own with three guns and two loaders to 'larn' the Prince of Wales, His Royal Highness having declined his invitation and gone instead to Bolton Abbey where he 'could be sure of there being some birds'. Whereupon Lord W. strode up in dudgeon to his moor and in a one-man fusillade dispatched 1,070 grouse, thus proving his point and placing his name imperishably in the record books.

I suppose that under shootin' should also come stalkin', and this is a gap which few mere Southerners are fortunate enough to fill. I have mentioned our little cavalcade proceeding up the mountain at Killarney, with Castlerosse in the front and the man with the pail bringing up the rear. This was an occasion when I really did have cause to bless old Sillar for initiating me into the mysteries of the rifle. On the day in question I walked and scrambled for hours without result, only to find to my intense mortification that his lordship had shot a stag, which I had probably disturbed miles away, without even moving from his place. I got home stiff and aching in every joint and on the following Sunday my host's 'Londoner's Log' concluded: 'Finally, Mr Longhurst has been out stalking. He started the day most jauntily and finished nobly and yet, when 8.30 p.m. struck, namely the dinner hour, I said, 'Where is Mr Longhurst?' and received the reply that, 'Mr Longhurst is trying to get down the stairs.'

Next day I shot three buck, but no stag. On the following morning we climbed up to the forest of Muckross, where I was dispatched under the charge of perhaps the most extraordinary man for his years that I have ever met. A wizened, round-faced little man, his name was Dan Donohue and he was seventy-nine, still, I was assured, the best stalker in all Ireland. He moved rapidly over the steep, rock-strewn ground, using his stick as a third leg, and soon had me pretty well breathless. He could pick out a stag with the naked eye when it was all I could do to detect it with the telescope. One of the fascinations of stalking is that the slightest false move, a tiny movement of a cap in the grass at a range of half a mile, the slightest whiff of man from upwind, the movement of other beasts you had not noticed, means game, set and match to the stag. I should think we had made a detour of at least an hour before almost at the top of the highest mountain in the forest the great moment came. We overtook our quarry, a big solitary stag, standing majestic and unaware in the glen below. I squirmed my way down, feeling like a tribesman on the North-West Frontier, to the point where a ledge jutted out over the glen and drew a bead on the stag. For a moment, instead of pressing the trigger, I laid the rifle down and gazed at this magnificent creature I was about to kill. Had I been alone, I should have taken a picture of the beast and let him go, but faced with the prospect of explaining away such faint-hearted unorthodoxy to Castlerosse, and more especially to old Dan, my courage deserted me. I raised the rifle again and a second later the stag was dead. As it fell, there rose from the grass beside it a second stag. I shot that too, and I knew how the Ancient Mariner felt when he shot the albatross.

Dan Donohue was beside himself. '*Good*, gentleman, *good*,' he kept saying. We went down to examine the victims and found that the first was a 'royal', in other words it had twelve points to its antlers, and this was indeed a memorable debut, for to shoot a royal ranks high among deer-stalkers – though, as I did not like to point out, you shoot first and count up the points afterwards. My conscience seemed to detect a puzzled, reproachful look in the eyes of the dead stags and I reflected with little satisfaction that they had died not because I had been clever enough to shoot them but because I had not had the moral courage not to. No such thought, however, entered the mind of Dan Donohue as he launched himself into the usual operations with the jack-knife. Moved perhaps by the strange primitive instincts that were viewed with such apprehension by the Italians in their campaign against the Abyssinians, he attacked first the stags' genital organs and with a wild frenzy flung them over his head.

This was the beginning in me, as I now see, of a sentiment which overtakes many as they get older. Soon after the war I attended a hare shoot near Newmarket. We stood behind hedges, and on the beaters' approach the flat fields became alive with hares, lolloping along towards us, which we were to blast in the face as they came within range. No doubt if I were a farmer, since three hares eat as much as one sheep, I should have felt different, but I confess that I tended to wave my gun to encourage them to go to either side. Soon even the humble rabbit was added to stags and hares as creatures to be killed by someone else but not by me, and now I have reached the stage where I even shoo bluebottles out of the window rather than attack them with a rolled-up copy of the *Sunday Times*. As one gets older, one comes to feel that it is not their fault that they are bluebottles, and that they have their lives to live too. On the other hand, if anyone offered me a day after the grouse, my conscience would be sorely pressed.

As to fishin', I am afraid I never feel qualms about the quarry, perhaps because I so rarely succeed in giving myself the chance. Having saved it up for my old age, it was somewhere around my fiftieth birthday when, inspired, as I have said, by the purchase of a little book in a Melbourne second-hand bookshop, I decided

that the time for flyfishing had now come. No point in setting
one's sights low, so in view of the fact that I lived just about within
range I looked around for a chance of getting on one of the
Hampshire chalk streams. It came, once again, not by design but
from happening to be in the right place at the right moment, in
other words at the launching of a BP tanker on the Clyde. This
was performed by the greatest woman golfer of her time, perhaps
of all time, Miss Joyce Wethered, more correctly known as Lady
Heathcoat-Amory. She named the ship *British Curlew*, and I
found its launching a most moving experience, and myself, in
company with many a stronger man, wiping a tear from my eye.
(I have always loved a quotation from the memoirs of that very
grand Edwardian lady, Lady Maud Warrender: 'There is something extremely moving about the launching of a great ship,
especially when it is done personally'!) At any rate I found
myself at the ensuing luncheon sitting next to a charming lady
whose husband, Ralph Vickers, turned out, and how we had come
to talk about fishing I cannot guess, to run a syndicate on the
Upper Avon near the village of Enford. This I was able to join and
thus in a modest way to become initiated into the mystique of
chalk stream fishing. I was also able to visit the church at Nether-
avon, where the Rev. Sydney Smith was curate from 1794 to 1797
and to stand in the actual pulpit from which, he said, when he
thumped the cushion to emphasize a point during the sermon,
the dust flew up in such clouds as to obscure the congregation.
Looking round the windswept, barren Salisbury plain, one could
see what he meant when he said that in the country he always
feared that creation would expire before teatime. Sydney Smith,
possibly the greatest wit in an age renowned for its wits, is almost
my favourite character and, if I entered one of those games of
choosing which man or woman of the past you would most like
to have dinner with, you could have all your Wellingtons and
Napoeons. I should pick Sydney Smith. (Hesketh Pearson's *The
Smith of Smiths** might give you many a happy hour, as it has
done me.)

However, it took the best part of three hours to drive to Enford
and it soon became apparent that fishing there would have to be
an overnight job – and even then one was liable to miss the morning
rise through being on the way and the evening one through being

* Hamish Hamilton, 1934.

in the pub – and that to get the best out of chalk stream fishing one ought almost to live on the river, with the rod made up and a small boy watching the water and earning a shilling by running up to report the beginning of a rise. One day I thought I had got it right at last. Having set off on a perfect summer morning in the Duck-egg Blue, 'down the drive at half-past five', I arrived on the water after a furious drive at about eight o'clock. It was a heavenly morning and, as I began to put up my rod, the water became covered with the rings of rising trout. Alas, after wrestling with the Duck-egg Blue for two and a half hours my hand shook so much that it was all I could do to attach the fly. When I began to cast, I might as well have been casting a steel hawser and I cleared the whole river in about ten minutes. You can't win in fishing. Nevertheless of all the pastimes that one can enjoy almost as much by reading about them as in practice, chalk stream fishing stands, to me, highest in the list: Earl Grey, for instance, who must have been one of the nicest men who ever lived; or C. W. Hills's *A Summer on the Test*,* or perhaps best of all that classic which friends had so long been telling me about, long out of print and now reprinted by Witherby, Harry Plunket Greene's *Where the Bright Waters Meet*.

My first introduction to salmon came on the Lune at Castle Hornby in Lancashire before the days when stretches of such water began fetching £30,000 a mile or whatever it is. We used to look down from the viaduct at Arkholme and see perhaps a dozen fish queuing up in the pool below, totally uninterested in our wares, so that only a grappling hook would have got them out, which I have no doubt on a few occasions it did. Among our number was a well known member of the Royal Liverpool Golf Club, Mr Noel Cornelius, who, dissatisfied with constant lack of success, floated some long-deceased prawns down the river supported by an apparatus made largely of gin corks. Within a moment or two it had disappeared and a few minutes later he was bashing a fifteen-pounder on the head with a stone. Furthermore, a quarter of an hour later he did it again. I christened him Prawn-elius and the name stuck till the day of his death.

However, fishing for the noble salmon is not a subject about which to be facetious, though I dare say I caused as much laughter with one episode as anyone in the history of the sport. This was

* Bles, 1924.

on the Tay not far from Perth when I was fishing from a boat with Juan Dominguez Guedes, who is the uncrowned king of Las Palmas and speaks English rather better than most of us. We were fishing about fifty yards above some rocky rapids, with the ghillie holding the boat against a considerable stream with the outboard motor, and had secured a fish apiece, when a screaming of my reel and a strong tugging at the line indicated that this time I really was onto something big. I looked up to find, away down by the rapids, a large gull going through the most peculiar contortions on the surface of the river. A moment later it managed to take off and I found myself flying it like a kite, the wretched bird having swooped down upon my artificial minnow. Yells of ribald laughter and a variety of instructions got through to us from spectators on the bank, but soon the bird fell once again to the surface, where it flapped and struggled, dragging in the strong current like a sack of coals, far too strongly to reel in. I tried to persuade the ghillie, a long, gaunt Highlander with little command of my brand of English, to let the boat drift gradually back to the rapids but could not get the message through, and now what had become a splendid joke was becoming intensely unfunny. I could of course cut the nylon line, but the prospect of the bird flying off with fifty yards of it for ever dangling from its beak was not an engaging one. On the other hand we had now been here for about a quarter of an hour and could not stay here attached to a gull for ever. At last the line parted right down by the minnow, and the bird, believe it or not, flew off apparently none the worse except for the triple hook it must still have had in its beak. My friends consoled me with the thought that without doubt the salt water would eventually rust it till it fell out.

Most salmon rivers, including the Tay, the Spey and on one occasion the Wye, when I had driven 167 miles (a long way, cross country, in England) to Symonds Yat, have a habit of turning the colour of chocolate on warning of my approach, sometimes bearing down great tree trunks in the swirling brown waters. The Spey once on my arrival had not only risen but totally obscured the white water-level post. I have, however, once waded in the Spey and from what I later gather am lucky, as a novice, to have lived to tell the tale. I was gratified to read that it is the most difficult of all rivers to wade and there were moments when, stuck among a lot of invisible boulders and with this tremendous inexorable pressure on my back, I began to wonder what the devil I was doing there at all. Exhaustion sets in and a single false step with any of one's three legs, including the wading pole, may see one in tomorrow's headlines. I could not help remembering at one such moment how the ghillie had casually said, just before I entered the water, 'Aye, this is where the bishop was swept to his death. They picked up his body away doon at Craigellachie.' My most vivid memory, however, and it could almost turn into a nightmare, was of the time when I turned cautiously round to look for my companion and saw instead this gigantic, inexhaustible wall of water surging down upon me, apparently from above, million after million tons of it, now and year after year to come. Nothing in my life, including mountains, has ever made me feel so small as did the River Spey.

30
Jack and Jill

On leaving 10 Markham Square (rather to my wife's disappointment but what with the fleas and the tomcats and the stairs I could
abide it no longer) we moved to a flat on the first floor of Carlyle
Mansions, a solid Victorian red-brick block in Cheyne Walk,
looking down on a little garden presided over by a vast seated
statue of Thomas Carlyle and almost next door to the celebrated
pub, the King's Head and Eight Bells. The flat had two magnificent
tall-ceilinged rooms facing the river, whose traffic gave me increasing delight as I got to know more and more of the vessels
passing up and down, but apart from these rooms it burrowed
darkly into the interior. In the flat above lived T. S. Eliot, and at
the top Ian Fleming – and how interesting to see whose works
last the longer of the two! Our children, however, were beginning
to get too big for 'flat' life and it was difficult in the holidays to
think of anything better than to give them half a crown apiece to
push off to the newsreels. Faced with a large flat and a similar
problem were our oldest friends, Alan and Margaret Garrow, he
having been my best man and I his, but they had a cottage in the
country as well and it was agreed that we should share it. The
cottage – it was a small house really – was on a secluded little green
whose location, since it is still miraculously unspoiled, I will not
reveal, except to say that it was near enough to enable us to play
golf on my second favourite inland course, Huntercombe.

The course and the enormous dark clubhouse on the wrong side
of the road, built originally, I believe, for an insurance company
but now replaced with a charming modern affair on the other side
of the course, were owned by the then retired Lord Nuffield,
whose creation of Cowley in rural Oxfordshire left him much to
answer for, though he was hardly to know it at the time. He lived
in a rather dark, plain house behind the clubhouse and from time

to time would come in of a Sunday morning and stay and chat till his wife, having inspected the electric light bulbs to see that they were not of an unnecessarily high wattage, made him go home. Despite all the millions he had made and given away he remained an essentially simple man, but altogether it seemed rather a drab conclusion to a remarkable life. As it turned out, I became rather a favourite of his and could generally bring a smile to his tired face with what was really a standard joke. Beside his house a drive led down to Huntercombe Place, which is one of those country houses which I always think of as the first prizes of life but which in this case, by the curious reversal of modern values, had been turned into a Borstal. One day he started holding forth to me about the Borstal Boys, and a heart-rending tale it was. His cook had baked an exceptionally fine cake and, having left it near the kitchen window, had turned round to find it gone. Twice they had stolen his car (an ancient Wolseley which he had refused to change in twenty-odd years) and now he had had to barricade the windows and have huge locks fitted to the gates. More than once the so-called 'Boys' had broken into the club and pinched all the drinks and cigarettes, and three times had 'done' the neighbouring pub, the Crown. What is more, he had the daily mortification not only of seeing lorryloads of rationed coke, which he himself could not get, going down past his gate, but also of seeing them driven by a much-valued greenkeeper lured away by higher wages furnished by the taxpayer.

There seemed somewhere in all this an underlying wry humour but it came to the surface when he protested with the utmost solemnity that, furthermore, he had given £10,000 to a fund to enable Borstal parents to visit their errant offspring. At this I let out a loud guffaw, slapped my thigh and said, 'That's the best thing I have heard for years!' He seemed completely taken aback and it took me some time to convince him that it really was inordinately funny. I succeeded, however, and whenever I saw him thereafter I would make sure that one or two people were standing around and then ask him how his Boys were getting on. At last he came to love it and it became almost *his* joke. His eyes twinkled when he saw me and I do believe I brought a few little rays of sunshine to his rather dull declining years.

Eventually the cottage where we had spent what was for all of us perhaps the happiest years of our lives became too small for

SUSSEX DOWNS

CLAYTON WINDMILLS, NEAR BRIGHTON. THESE WELL-KNOWN WINDMILLS, JACK & JILL. together with a SEMI-BUNGALOW of 9 rooms and about 2 acres. FOR SALE FREEHOLD. View only by appointment with the local agents, Messrs. YOUNG & JAMES. 1, Keymer Road. Burgess Hill. Particulars in first instance from Messrs. YOUNG & JAMES or HAMPTON & SONS, LTD.

As we searched for a house in the country this advertisement kept on turning up. Only gradually did I appreciate how much these mills, high on the skyline, meant to how many people and in what distant parts of the world. I was presented with this etching of Jack and Jill, dating from about 1890, in Nairobi.

four grown-ups and three rapidly growing children. As I did not want, and probably could not afford, two homes of our own, it was a question of London or the country. For the children's sake it had to be the country, especially as I did not have to go to a place of work every day. My thoughts turned naturally to the Downs. As we scanned the advertisements, one which had caught the eye early on kept turning up.

The property was evidently a drug on the market, but the thought of two derelict windmills and a nine-room wooden bungalow fascinated us enough to make us determined to see them. We were met at Burgess Hill station by the agent one dreary November afternoon and at the top of Clayton Hill turned left up a lane beside one of the 'chimneys' of Clayton Tunnel (scene on 25 August 1861, incidentally, of the greatest tunnel disaster in railway history), to find ourselves almost immediately in the clouds. Though it was only half-past two, the bungalow, which was in fact the shepherd's cottage and the miller's combined, was almost completely dark, the hall illuminated only by a microscopic Calor Gas jet. We were taken round by Miss Jones, an elderly Victorian lady, passing from one tiny dark room to another, many with names, like the Captain's Cabin, Mrs Anson's Room, the Parlour, and so on, and there were two little bedrooms up a twisting staircase concealed behind one of the five doors leading out of the kitchen. A companionway led out of the hall and up into the Granary, and here indeed was a most remarkable room, whose character at once shone through, even if the Calor Gas lighting hardly did. My wife and I at once had the same thought. What a wonderful room for Christmas! The windows let in just enough light to see a long workbench, complete with vice, along one side, and on the wall hung samples of the incredibly fragile aeroplane struts and stays, almost as though of the balsa wood which children have in 'kits' today, which the inhabitants, including Miss Jones, had sat at this bench and made during the first war. The two windmills were known as Jack and Jill but in the clouds one could not see one from the other nor the top of either. There was no water, apart from what they caught off Jack, and this passed down into an underground charcoal filter outside the kitchen door, whence it took two hundred turns to and fro with the pump handle to raise a bucketful. They bathed in what Miss Jones called a 'splash bath' in front of the old Rayburn cooker in the kitchen.

What urged us to visit this uninhabitable warren again I do not know: sheer curiosity perhaps, but each of us felt some second sense beckoning us to try again. This we did, on a marvellous bright December day and this time by car, the Duck-egg Blue in fact. As we twisted out of the village of Cuckfield the Downs came suddenly into view six miles away and there on the skyline were two little dots. These proved indeed to be the mills and, now that we could see where we were, we could begin to take in the unique character of the place. An underground passage ran from the Granary to some steps leading up to the ground floor of Jack and from here one passed through to the stump of a third and much older mill called Duncton, a single round room in which you could almost feel the peace and hear the silence. In a glass case on the wall were a red and gold baton and some ancient medals, and it was these which led us round to the history of this extraordinary place. The medals, it seemed, had been struck for the great Admiral Anson on the occasion of his victory off Finisterre in 1747. The baton was the 'Gold Stick' carried by his descendant, Captain Anson, RN, at the Coronation of George V. This Captain Anson had an overwhelming desire to retire to a lighthouse but, none appearing to be available, he did the next best thing and determined to 'civilize' the then deserted windmill, Jack, which would still as a matter of fact make a perfect lighthouse. Jack has four ever-decreasing circular floors and then a ladder up to the cap and on the third of these the Captain installed the tank for a complicated central-heating system, the heating being provided by an old stove stoked by an ex-naval stoker down in the Granary. For a while, said Miss Jones, they lived in Duncton and the ground floor of Jack, often in their overcoats for all the captain's central heating, and Miss Jones herself slept on the first floor.

The captain died soon after the First War and Miss Jones stayed on as companion to Mrs Anson. It took no time to appreciate that the presiding genius of the place had been Mrs Anson. When they got there – and one wonders how such a woman came to let the captain pursue this act of lunacy at all – there were only the bare empty structures and the wide, open downland. Now one noticed substantial trees, windbreaks and hedges surrounding the whole two acres, flower-beds, fruit-trees, flowering shrubs, and a fine kitchen garden, all planted or created by Mrs Anson. The second floor of Jack she had turned into a chapel, dedicated by her uncle, Archbishop Temple of York.

Nevertheless the place, as it stood, was unplayable and no wonder Miss Jones and her two companions felt they could hang on no longer. It was hardly surprising that they could not sell it, and the time must soon come when there would be nothing for it but to walk away and leave it, just as the miller had done in 1909. My wife and I, following our original instinct, determined not to give up until demonstrably beaten and agreed that, if we could get water, never mind the electricity, we would take a chance and have a go. We even investigated the idea of getting water up by cart. A chance remark of Miss Jones's, however, turned the scale. 'They've got water up at the farm,' she said. This was subsidiary to the main farm down below and, invisible in a fold in the Downs a few hundred yards away, was the only other building up there. The farm's water, essential for the milking herd, was pumped up by a little electric pump down by the Pyecombe Golf Club. Might it not be possible to take a line off this and share the cost? The farmer, Mr Jesse, had the reputation of being a bit 'awkward', but I rang him there and then and to this unknown caller in words which redirected the course of my family's life, he said at once, 'I would do anything to help anyone get water.' Thus it was arranged and, when anyone hints that Mr Jesse, now in his eighty-first year, is 'awkward', I tell them this little story. Miss Jones and her companions went happily down the hill; a water line was brought off the nearest point of Mr Jesse's, for which, it being Crown land, we pay Her Majesty five pounds a year and I hope she appreciates it; and in July 1953 a new set of eccentrics moved into Clayton Windmills.

Even before we did so our suspicion that this was to be no ordinary home was dramatically confirmed. The captain had organized a system of those old-fashioned bells hanging like inverted question-marks and activated by a vigorous pulling on the wire in some distant room, the servants being able to detect from which room the summons comes by which bell is jingling to and fro. Two of the wires actually went right up through the Granary, along the secret passage and up into Jack and Duncton, from which it must have needed no mean pull to set a bell going in the kitchen. My wife was there one day with the builder, the two of them completely alone in the unfurnished cottages, when all six bells rang vigorously at once. Nor was it a case of their thinking they heard bells ringing: they could see them ringing. They confirmed that there was not a soul in the place. It is conceivable that an outsize rat, of which we had none anyway, might have very slightly agitated one bell by clinging to the wire, but not six. When the bells had settled down again, the builder opened a cupboard door in the kitchen and an old broom shot out at him, several inches off the ground and going well. At last the time came to spend our first night there and, if you had offered me a hundred pounds to go up the secret passage in the dark, I should not even have considered it. Our bedroom door opened onto the kitchen within three or four feet of the bells and it was about half-past three that I heard one ringing. I got hold of my torch. 'If I don't look now and find out which one it is,' I thought, 'we shall never be able to live here.' I flung open the door, shone the torch, and saw the third bell from the left swinging merrily to and fro. I thought of following its wire along, but my nerve failed. Time enough in the morning. In due course I traced it to the little room next door, which was in fact occupied by our ex-nanny, who had come down to lend a hand with the move. The wire terminated at the ceiling of the room but there hung from it a piece of meagre string about six inches long. Nanny Emerton, wife of Regimental Sergeant-Major Emerton, had spent her whole life in an atmosphere of army discipline and I am certain that even today, if my thirty-year-old son heard a sharply pitched voice crying, 'Oliv*ah*!' he would still jump a foot in the air. This was hardly, then, the sort of person to get up, unbeknownst, at three in the morning, light the gas, stand up on the bed, and pull sharply on six inches of string of whose existence she was totally unaware. A little later my wife and French mother-in-law were sitting over the Granary fire when a pair of tongs took off and shot rapidly across the fireplace. 'Oh, Clo-deen,' said my French mother-in-law in her best English, 'it jamp.' I was not there to see it, but there is no possible doubt that 'jamp' it did. My mind went back to our first visit to Miss Jones, when the whole place had seemed so dark and eerie and I had said to her as casually as possible, 'Is this place, er . . . I mean, are there any, er . . ?' I can see her now, struggling with her conscience, desperately anxious to sell the place but unable to tell a lie. 'Well,' she said, after a long pause, 'if there are, they're very pleasant ones.' She meant, of course, Mrs Anson, who none of us had any doubt was with us for some time after we moved in. She had died of chest trouble and time and again we would hear her characteristic cough coming from 'Mrs Anson's room', sometimes with not a soul in the house, sometimes with somebody sleeping there. Miss Jones, however, was right. Nothing would induce me to sleep in a haunted house but I never had any fear of Mrs Anson – she was undoubtedly one of the 'pleasant ones' – or indeed of one or two other eerie experiences the like of which have never happened to me anywhere else.

About ten years ago, for instance, my wife went off to India to assist with the birth of a grandchild, leaving me in the care of Bettine, this being held to be quite proper since, though unrelated, she had been our principal bridesmaid and we had all known each other long enough, etcetera, etcetera. Bettine had one of the little rooms upstairs, I had a little one off the hall, and the telephone was in the kitchen mid-way between the two. The night was almost gone when the telephone rang and I remember waiting, rather ungallantly, to see whether Bettine would answer it, and soon I heard her do so. Her mother was seriously ill in some guest-house in Hove at the time and one could soon tell that this must be the subject of the call. At a range of no more than ten or twelve feet I could hear Bettine's part of the conversation as though in the next room. It seemed clear, when she had rung off, that she would have to go to her mother and the least I could do would be to get up and see her off. I swung my feet over the edge of the bed and lit the gas. There was an almost positive silence and suddenly it dawned on me. 'My God,' I thought, 'I'll bet there's no one there' – and, of course, there wasn't. In a moment I had grabbed a piece of paper and was writing. I have it before me now and reproduce it exactly as I wrote it at the time:

6.15 a.m. 20 January 1961. Half asleep, left ear on pillow. Four coins in phone box *very* clear. Anguished common woman's voice, 'Mr Longhurst?' B. answered. I thought must be early: however did she hear and not me? (very definite this). Anyway, let her go on. Impression that it was Miss Evans. Definitely about her (B.'s) mother. Come at once. She, Miss Evans, did not like to go in. Something about noises. 'She has got to wash' – twice B. said, 'Good God, there is time for me to dress, isn't there?' as though impatient at Miss Evans's insistence. Word 'dead' came in somewhere and possibly a Mrs Richards who might go in. B.'s voice *unmistakable*. I actually stopped right ear with finger to hear this better coming through pillow. Remember thinking it was strange but I could work it out when talk ceased. When it did, I made to get up and talk to B. Then suddenly thought, 'My God, I'll bet she isn't there.' If so, this is the clearest ever. No one in the kitchen.

No one seemed to know Miss Evans – but Mrs Richards, of whom I had never heard, was the landlady!

Really the most extraordinary things used to happen when we lived in the cottages and it was even more extraordinary perhaps that one should have come to take so casually events which would have caused a sensation down below. Late one night there was a tinkle at the front door.

A dark little man was standing outside.

'Clayton Windmills?' he said.

'Yes.'

'Well, I've brought the hearse.'

After a certain amount of manoeuvring in the light of my torch I sent him on his way up the lane, where he succeeded in finding the object of his visit, the mortal remains of some poor old lady, not quite all there, who had wandered away up the Downs and laid herself down to die.

On another occasion I arrived home in the dark to find two large policemen, and a lady lying on the ground having a fit, I forget what about, but it was the most natural thing in the world to say, 'Come in, all of you.' This casual, take-it-as-it-comes approach, which one could never have developed in a normal house, might have landed me into serious trouble. A man arrived late one evening when Bettine had gone to bed. He had got a boy scout with him, he said, whom he had picked up somewhere near Crawley, the boy having missed the truck which was to take his troop up to camp at Clayton Windmills. We circled the place in the dark but could find no boy scout camp. 'Oh, well,' I said, since the man wanted to get on, 'leave him here and we will fix it all up in the morning.' I showed the boy, who was ten or eleven, into my son's room, where he undressed, got into bed and was rapidly asleep. I was now in possession of a naked, 'missing' boy scout, about whom – take 'em as they come! – I proposed to do positively nothing whatever. Luckily, though I had forgotten it, the man had said he would try to inform the police and later on there was yet another disturbance on the arrival of two constables, to whom I at least had the sense to make clear that the boy was in my son's bed, not mine. On interrogating him in the morning, I learned that he belonged to a troop in Redhill. He tucked in to a hearty breakfast and I took him down to the station. Where would he go when he got to Redhill? Oh, the scouts' hut. How would he get there? By bus. Had he got any money for the fare? No. So I gave him a shilling, bought him a comic and a bar of chocolate, and in due course asked the ticket clerk for a half single to Redhill. 'Excuse me,' he said, 'but have you got a boy scout with you?' The clerk said he had had a message from the police and would I please keep the boy till they arrived. He proved to be the most plausible liar I have ever encountered. There never was a scouts' camp at Clayton Windmills or a truck to pick him up. He knew of no scouts' hut in Redhill and had never been there. He had run away from home, and for about the tenth time. 'Ah, you again,' said the police when they came to take him away. I damn nearly made him give my bar of chocolate back.

Fortunately I have never been 'that way' – though sometimes I almost wish I had, for by all accounts it could have left one with some interesting memories – but, had this boy at some previous time been what is politely called 'interfered with', one could imagine the kind of evidence and the horrifying details which so accomplished a liar would cheerfully have come out with. I could see the headlines GOLFER ON SERIOUS CHARGE and the magistrate's, 'Are you seriously asking the court to believe, Mr Longhurst . . ?'

On the whole a very near thing, a very near thing indeed.

The mills overlook the twin cities of Hassocks and Hurstpierpoint, the latter known as Hurst, and nestling invisible at the foot of the Downs below is the hamlet of Clayton with its little Saxon church. When I told my mother of our impending move and tried to explain all about it, I was soon cut short, for by the most fantastic coincidence it seemed that I was moving not farther from home but in a sense nearer. Her grandfather, she said, had lived in the beautiful old farmhouse known as the Ham, brewing his own beer and at one time running my present morning rendezvous, the New Inn, and a tombstone in Hurst churchyard to 'Thos and Philadelphia Smith' bears witness to his memory. Her father, who used to sign his letters to her 'yr affectionate father, THOS SMITH', was born in the Ham and apprenticed to the well-known

Brighton firm of Hannington's. Thence, on setting out on his own and moving to Farnham, he called his house Claytonhurst, and when my mother married and moved to Bedford they called their house Claytonhurst, and I only just missed being born there. Now the wheel had turned full cycle and I felt that, far from being an outsider, I had come home – a feeling that was emphasized when Miss Jones gave me the beautifully bound and meticulously kept book of the miller's accounts for 1849 (and his bit of blotting paper, which last blotted 122 years ago) and I found my great-grand-father's account therein.

The sense of continuity was also brought home by a book called *Life in a Sussex Windmill* by Edward Martin, an expert on dew ponds and the geology of the Downs. Soon after the last miller had gone sadly down the hill, the business of grinding corn having been usurped by the new-fangled roller mills, Mr Martin moved into Jack and Duncton. In his book, which is something of a collector's piece in Sussex, he tells of the rigours of camping out up here, with everything open to the bare downland, the occasional tramp dossing down in the angle between the two mills and people for ever peering in at the windows to see what strange manner of persons inhabited the place, and even asking if he sold ginger beer. Nor, he said, could they ever get the natives to realize that this was a private residence, to which one could add in this respect at least that there has been little change in the intervening sixty years. His first summer, he says – it must have been 1909 – was the year of the grey slugs, 'bonny creatures indeed: they beat any that I had ever seen before and when on the move must have reached in some instances a length of four inches'. If only he had been alive today, we could have shown him one of their descendants accu-rately measured at six and a quarter inches!

> When alone in the place at night [he wrote, and it will have been in the very room in which I am writing now], the silences were almost appalling; no other word seems applicable to it. People who are ac-customed to town life find the silence of a country village rather un-comfortable after nightfall, but up aloft in the Mill, above the level of the villages all around, one *felt* the silence. There was not even the occasional passer-by, not even the step of the public house loafer going home later than the rest of his kind. At such a time the smallest sound is heard; even a mouse squeaking seems pleasant to the ear. And if it began to rain there was always the friendly patter of the raindrops on the roof. . . .

The fact that I enjoy the friendly patter of the raindrops on the same roof and that later generations of the same mice are at this very moment pattering and squeaking and chasing each other over my head gives me a strangely satisfying sense of contentment.

One sound that he used to hear we can now only imagine. This was the cap of Jack revolving on its iron 'railway' (still there) at the top, set in motion by the fanwheel to bring the big sails into the wind. 'Sometimes there was a decided change of wind, and that rather suddenly, and the movement of the circular rail could be heard like a long drawn-out groan throughout the Mill. The Mill in fact spoke. Then the groaning would be like a thousand demons set loose. . . .' The fanwheel eventually perished, leaving the huge sails poised over the roof of Duncton, and for safety they were taken way. At other times Mr Martin (whose son was up here as a boy and suddenly turned up to visit us only a few years ago), waxed lyrical, just as we are inclined so often to do today. 'As I write, the sun is sinking over Wolstenbury Hill. Everything seems quiet and subdued. The Weald lies lifeless below; but no, not lifeless, the church bells are ringing. Devotional life is active somewhere. Is it a service? Scarcely just now. It is too early or too late for that . . . but the effect up on the height is grand. But a few hours ago, I left the great capital of the world, where all was rush, where all was excitement. And now I am alone: alone with Nature: alone with God.' In this very room. Rather nice.

Often when I am sitting up here in Duncton late at night, the silence broken only by the descendants of Edward Martin's mice, there is a scratching at the door and I get up to admit our black cat, imaginatively christened Nigger, for which doubtless we shall be reported to the Race Relations Board. He is sitting draped around the back of my neck, purring, at this moment and I think, as so often, of the old ninth-century Irish monk, quoted by Sir Arthur Bryant, who in much similar circumstances wrote the charming lines (which, if you happen to be alone, are rather fun to read aloud):

> I and Pangur Ban, my cat,
> 'Tis a like task we are at.
> Hunting mice is his delight,
> Hunting words I sit all night.

'Tis a merry thing to see
At our tasks how glad are we,
When at home we sit and find
Entertainment to our mind.

'Gainst the wall he sets his eye,
Full and fierce and sharp and sly:
'Gainst the wall of knowledge I
All my little wisdom try.

So in peace our task we ply,
Pangur Ban, my cat, and I.
In our arts we find our bliss,
I have mine and he has his.

Some time after we arrived at the Mills I had a letter from the
local council asking whether I would object to a preservation
order being placed upon them. This is nothing to do with 'national
monuments' and such like: it means merely that you must not
'mess them about' or substantially change their looks or character
without previous agreement. I replied that my one desire was to
preserve them and added craftily as an afterthought that perhaps
in that case the council might care to assist in doing so. The sails
of Jill were already in bad shape, there was woodworm inside, and
it would not be long before the cap of Jack would need repair.
Nobody who took on Jack and Jill could contemplate being the
person in charge – I will not say 'owner', since one could only
regard oneself as being a sort of trustee for life till the time came
to hand them over to another – when the mills were seen to have
fallen down from the lack of care. On the other hand no one could
maintain two ancient windmills for the public benefit out of the
remains of taxed income. It was only later that I came gradually
to appreciate just how much these mills on the skyline meant to
how many people and in what distant parts of the world. In the
late fifties the writing of my book for British Petroleum took me
to the Persian Gulf and to some of the most remote outposts and
islands, often with only a handful of people. They would ask, of
course, the standard question, 'Whereabouts do you live?' to
which I would reply, 'I am the proud owner of two celebrated
windmills on top of the Downs not far from Brighton.' On no
fewer than seven different occasions someone said, 'You don't

mean Jack and Jill?' My finest capture, however, was Lady Dean, the wife of Sir Patrick Dean, Our Man in Washington, who had invited me to the family Sunday lunch at the embassy for no better reason than that we had been at Cambridge together. The going was a little slowed by the atmosphere of protocol which even on Sundays is liable to be felt in an establishment which has to divide the guests for the Queen's birthday into two parties, since it will only hold two thousand at a time. The mills, however, came to my rescue. 'Not Jack and Jill?' Her Ladyship said. 'Why, I was at school at Burgess Hill!'

Miss Jones told me a story, which I did not believe at the time, of the miller's chickens taking off in a gale and pitching in the farm down below. Also that, when caught in the depression hollowed out for the building of Jill, she had had to crawl out on her hands and knees. We have had only three really good 'blows' in eighteen years, the first of them on 3 August, when I at once perceived that Miss Jones was not exaggerating. No hen could have failed to become airborne in that and now, whenever it really blows, I think of these hens swept squawking and protesting over the steep edge of the Downs, tossed in the sky like ragged bunches of feathers and pitching finally in Vincent's Farm. They must have been the highest-flying hens in the history of poultry, at one time at something like four hundred feet. I take unceasing delight in another simple jest based on the wind. After any good 'blow' I stand around in the village, or maybe the New Inn, and I can see them coming a mile away. I know what they are going to say. They're going to say, 'Doesn't it blow up your way?' to which I shall reply, 'Yes, it does. That's why they put the windmills there!' Never mind, little things please little minds. People often ask why one mill has sails and the other not, and another little joke which, believe it or not, practically never fails is the dead-pan reply, 'Well, they found in the end that there was not enough wind for two.'

At any rate the Cuckfield RDC, aided later by the East Sussex County Council, came nobly to the rescue. A firm was called in from Winchester to look first at Jill and produced a horrifying estimate, quite justified, I am sure, but based on restoring the mill's interior as well. The sum was out of the question and I like to think it was I of all people who suggested that, since we only aimed to keep the exterior as a landmark, though of course as much of the interior as possible, would it not be possible to put up a framework of RSJs inside the mill and hold it up that way? RSJs are Rolled Steel Joists. I forget where I picked them up but, as they are positively the only building term I know, I always toss them in when I can. To my astonishment I hit the bull's-eye first shot and Jill today, though frail outside, is held securely up from inside by RSJs. Some beautiful new sails were made with loving care by Mr E. Hole in Burgess Hill but, perhaps from insufficient painting, they only lasted eleven years and the whole of the 1970 allocation was spent on a new set, this time by Harold Paris of Hove. I marvelled at the skill of youngish fellows who could never have made a sail for a windmill before. So Jack and Jill are still up the hill and delighted I am to have played some part in preserving them. In return for the expenditure of public money, I said, I would like to give something back by letting unlimited parties of schoolchildren, suitably accompanied, see over the mills. The first lot came to ninety-six, and you may imagine the squealing and squeaking as they made their way up the underground passage in the dark. Since then we must have had hundreds and I love to see them and to think of the mills giving such happiness in their old age. I always think, however, of the lines about: 'Regardless of their doom, the little victims play.' They little know, as I know, that they are all going to be made to write an essay about it next day.

Nor are schoolchildren our only visitors. We have had the beautiful Arlene Dahl and Jack Hawkins making a film up there, with the lady driving dashingly off over the Downs in a jeep, the cameras not showing, one need hardly say, the chaps who were bent double pulling it forward with a rope since in fact she could not drive. And the child star Mandy Miller with an artificial fire in Jill which flooded the local fire brigade with emergency calls. In earlier days the boys of Hurstpierpoint College, so help them, had to run round the mills, with a beak up there taking their names, so in one of their Old Boys' cricket weeks I incautiously said that to pay back the debt I would entertain to gin in the Granary anyone who could honestly declare that he had run round the mills. We still claim, unlike the other Windmill, 'We never closed.' Word got round, however, and this one was a near thing.

Other visitors come up to the unofficial car park at the bottom of the kitchen garden, twenty or thirty cars at a time, and it gives me a smug feeling to think that they have come for a glimpse of the view while I have it all the time. A good deal of courting goes on and that makes me happy too, except that I could wish that they would take their tackle home instead of chucking them out of the car or, as one triumphant fellow did, as though flying the signal of victory, tying three of them in a row on my barbed wire.

The kitchen garden is my pride and joy, though I suspect this to be a sign of old age and that a keenness on cabbages may well indicate the approach of the close of play. The garden was managed in Miss Jones's time by a shiny rubicund little man called Peter Miller, who must then have been in his late seventies since he is now ninety-five, still around the village and still looking after himself. 'My wife's inside's gone all to pieces,' he once said, and I am afraid it did not recover. My own wife developed on the sole of one foot a whole cluster of what I believe are called verrucas, rather like warts. Peter at once offered to buy them off her for a halfpenny, the only conditions being that she must accept the halfpenny and must tell no one. The transaction was effected and the whole lot disappeared in a matter of days. Since we may number a few fellow-gardeners among our readers, I will mention that four years ago I went over to 'no-digging', the theory being that Nature simply lets leaves fall, become compost and get taken into the ground by worms and the weather. The worms also aerate and drain the soil, so why break your back digging and messing up all their good work? Why not make your own compost, plus perhaps mushroom compost or peat, and just chuck it on the surface? Four years' experience has proved the point; you can take it from me that the best place for the spade is in the toolshed.

We also tried bees. I had always wanted to sit in a deck-chair listening to the steady hum of thirty thousand industrious unpaid agents collecting honey on my behalf, so I got hold of a couple of hives, each with a resident swarm, and set them to work. We did have about a pound of rather indifferent honey but next time the man came to extract it he left it in the outside safe, the contents of which could be reached by opening a little glass window in the scullery. Naturally enough the ancient gauze on the outside had the odd hole or two in it and by the time I returned the bees were running an angry shuttle service taking the honey back to the hive. Nor could I snatch any for the household since the glass window was crawling with them. Soon after that they all beed off and I reckon my pound of honey cost about £35.

Eventually, much as we had loved the strange life up there and the pleasure it had given to so many in addition to ourselves, we began gradually to feel that the time was coming for us in turn to go down the hill and leave to some younger people the delights of pressure lamps, Calor Gas and the old Rayburn that would not go when the wind was in the east. I entrusted the matter to Messrs Knight, Frank and Rutley and caused, I believe, a little innocent amusement in that austere office by insisting on writing my own account of what life was like up at the mills, outlining the bad points as well as the good, a practice which I gathered to be unusual in the world of estate agency. At any rate it drew quite a number of celebrities, including that talented and charming actor Clive Brook. Many devious schemes were worked out for modernizing the cottages but the truth was that the only thing to do was to knock them down – they were of no architectural merit – and start again. What, with no electricity?

At the critical moment I was saved by the bell – literally. Some-one rang to say he had heard that there was a chance of getting the electricity, shared with the farm, and so it turned out. They brought it in a trench up the side of the Downs, thus automatically increasing the value of the property by ten times the £500 which was my share of the cost. We moved out for the best part of a year while Vinall's of Henfield built us the somewhat spectacular house, though I say it, to which we moved back in 1963 and which a year or two ago featured in *Ideal Homes*. I will let one of the fine pictures taken by Jerry Harpur tell the story and will add only something which may be of interest to anyone intent on building a house and even, though I do not expect so, to builders, who ought to have seen it long ago. This is the very elementary point that, if you are going to have a home with two storeys, you must live on the first floor and not on the ground. Whether I should have detected this for myself in any other circumstances I cannot say but, if you have lived with a sixty-mile view, looking out of windows none of which take you farther than a hedge or the nearest lilac bush, the point speaks for itself and it soon becomes obvious that, whether you are on top of the Downs or in a council estate in Wigan, you see more from the first floor than you do from the ground, even if it is only how long the milkman has been at No. 10. Moreover, you enjoy a splendid bonus in that what they teach you at school, namely that hot air rises, turns out to be true, so that, when some-

This is Jack, with our modern house designed
so as not to obtrude on the skyline.

one leaves the front door open to an icy blast, all it does is to send the warm air upwards, where it is neatly trapped by the insulated walls and roof.

The pier, as we call it, was the idea of Peter Farley, the architect, who is due, his friends hope, to make a fortune from his work on the huge property development in Brighton masquerading under the name of a 'Marina'. From the pier we look over to the Devil's Punchbowl at Hindhead, forty-odd miles away; then across the Weald to the North Downs, and away on the right to the wireless masts of Crowborough – a stupendous, ever-changing scene – and at night the distant lights of Burgess Hill's main thoroughfare look exactly as though we were approaching the runway. Often in the morning we are in brilliant sunshine with the world below entirely shrouded by cotton wool and it is hard not to think patronizingly of all the people invisible down below with their foglamps and windscreen wipers. Sometimes we can hardly hear ourselves speak above the wind, as though on a ship in mid-Atlantic. At others it is so still that we can hear Miss Lindsey's geese over on the opposite hill or the clank of a bucket down in the farm. Altogether, rather a wonderful place and, as I have said, I am happy indeed to have had a hand in preserving it.

31
A Butterfly
Sanctuary

My mother, together with a truly rural upbringing, gave me a love of Nature which has stood me in good stead all my life, but it was R. L. Sillar at St Cyprians who instilled into me and dozens of other boys a special delight in butterflies. One never thought of going up on the Downs in the summer term without the full equipment of net, pill boxes and killing-bottle, while back at school setting-boards, pins and transparent paper awaited the catch. Many of us with the help of George, the carpenter, made wooden boxes with sliding glass front and a hole in the bottom for the food plant, in which we reared caterpillars, mainly Puss Moths, Hawk Moths and Tiger Moths. I remember to this day, and so does he, the delight with which, hanging about behind the Armoury, the aforementioned Earl-of-Essex-to-be and I discovered a hatch of Puss Moth caterpillars on the poplar tree, tiny little black things almost invisible then but due to grow into green monsters with square pugnacious faces and a pair of intimidatory whiplash tails, perhaps the most exciting caterpillar of them all.

The Downs of those days were a bug-hunter's paradise, though you never see a boy with a butterfly net on them today as the farmers have been allowed to plough them all up, and with a subsidy from the tax-payer at that. To anyone who really loved the Downs it makes your heart ache to see them turned into nothing more than a prairie, but it is no good crying over ploughed-up turf, so I will not bore you by 'carrying on' about it. Suffice to say that for a boy in those days the Downs were heaven.

Sometimes at half-term we were even able to sneak a visit to Abbot's Wood, on the London side of Polegate, which many millions of motorists careering down the double road must pass every year without suspecting it to have been, and from the look of it still to be, the haunt of that most coveted, high-flying and uncapturable of all butterflies, the Purple Emperor.

Anything light blue thrives on chalk and this is true of butter-flies. Every kind of 'Blue' was to be found – Holly, Small, Chalk-hill – and in such quantities that one soon became blasé and began to look for 'varieties', in other words specimens with something unusual about them. The greatest expert I ever met was Mr Nichols, a plumpish figure with a walrus moustache who kept a very small beerhouse in a back street in Bedford, one of the most unlikely characters, perhaps, to find among the country's leading authorities on lepidoptera and a collector for the Birmingham Museum. He knew not only the day but, given normal weather, the hour at which Chalkhill Blues would hatch on Royston Heath (now ploughed-up, of course) and one year my father drove us over. Mr Nichols was exactly right and soon the heath was alive with Chalkhill Blues. It was the proudest moment of my life when I wiped the great man's eye by spotting and capturing a 'variety' which had markings half male and half female. He was very good about it and my heart swelled as he said, 'A fine fly. A very fine fly indeed.' Apparently it was worth a fiver even in those days. And now I have lived on the top of the Downs for eighteen years and never seen a single Chalkhill Blue.

The farmers having poisoned almost every living thing except a few skylarks, I have tried to turn our modest couple of acres into a bird and, especially, a butterfly sanctuary – with only limited success, I am afraid, but every little helps. I enlisted the aid of Hugh Newman, whose father founded the Butterfly Farm at Bexley in 1894, which he himself carried on till a few years ago. Newman, in case the subject appeals to you, is the author of two charming books *Living with Butterflies*,* the story of his and his father's seventy years as butterfly farmers, and *Create a Butterfly Garden*,* which might suddenly catch the imagination of anyone who lives in the country and has not really given it a thought before.

I remember his telling me of receiving an order from New Zealand for tens of thousands of Cinnabar Moth caterpillars, which it was hoped would keep down the ragwort which was in-festing the land. The caterpillars were duly delivered and the birds of New Zealand could hardly believe their eyes. The last one was gone within a matter of hours. Newman also had no less distinguished a customer than Winston Churchill, who wrote in *My Early Life*: 'I have always loved butterflies . . . The Butterfly

* Both published by Baker, 1967.

is the Fact – gleaming, fluttering, settling for an instant with wings fully spread to the sun, then vanishing in the shades of the forest.' He ordered Newman to send five hundred Peacock caterpillars to Chartwell and put them out in the grounds. Newman did so and was most entertaining on the subject of his battles with Churchill's head gardener on leaving nettles, without which, of course, a Peacock caterpillar cannot live.

I planted a couple of poplar trees for the Puss Moths and Poplar Hawks, and buddleias of various kinds (is it really true, as I have read, that they were named after a Dr Buddle?) for the Vanessae – Tortoiseshells, Commas, Painted Ladies, and Red Admirals, all of which were too 'common' to be even noticed in the days of plenty – and we already had plenty of privet for the Privet Hawks and some blackthorn for the Emperor Moths, whose big green caterpillars you more normally find on heather. To found our little colony I bought mostly eggs, though with moths you rarely see the finished product since they only fly by night. I was looking at some Emperor eggs – I really ought to call them 'ova' – white and about half the size of caviare, when I thought I noticed movement. In a matter of minutes the tiniest little fuzzy black caterpillars had emerged and started their life by eating the shells. I brought them up inside for a while, then put them out in a muslin 'sleeve' on the blackthorn till they chrysalized in cocoons, upon which they were returned to store, and one day the following year I gazed with awe at the first newly emerged specimen on the wall of the potting-shed. With the huge 'eyes' on its wings the Emperor must be one of the most beautiful creatures of Nature and it was the best part of fifty years since I had seen one. Not that one is always so fortunate. I 'sleeved' some magnificent Poplar Hawks until the time came when they would be wanting to climb down the tree to bury themselves and chrysalize. I took off the sleeve and, when I came back a few minutes later to admire them, the sparrows from the mill had had the lot.

Still, we have our little successes. I once saw a Privet Hawk caterpillar marching across the bottom of the drive in the purposeful way that meant that he wanted to chrysalize, so I picked him up and put him under the base of an aubretia plant which seemed to me a suitable place. To my infinite delight he seemed to agree and at once began digging himself in. It took him less than five minutes to disappear completely, leaving no trace on the surface, and we dug him up next spring. Little things please little minds, but at least it helps to keep you young.

In 1969 we had an enormous hatch of Peacocks and I watched the whole process of one emerging from the chrysalis. It lay on its back and twisted the casing round and round with its legs till it broke the equivalent of the umbilical cord and was free. It was hardly an inch long, with flattened, damp, rolled-up wings. Within an hour it had turned into one of the most handsome of all our butterflies.

I am afraid I cannot boast any spectacular success with my butterfly farming, but when you look round at the barren prairie which used to be the South Downs, on which no insect can any longer survive and breed, we may not after all have done so badly. We have bred Puss Moths; and Privet, Poplar, and Elephant Hawks; and have managed to attract the occasional Humming Bird Hawk round the flower borders. On the more modest side we have provided sanctuary for Brimstone, Speckled Wood, Wall, Meadow Brown (much despised at school, very much the poor relation), Small Copper, Small Skipper, Small Heath, Common Blue, Cinnabar, Green-Veined White (even if it does lay eggs on the cabbages) and that happy harbinger of spring, the Orange-Tip. We also have a fine colony of Burnet moths, the little black ones with either five or six red spots on their wings, whose golden chrysalises you see attached to tall stems of grass in June. They generally emerge during the Open Championship, but I get back in time to see them hanging on the grass stems attached in pairs, busily mating. They have another golfing connection in that I renew my stock annually from chrysalises on the 6th fairway at the Brighton and Hove club and occasionally from Rye.

The great triumph, however, was when I bought and managed to hatch out some Swallowtail chrysalises, this supremely beautiful butterfly being a sort of Holy Grail of collectors and occurring in its natural state only on Wicken Fen. Perhaps mine were imported, but at any rate I released a couple on a sunny day and thus joined the small and select company of those who have actually seen them in flight in England. I watched enchanted as they alternately flitted and floated over the flower beds and I hoped that they might prove to be a male and female and mate and find our clumps of fennel on which to breed. Alas, we have never seen any since.

32
Costly
Infatuation

My family's connection with the turf goes back a long way and may be said on the whole to have been unfortunate in its good fortune. It started, so far as I know, with my mother's uncle William Gilbert, whom the whole family obviously adored, if only for the fact that he always had the pony brought into the drawing-room and paraded round the table during Christmas Dinner. He was a corn merchant in Farnham, Surrey, and lived in extremely good style, though heavily indebted to one of the many private banks of the 1870s and '80s. Unhappily the bank was 'taken over' – it happened even in those days – and the new manager's insistence that Uncle William adjust his account put his finances into a parlous condition. 'What?' he was heard to say. 'Haven't you got any money in your blasted bank?' He had already won the Two Thousand Guineas with Sailor Prince and in 1886 he decided, as they so often seem to have done in those days, to risk the lot on him in the Royal Hunt Cup at Ascot. He also had another horse running, ridden by a boy, called Despair.

He won the Royal Hunt Cup all right but, alas, it ruined him, for the winner was not Sailor Prince but Despair. I hardly like to think of his feelings as he led in the winner to the cheers of the multitude, with the boy saying, "'E was away with me, sir. Honest, sir. I couldn't 'old 'im, sir.' Of course, to make the story right Sailor Prince should have been second, but in fact he was nowhere. Rubbing salt unconsciously in the wound my great-uncle's friends presented him with a printed Memento, in blue and gold, a copy of which I have before me, dedicated to W. Gilbert, Esq. and the Victory of Despair, complete with some absolutely frightful verse, beginning: 'Loyal to the sport yclept the "Sport of Kings"/Gilbert gains success that honour brings/Loyal to the steed who oft his banner bore/ right in the front, yet never to the fore.' The Royal

Hunt Cup was a huge piece of presumably silver statuary showing St George slaying the dragon. 'We always wondered why it had to be kept in our house instead of his,' my mother used to say. The answer was that otherwise the bailiffs would have had it.

When my friend Wreford-Brown, who used, if I remember, to make a book among the Lower School at Charterhouse and remained word perfect on Ruff's *Guide to the Turf* during twenty-five years of soldiering in parts of the world as remote as Abyssinia and the Sudan, suggested that we might go into partnership in a horse which had taken his fancy, it was only natural that our family half should be registered in my mother's name rather than mine, not only in memory of her uncle but because she seemed to have a knack of spotting winners. In her mid-seventies she brought home a whole succession of long-odds big race winners, to such an extent that, when she lived in the village of Goldington on the outskirts of Bedford, nobody was inclined to place a bet until it became known, via the hairdresser, 'what old Mrs Longhurst was on'.

Our horse was a smallish chestnut called Infatuated, of an exceptionally nice disposition, though no longer destined to earn us anything for stud purposes, and was trained by Toby Balding, son of the great polo player, at Weyhill. My mother being eighty-five when we bought him, there was a good deal of 'Don't be so ridiculous. Me at my time of life,' and I cherish the memory of her, cheque-book open and pen poised, saying solemnly, 'But what would the rector say?' to which I am afraid I replied, 'I know exactly what the rector would say. He would say, "Shall I put the Easter offering on him at Plumpton on Monday?".'

Our first venture was at Newbury, where I at once began to sense the vanity of being an Owner. You turn importantly into the car-park marked 'Owners, Trainers and Jockeys'; watch your horse being saddled up; walk importantly into the ring and talk to the jockey, in our case Bill Palmer ('Haven't had a winner in my family for seventy-six years,' I said. 'I'll do my best, sir!' he replied); and furthermore you get a free lunch or, if too excited to eat it, the equivalent of 7s. 6d, in sandwiches, which comes to one round of smoked salmon and one of ham.

We hoped that at the best we might get a place. They were half-way round the second time before we were so much as mentioned by the commentator, lying about twelfth among an apparently impenetrable mass of horses. Then it was eighth; then fifth; then fourth. Then suddenly, as they came over the last hurdle ('flight' to us racing men), it was 'Infatuated and So-and-so'. In fact I have mentioned our modest incursion into racing partly for the sake of a wonderful picture of him taken at this very moment, which Palmer will be able to show with pride to his grandchildren as a masterpiece of poise and motion. A few seconds later I was lifting my hat to the pair of them as they passed the post, winners by twelve lengths – and 16–1 on the Tote. The racing press got hold of the story of my mother's uncle and she found herself featured in nearly all the papers next day, one account being headed in inch-high letters MOTHER'S JOY.

Infatuated then won a race at Warwick, beating a horse that cost ten times the £600 we had paid for him, and was an odds-on favourite at Wye, his value apparently increasing by about £1,000 a month – but there, alas, ended our saga of success. He got within an hour of Wye racecourse when they abandoned the meeting, thus robbing us of a certain £300. Then he got to Plumpton and they abandoned the meeting at 1.00 p.m., robbing us, as we like to think, of another £300.

Never mind. All would come right at Fontwell – but a lovely sunny day turned out to be only Black Monday. It was my first experience of being a Losing Owner and I found it painful. All that I had gained went down the drain. 'Never mind,' said my mother, 'so long as the little horse is all right!' She was right. If he had fallen and had to be destroyed, I am sure I should never have set foot on a racecourse again.

Later Infatuated won a race at Chepstow at a starting price of 5–2, at which we backed him and which turned out to be almost exactly half the price paid out on the Tote, and his next engagement was to be on the flat at Folkestone, in a race for which, since he had so obvious a chance, none other than Doug Smith was engaged to conduct him round. He had rather delicate ankles – the horse, I mean, not Doug Smith, and I suppose I should call them fetlocks anyway – and was therefore liable to injure himself if pressed on hard going. The overnight report had the going as 'fair' but this proved entirely inaccurate and the ground was hard as a board, and here comes one of the monstrous iniquities of horse racing. It was obviously dangerous for the horse to run, especially if the fiction were to be maintained that he was 'flat out', but if we scratched him and did not let him run we should have had to pay a fine of £50 out of our own pockets (*and* the jockey *and* the horse-box from Weyhill *and* the head lad) simply in order not to inconvenience the patrons of the betting-shops, should they find that they had backed from the morning papers, at no cost to themselves, an 'overnight runner' which did not run because, if it did, it might do itself a serious injury.

This, in fact, is precisely what poor Infatuated did, so that, at about the equivalent of an old-age pensioner's weekly stipend, he had to go out to grass for a year at our expense as a result of an injury he incurred solely on behalf of the betting-shops, or, as meaner observers might declare, our own reluctance to be fined fifty quid. At long last, when he seemed fit again and a farmer in the West Country had taken a fancy to him, our adventure on the turf seemed ripe for conclusion. Toby Balding decided it might sharpen the horse up and perhaps make him look worth a hundred or two more if he had a go round Newton Abbot, not too expensive for the horsebox from Weyhill, and there he was duly dispatched. While I had found by this time that you certainly did not know when your horse was going to win, I was still under the impression that you knew when it wasn't. Not so. I have a picture of the Newton Abbot party, grinning all over their faces, including the horse, having won the main race of the day and a handsome challenge cup. Thirty-two and a half to one on the Tote and not one of us had a penny on him. Talk about a mug's game!

33
The Blasted
Baker

My friend and neighbour Mr Harold Potter, OBE, having been compulsorily retired at his peak from the Civil Service for no better reason than that his birth certificate showed that he had lived for sixty years, found that, modest as had been his reward for what had been a task of quite astounding responsibility, his pension left him still more inadequately placed for the years to come. I, being also one whose true worth had never been recognized, was in the same boat and the law of the day being, as it doubtless always will be, that the more work you do and the more successfully you do it, the bigger proportion you get taken away in tax, it was natural that we should seek means of augmenting our own rather than the Government's income. As this could not be done by working, there was only one thing for it – the pools.

The first snag, of course, was that neither he nor I had the faintest idea of how to fill the damned things in. This was soon overcome, for it turned out that his wife did, and she was at once appointed secretary to the syndicate. It was decided that we should enter for the Treble Chance – in which, for the uninitiated, you tried to get eight drawn games in one line of eight selections: maximum points 24 – 3 for a draw, 2 for an away win, 1 for a home win. From this it will be seen that the fewer the draws on the day's play the bigger the dividend was likely to be. We were to pick sixteen selections per week and, if we got eight or more draws among them, with any luck eight would come up on one line, or some such. I think we had about twenty-five shillings' worth at a penny a line.

It was evidently no use our selecting our teams each week from the book of form, partly because we did not know one from another and partly because, if you select the obvious ones, everyone else has got them too and the pay-out becomes infinitesimal. A dice was therefore extracted from the children's Snakes and Ladders and solemnly cast by the distinguished civil servant until sixteen numbers had been arrived at, these to be our permanent selections for the season.

We had hardly had time to forget all about them when Mrs Potter was reported to have come over strangely silent and pre-occupied. Interrogation revealed that on the previous Saturday there had only been nine draws in all – and on one line we had seven of them. And what about the other match? This turned out to be the well-known Scottish religious festival, Celtic versus Rangers, one of which is Catholic and the other Protestant, I never can remember which. At any rate such is the fervour of Christian brotherly love which prevails at this encounter that the Chief Constable of Glasgow declined to allow it to be held on Saturday at all and to lighten the casualties made them postpone it till the Monday. Only Mrs Potter knew that a postponed match counts, according to the rules, as an away win. We were, there-fore, in a week with only nine draws, sitting on 23 points. Would anyone get 24?

Was she sure she had filled the thing in right? Yes, quite. Was she sure she had posted it? Yes, a man came every week and collected it, pocketing half a crown in the pound commission, so he must have sent it. Did she know anyone who had been paid out before and, if so, when did it arrive? Yes, and it arrived on Thursday. We decided to wait till Thursday, when the son of the house, having waited for the postman in the hall, dashed upstairs with: 'Two for you, Mum.' Two bills. Ought we to send in a claim? No, better wait till Friday. And on Friday it came.

Out of the hundreds of millions of lines in permutations and combinations and the rest of it sent in to Messrs Littlewoods every week only one single line, believe it or not, had eight draws out of the nine. This was a Mr Wall, a sixty-two-year-old baker in New Malden, Surrey, and I confess that for many a week my lip curled in envy at the very thought of 'that blasted baker', as we called him. 'His wife, Alice,' said a contemporary account, 'still collects trading stamps and cigarette coupons – she wants some cut glass and a coffee table – and she continues to go to bingo and whist. All they have bought in the way of extras since their big win are two off-the-peg overcoats costing £13.13.0 and a £4 pair of shoes for Mr Wall.'

In a Walter Mitty sort of way I saw myself at Grosvenor House accepting the cheque from some busty young starlet or even the great Cecil Moores himself, and the television interviewer saying, 'Will this make any difference to your life, Mr Longhurst?' and myself replying, 'Will it indeed – and, if you're listening, Lord Thomson, my notice as from Tuesday.' Instead we had the mortification of seeing huge advertisements with the fatal figure of £275,235 for 1d. – I can scarce bear to write it down again – and a picture of Mr Wall with the caption, so help the man who wrote it, 'He'll never *need* dough again.'

On Friday the postman brought with him a cheque for the derisory sum of £1,039.3s. Like a man fishing for pike and catching a minnow I felt (then but not now) almost like throwing it back, and in a sense I did, for I found that the first reaction when you win money like this is, as with so many people, to give it away. The children and their spouses got a hundred apiece; my own spouse, after a few harsh words, seeing that she wasn't in the syndicate at all, extracted a hundred in silence money; and the rest I spent on champagne, with every bottle of which we drank to 'Cecil Moores and blast the baker'.

To which bittersweet episode I would add two postscripts. The first is that if you believe in horoscopes you want your head examined *but* the *Daily Express*'s feature for the day had, for myself, bearing in mind my wife's intransigence: '*Pisces :* Get differences with friends sorted out today; do the same with partners.' For H. Potter: '*Sagittarius :* Financial negotiations reach climax, but you may not get all you hoped for.' For Mrs H. Potter, the secretary-manager: '*Aquarius :* You have to take on someone else's burdens, but this serves a useful purpose, financially.' It makes you think!

My second postscript is, as I think you will agree, a rather charming one. These huge pools wins so often bring disaster in their train, but not so in this case. Some time later *The Times* ran a follow-up story of some of the big winners and, after quoting the young coal-miner who picked up £150,000 and whose wife said she was going to 'spend, spend, spend' – he killed himself in his Jaguar on his way back from inspecting his racehorses and eventually she was down to £12 a week – the story went on:

> Mr and Mrs Frank Wall were planning how to make ends meet on
> their retirement, until a knock on the door of their council house in

Malden brought the news that they had won a fortune on the pools. It turned out to be £275,235.

Frank Wall, aged 63, was a baker, earning £17 a week, on nightwork £27. His wife was bringing in £7 as a canteen cook. Spare and fit, with white hair and a pink complexion which, after a lifetime in bread bakeries, looked as if it was permanently dusted with flour, Frank Wall meant to carry on as long as he could. Plump and homely, his wife was still managing to look after him, and a job, too. But they were both approaching their middle sixties, their three children were grown up, and the prospect loomed of how to manage on an old-age pension of £4 a week. Obviously, they wouldn't be able to afford the £3 a week rent of their council house. The notion they had was to make their home in their old age in a caravan.

Suddenly, Frank Wall, who had never had a bank account in his life, had a bank balance of well over a quarter of a million. The pools people asked him how he wanted to apportion the money. No, he didn't want a car; he didn't want a holiday abroad; and his wife didn't want a mink coat or jewellery. What he wanted was a house in Bournemouth, which he and his wife had once visited on a day's holiday outing. He bought the freehold of a new house for £8,800.

To each of his three children, his 36-year-old son, a carpet layer by trade; his 38-year-old daughter married to a surveyor in Scotland; and his 28-year-old daughter, married to a bus driver, be provided £20,000 to buy a house and a car. He put £1,000 in trust for each of his seven grandchildren when they are twenty-one. Next, he gave £2,000 each to his eight brothers and sisters. Finally, he made a present of £10,000 to an old drinking pal and neighbour, another baker, to enable him to retire. In total, he gave away £93,000 immediately.

His change of fortune came on New Year's Day, 1966. He is now sitting with his legs up at 6 Ashling Close, Charminster, near Bournemouth, where he has provided a swing in the garden for the entertainment of his grandchildren.

What a happy tale that is and what a very nice man Mr Wall must be – 'blasted baker' or not! All the same I cannot help dreaming of what would have happened if the Chief Constable had let the religious maniacs of Glasgow hold their match and it had ended in a draw.

34
Starvation Cure

My deep-seated loathing of PT, together with my successful determination never to play football except in goal, conspired to turn me into a strictly non-exercise type. All this, and a liking for the good things of life, has left me with a constant and generally losing battle against avoirdupois. I am not much given to envy. I covet no man's possessions, neither his ox nor his ass nor even, any longer, his wife. I do, however, confess to one exception: I envy those slim people who can eat like a horse and drink like a fish and never put on an ounce – and let no man say it is due to 'character' on their part and lack of it on mine. It is how you are made. Metabolism, I believe, is the word. Henry Cotton, for instance, came to my own wedding and to my son's and my daughter's in the same tail coat and, as the ever more portly host, I found it infuriating. Being one who can easily put on three pounds in a day, I found that it was a case of either permanently 'going without' or letting Nature take its course and then, so to speak, giving a violent tug on the reins. The violent tug on the reins consists of the annual visit to Enton Hall, near Godalming, one of those establishments rather ludicrously described as 'health farms', from which, as I write, I have just come back minus thirteen pounds in eight days, feeling minus thirteen years as well.

All this renders one subject to much ridicule and badinage by the unthinking. 'Fancy paying them all that money to live on orange-juice,' they say, or, 'Why can't you do it at home?' The answer is that it is a matter not only of 'Oh, that this too, too solid flesh would melt' but also of going into retreat. Enton is a huge red-brick monstrosity erected by some rich character in the early eighties up a minor road behind the village of Witley, from which only a single habitation is visible on top of a neighbouring hill. It boasts a variety of magnificent specimen trees and a background

The pleasure of living in the mills was enhanced for me by a satisfying sense of continuity : I discovered that my great-grandfather had lived nearby – indeed I found his account in the miller's book of 1849.

of woods and, apart from the occasional aeroplane descending to Dunsfold, an air of unbelievable peace prevails. In the garden is a row of chalets, of which No. 5 is my home-from-home, where one may sit in bed gazing out at the lawns and the trees, of a simple yet comfortable austerity, like a very good officer's bedroom in the war – beds, one; mats, foot, one; basins, one; blankets, electric, one; and so on. As there are broadly speaking no meals and therefore no mealtimes, one may without a twinge of conscience be in bed or sleeping at one in the afternoon. Fasting is a wonderful thing, as previous generations knew and we have perhaps forgotten, though I will not start a sermon on the subject. When I first went 'inside', many years ago, I was hungry on the second day but only, as I later realized, because I imagined I ought to be. Now I can go for six or seven days on hot water and lemon until I begin to wonder, rather as one reads of long-term prisoners reluctant to face the outside world, whether one must really go out and start eating great lumps of grilled dead cow and suchlike, with all the attendant processes and results of digestion. Nearly everyone feels 'ropey' after two or three days as all the poisons work their way out, but there comes the magic moment when you see light at the end of the tunnel and day by day begin to see with both eyes and hear with both ears and breathe through both sides of your nose, till you feel that you could cheerfully take on anything or anybody. As for the crossword, you fill in the letters almost before you have finished reading the clues. It is a great and glorious feeling, even if you do begin soon to slip back into your old ways.

There are, of course, innumerable stories of so-and-so, who was expelled with ignominy for being detected with a bottle under the bed, but for myself, despite drink having been an occupational hazard for the best part of forty years, I find no temptation in this matter and in my morning walk can cheerfully stride by the White Hart at Witley during opening hours. My only concession, in fact, is that towards the end I go out on the occasional evening for a half-bottle of champagne with one or two friends in the neighbourhood, this having been proved to cast no reflection on the scales next day.

I was, I fancy, the first to discover the alarming statistic that, as the average golf club weighs less than 13 ounces, a full set of 14 does not weigh a stone. So when I weigh-in at Enton at 15

stone, I am carrying the equivalent of 60 wooden clubs, 150 irons
and almost exactly a gross of balls. I told this to a substantial friend
of mine, Lord Banbury, one day and next morning the noble naked
Lord stepped off the scales saying with much pride, 'I've lost all
the irons and two of the woods!' To another even more substantial
friend, who leads a sedentary life, sitting up half the night invent-
ing things and drinking so much coffee in the process that he
consumes six pints of milk a day, I revealed that every time he gets
up from his chair he has to lift 100 wooden clubs and 200 irons.
He wrote for the brochure next day.

Enton is the basic original of Ian Fleming's 'Shrublands', where
James Bond and the villain nearly kill each other by switching full
on the various rack-like apparatuses by which the other is being
treated. I forget the name of the book but I think it is *Moonraker*
in which the masseur insists on the villain taking his watch off,
Bond notices a sign tattooed underneath it, and is overheard by
the villain as he telephones headquarters to know what the emblem indicates. All this could well be, but whether the fearsome
rack-like devices exist, presumably in the osteopathic section, I
should take leave to doubt. At any rate our massage, hot blankets
and sitting in little sitz-baths of cold water with our feet in hot,
waiting for the pinger to indicate that it is time to transfer to the
hot one with our feet in cold, all seem mild by comparison. I can,
however, claim to have given Fleming, just in time to include it in
the book, the rather splendid line, 'See you later, Irrigator.'

35
Television
Cavalcade

Just when I thought the time of life was coming when I could sit back and so to speak, freewheel home, the extraordinary increase in interest in golf set me working harder than ever, not only through finding favour as a commentator in America, involving as many as five trips in one year, but also through the decision of the BBC to co-operate with Mark McCormack's organization in America in producing a series of filmed golf matches. McCormack is the man who altered the whole professional scene all over the world by managing first Arnold Palmer, then Gary Player and then Jack Nicklaus and styling them 'the Big Three', which for some time it is fair to say they were. He was to provide the players and prize money; the BBC were to make the films. McCormack hoped to recoup himself by selling the films to American television, while the BBC would be filling time which they would have to fill anyway, though at a pretty considerable cost.

McCormack planned first a three-round series entitled *The Big Three in Britain*, then a thirteen-match series labelled *United States versus the World*. The Big Three were to play at Gleneagles, Carnoustie and St Andrews, which were adjacent enough to do the three rounds in successive days, though, by God, if any of us had known what this entailed there would have been a strike before ever we started. We got off the first tee at Gleneagles at 9.00 a.m. and finished nine and a half hours later. We then drove to Carnoustie, arriving long past any hope of dinner (this became quite a routine: no dinner, put in a call for 7.00). Next morning we were on the bleak and windswept Carnoustie course at 8.00 a.m. and off it eleven hours later, just in time to catch the last ferry over the Tay to St Andrews: no dinner and a call for 6.30 this time: on the course at 7.00 a.m. and off at about 5.30 with the players dashing to escape in time via Prestwick.

Our start at Gleneagles remains one of the moments of my golfing life. The producer, Phil Pilley, had never conducted such an operation before; nor had any of the cameramen or assistant producers; nor had the commentator. What is more, Pilley had broadly speaking no experience of golf and was strictly a non-player. He was now in charge of what looked more like part of an armoured division that had strayed onto a golf course: a whole troop of Mini-Mokes, Land-Rovers, a tea wagon and two of those mobile extendable crane-like affairs for hoisting cameramen aloft. My own 'establishment' was two Mini-Mokes, with two sound-engineers and their equipment in one and myself, a 'minder', a girl to record everything I said, and a driver in the other. My job was to describe each hole – length, par and characteristics – theoretically before they played it, but that often had to go by the board. Then one had to make a comment on every shot as it was played, and that soon went by the board too, sometimes because we had not managed to go ahead and get a suitable pitch in time, sometimes because someone zoomed by in a vehicle or some spectators started talking, but most often because of aeroplanes. Till you have tried a job like this, you do not appreciate how rarely the sky over our small island is any longer silent. One also had to announce how the players stood at the end of each hole, adding in the meantime bits about their background, in what year they won what (being careful not to say 'this year', thus identifying when the matches were played), the background of the club and great events which had been played there, together with any local 'stories' that came to mind or could be ferreted out of books. Most difficult of all were the interviews, opening, closing, at half-time, and at a moment's notice when anyone got into specially photo-genic trouble, in which case there were cries of 'Rimas!' this being Rimas (pronounced 'Remus') Vainorius, a tall, lithe fellow with a bizarre taste in hats, who carried round an immensely heavy camera without any vehicle at all and was said to be the 'best holder of a camera in the business'. If you happen to have seen any of these films, you may be sure that any shots of balls entangled in the rough or deep in the woods were the work of Rimas.

At Gleneagles we opened with myself high up on the edge of the first green and the Big Three walking into shot, and I duly said something about the three best players in the world and three of our best courses for them to play on and then got each of them to

338

say something. All three being wholly articulate, this was not difficult, but interviewing is basically a very difficult art and, when you get a naturally uncommunicative type, it is murder. This done, they were motored back to the first tee, and Pilley set the whole, untried apparatus into motion. He proved to be one of the most thorough, painstaking and methodical people I have ever met, and the amount of work he did was positively horrifying. He had to make all the arrangements with the club and 'recce' the course with a view to writing a huge script indicating exactly where the 'leapfrogging' teams of cameramen were to proceed to in readiness for the next shot; he had to order the vehicles; arrange accommodation for everyone and transport for the players; arrange terms and payment for the whole regiment; and heaven knows how many other things as well. At Gleneagles our nine and a half hours, including a break for an alfresco lunch, with three players and everyone doing it for the first time, was by no means bad. Later with two players our 'par' became about seven and a half hours, depending somewhat on how well the players played. With the assistance of the local professional Pilley would have placed the cameras in position to receive a well hit shot. It was when they drove into the woods and suchlike (cries of 'Rimas!') that the whole cavalcade had to stop and be reorientated, not only to capture the shot out of the woods but to place cameras on a new receiving end. This would also mean that the vehicles which had been so carefully hidden out of shot from any camera would now have come into shot and be causing the familiar cry: 'Move that Moke!' Or it might be, 'Get some people to stand in front of that Land-Rover,' or maybe children to squat down on the green to hide the legs of a camera tripod. In all we did forty-six of these films and, though you will sometimes see a crane in the background, the only time I remember seeing a Moke was in the very opening hole, years ago as it now seems, at Gleneagles.

Sometimes, if all went well, we would get ten or eleven, and once even twelve, holes done before breaking for lunch and this was a great encouragement. Nine more to go after lunch was a very different thing to 'Only seven to go, thank God', when the reluctant troops were made to fall in and get on the march again. My own routine soon became one 'purple heart' jerker-upper pill at about the 7th: contents of hip flask with lunch, giving my beer ration to the nearest deserving case; and a half purple heart at about the 13th. I cannot tell you the relief with which I personally, being a bit long in the tooth for field manoeuvres on this scale, would realize, on repeating my closing formula 'And so in this game in our thirteen-match series Snooks of the United States beats Smith of Australia, representing the World, by x strokes', that a day which at the beginning one thought would never end had really done so. As I collapsed over the first large Bell's in the clubhouse, I felt I had really earned it.

Pilley's work, of course, was never done. There was always work on the next film but each one already filmed was going to take a highly experienced hand some six weeks to edit, with Pilley directing the operation. More than twenty thousand feet of coloured film, costing heaven knows what, would be cut to about 1,800, exactly fifty minutes, so as to allow for commercials in case it was sold to America. It seemed terrible to think of how much good stuff had to go by the board – including my comment at Gleneagles, 'Within a quarter of a mile of where we are standing now I once counted more than two thousand wild geese on one small potato field.' I thought this a very interesting aside, the sort which appeals to a man sitting over his television, and I still do. I have now made it three times. The first two were unlucky. The third Gleneagles film is at the moment of writing being edited and I wait to see whether my geese get in at last. Also edited out was the bit where apparently a baby squalled and I referred to it, though I would swear on oath that I didn't, as a 'pestilential infant'. It was thought that Mother might see the film and protest to the BBC (P.S. My geese never got in.)

The Big Three series, as it turned out, was rather a success and was in fact sold for a large sum to America, possibly because the final scene stood out from anything in any of our own matches or such as I have seen in the comparable series, the Shell *Wonderful World of Golf*. If one had stage-managed the Big Three, which of course we did not and could not, one would have had them after fifty-three of the fifty-four holes all with identical scores and on the last tee of the Old Course at St Andrews. One would then have had all three drive up the middle and all three put their seconds on the green with a longish putt for a 3. First Player, then Nicklaus would miss by inches, leaving the whole series with Arnold Palmer and 'this to win' – and so, believe it or not, it came to pass. Palmer's putt in fact came right up to the middle of the hole and only in the last few inches faded and hung on the lip. A triple tie! What 'made it', however, was the scene looking down from the top of the clubhouse at perhaps fifteen hundred or two thousand people dashing madly up the last fairway to the green, a truly startling picture. The tie had a pleasurable aftermath, since it was decided to throw in an extra match as a play-off. The light would not be good enough in Britain by the time the players could next be got together, so someone had the bright idea of playing at the Dorado Beach Club in Puerto Rico, a lush fifteen-million-dollar Rockefeller development designed to bring money into a poverty-stricken island. I had been there before and found the prospect of a week there in November not unattractive. Everybody uses the lavish hotel but right at the end of the course I had discovered the original plantation house which now served as a half-way house. It was only about fifty yards from the ocean and one could look out from the cool stone balcony, with a glass in one's hand, speculating that over those waters Drake almost certainly sailed, and perhaps he even landed here. At any rate the BBC put down some £4,500 for our fares and away we went to finish it off. Player had rather an off day and was eliminated, but after about nine hours we found ourselves once again up the long first hole, with Palmer and Nicklaus still tied, playing it as the 19th and with sufficient light for only this one hole. Mercifully Nicklaus hit his drive behind a tree and we finished with Palmer the winner and ten minutes to spare.

When we had done the Big Three in Britain and two thirteen-match series, McCormack thought up the idea of Arnold Palmer, probably the best known sportsman in America (and sportsman is indeed the word, though I am always telling him he ought to chuck the golf and go into public life, never mind on which side) and Tony Jacklin, who at the time was Open Champion of both Britain and the United States, playing 'The Best 18 in Britain'. The so-called 'Best 18' could naturally be only a matter of opinion, but in this case was limited by geography and the availability of the players. Thus it had to be done just before the 1970 Open Championship at St Andrews, which meant, broadly speaking, Scotland and the coast of Lancashire and, though the series produced much lively argument in golfing circles, people mostly understood that we were not implying that there were no 'best' holes at, say, Sandwich or Westward Ho! We just could not reach them.

In parentheses, for the golfing reader only, I would add that the holes we did were: St Andrews, 11th, 14th, 17th (the Road Hole); Carnoustie, 6th, 16th, 17th; Troon, 8th (the Postage-Stamp) and 11th; Turnberry, 9th, 15th; Prestwick, 3rd; Muirfield, 9th; North Berwick, 14th (the Redan); Birkdale, 6th, 15th; Hoylake, 1st, 7th (the Dowie); and Lytham, 17th.

Few people have survived so brilliant or so sudden a limelight with better grace than Jacklin, at fifteen a steamfitter's apprentice at £3.15.0. a week in the steel works at Scunthorpe, at twenty-five facing a truly fascinating problem, namely that money will never, ever, mean anything in his life again. He proved to be an easy, fluent talker and this meant everything, since the essence of the film was that both should talk about each hole before they played it. Considering that he was just about to defend his British Open title and that the prize money, whatever it was, meant nothing to him, and considering the inevitable amount of being 'mucked about', I thought he came out of it all extraordinarily well. The procedure was that they first played the hole with as many practice balls as they liked and then came back to play it as 'the real thing' – and no funny business. Incidentally, since so many people asked me, there was no funny business in any of the matches. Nobody was allowed to 'have it over again'. The players mostly tried very hard, if only through not wishing to be seen by millions of people being beaten by so-and-so. People also said how tiring it must be for them to have to wait so long between shots, to which I would reply, 'What, when you get £1,000 for losing?' Each hole in the 'Best 18' took thirty or forty minutes, after which we would proceed to another hole on that course or, if there were only one, to the next course. In one memorable day we did two holes at Birkdale, then drove through Liverpool and the Mersey Tunnel to do two at Hoylake, then all the way back through Liverpool to do one at Lytham, then a chartered plane from Blackpool to Prestwick and finally a twenty-mile drive to Turnberry. Sometimes we actually did two or even three holes on one course and then after the briefest of breaks, set out to do an eighteen-hole match for the U.S. v. the World series on the same course. Meanwhile Pilley thought up 'links' such as the two contestants and myself sitting in the back of an opulent limousine, with him, Pilley, shining a light on us through the partition and Rimas and the sound engineer squatting on the floor. Another time it was

myself leaning out of a train window at Prestwick as the train left
for Troon – one that had to be got right first time, or else. The
limousine shots were made, it may now perhaps be revealed,
between Muirfield and a small disused wartime airfield near by.
'Now we are approaching Hoylake,' Pilley would say, whereupon
I would set my distinguished companions going on the subject of
Hoylake. 'That's all right. Now we are approaching Birkdale,' and
so it went on. At the far end of the runway we detected a single-
engined aeroplane, like a tiny white moth, and in this the two
contestants were to fly across to St Andrews, where they had a
starting time for a practice round for the Open. The machine
would not, however, take their vast bags of clubs and these were
to come along in the 'limmo', as the Americans call it. They
crammed into their fragile craft, Jacklin looking extremely appre-
hensive in the back, and in a few moments were being tossed by
the wind to one side and the other like a feather. Talk about not
putting all your eggs in one basket! If only McCormack could see
them now, I thought. His two most valuable properties, worth at
a conservative estimate ten million dollars the pair, tossed around
like this, all to save an hour or so to St Andrews. And, after all that,
the limmo and their clubs did not arrive in time.

For myself, what with the 'Best 18' and the other series, often
on the same day, and the Open Championship itself in the middle,
I did twenty-two days without a break and it bloody near killed
me. Never again! Or anyway not till the next time. On the whole,
though, the films seem to have gone down well, especially with
anyone with coloured television, and many non-golfers were
found to enjoy them. For this reason they seem, on looking back,
to have been a worth-while episode in my life. I even got letters
from New Zealand where, said one correspondent, nobody in his
area ever made engagements for Wednesday evenings and everyone assumed next day that everyone else had seen them, to such
an extent that, when he had driven past a friend's dairy that
morning, the man had looked up and shouted, 'Pity he missed that
putt!'

Perhaps the richest moment of the whole series was the very
last, when for some technical reason we had to re-do the closing
scene and went out in the 'limmo' one morning to Ealing, as being
the nearest course to London where a suitable background might
be obtained. Including the players there were only about eight of

us and we hung around in little groups, waiting for two ladies to play to the short-hole green beside the clubhouse, which was to form our background. One hit her ball into the filthy, tin-can-ridden, polluted stream which was once the River Brent and had to play another, and it was clear that neither was a potential winner of the Ladies' Championship; just two ordinary lady golfers, in fact, playing their ordinary game on a mid-week morning on an almost deserted course. Eventually they reached the green and while one was putting I saw the other look unsuspectingly up. She froze for a moment and looked away, then, pulling herself together, looked again. It was true. The first gallery in front of which either of them had ever played contained Arnold Palmer and Tony Jacklin!

36
My Favourite
Land

Finding myself two or three years ago in South Africa, over which it occurs to me the great British public may have been subjected to one of the biggest brain-washing operations of all time, I thought I must pay a visit to the wicked rebels in Rhodesia, from which country I had met so many fine fellows in England and to which it seemed, from what they had told me about it, I might one day retire. Almost the first person I met in Salisbury was Colin Kirkpatrick. Really this 'old school' business is rather extraordinary! He and his brother had been at St Cyprians; I recognized him immediately, and we took up again just as if we had not met for a year or so instead of the best part of fifty. He drove me all the way up to the superbly beautiful Eastern Highlands and it was a strange and singular thrill to think that somewhere up in those mountains might lie my last resting-place. We went as far up as Troutbeck, which might reasonably be termed the Gleneagles of Rhodesia, with its trout-stocked lake, golf course and mountain background. In the hall they have a picture of Loch Earn in Scotland and the likeness is quite extraordinary. Troutbeck was thought up when the road into the hills was only a mere track and was entirely created by the redoubtable Major Herbert MacIlwaine, whom older rugby footballers will remember as a fifteen-stone forward of renown. On the way back we made a diversion to enable me to see the Mare Dam and its little holiday cottages, which Kirkpatrick thought might suit me, and passed on the way, without calling in, the little Rhodes Inyanga Hotel, which caught my fancy through the riot of flowers hanging down the bank that keeps the hotel itself out of sight from the road.

The game of golf, I have often said, is the esperanto of sport, the universal letter of introduction and opener of doors, and so, once again, it proved. I presented myself at the Royal Salisbury Club and was welcomed as though my country were aiding Rhodesia instead of trying to bankrupt her. Nothing was too much for anyone to do to make my stay enjoyable and I was not surprised when later I learned that hospitality is a great Rhodesian tradition. I can remember the exact place in which I was standing in the crowded bar one evening when the thought ran through my mind: 'What a wonderful thing it would be for the Royal and Ancient club of St Andrews, the very heart of golf, to send a team on a goodwill tour of Rhodesia!' On arriving home, I suggested this to the then captain, Gerald Micklem, but the club, he said, had now given up sending out touring teams. The tide, however, was turned by that large and sterling Scotsman Wilbur Muirhead, who was chairman of the championship committee. 'I'd come,' he said. That was good enough for me, and it was not long before we had completed a party prepared to venture into rebel territory, and be damned to Harold Wilson. They consisted of my old friend Peter Wreford-Brown, Edward Bromley-Davenport, Alec Hill, Donald Steel, Bill Callendar, Ronnie Alexander, John Salvesen and Mesdames Alexander and Salvesen. Our hosts in Rhodesia, having in the meantime arranged a truly wonderful schedule for us, were there to meet us on the tarmac, with a room full of refreshments to while away the short time it took the customs to pass ourselves and our baggage through without formality. We were each given a pass instead of having our passports stamped – in case we passed through any of the emergent dictatorships on the way home, where the locals might take it out on us if they saw that we had been visiting our rebellious fellow-countrymen.

Incidentally, one of the best laughs for some years was when a number of British professionals decided to play in Zambian tournaments on the way home from South Africa rather than Rhodesian because there was more money to be won. Their reward on arrival was to be thrown instantly into gaol on the grounds that they had been playing golf in South Africa – not that there was any known law against doing so but once Africans are 'independent' they tend to make up the law as they go along. I managed to get an article into the *Sunday Times* headed 'Giving them the old Zambian Welcome' and this greatly pleased me, for it was almost impossible to get anything pro-white into the papers in those days – and for that matter still is.

All the way along the line our friends put us up in their houses, and clubs gave parties for us at which we were able to meet and listen to the views of the leading citizens, including the arch-rebel himself, Mr Ian Smith, and his then chief administrative officer, Mr Clifford Dupont, now the country's first President, to say nothing of the occasional sanction-buster, one of whom told me that he reckoned the trade loss to Great Britain up to then, January 1970, was about £300,000,000. All the new cars were French, German or Japanese and it grieved one's heart to see it in a community that was in many ways more British than present-day Britain.

In the Prime Minister's ante-room there is a most magnificent copper rosebowl which they had presented, suitably inscribed, to the officers and men of HMS *Tiger* in appreciation of their hospitality when the Rhodesian delegation were accommodated in the ship during talks with the Labour Government. You will scarcely credit it, but the ship was not allowed by the British Government to accept it.

Having played at five clubs around Salisbury, we got into a magnificent coach – Mercedes, of course, not Leyland – complete with hot and cold water and lavatory at the back, and set off on the long haul up to Troutbeck, which made our four Scotsmen feel very much at home. Thence to Umtali, over Christmas Pass, which the pioneer column reached on Christmas Day 1900, and a night in the hotel at Chimanimani, one of the most beautiful spots in the world, I dare say; thence to Turner and Newell's vast asbestos mine at Shabani, with one of the best courses in the country; a long haul to Gwelo and finally Bulawayo.

From Bulawayo we made a diversion to enable us to climb up to Rhodes's grave at a beauty spot which he chose in advance high up in the Matopos – just a stone slab in the rock bearing the words CECIL RHODES, singularly impressive in its simplicity. The hillside is covered with what appeared to be dead, trampled-down heather known as the Resurrection Plant, and I still have a piece of it in my travelling-case. Its name comes from the fact that, though apparently dead, it will come out in leaf months later if you put it in water. How long it will do this I do not know, but I have had my piece for the best part of two years and a little sprig torn off now and put in water still comes out with bright green little leaves, like thyme, within the hour.

We also took in the Victoria Falls, beside which Niagara seems no more than a couple of burst pipes, and, however 'touristy' it may have become, one could not without genuine awe gaze at this stupendous cataract, wondering what must have been Livingstone's impressions as he first saw it and then retired to sit under this very banyan tree under which one is sitting now. Incidentally, we must be among the very few who can claim to have been decimalized at the Falls, and a very painless process it turned out to be by comparison with a year later at home. The twenty-shilling Rhodesian pound became a ten-shilling dollar, or 100 cents, so that what had been 16s. was now $1.60, which the meanest intelligence could understand. On arriving home early in 1971 I found myself being decimalized once again but by the wisdom of the financial wizards concerned this turned out to be based on units of twenty instead of ten (which I thought was what decimal meant anyway), so that a tot of the hard stuff became 16½p. At school I used to be quite good, though I say it myself, at elementary arithmetic. Perhaps my powers are failing but I still have to turn to my little pocket calculator to find the equivalent of 16½ hundredths of twenty shillings.

As our bus, driven by a splendid character called Solomon, who had a huge hole in his right ear through which, sitting behind him, I was able to watch the road, made its original leisurely way up into the Highlands, we had called in for a refresher at the aforementioned Rhodes Inyanga hotel. Though it unaccountably has no official stars, this is one of the most completely civilized small hotels I have ever seen. I know because I have now, in the year following our tour, been there nearly a month, getting on with this book against constant temptations not to.

This was once Cecil Rhodes's farmhouse, and after the morning session working on this positively final autobiographical testament I took the Alsatian, Queenie, for a stroll down the avenue between the huge 100-foot gum trees and the row of oaks which Rhodes planted seventy years ago, then down across the nine-hole golf course to the trout stream at the bottom. We have no piped-in music, no television, no radio, no traffic, no aeroplanes, and the paper comes up at around teatime if someone happens to go down to the store five miles away. We have no hippies, no strikes, no demonstrations, no Rentacrowd, and by comparison with the England I left no nudes is indeed good nudes. The lawn is bordered by all the old-fashioned English cottage flowers, and I see from my window roses, dahlias, nasturtiums, nemesia, michaelmas daisies, stocks, begonias, and gladioli, all in bloom in January. Large butterflies flit from flower to flower and a pair of little honey birds hang upside down in the fuchsia bushes probing the blossoms with their long curved beaks. Also we have 'Horatio', the little widow bird, who is about the size of a small sparrow, black and white with a red beak and two black feathers about eight inches long trailing behind. His favourite perch is on top of one of the mushroom-shaped thatched shelters on the lawn and from there he makes awkward passes at his half-dozen rather drab little wives. Soon he is due to lose his tail feathers and migrate south for a few months, but he is already in his fourth season here and everyone, including myself, hopes to see him again for a fifth.

On this same visit I was invited to attend the Captain's Dinner – a Scotsman of course – at the Royal Salisbury Club. It might have been a similar occasion at any of the senior clubs at home and it occurred to me half-way through that I and almost any Rhodesian member present could adjourn to the secretary's office and come back with a settlement, fair to every race, party and creed, by the time we had got to the coffee. One of the most familiar reactions of the politician, however – and how well I remember it! – is: 'Ah, yes, but it's not as easy as that.' Even so, perhaps it is not really so difficult as they have made it for so many years and maybe, even before these words see the light of day, we shall be able to welcome a team of Rhodesian golfers to their homeland without having to row them ashore with all the other illegal immigrants, however handy may be the fact that most of them seem to land beside the first fairway at Prince's, Sandwich.

Meanwhile a British frigate was still frigging up and down outside the port of Beira, which belongs to our oldest ally, to ensure that no oil made its way down to the rebels, though as a visitor I was at once most courteously issued with enough petrol for fifteen hundred miles and 'do let us know if you need any more', and indeed the rationing itself is now a thing of the past. No doubt the Admiralty were bound to maintain this ludicrous blockade but one wondered whether they were really so short of frigates as to have to do it with one called HMS *Salisbury*? The Rhodesians made a wry jest out of this, as you might expect, just as they had done during our previous visit out of the fact that at least one senior blockading officer spent the whole of every leave playing golf in Bulawayo!

In the evenings I used to sit in the little room that was Rhodes's kitchen, in one of his own chairs. An astonishing air of peace and continuity prevailed and more than ever I sensed that somewhere up here I might end my days. Meanwhile the time had come to leave, but the link with home seemed stronger than ever when no fewer than four families asked me, this being the time of the postal strike, to act as courier between them and children or parents within no more than two or three miles of my own home. South African Airways advertised the arrival time of their flight as 08.15 and when the wheels touched the ground my watch actually said 08.15 and 30 seconds, so I was able by midday to deliver in rural Sussex letters that had been 'posted' seven thousand miles away some sixteen hours before.

One may be allowed to hope the time will soon come when this tragic farce no longer keeps British people apart, but I will not bore you by becoming 'political'. Let me end on a lighter and more personal note. I have recalled how on D-Day 1968 I put my golf clubs up in the loft with the water tanks and walked away. Secretly I thought that, when eventually put out to grass, I might try modestly again. In Rhodesia, alas, I found the answer. On the day I was due to take my reluctant farewell some of the rebels made me play croquet. I grasped the instrument instinctively in golfing fashion, and suddenly it all came back. 'Once you've had 'em,' they say, 'you've got 'em.' I even had the twitch with a croquet mallet.

Afterword

Well, there you have it, or at any rate some of the more agreeable parts of it, and, anyway, who wants to read about the others? Looking back, I can sense the incredible good fortune, denied to so many a better man, of falling in at the outset with that happy band 'whose work and pleasure are one', and indeed whose work, if it is to be rewarded, must itself give pleasure. Also of becoming, on however modest a subject, a descriptive writer, since beyond question you see life and people in sharper focus if you know you have got to make a living by writing about them. I can see that becoming an observer rather than a participator, even though from time to time participating oneself, determined my entire outlook on life, so that even now, living on the top of a hill over-looking the whole of the Sussex Weald, I find myself, rather than feeling part of the scene, wondering loftily what they are all up to down there.

I used to think the previous generation had lived through more changes than any in history but now it seems that my own has done so, though I cannot say I fancy the technological age of glass-box architecture, people motoring on the moon, pylons, pollution, and the little man who buzzes his miserable little aeroplane round and round over my garden on a Sunday afternoon, learning to fly.

Like every boy of my age I was brought up on the principles of putting something by for a rainy day and trying to leave the family inheritance, if any, a little better than you found it. Now it is not worth trying to save, and the great thing is not to be caught with anything on you when you die. In this latter at least, if I can live a year or two more, I shall succeed, and the thought consoles me for the memory of innumerable chances of making small fortunes which I either bungled or never even detected.

Where we go from here I am hanged if I know. A couple of

years will see me free of writing little pieces about golf but I shall still be younger than was Winston Churchill when he undertook the direction of the war, so perhaps there is something useful left in the old dog yet. What's done is done and what was missed is gone. As a wise friend once put it, it is not what you have had that you miss. Like the fisherman, you miss the ones that got away.

If I have a regret, it is to find myself living in the 'permissive society' at the age of sixty-plus. Rather like opening the stable door when the horse is no longer fit to bolt. With which elevating thought I wish you, for a while, farewell.